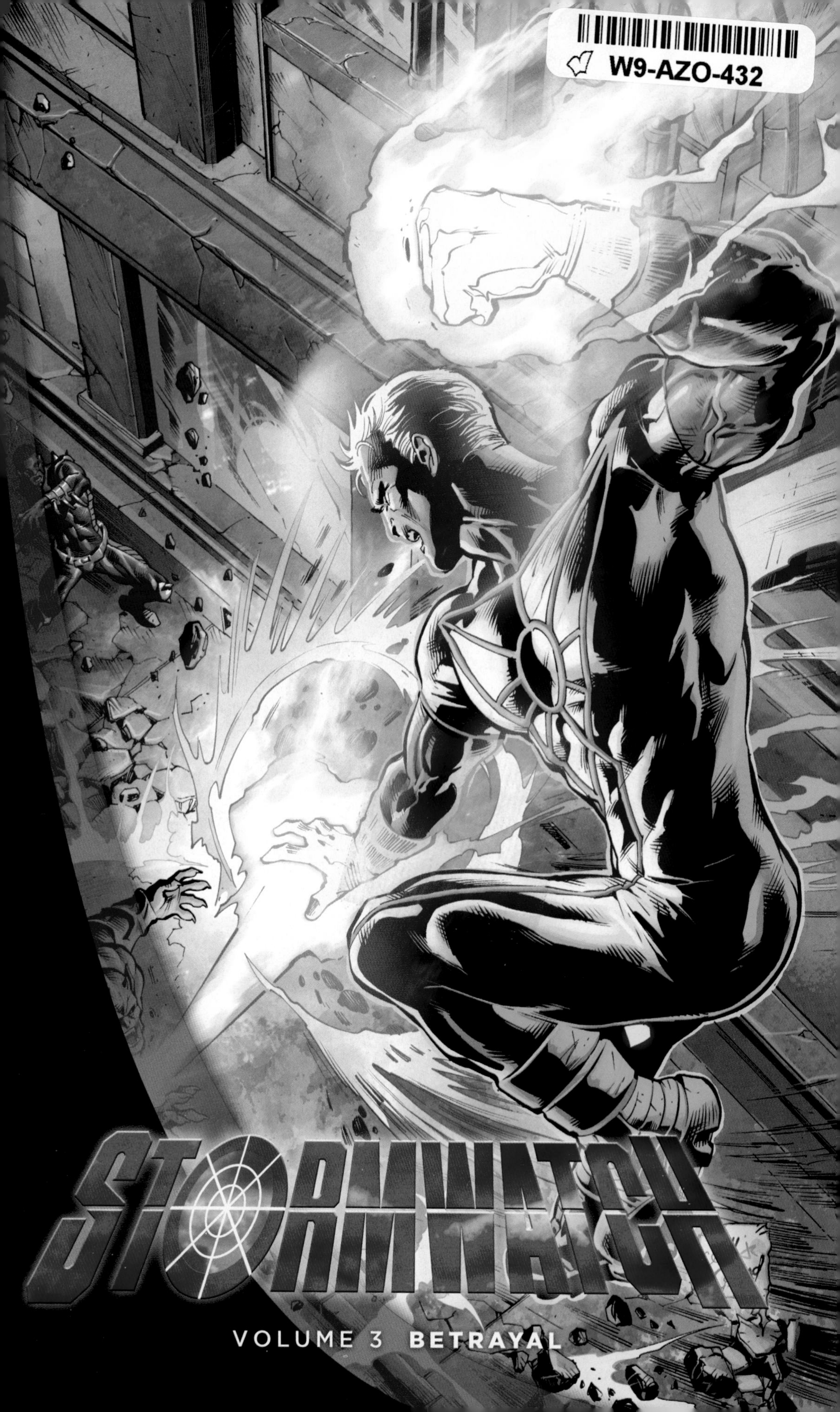
STORMWATCH
VOLUME 3 BETRAYAL

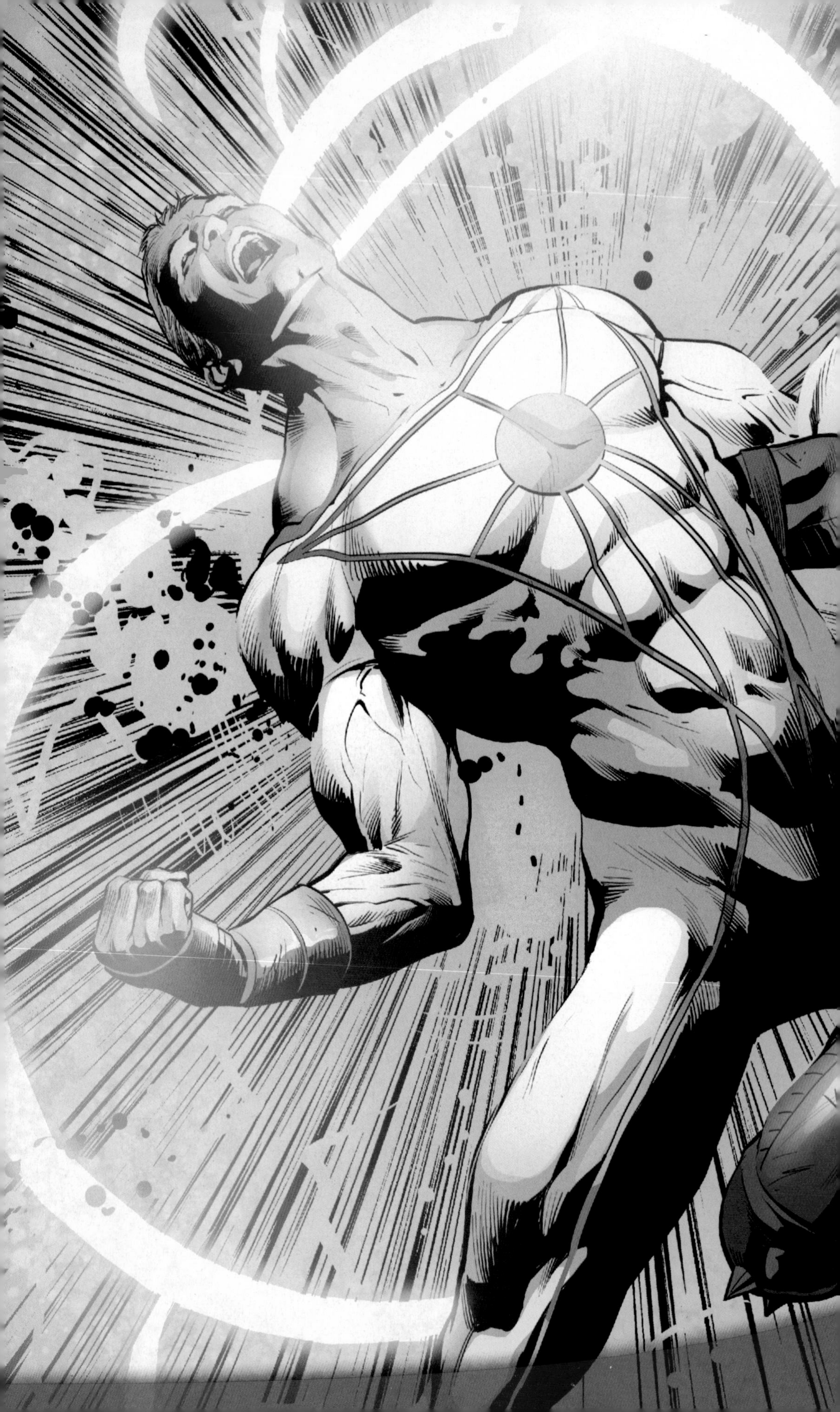

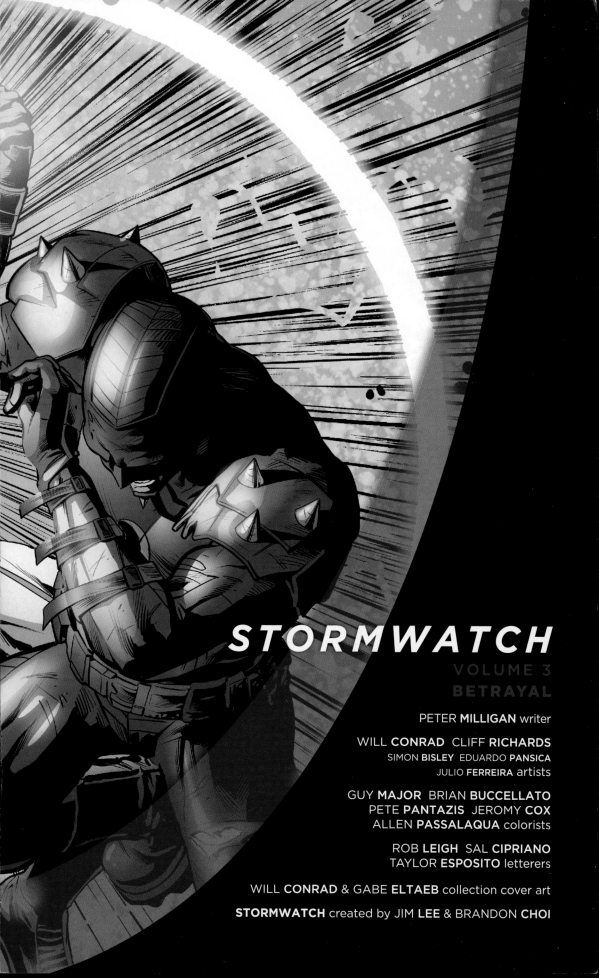

STORMWATCH

VOLUME 3
BETRAYAL

PETER **MILLIGAN** writer

WILL **CONRAD**   CLIFF **RICHARDS**
SIMON **BISLEY**   EDUARDO **PANSICA**
JULIO **FERREIRA** artists

GUY **MAJOR**   BRIAN **BUCCELLATO**
PETE **PANTAZIS**   JEROMY **COX**
ALLEN **PASSALAQUA** colorists

ROB **LEIGH**   SAL **CIPRIANO**
TAYLOR **ESPOSITO** letterers

WILL **CONRAD** & GABE **ELTAEB** collection cover art

STORMWATCH created by JIM **LEE** & BRANDON **CHOI**

PAT McCALLUM SHELLY BOND EDDIE BERGANZA Editors – Original Series CHRIS CONROY Associate Editor – Original Series
SEAN MACKIEWICZ GREGORY LOCKARD KATE STEWART DARREN SHAN Assistant Editors – Original Series ROWENA YOW Editor
ROBBIN BROSTERMAN Design Director – Books ROBBIE BIEDERMAN Publication Design

BOB HARRAS Senior VP – Editor-in-Chief, DC Comics

DIANE NELSON President DAN DIDIO and JIM LEE Co-Publishers GEOFF JOHNS Chief Creative Officer
JOHN ROOD Executive VP – Sales, Marketing and Business Development AMY GENKINS Senior VP – Business and Legal Affairs
NAIRI GARDINER Senior VP – Finance JEFF BOISON VP – Publishing Planning
MARK CHIARELLO VP – Art Direction and Design JOHN CUNNINGHAM VP – Marketing
TERRI CUNNINGHAM VP – Editorial Administration ALISON GILL Senior VP – Manufacturing and Operations
HANK KANALZ Senior VP – Vertigo & Integrated Publishing JAY KOGAN VP – Business and Legal Affairs, Publishing
JACK MAHAN VP – Business Affairs, Talent NICK NAPOLITANO VP – Manufacturing Administration
SUE POHJA VP – Book Sales COURTNEY SIMMONS Senior VP – Publicity BOB WAYNE Senior VP – Sales

STORMWATCH VOLUME 3: BETRAYAL

DC Comics, 1700 Broadway, New York, NY 10019
A Warner Bros. Entertainment Company.
Printed by RR Donnelley, Salem, VA, USA. 8/16/13. First Printing.

ISBN: 978-1-4012-4315-9

Library of Congress Cataloging-in-Publication Data

Milligan, Peter.
Stormwatch. Volume 3, Betrayal / Peter Milligan, Will Conrad.
pages cm
"Originally published in single magazine form in Stormwatch, 13-18, Young Romance 1."
ISBN 978-1-4012-4315-9
1. Graphic novels. I. Conrad, Will. II. Title. III. Title: Betrayal.
PN6728.S76M56 2013
741.5'973—dc23
                    2013016909

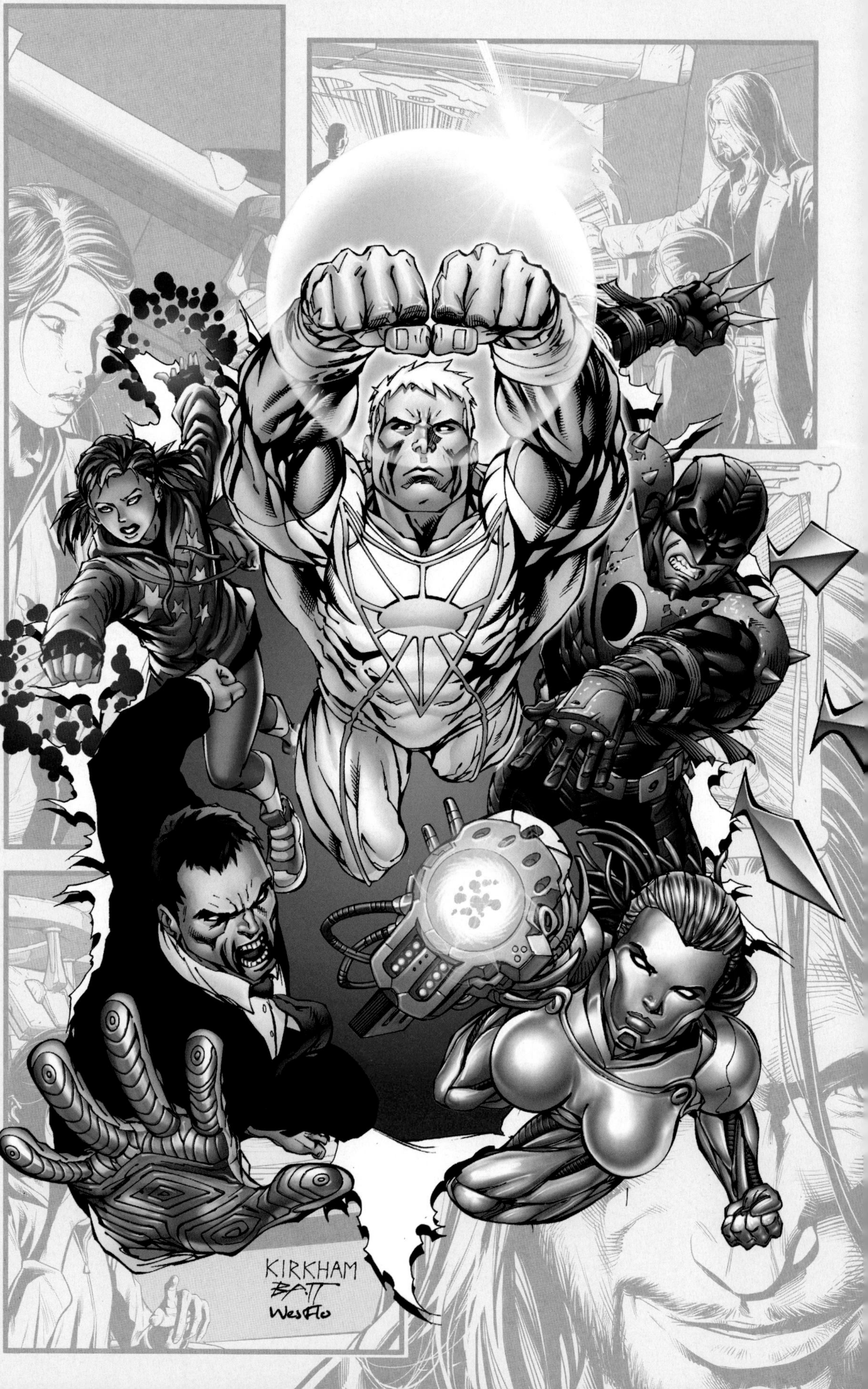
KIRKHAM
BATT
WesFlo

CRASH COURSE

PETER MILLIGAN writer WILL CONRAD artist cover art by TYLER KIRKHAM, BATT & WES HARTMAN

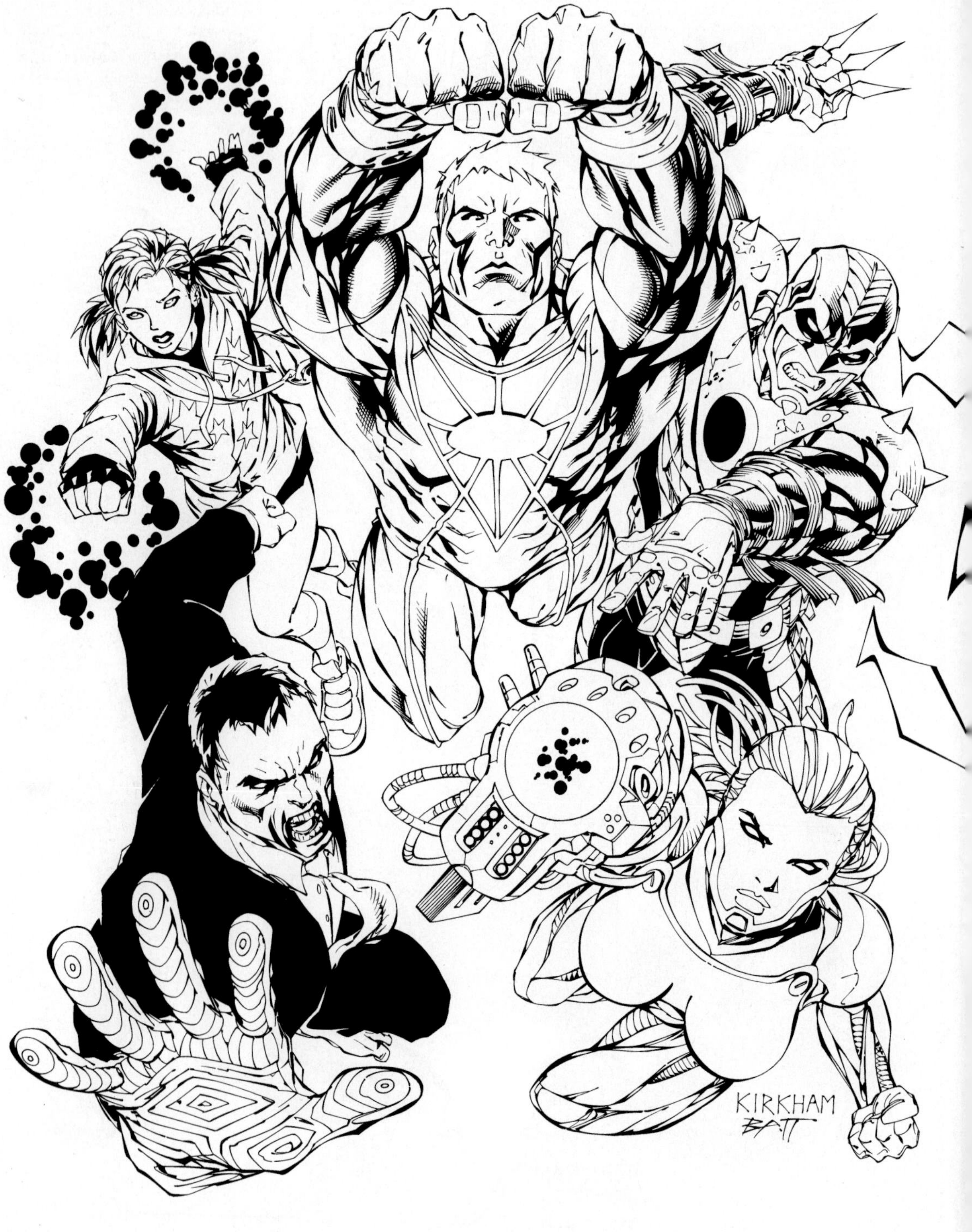
KIRKHAM
BATT

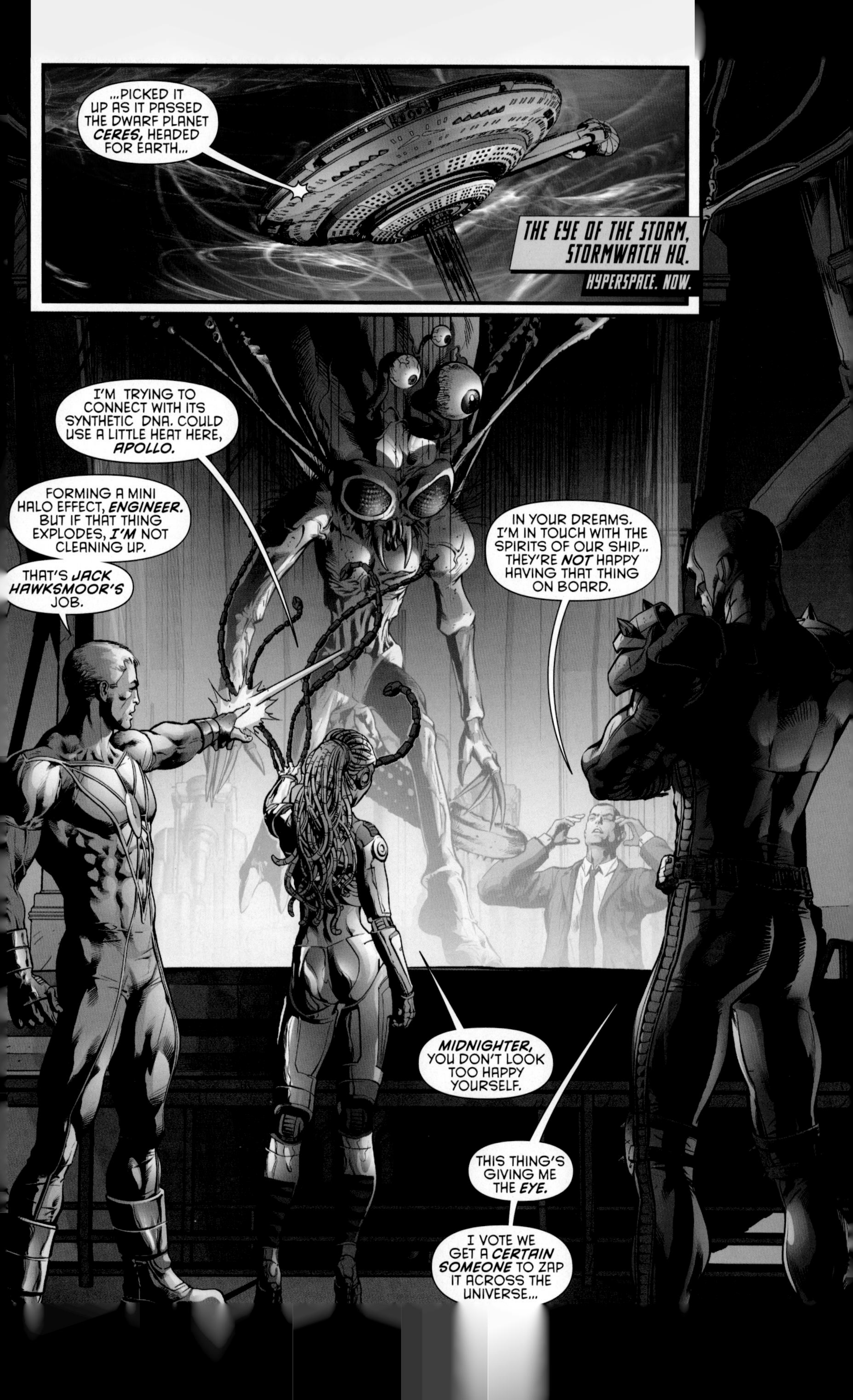
...PICKED IT UP AS IT PASSED THE DWARF PLANET CERES, HEADED FOR EARTH...
THE EYE OF THE STORM, STORMWATCH HQ.
HYPERSPACE. NOW.
I'M TRYING TO CONNECT WITH ITS SYNTHETIC DNA. COULD USE A LITTLE HEAT HERE, APOLLO.
FORMING A MINI HALO EFFECT, ENGINEER. BUT IF THAT THING EXPLODES, I'M NOT CLEANING UP.
THAT'S JACK HAWKSMOOR'S JOB.
IN YOUR DREAMS. I'M IN TOUCH WITH THE SPIRITS OF OUR SHIP... THEY'RE NOT HAPPY HAVING THAT THING ON BOARD.
MIDNIGHTER, YOU DON'T LOOK TOO HAPPY YOURSELF.
THIS THING'S GIVING ME THE EYE.
I VOTE WE GET A CERTAIN SOMEONE TO ZAP IT ACROSS THE UNIVERSE...

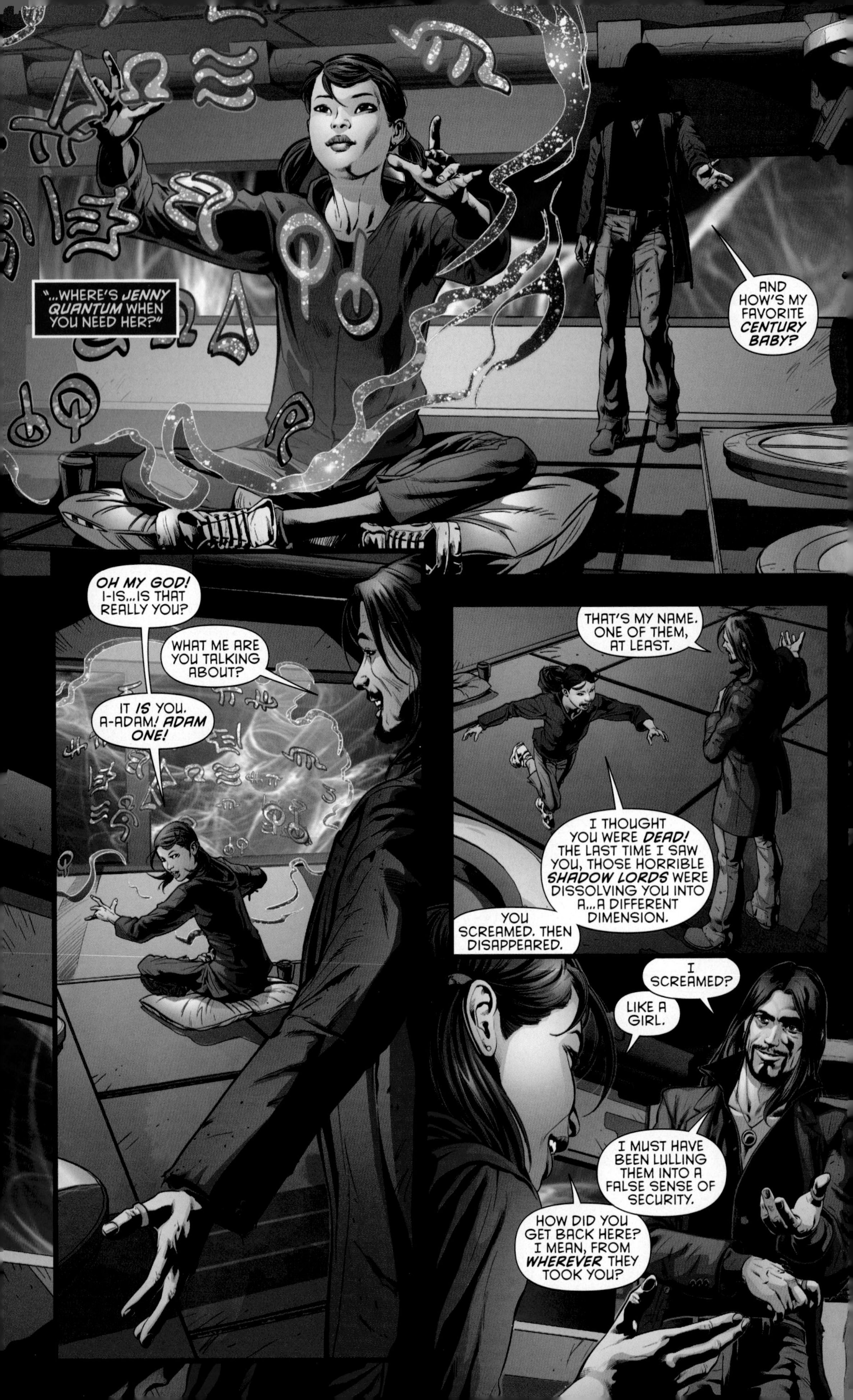
"...WHERE'S *JENNY QUANTUM* WHEN YOU NEED HER?"
AND HOW'S MY FAVORITE *CENTURY BABY?*
OH MY GOD! I-IS...IS THAT REALLY YOU?
WHAT ME ARE YOU TALKING ABOUT?
IT *IS* YOU. A-ADAM! *ADAM ONE!*
THAT'S MY NAME. ONE OF THEM, AT LEAST.
I THOUGHT YOU WERE *DEAD!* THE LAST TIME I SAW YOU, THOSE HORRIBLE *SHADOW LORDS* WERE DISSOLVING YOU INTO A...A DIFFERENT DIMENSION.
YOU SCREAMED. THEN DISAPPEARED.
I SCREAMED?
LIKE A GIRL.
I MUST HAVE BEEN LULLING THEM INTO A FALSE SENSE OF SECURITY.
HOW DID YOU GET BACK HERE? I MEAN, FROM *WHEREVER* THEY TOOK YOU?

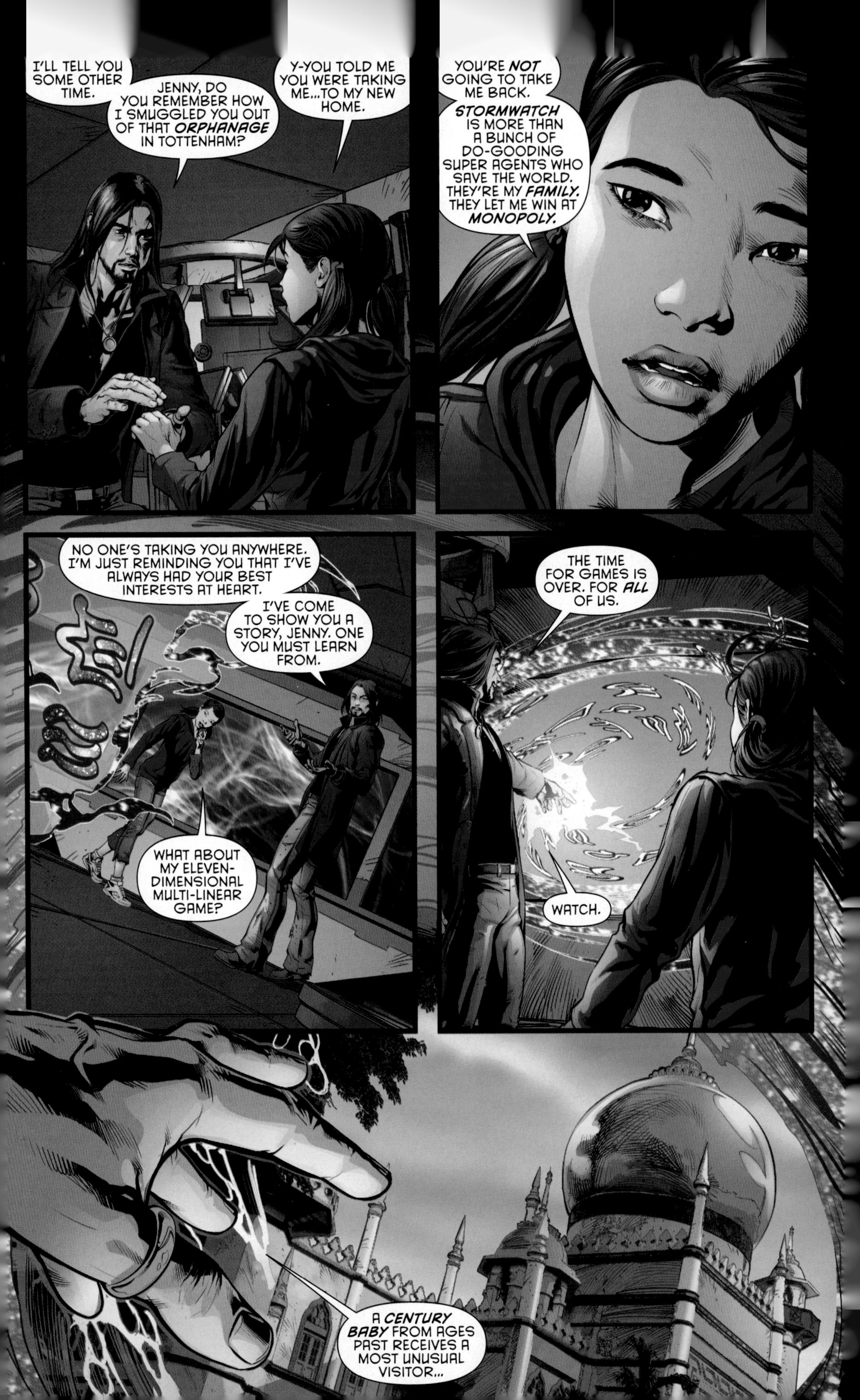
I'LL TELL YOU SOME OTHER TIME.
JENNY, DO YOU REMEMBER HOW I SMUGGLED YOU OUT OF THAT ORPHANAGE IN TOTTENHAM?
Y-YOU TOLD ME YOU WERE TAKING ME...TO MY NEW HOME.
YOU'RE NOT GOING TO TAKE ME BACK. STORMWATCH IS MORE THAN A BUNCH OF DO-GOODING SUPER AGENTS WHO SAVE THE WORLD. THEY'RE MY FAMILY. THEY LET ME WIN AT MONOPOLY.
NO ONE'S TAKING YOU ANYWHERE. I'M JUST REMINDING YOU THAT I'VE ALWAYS HAD YOUR BEST INTERESTS AT HEART.
I'VE COME TO SHOW YOU A STORY, JENNY. ONE YOU MUST LEARN FROM.
WHAT ABOUT MY ELEVEN-DIMENSIONAL MULTI-LINEAR GAME?
THE TIME FOR GAMES IS OVER. FOR ALL OF US.
WATCH.
A CENTURY BABY FROM AGES PAST RECEIVES A MOST UNUSUAL VISITOR...

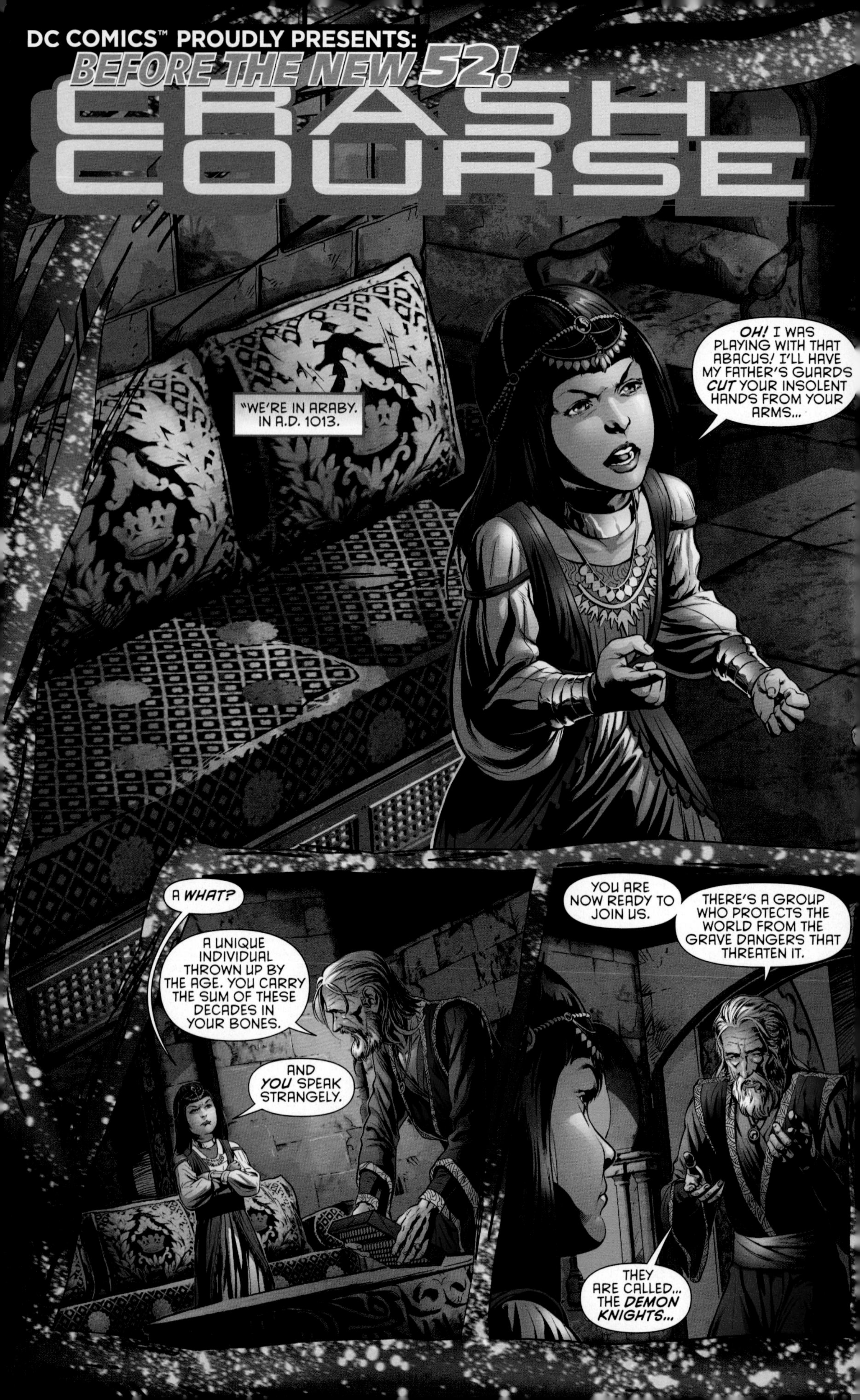
DC COMICS™ PROUDLY PRESENTS:
BEFORE THE NEW 52!
CRASH COURSE
"WE'RE IN ARABY. IN A.D. 1013.
OH! I WAS PLAYING WITH THAT ABACUS! I'LL HAVE MY FATHER'S GUARDS CUT YOUR INSOLENT HANDS FROM YOUR ARMS...
A WHAT?
A UNIQUE INDIVIDUAL THROWN UP BY THE AGE. YOU CARRY THE SUM OF THESE DECADES IN YOUR BONES.
AND YOU SPEAK STRANGELY.
YOU ARE NOW READY TO JOIN US.
THERE'S A GROUP WHO PROTECTS THE WORLD FROM THE GRAVE DANGERS THAT THREATEN IT.
THEY ARE CALLED... THE DEMON KNIGHTS...

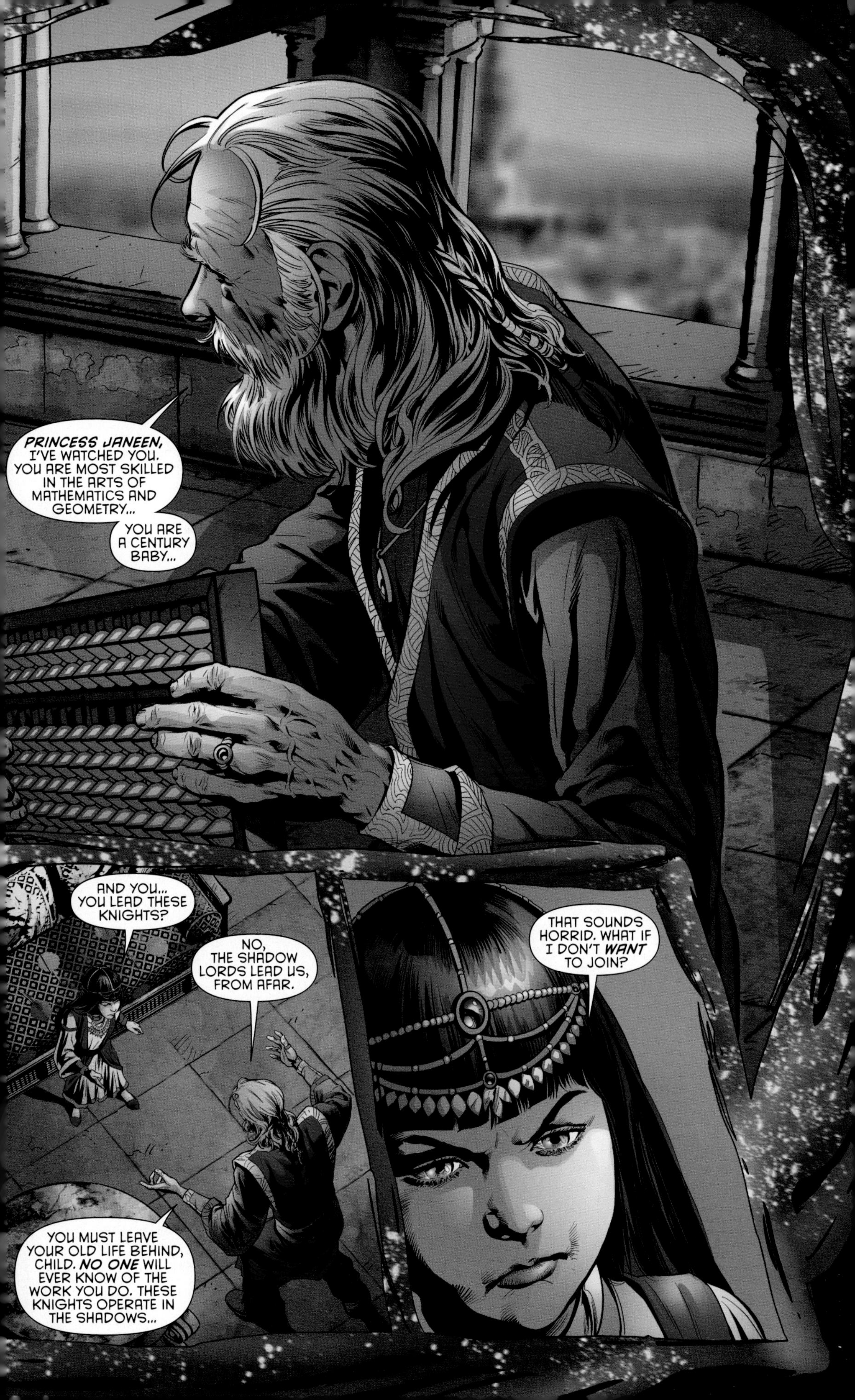

PRINCESS JANEEN, I'VE WATCHED YOU. YOU ARE MOST SKILLED IN THE ARTS OF MATHEMATICS AND GEOMETRY...
YOU ARE A CENTURY BABY...
AND YOU... YOU LEAD THESE KNIGHTS?
NO, THE SHADOW LORDS LEAD US, FROM AFAR.
YOU MUST LEAVE YOUR OLD LIFE BEHIND, CHILD. NO ONE WILL EVER KNOW OF THE WORK YOU DO. THESE KNIGHTS OPERATE IN THE SHADOWS...
THAT SOUNDS HORRID. WHAT IF I DON'T WANT TO JOIN?

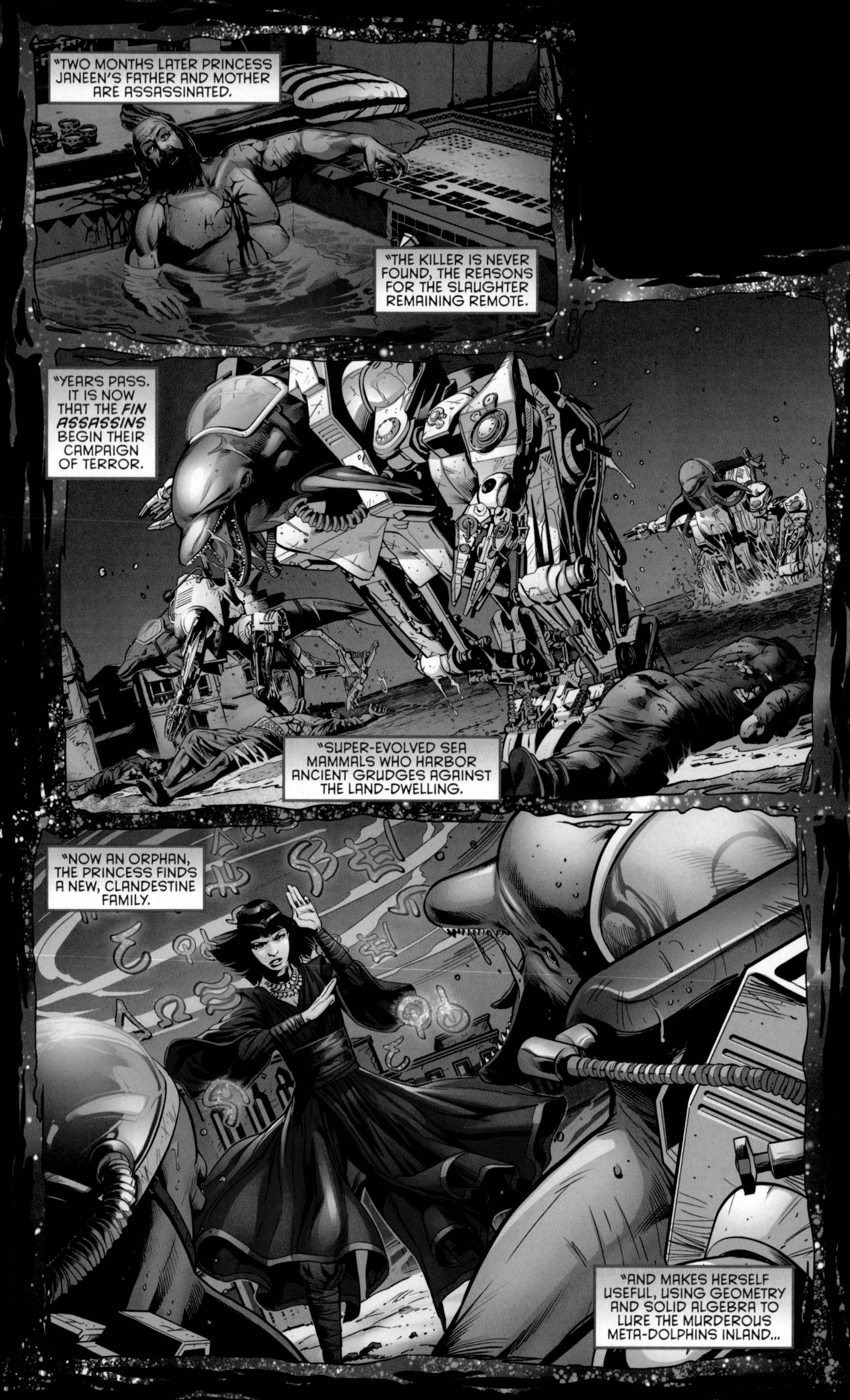
"TWO MONTHS LATER PRINCESS JANEEN'S FATHER AND MOTHER ARE ASSASSINATED.
"THE KILLER IS NEVER FOUND, THE REASONS FOR THE SLAUGHTER REMAINING REMOTE.
"YEARS PASS. IT IS NOW THAT THE *FIN ASSASSINS* BEGIN THEIR CAMPAIGN OF TERROR.
"SUPER-EVOLVED SEA MAMMALS WHO HARBOR ANCIENT GRUDGES AGAINST THE LAND-DWELLING.
"NOW AN ORPHAN, THE PRINCESS FINDS A NEW, CLANDESTINE FAMILY.
"AND MAKES HERSELF USEFUL, USING GEOMETRY AND SOLID ALGEBRA TO LURE THE MURDEROUS META-DOLPHINS INLAND...

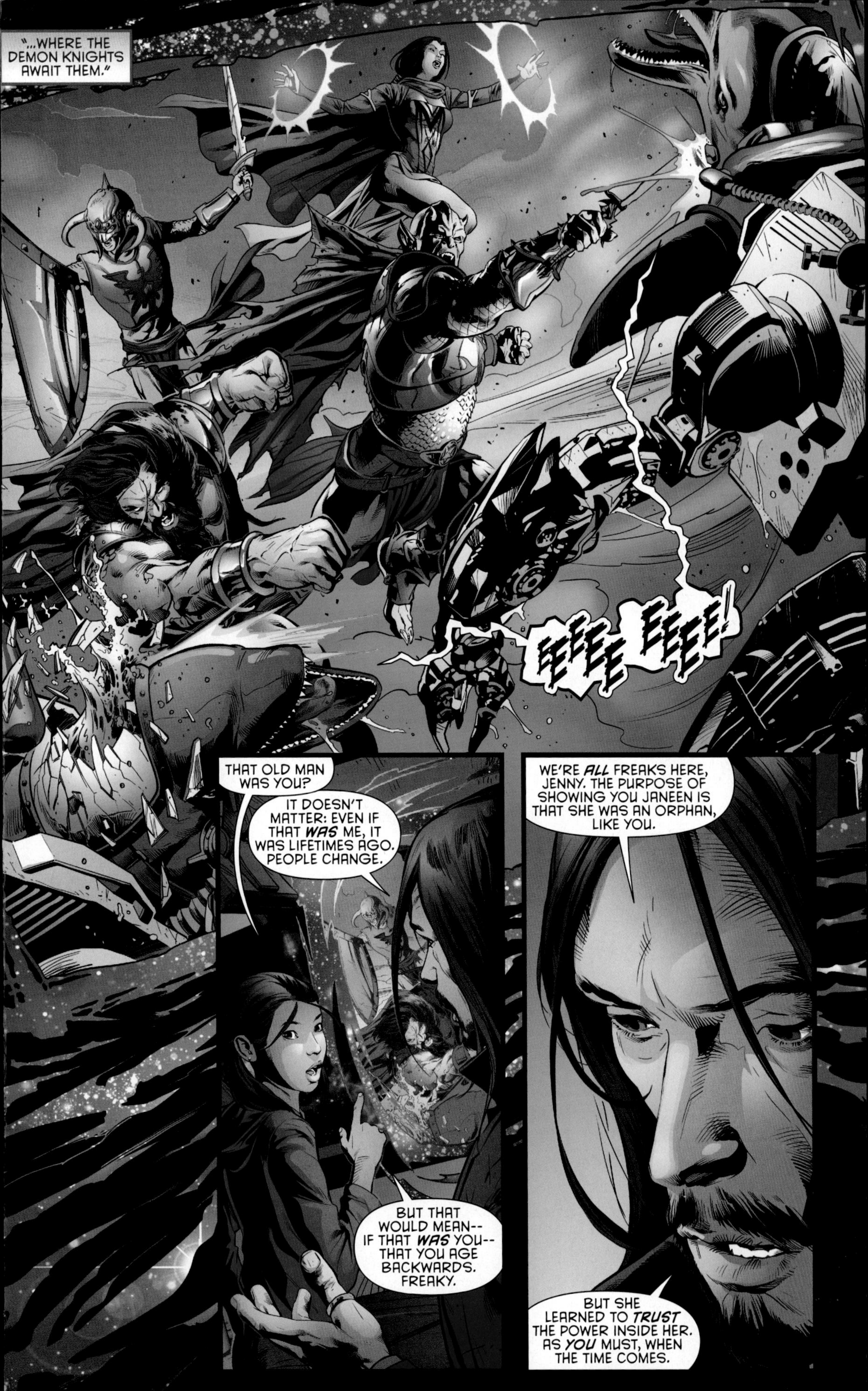
"...WHERE THE DEMON KNIGHTS AWAIT THEM."
EEEEE EEEE!
THAT OLD MAN WAS YOU?
IT DOESN'T MATTER: EVEN IF THAT *WAS* ME, IT WAS LIFETIMES AGO. PEOPLE CHANGE.
BUT THAT WOULD MEAN-- IF THAT *WAS* YOU-- THAT YOU AGE BACKWARDS. FREAKY.
WE'RE *ALL* FREAKS HERE, JENNY. THE PURPOSE OF SHOWING YOU JANEEN IS THAT SHE WAS AN ORPHAN, LIKE YOU.
BUT SHE LEARNED TO *TRUST* THE POWER INSIDE HER. AS *YOU* MUST, WHEN THE TIME COMES.

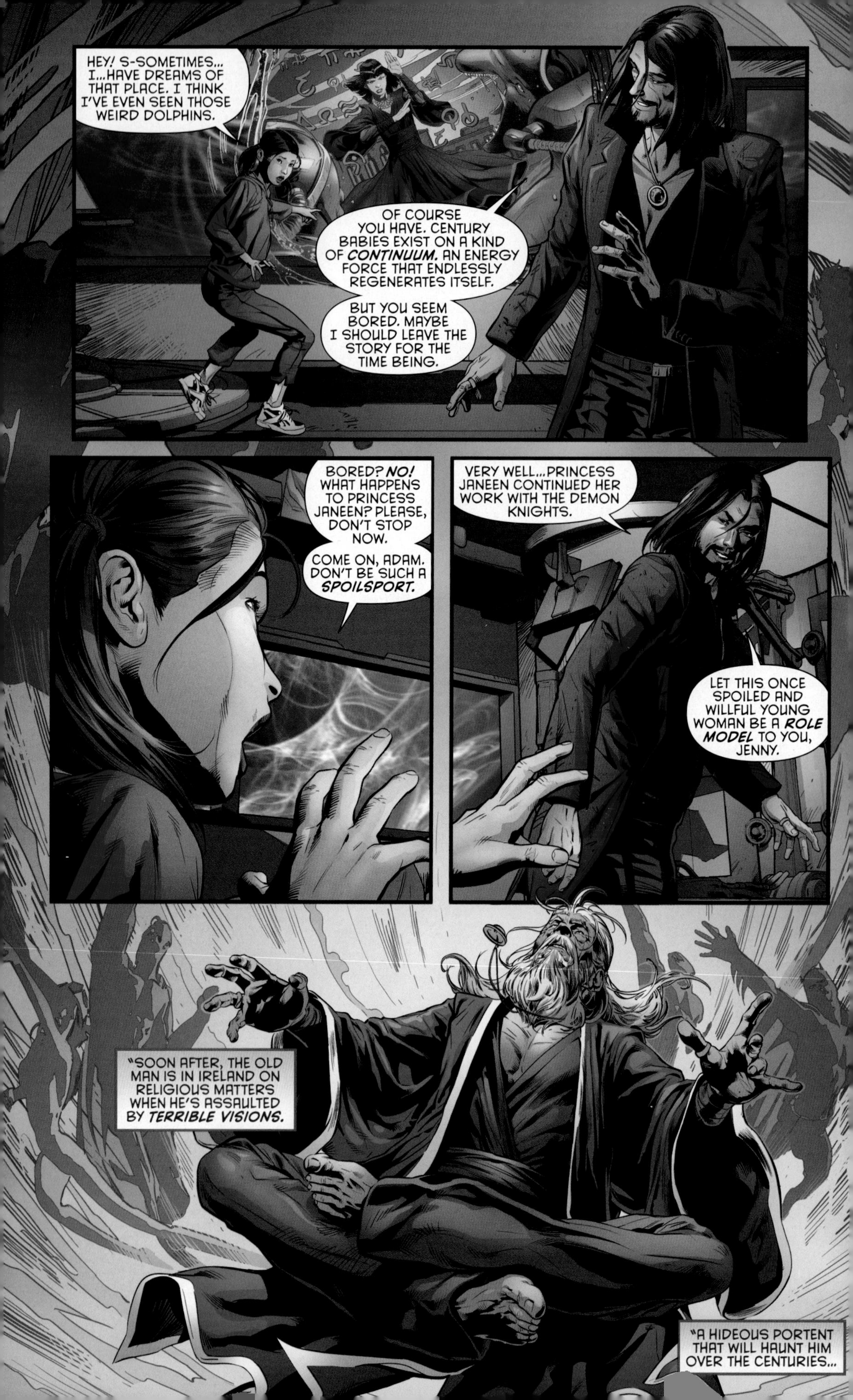
HEY! S-SOMETIMES... I...HAVE DREAMS OF THAT PLACE. I THINK I'VE EVEN SEEN THOSE WEIRD DOLPHINS.
OF COURSE YOU HAVE. CENTURY BABIES EXIST ON A KIND OF *CONTINUUM.* AN ENERGY FORCE THAT ENDLESSLY REGENERATES ITSELF.
BUT YOU SEEM BORED. MAYBE I SHOULD LEAVE THE STORY FOR THE TIME BEING.
BORED? *NO!* WHAT HAPPENS TO PRINCESS JANEEN? PLEASE, DON'T STOP NOW.
COME ON, ADAM. DON'T BE SUCH A *SPOILSPORT.*
VERY WELL...PRINCESS JANEEN CONTINUED HER WORK WITH THE DEMON KNIGHTS.
LET THIS ONCE SPOILED AND WILLFUL YOUNG WOMAN BE A *ROLE MODEL* TO YOU, JENNY.
"SOON AFTER, THE OLD MAN IS IN IRELAND ON RELIGIOUS MATTERS WHEN HE'S ASSAULTED BY *TERRIBLE VISIONS.*
"A HIDEOUS PORTENT THAT WILL HAUNT HIM OVER THE CENTURIES...

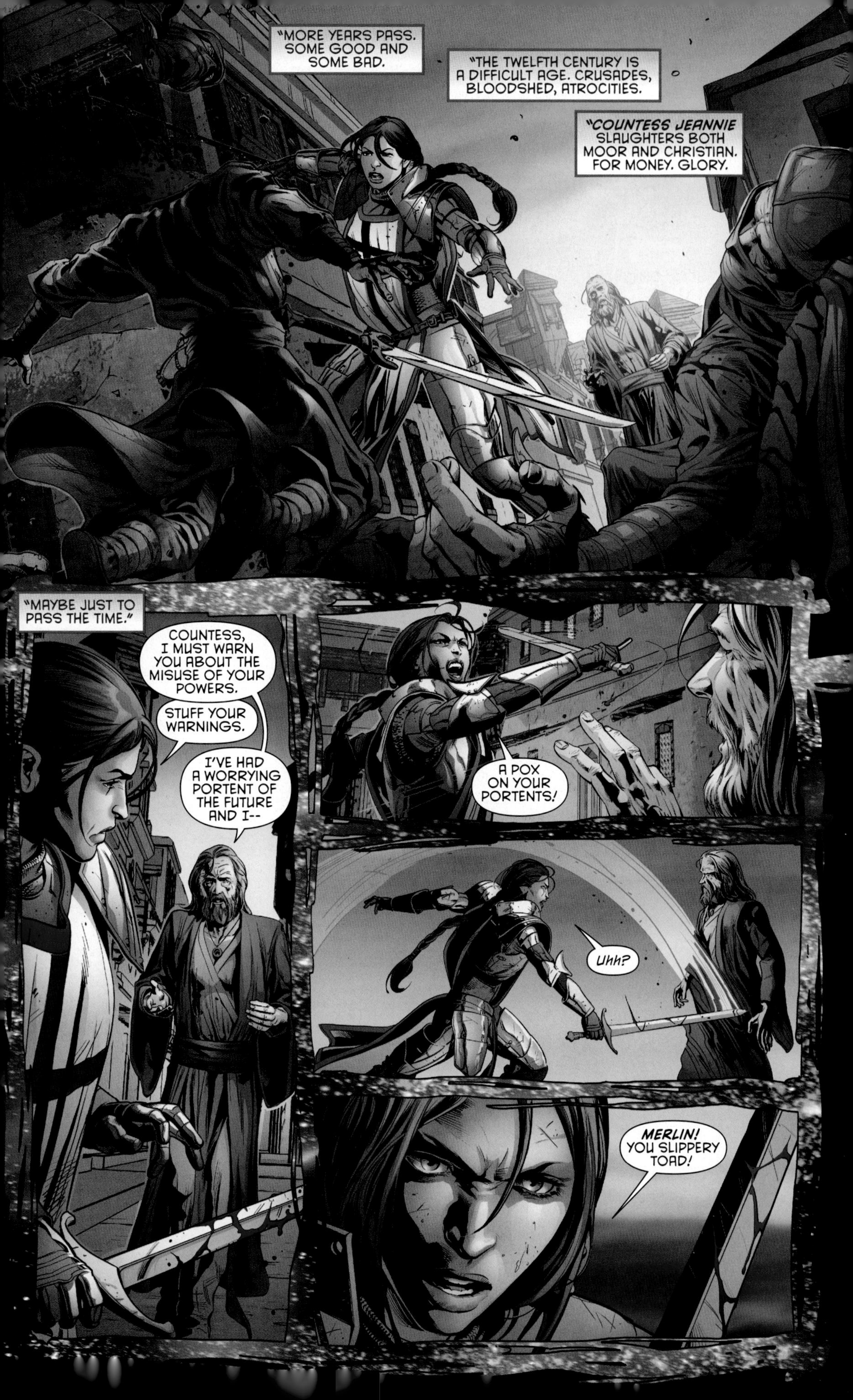
"MORE YEARS PASS. SOME GOOD AND SOME BAD.
"THE TWELFTH CENTURY IS A DIFFICULT AGE. CRUSADES, BLOODSHED, ATROCITIES.
"COUNTESS JEANNIE SLAUGHTERS BOTH MOOR AND CHRISTIAN. FOR MONEY. GLORY.
"MAYBE JUST TO PASS THE TIME."
COUNTESS, I MUST WARN YOU ABOUT THE MISUSE OF YOUR POWERS.
STUFF YOUR WARNINGS.
I'VE HAD A WORRYING PORTENT OF THE FUTURE AND I--
A POX ON YOUR PORTENTS!
Uhh?
MERLIN! YOU SLIPPERY TOAD!

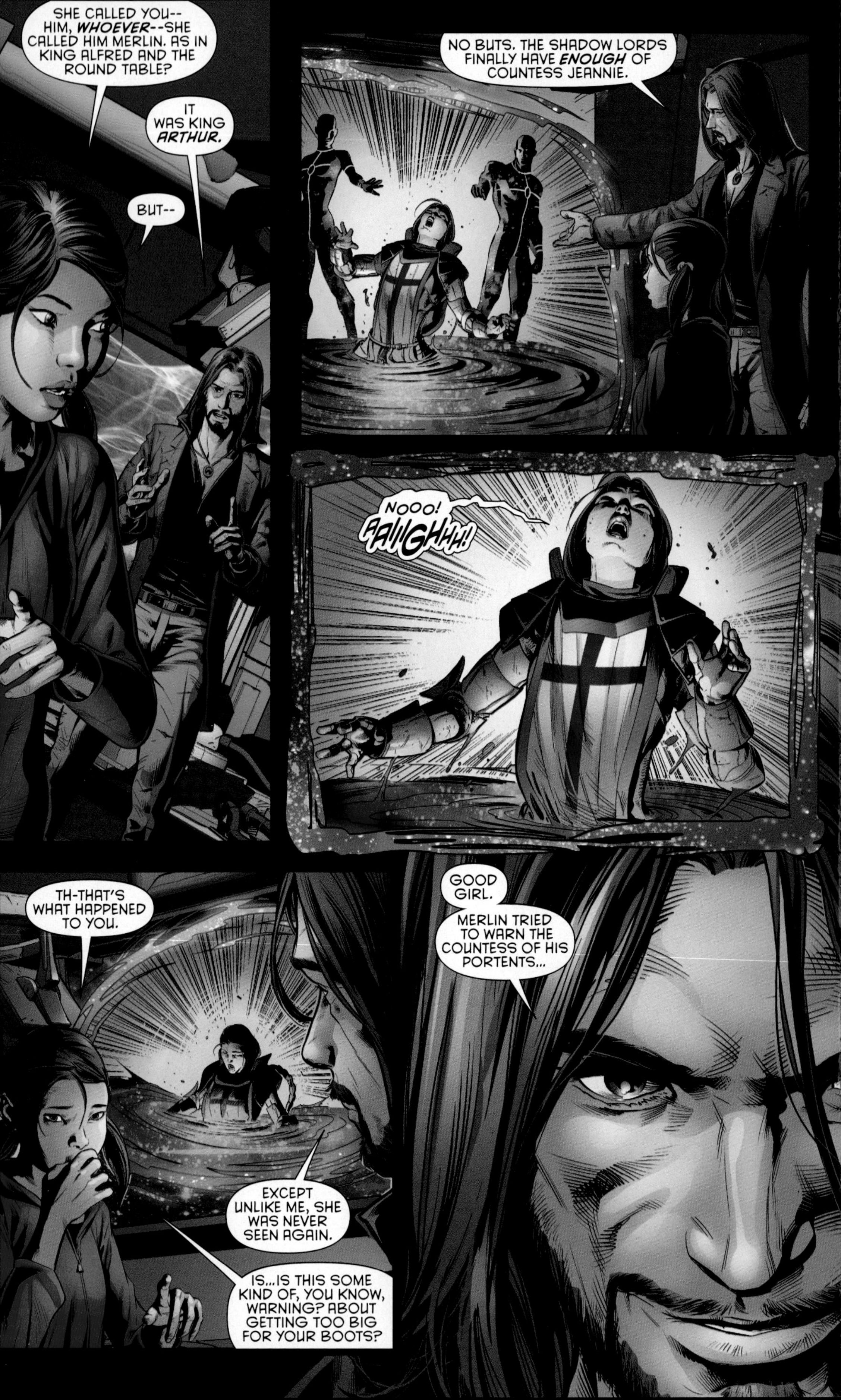

SHE CALLED YOU-- HIM, WHOEVER--SHE CALLED HIM MERLIN. AS IN KING ALFRED AND THE ROUND TABLE?
IT WAS KING ARTHUR.
BUT--
NO BUTS. THE SHADOW LORDS FINALLY HAVE ENOUGH OF COUNTESS JEANNIE.
NOOO!
AAUGHHH!
TH-THAT'S WHAT HAPPENED TO YOU.
GOOD GIRL.
MERLIN TRIED TO WARN THE COUNTESS OF HIS PORTENTS...
EXCEPT UNLIKE ME, SHE WAS NEVER SEEN AGAIN.
IS...IS THIS SOME KIND OF, YOU KNOW, WARNING? ABOUT GETTING TOO BIG FOR YOUR BOOTS?

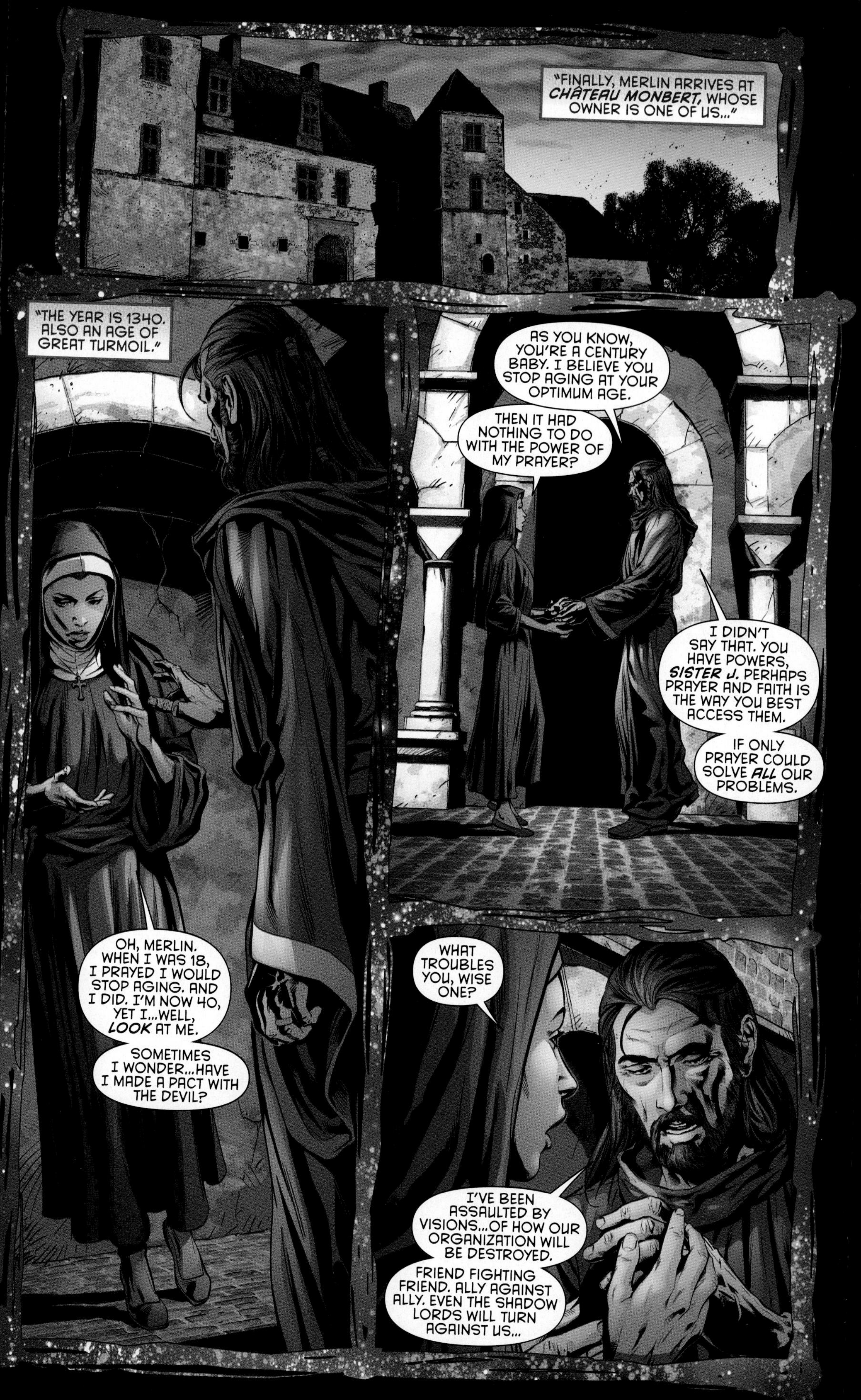
"FINALLY, MERLIN ARRIVES AT CHÂTEAU MONBERT, WHOSE OWNER IS ONE OF US..."
"THE YEAR IS 1340. ALSO AN AGE OF GREAT TURMOIL."
OH, MERLIN. WHEN I WAS 18, I PRAYED I WOULD STOP AGING. AND I DID. I'M NOW 40, YET I...WELL, *LOOK* AT ME.
SOMETIMES I WONDER...HAVE I MADE A PACT WITH THE DEVIL?
AS YOU KNOW, YOU'RE A CENTURY BABY. I BELIEVE YOU STOP AGING AT YOUR OPTIMUM AGE.
THEN IT HAD NOTHING TO DO WITH THE POWER OF MY PRAYER?
I DIDN'T SAY THAT. YOU HAVE POWERS, *SISTER J.* PERHAPS PRAYER AND FAITH IS THE WAY YOU BEST ACCESS THEM.
IF ONLY PRAYER COULD SOLVE *ALL* OUR PROBLEMS.
WHAT TROUBLES YOU, WISE ONE?
I'VE BEEN ASSAULTED BY VISIONS...OF HOW OUR ORGANIZATION WILL BE DESTROYED.
FRIEND FIGHTING FRIEND. ALLY AGAINST ALLY. EVEN THE SHADOW LORDS WILL TURN AGAINST US...

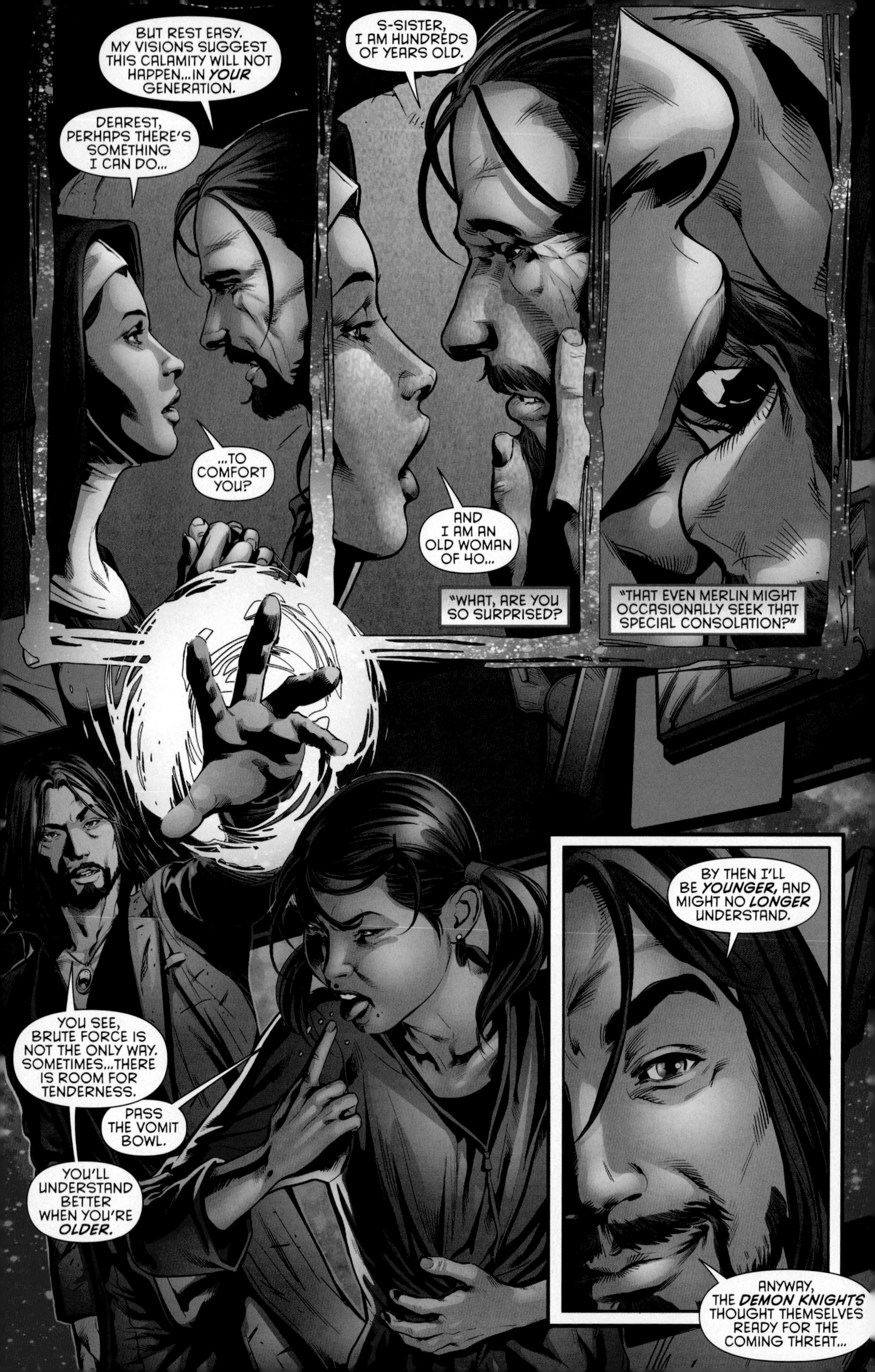

BUT REST EASY. MY VISIONS SUGGEST THIS CALAMITY WILL NOT HAPPEN...IN *YOUR* GENERATION.
DEAREST, PERHAPS THERE'S SOMETHING I CAN DO...
...TO COMFORT YOU?
S-SISTER, I AM HUNDREDS OF YEARS OLD.
AND I AM AN OLD WOMAN OF 40...
"WHAT, ARE YOU SO SURPRISED?
"THAT EVEN MERLIN MIGHT OCCASIONALLY SEEK THAT SPECIAL CONSOLATION?"
YOU SEE, BRUTE FORCE IS NOT THE ONLY WAY. SOMETIMES...THERE IS ROOM FOR TENDERNESS.
PASS THE VOMIT BOWL.
YOU'LL UNDERSTAND BETTER WHEN YOU'RE *OLDER.*
BY THEN I'LL BE *YOUNGER,* AND MIGHT NO *LONGER* UNDERSTAND.
ANYWAY, THE *DEMON KNIGHTS* THOUGHT THEMSELVES READY FOR THE COMING THREAT...

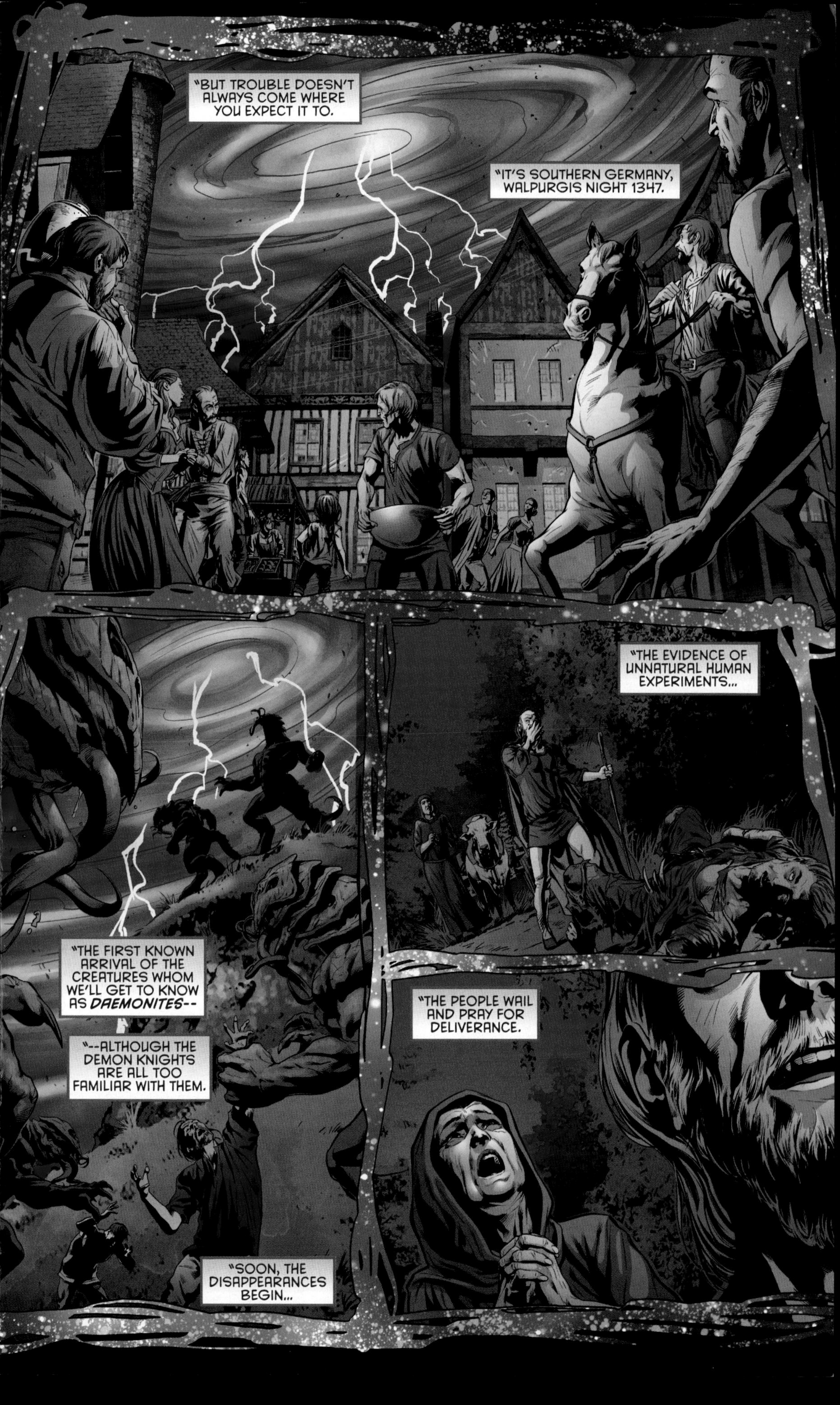
"BUT TROUBLE DOESN'T ALWAYS COME WHERE YOU EXPECT IT TO.
"IT'S SOUTHERN GERMANY, WALPURGIS NIGHT 1347.
"THE FIRST KNOWN ARRIVAL OF THE CREATURES WHOM WE'LL GET TO KNOW AS *DAEMONITES*--
"--ALTHOUGH THE DEMON KNIGHTS ARE ALL TOO FAMILIAR WITH THEM.
"SOON, THE DISAPPEARANCES BEGIN...
"THE EVIDENCE OF UNNATURAL HUMAN EXPERIMENTS...
"THE PEOPLE WAIL AND PRAY FOR DELIVERANCE.

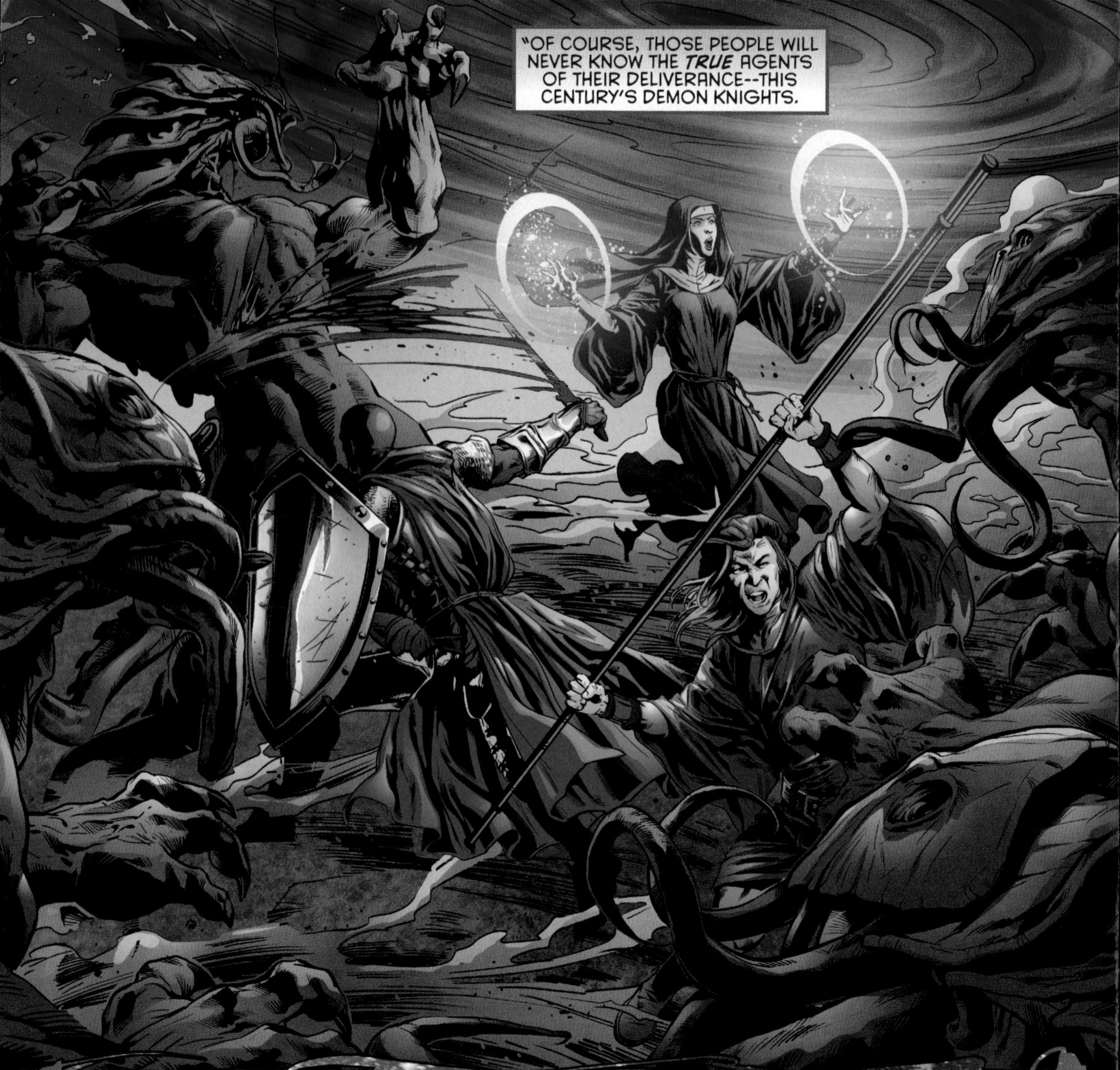
"OF COURSE, THOSE PEOPLE WILL NEVER KNOW THE *TRUE* AGENTS OF THEIR DELIVERANCE--THIS CENTURY'S DEMON KNIGHTS.

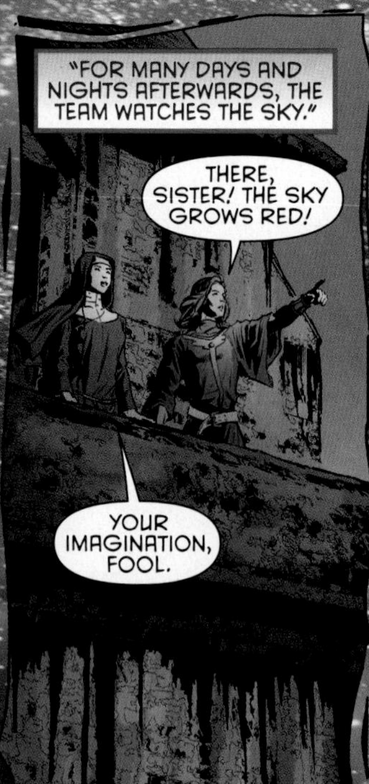
"FOR MANY DAYS AND NIGHTS AFTERWARDS, THE TEAM WATCHES THE SKY."
THERE, SISTER! THE SKY GROWS RED!
YOUR IMAGINATION, FOOL.

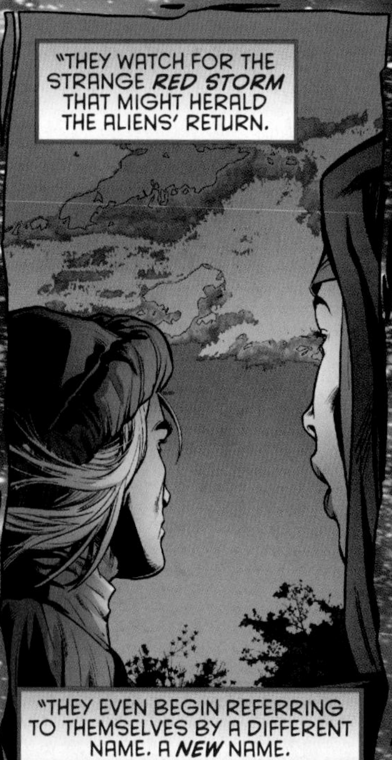
"THEY WATCH FOR THE STRANGE *RED STORM* THAT MIGHT HERALD THE ALIENS' RETURN.
"THEY EVEN BEGIN REFERRING TO THEMSELVES BY A DIFFERENT NAME. A *NEW* NAME.

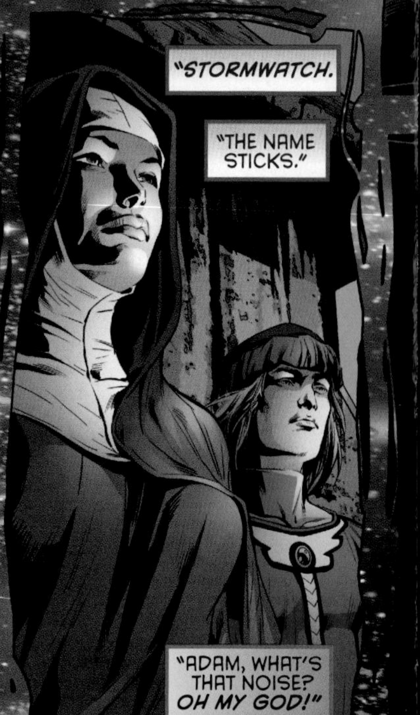
"*STORMWATCH.*
"THE NAME STICKS."
"ADAM, WHAT'S THAT NOISE? *OH MY GOD!"*

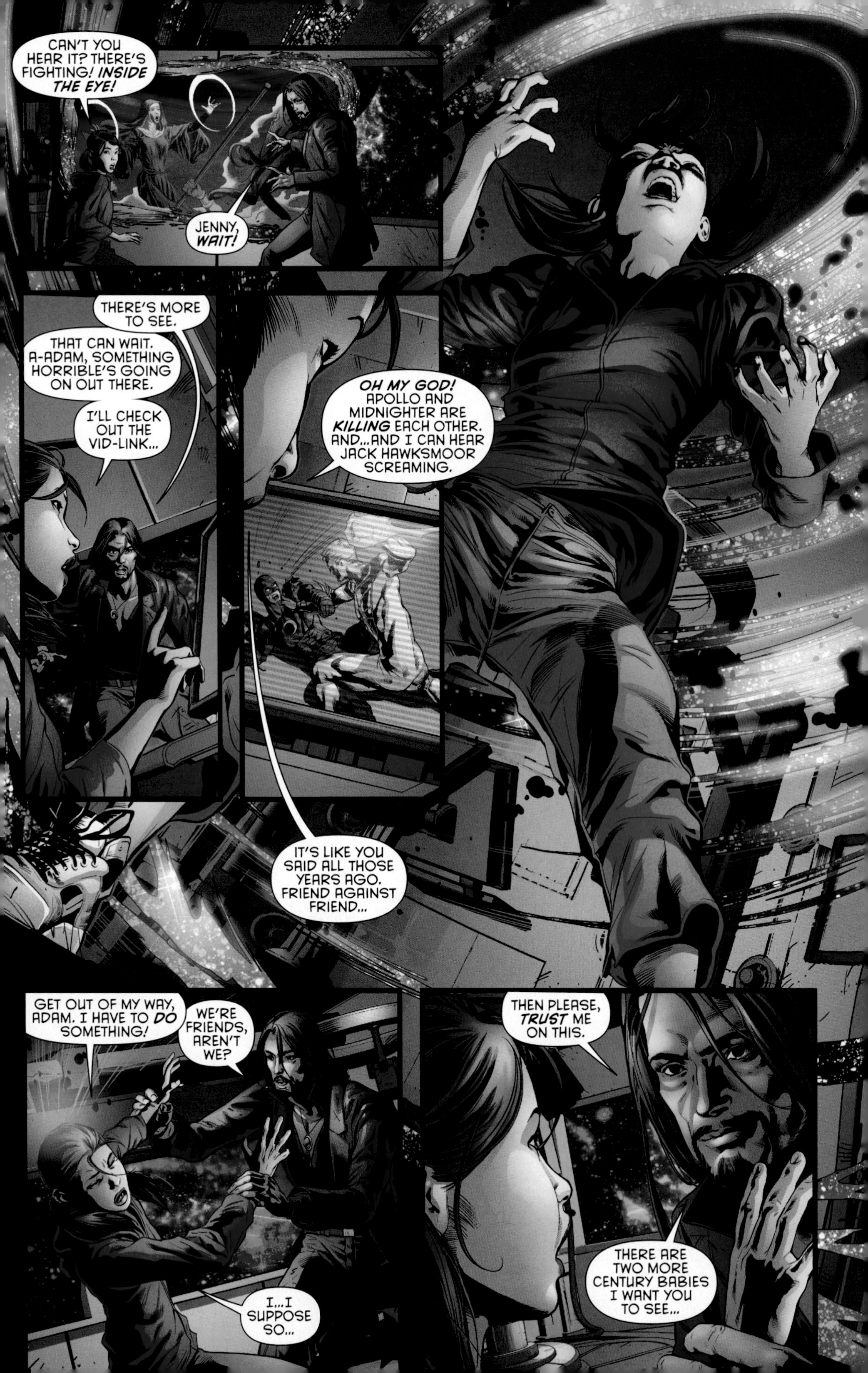
CAN'T YOU HEAR IT? THERE'S FIGHTING! INSIDE THE EYE!
JENNY, WAIT!
THERE'S MORE TO SEE.
THAT CAN WAIT. A-ADAM, SOMETHING HORRIBLE'S GOING ON OUT THERE.
I'LL CHECK OUT THE VID-LINK...
OH MY GOD! APOLLO AND MIDNIGHTER ARE KILLING EACH OTHER. AND...AND I CAN HEAR JACK HAWKSMOOR SCREAMING.
IT'S LIKE YOU SAID ALL THOSE YEARS AGO. FRIEND AGAINST FRIEND...
GET OUT OF MY WAY, ADAM. I HAVE TO DO SOMETHING!
WE'RE FRIENDS, AREN'T WE?
I...I SUPPOSE SO...
THEN PLEASE, TRUST ME ON THIS.
THERE ARE TWO MORE CENTURY BABIES I WANT YOU TO SEE...

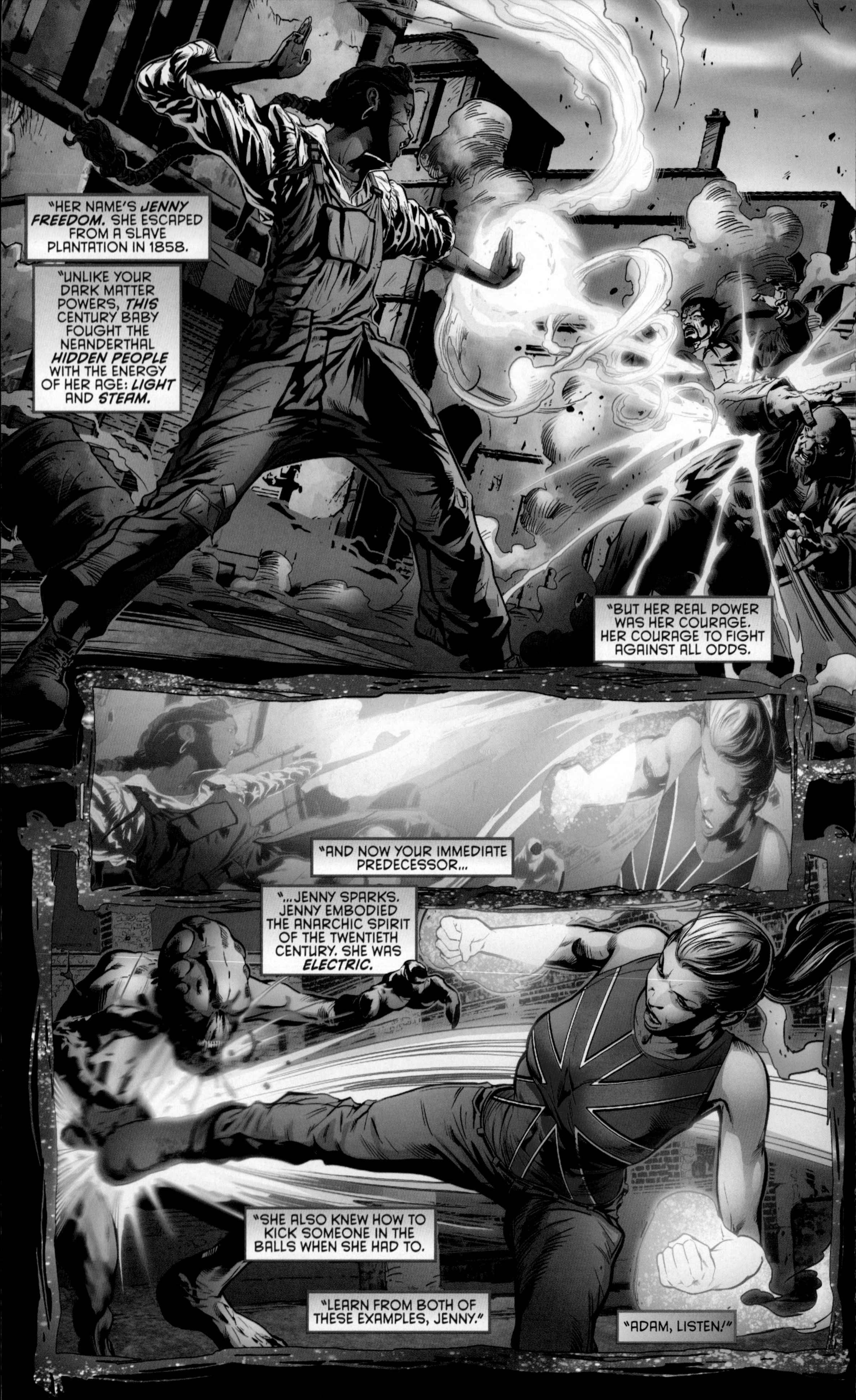
"HER NAME'S JENNY FREEDOM. SHE ESCAPED FROM A SLAVE PLANTATION IN 1858.
"UNLIKE YOUR DARK MATTER POWERS, THIS CENTURY BABY FOUGHT THE NEANDERTHAL HIDDEN PEOPLE WITH THE ENERGY OF HER AGE: LIGHT AND STEAM.
"BUT HER REAL POWER WAS HER COURAGE. HER COURAGE TO FIGHT AGAINST ALL ODDS.
"AND NOW YOUR IMMEDIATE PREDECESSOR...
"...JENNY SPARKS. JENNY EMBODIED THE ANARCHIC SPIRIT OF THE TWENTIETH CENTURY. SHE WAS ELECTRIC.
"SHE ALSO KNEW HOW TO KICK SOMEONE IN THE BALLS WHEN SHE HAD TO.
"LEARN FROM BOTH OF THESE EXAMPLES, JENNY."
"ADAM, LISTEN!"

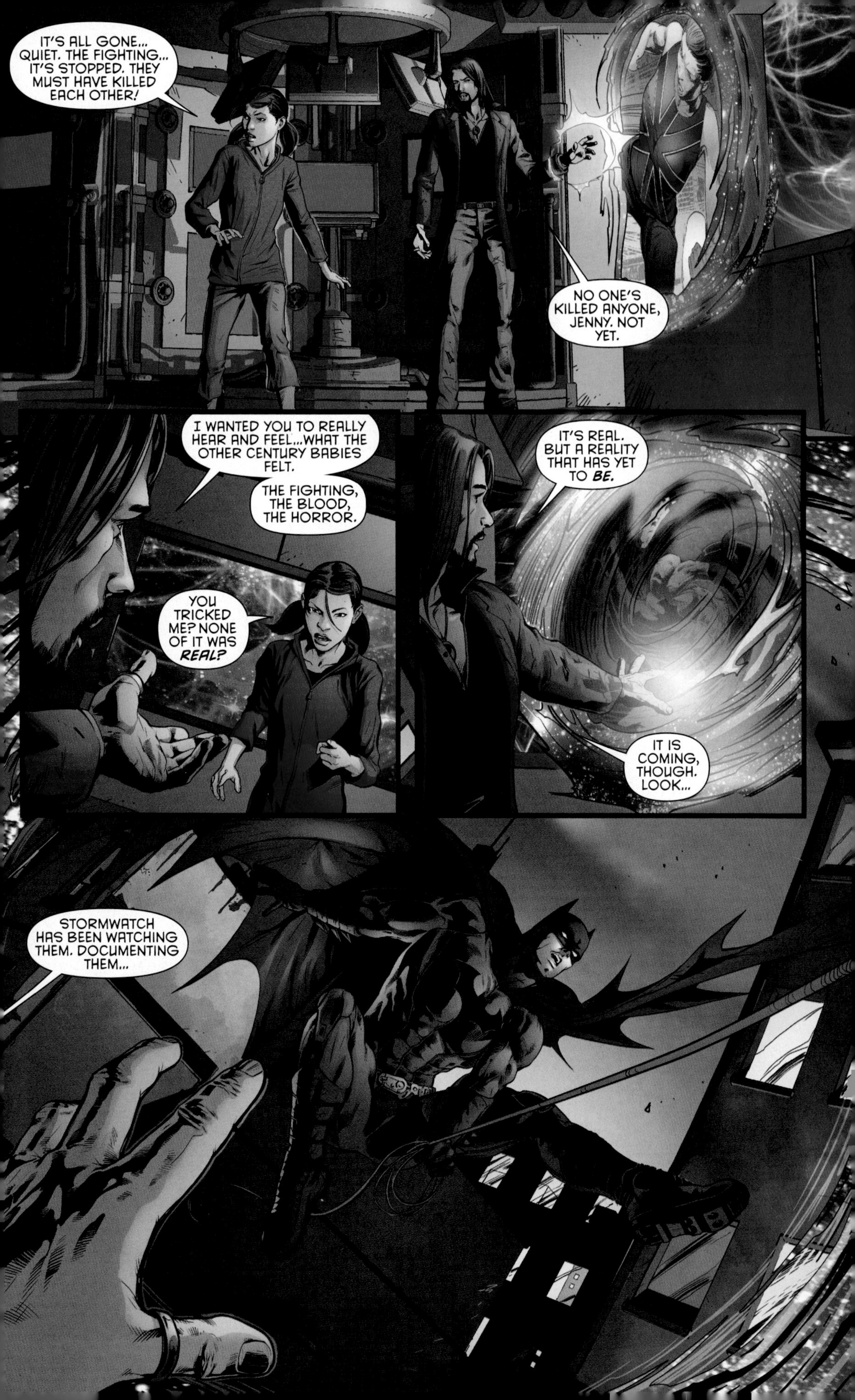
IT'S ALL GONE... QUIET. THE FIGHTING... IT'S STOPPED. THEY MUST HAVE KILLED EACH OTHER!
NO ONE'S KILLED ANYONE, JENNY. NOT YET.
I WANTED YOU TO REALLY HEAR AND FEEL...WHAT THE OTHER CENTURY BABIES FELT.
THE FIGHTING, THE BLOOD, THE HORROR.
YOU TRICKED ME? NONE OF IT WAS *REAL?*
IT'S REAL. BUT A REALITY THAT HAS YET TO *BE.*
IT IS COMING, THOUGH. LOOK...
STORMWATCH HAS BEEN WATCHING THEM. DOCUMENTING THEM...

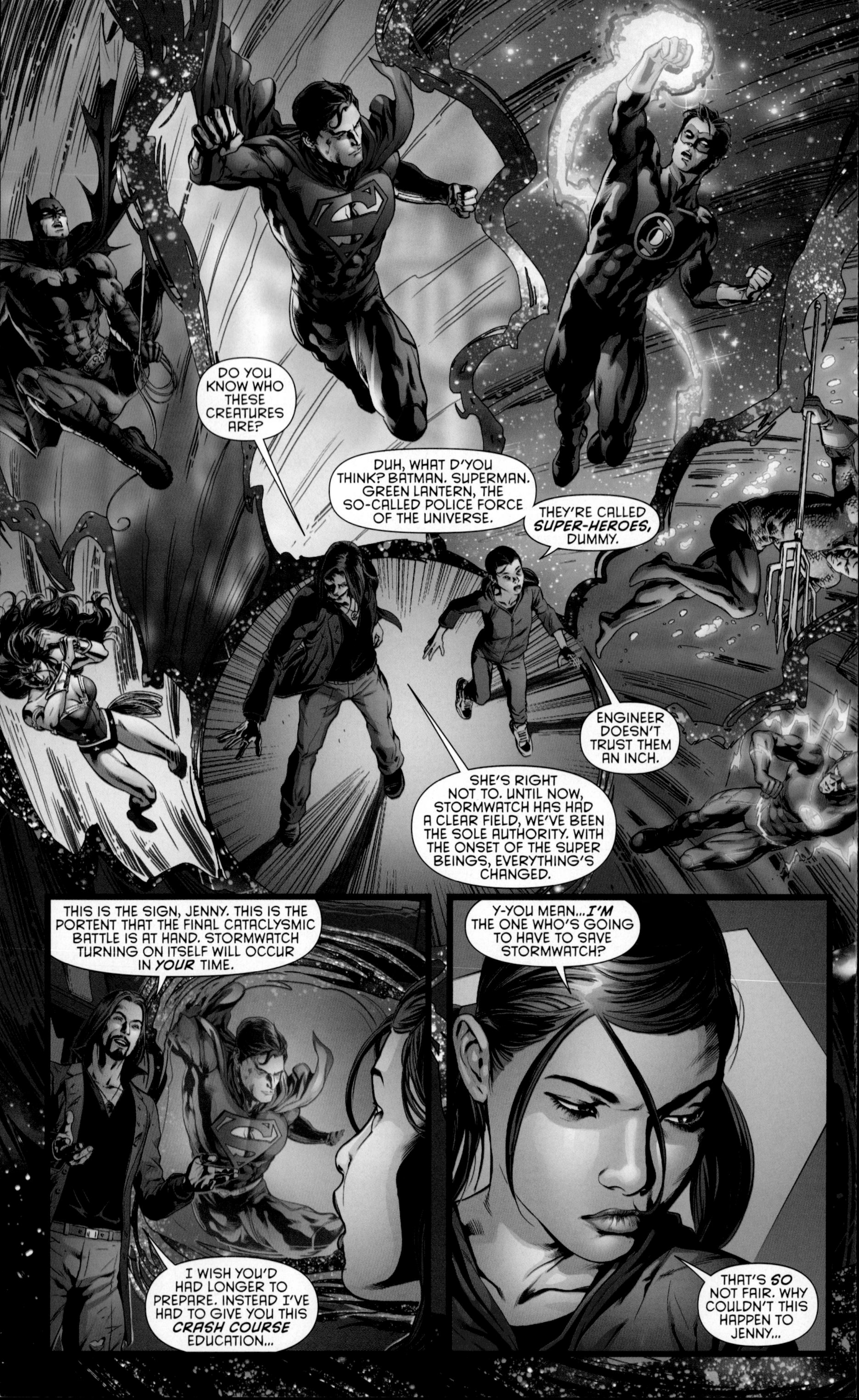
DO YOU KNOW WHO THESE CREATURES ARE?
DUH, WHAT D'YOU THINK? BATMAN. SUPERMAN. GREEN LANTERN, THE SO-CALLED POLICE FORCE OF THE UNIVERSE.
THEY'RE CALLED SUPER-HEROES, DUMMY.
ENGINEER DOESN'T TRUST THEM AN INCH.
SHE'S RIGHT NOT TO. UNTIL NOW, STORMWATCH HAS HAD A CLEAR FIELD, WE'VE BEEN THE SOLE AUTHORITY. WITH THE ONSET OF THE SUPER BEINGS, EVERYTHING'S CHANGED.
THIS IS THE SIGN, JENNY. THIS IS THE PORTENT THAT THE FINAL CATACLYSMIC BATTLE IS AT HAND. STORMWATCH TURNING ON ITSELF WILL OCCUR IN YOUR TIME.
I WISH YOU'D HAD LONGER TO PREPARE. INSTEAD I'VE HAD TO GIVE YOU THIS CRASH COURSE EDUCATION...
Y-YOU MEAN...I'M THE ONE WHO'S GOING TO HAVE TO SAVE STORMWATCH?
THAT'S SO NOT FAIR. WHY COULDN'T THIS HAPPEN TO JENNY...

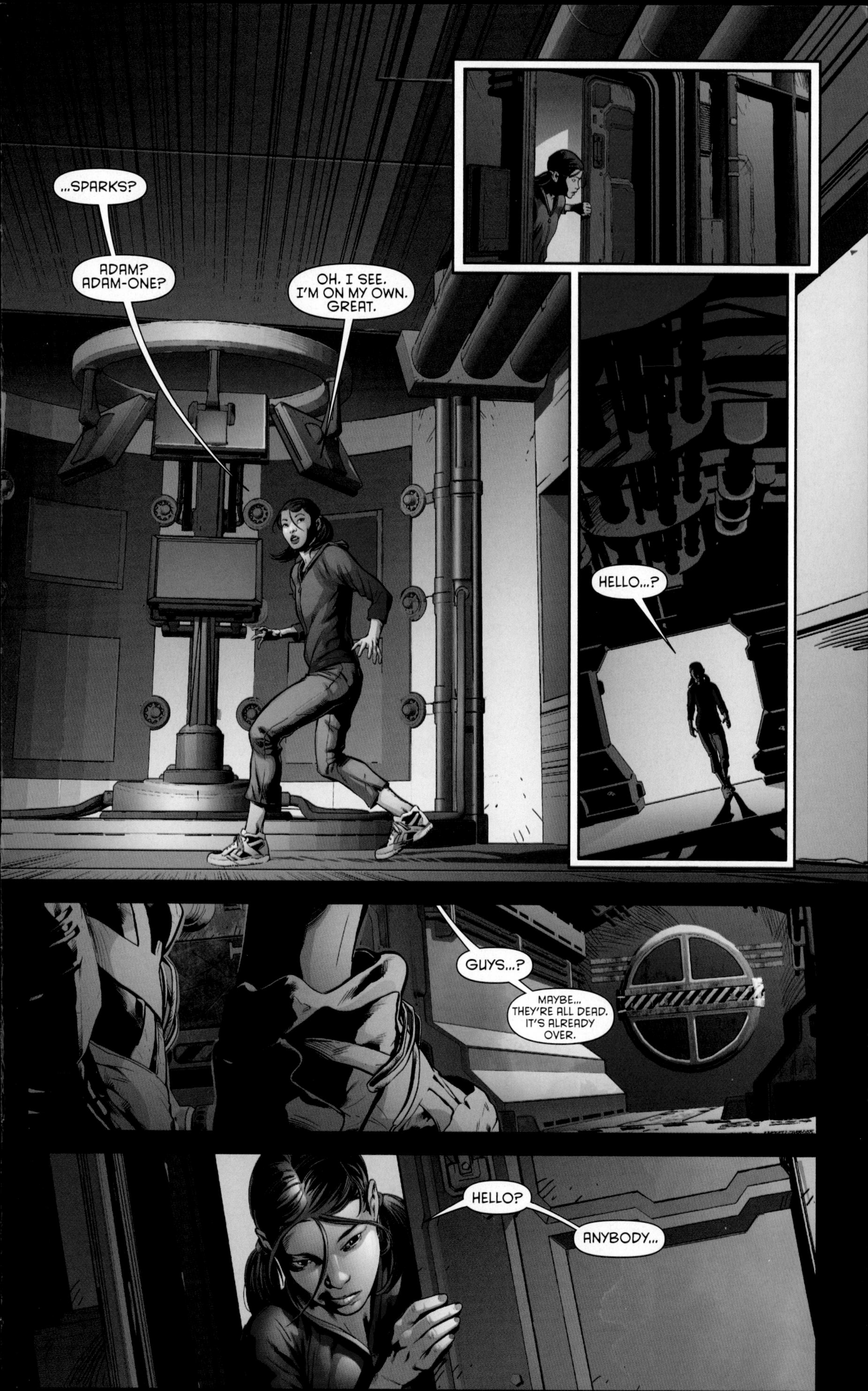
...SPARKS?
ADAM? ADAM-ONE?
OH. I SEE. I'M ON MY OWN. GREAT.
HELLO...?
GUYS...?
MAYBE... THEY'RE ALL DEAD. IT'S ALREADY OVER.
HELLO?
ANYBODY...

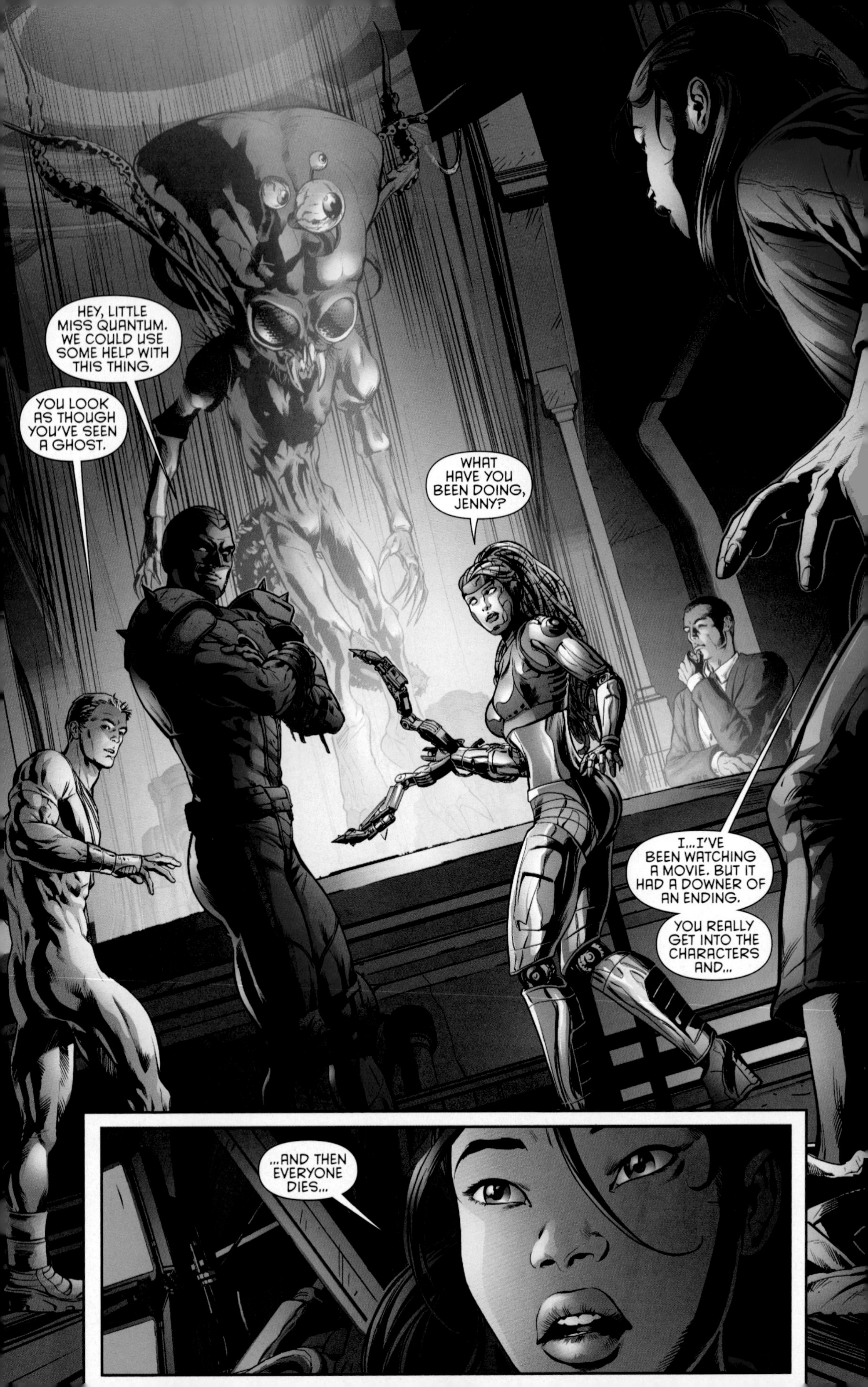
HEY, LITTLE MISS QUANTUM. WE COULD USE SOME HELP WITH THIS THING.
YOU LOOK AS THOUGH YOU'VE SEEN A GHOST.
WHAT HAVE YOU BEEN DOING, JENNY?
I...I'VE BEEN WATCHING A MOVIE. BUT IT HAD A DOWNER OF AN ENDING.
YOU REALLY GET INTO THE CHARACTERS AND...
...AND THEN EVERYONE DIES...

SEOUL BROTHERS

PETER MILLIGAN writer SIMON BISLEY artist

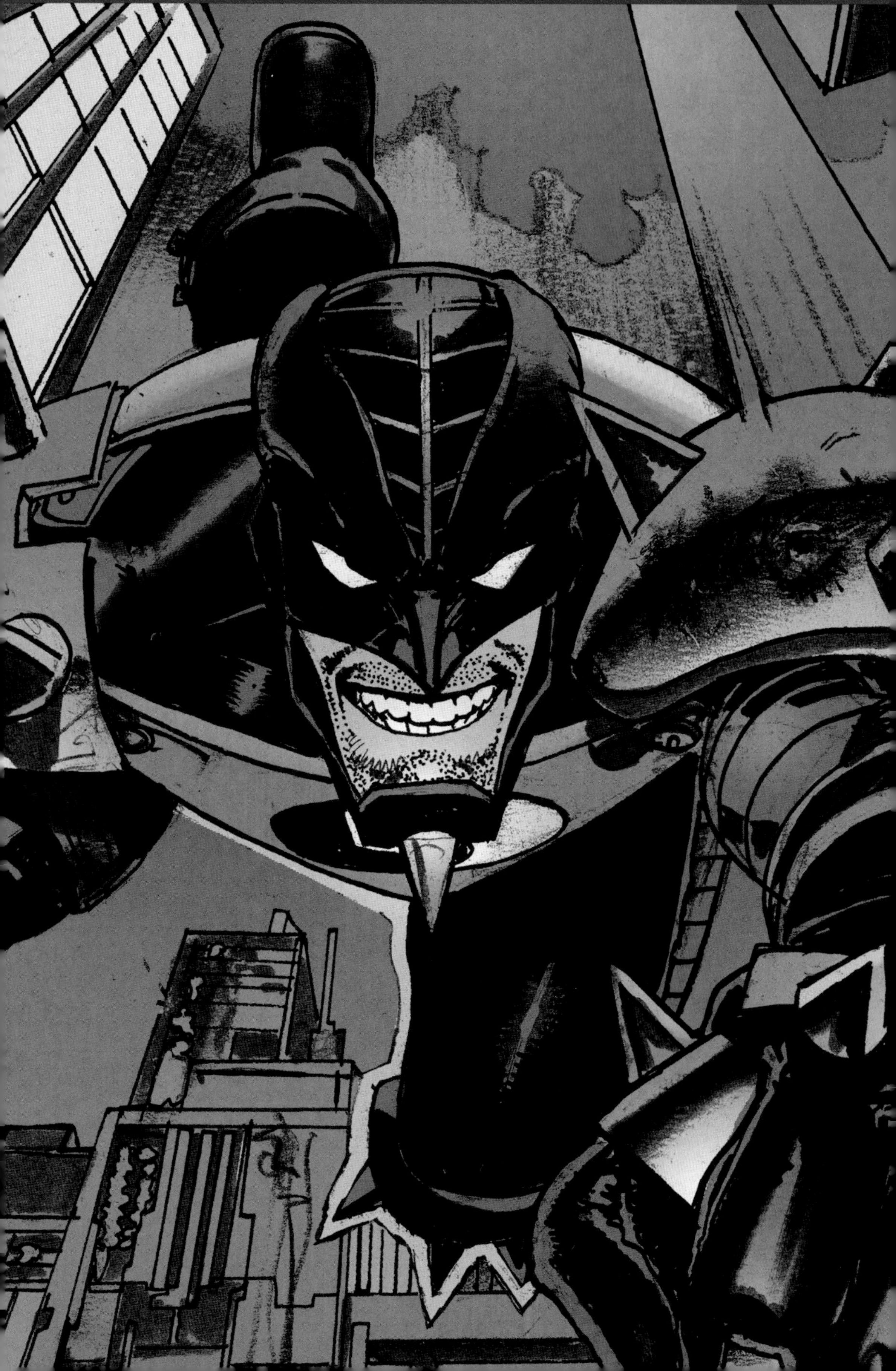

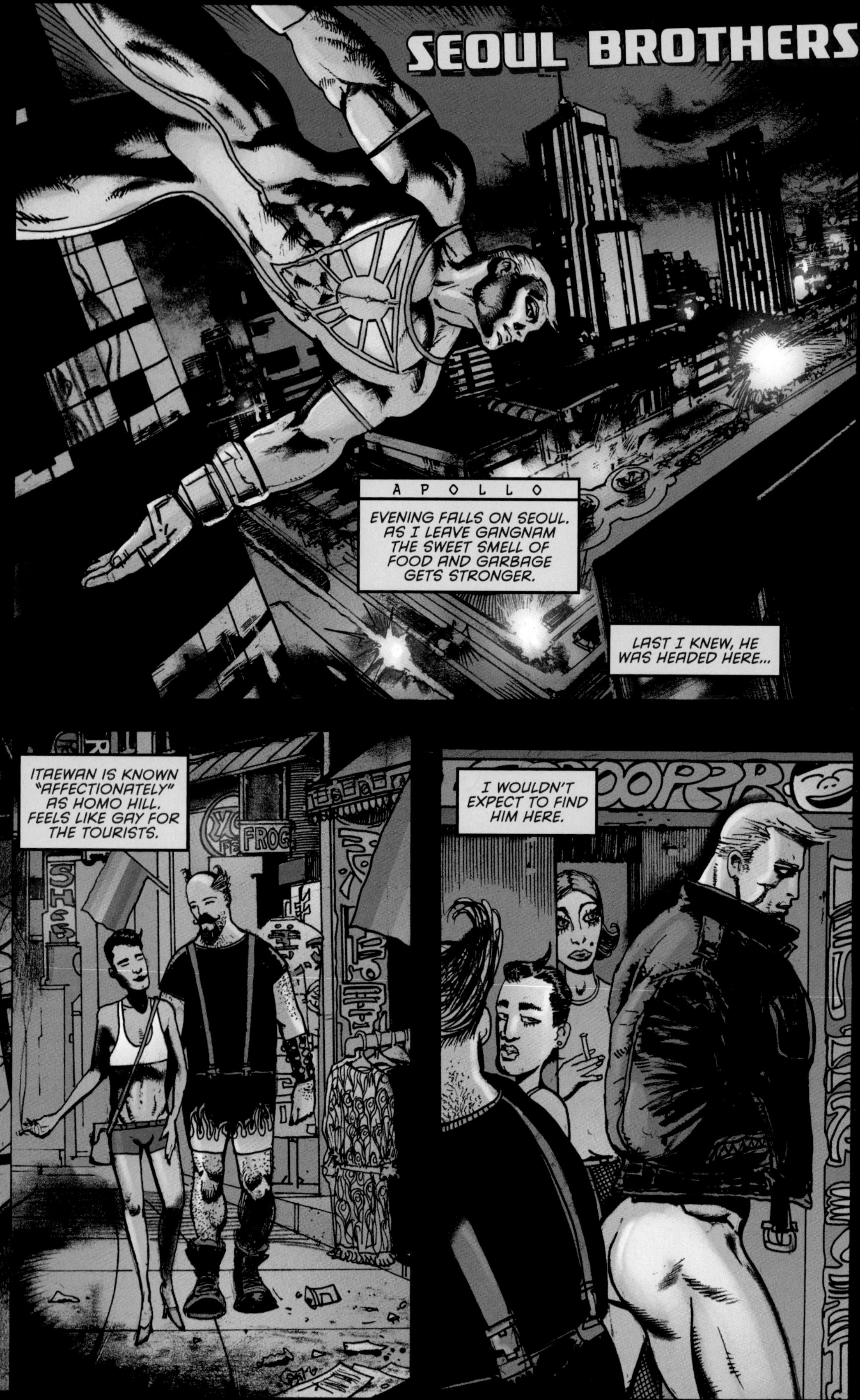
SEOUL BROTHERS
APOLLO
EVENING FALLS ON SEOUL. AS I LEAVE GANGNAM THE SWEET SMELL OF FOOD AND GARBAGE GETS STRONGER.
LAST I KNEW, HE WAS HEADED HERE...
ITAEWAN IS KNOWN "AFFECTIONATELY" AS HOMO HILL. FEELS LIKE GAY FOR THE TOURISTS.
FROG
I WOULDN'T EXPECT TO FIND HIM HERE.

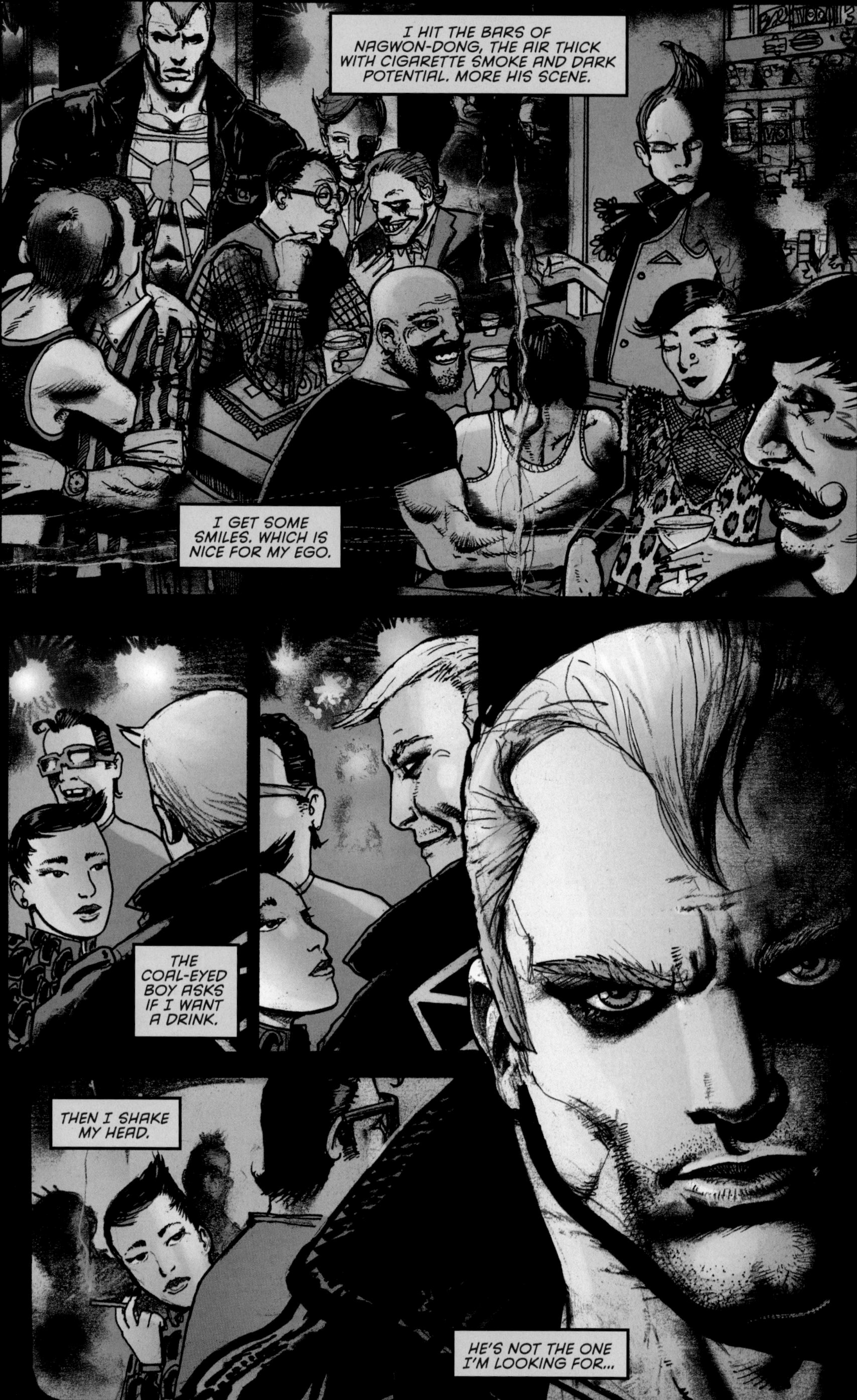
I HIT THE BARS OF NAGWON-DONG, THE AIR THICK WITH CIGARETTE SMOKE AND DARK POTENTIAL. MORE HIS SCENE.
I GET SOME SMILES. WHICH IS NICE FOR MY EGO.
THE COAL-EYED BOY ASKS IF I WANT A DRINK.
THEN I SHAKE MY HEAD.
HE'S NOT THE ONE I'M LOOKING FOR...

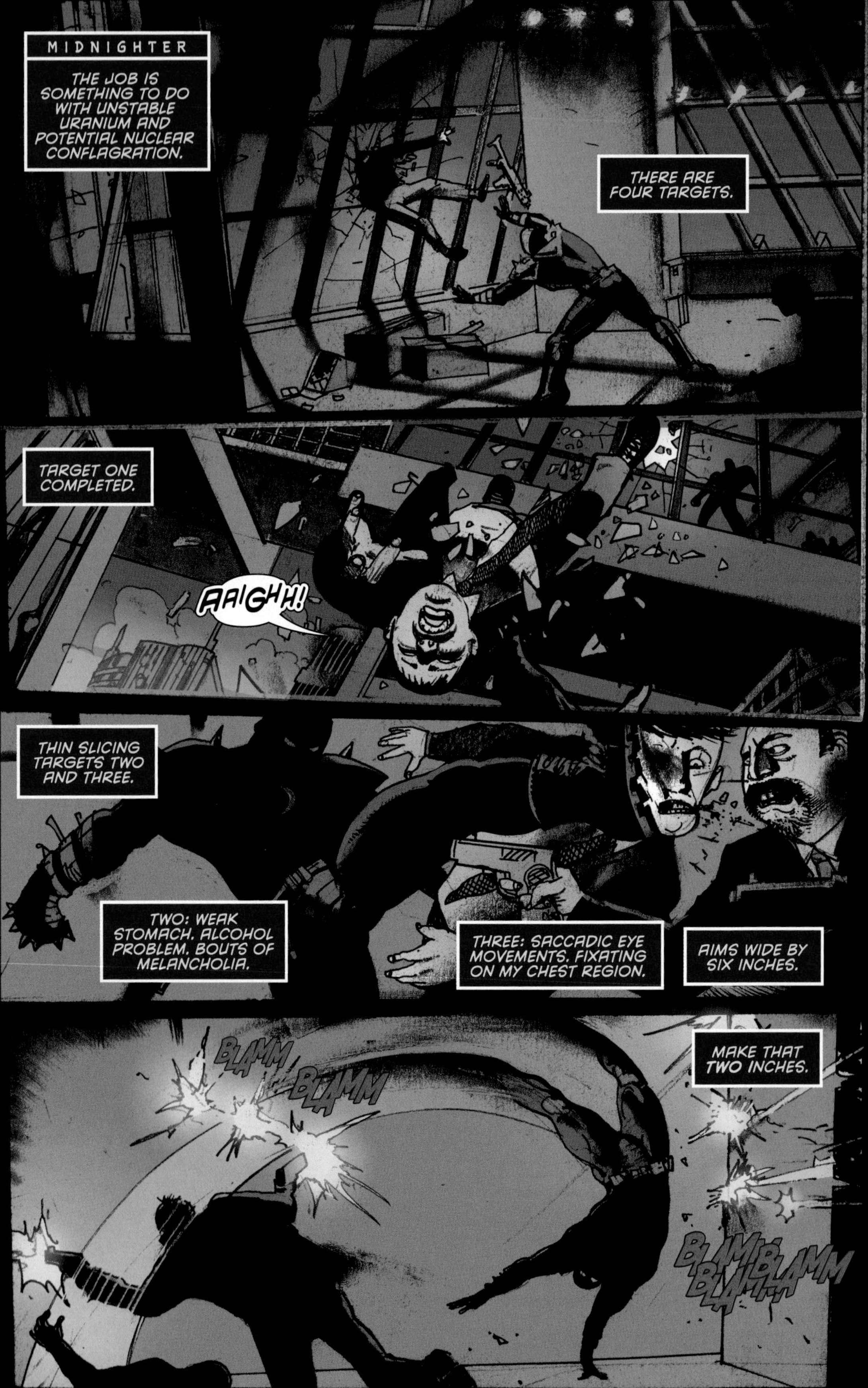
MIDNIGHTER
THE JOB IS SOMETHING TO DO WITH UNSTABLE URANIUM AND POTENTIAL NUCLEAR CONFLAGRATION.
THERE ARE FOUR TARGETS.
TARGET ONE COMPLETED.
AAIGHH!
THIN SLICING TARGETS TWO AND THREE.
TWO: WEAK STOMACH. ALCOHOL PROBLEM. BOUTS OF MELANCHOLIA.
THREE: SACCADIC EYE MOVEMENTS. FIXATING ON MY CHEST REGION.
AIMS WIDE BY SIX INCHES.
BLAMM
BLAMM
MAKE THAT TWO INCHES.
BLAM BLAMM
BLAM

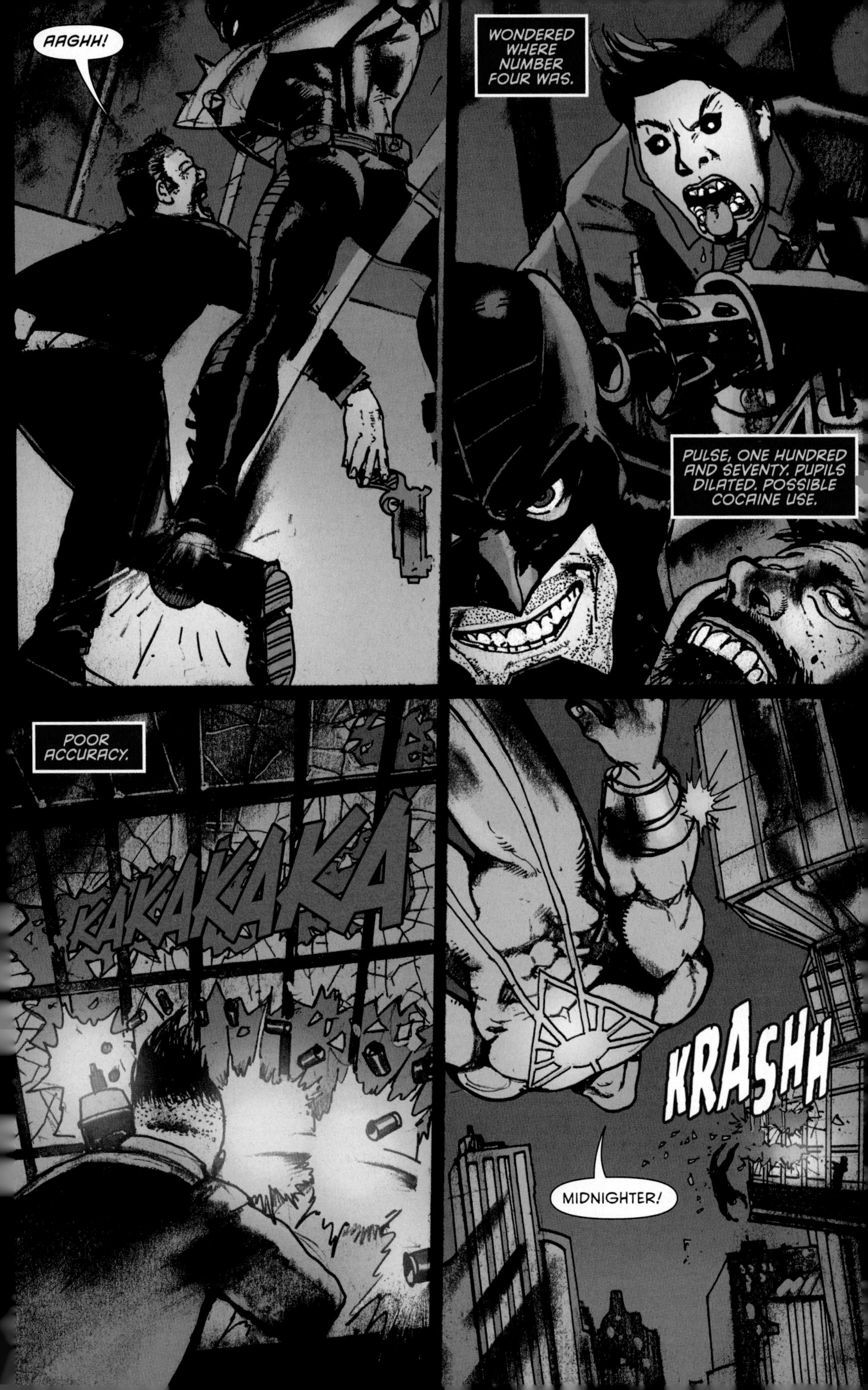
AAGHH!
WONDERED WHERE NUMBER FOUR WAS.
PULSE, ONE HUNDRED AND SEVENTY. PUPILS DILATED. POSSIBLE COCAINE USE.
POOR ACCURACY.
KAKAKAKAKA
KRASHH
MIDNIGHTER!

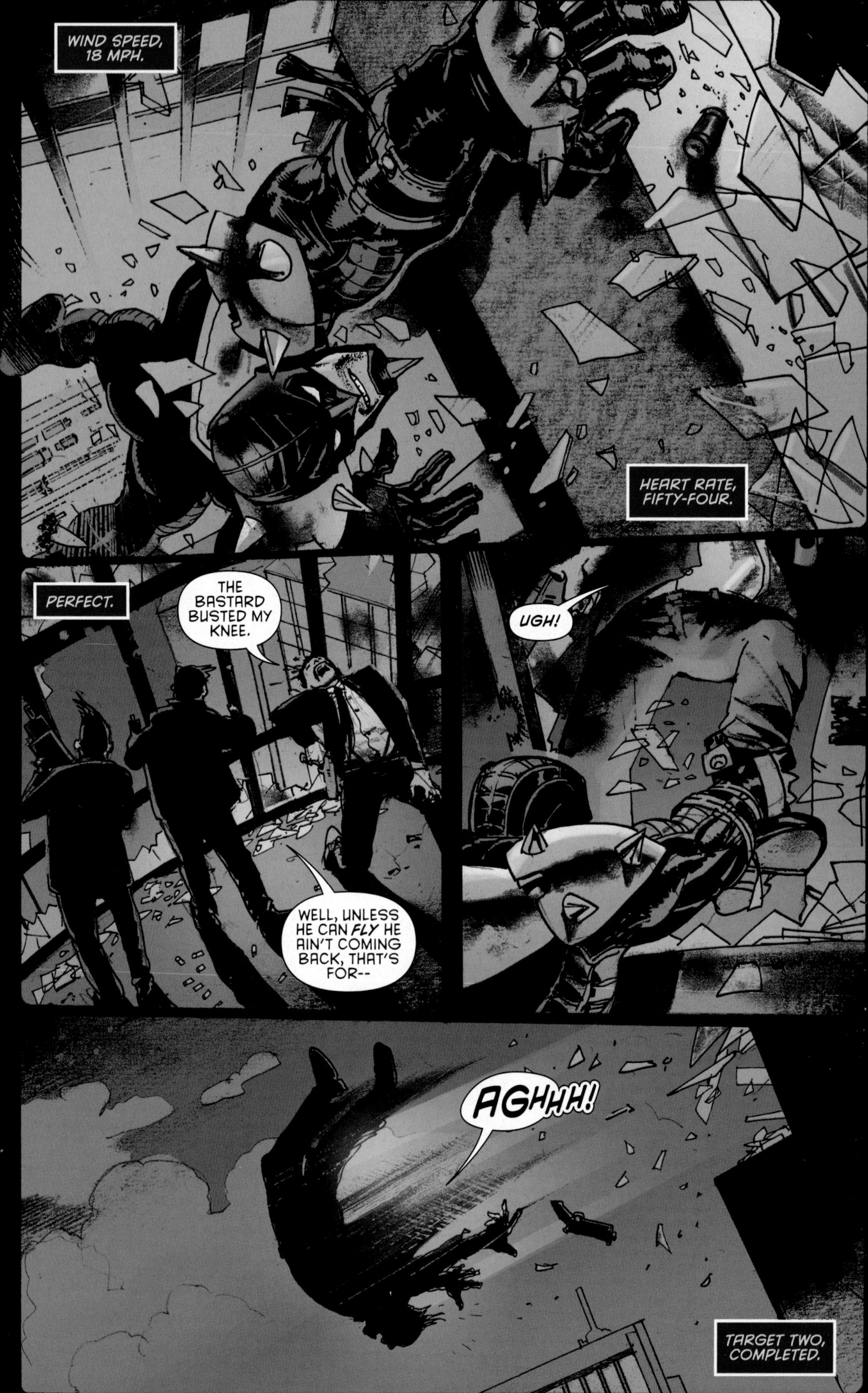

WIND SPEED, 18 MPH.
HEART RATE, FIFTY-FOUR.
PERFECT.
THE BASTARD BUSTED MY KNEE.
WELL, UNLESS HE CAN FLY HE AIN'T COMING BACK, THAT'S FOR--
UGH!
AGHHH!
TARGET TWO, COMPLETED.

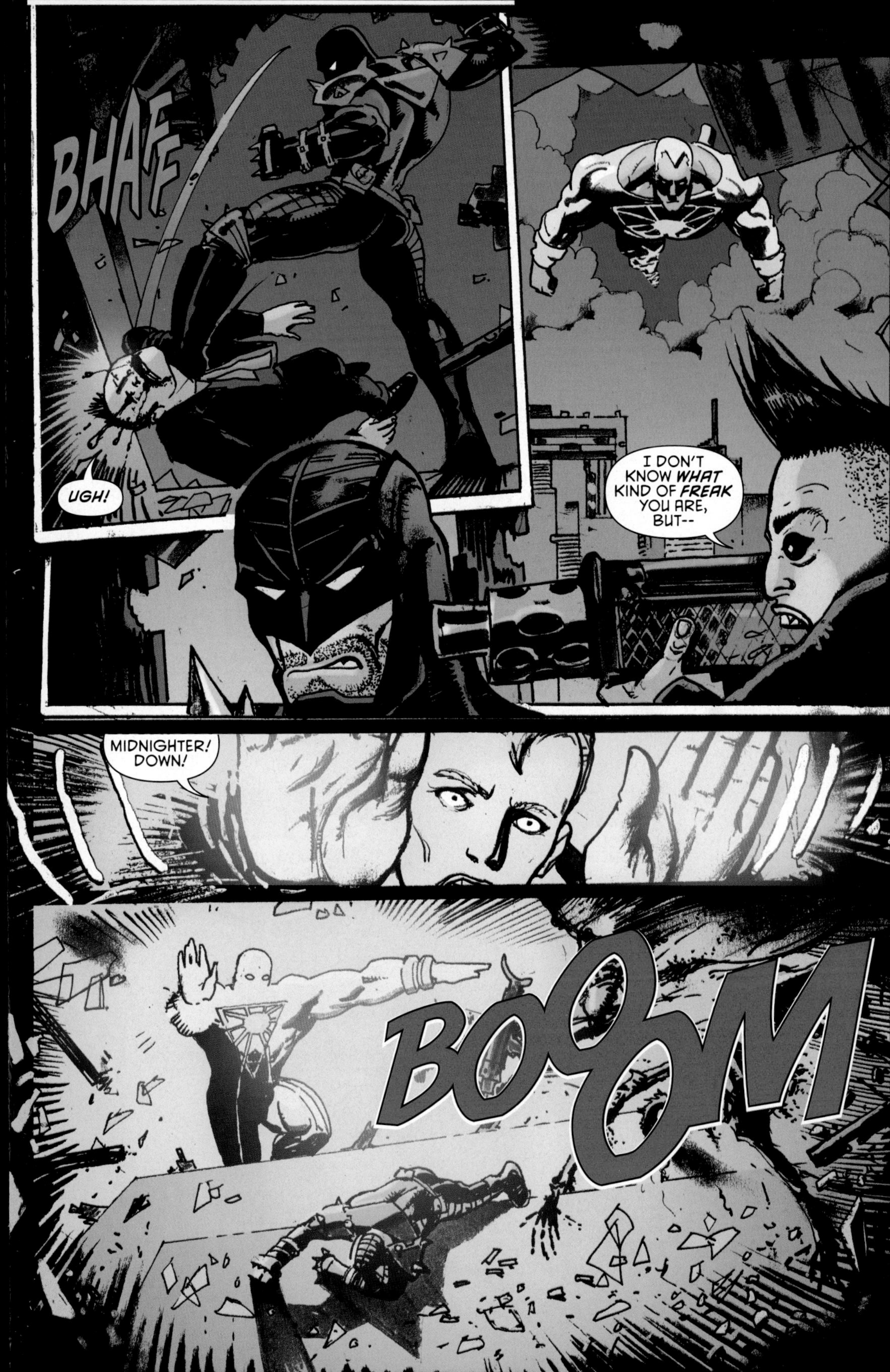
BHAFF
UGH!
I DON'T KNOW WHAT KIND OF FREAK YOU ARE, BUT--
MIDNIGHTER! DOWN!
BOOOM

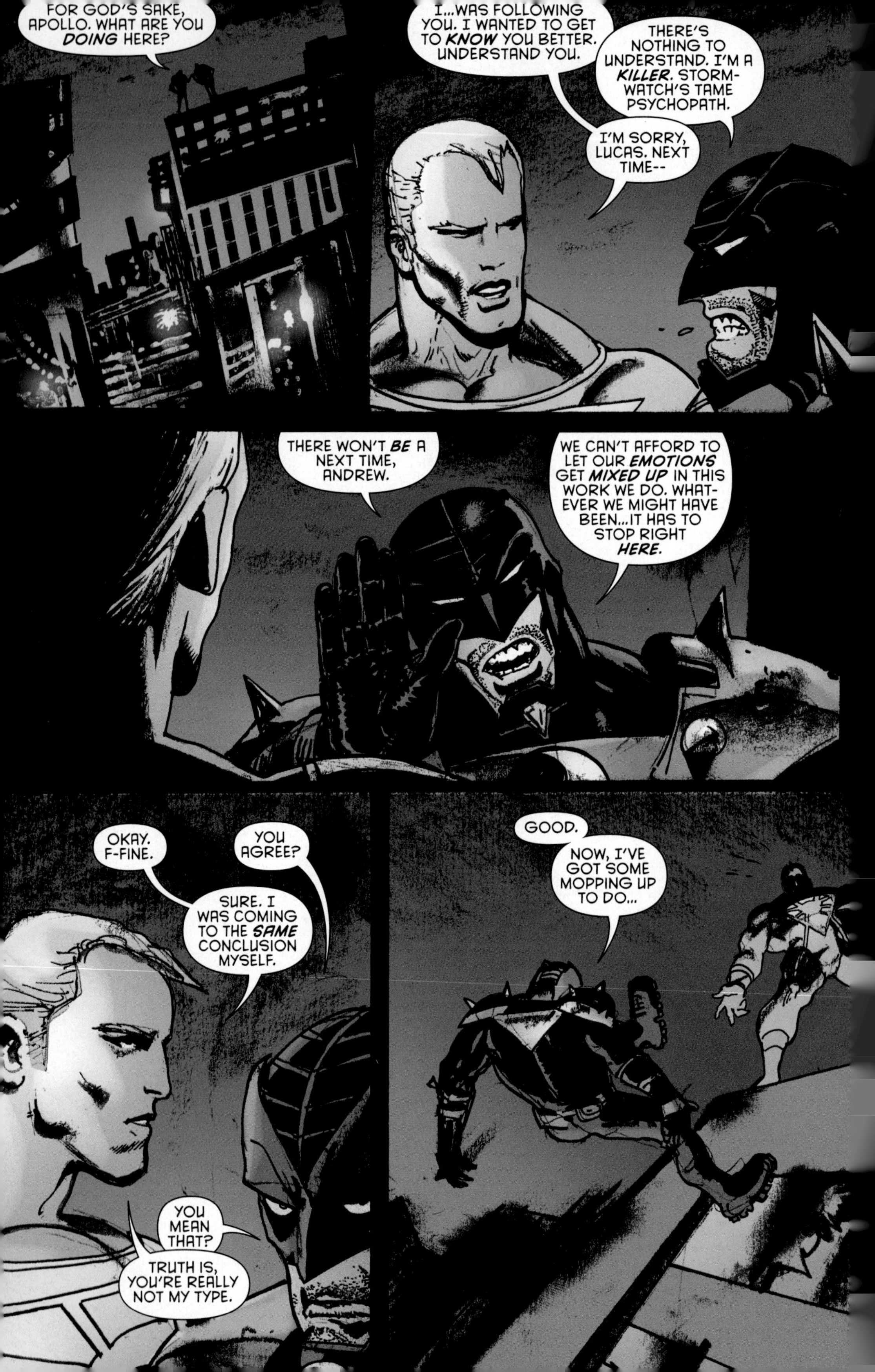
FOR GOD'S SAKE, APOLLO. WHAT ARE YOU DOING HERE?
I...WAS FOLLOWING YOU. I WANTED TO GET TO KNOW YOU BETTER. UNDERSTAND YOU.
THERE'S NOTHING TO UNDERSTAND. I'M A KILLER. STORM-WATCH'S TAME PSYCHOPATH.
I'M SORRY, LUCAS. NEXT TIME--
THERE WON'T BE A NEXT TIME, ANDREW.
WE CAN'T AFFORD TO LET OUR EMOTIONS GET MIXED UP IN THIS WORK WE DO. WHAT-EVER WE MIGHT HAVE BEEN...IT HAS TO STOP RIGHT HERE.
OKAY. F-FINE.
YOU AGREE?
SURE. I WAS COMING TO THE SAME CONCLUSION MYSELF.
YOU MEAN THAT?
TRUTH IS, YOU'RE REALLY NOT MY TYPE.
GOOD.
NOW, I'VE GOT SOME MOPPING UP TO DO...

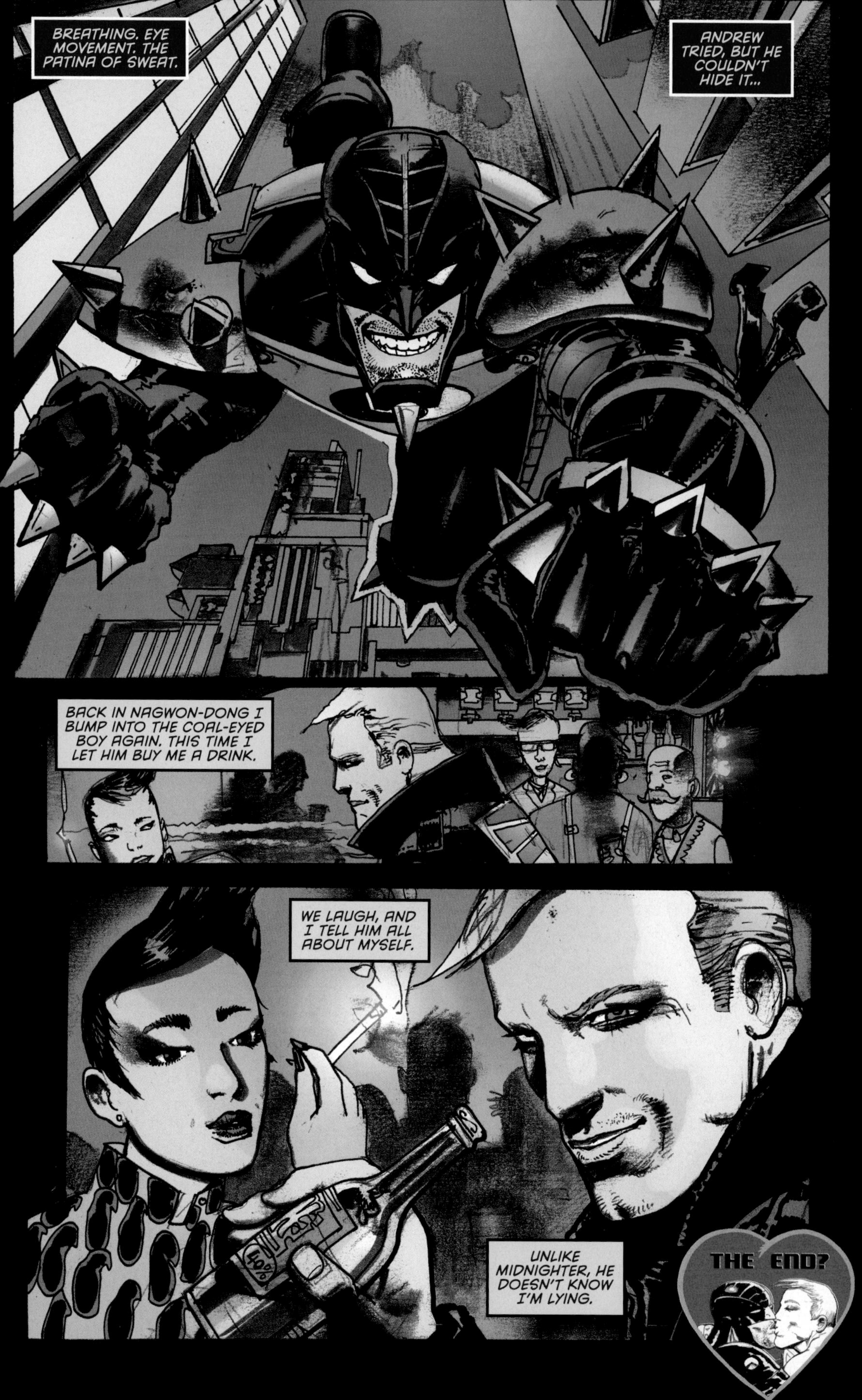
BREATHING. EYE MOVEMENT. THE PATINA OF SWEAT.
ANDREW TRIED, BUT HE COULDN'T HIDE IT...
BACK IN NAGWON-DONG I BUMP INTO THE COAL-EYED BOY AGAIN. THIS TIME I LET HIM BUY ME A DRINK.
WE LAUGH, AND I TELL HIM ALL ABOUT MYSELF.
UNLIKE MIDNIGHTER, HE DOESN'T KNOW I'M LYING.
THE END?

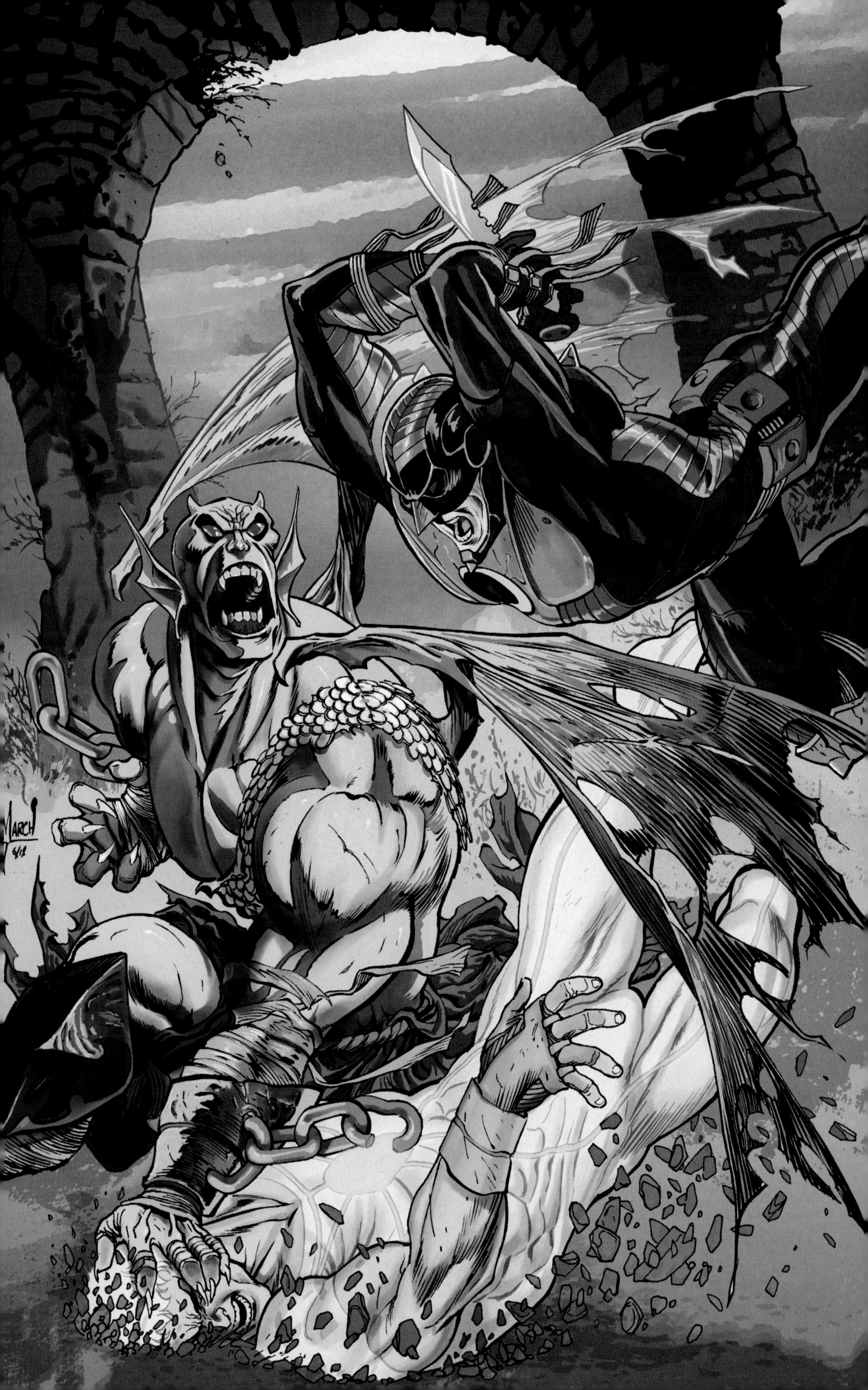
MARCH

THE RISE OF THE DEMON PART ONE: THE DREAMING TOWER

PETER MILLIGAN writer **WILL CONRAD & CLIFF RICHARDS** artists cover art by **GUILLEM MARCH**

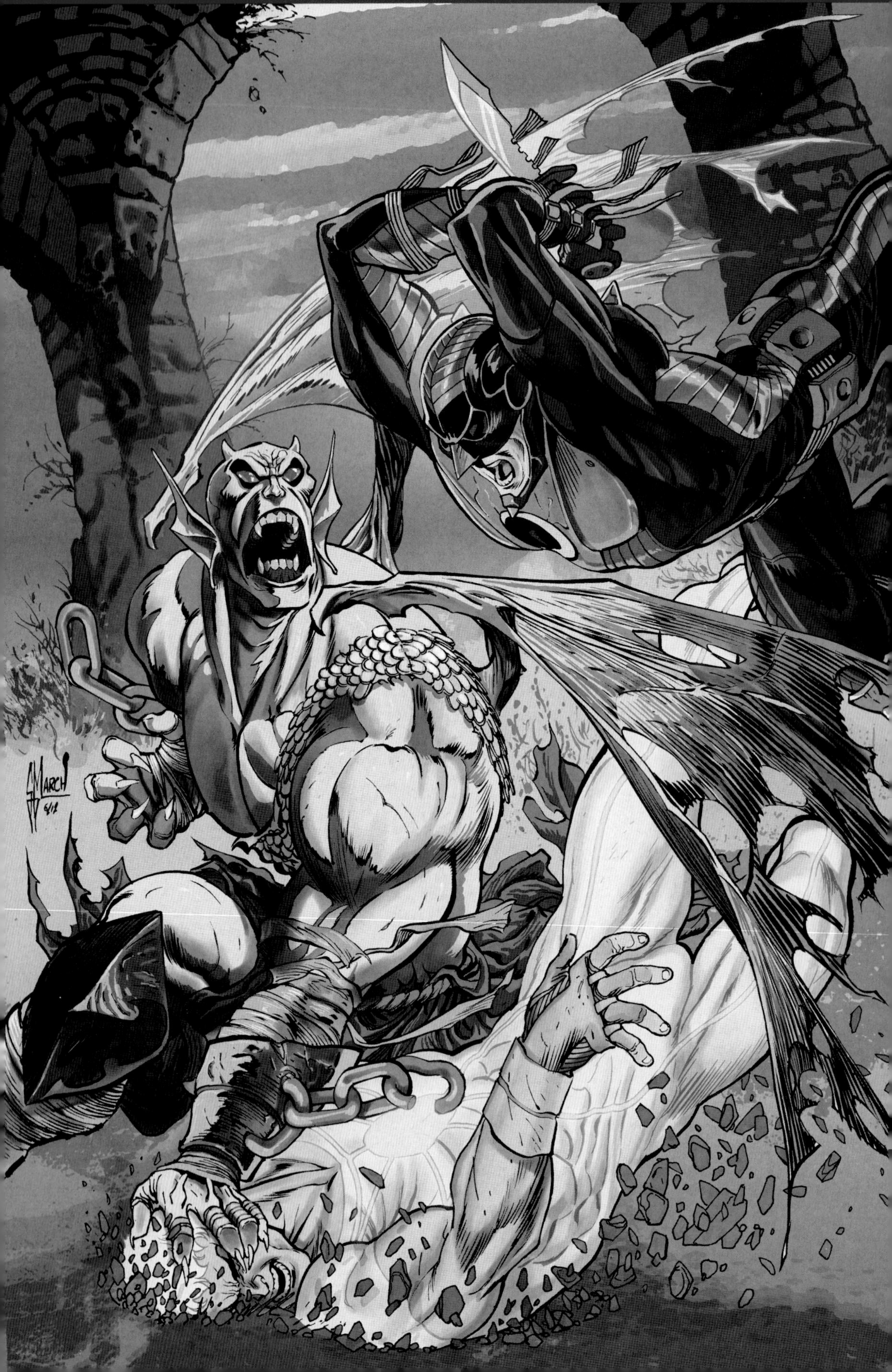

GMARCH

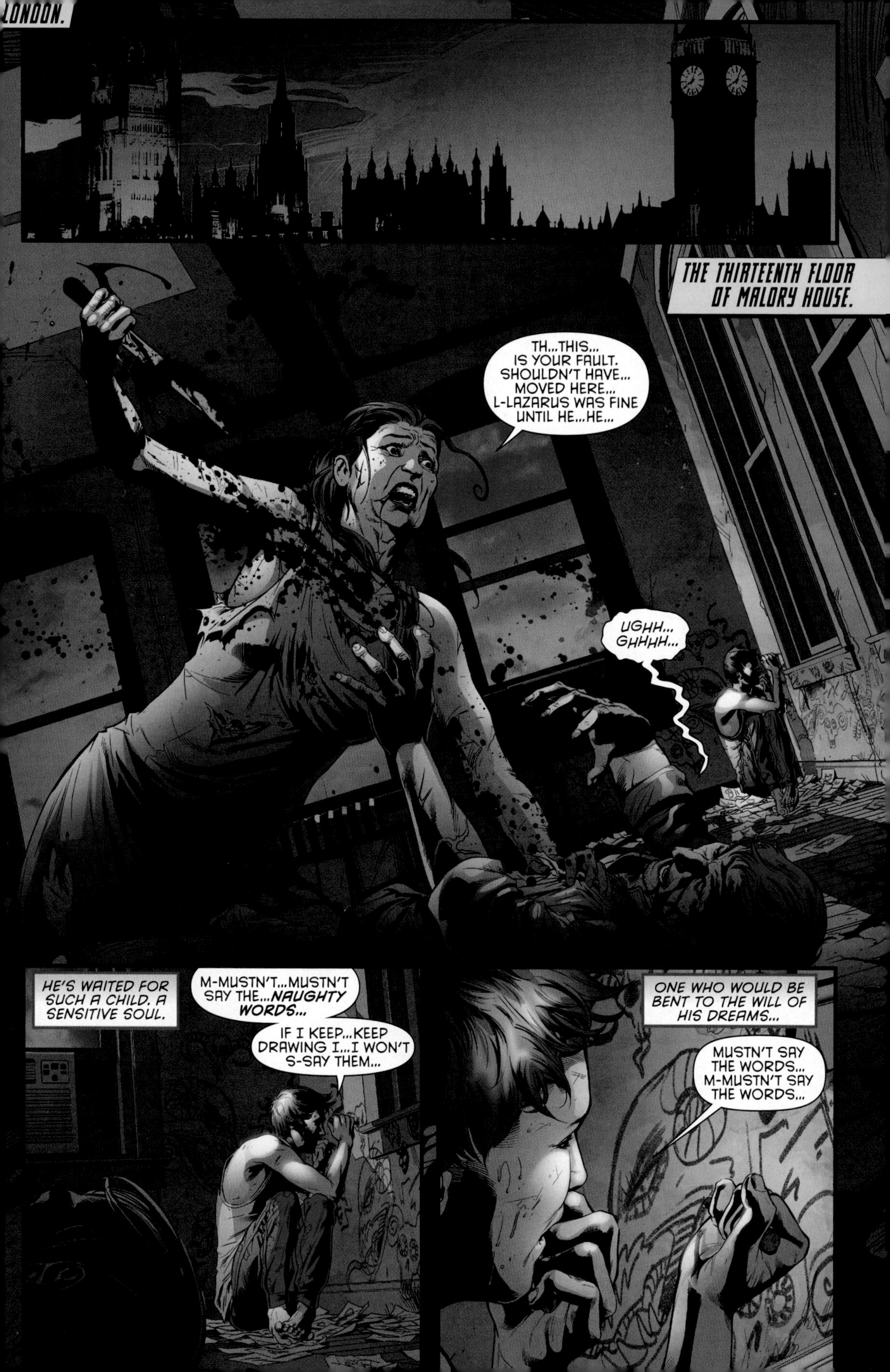
LONDON.
THE THIRTEENTH FLOOR OF MALORY HOUSE.
TH...THIS... IS YOUR FAULT. SHOULDN'T HAVE... MOVED HERE... L-LAZARUS WAS FINE UNTIL HE...HE...
UGHH... GHHHH...
HE'S WAITED FOR SUCH A CHILD. A SENSITIVE SOUL.
M-MUSTN'T...MUSTN'T SAY THE...NAUGHTY WORDS...
IF I KEEP...KEEP DRAWING I...I WON'T S-SAY THEM...
ONE WHO WOULD BE BENT TO THE WILL OF HIS DREAMS...
MUSTN'T SAY THE WORDS... M-MUSTN'T SAY THE WORDS...

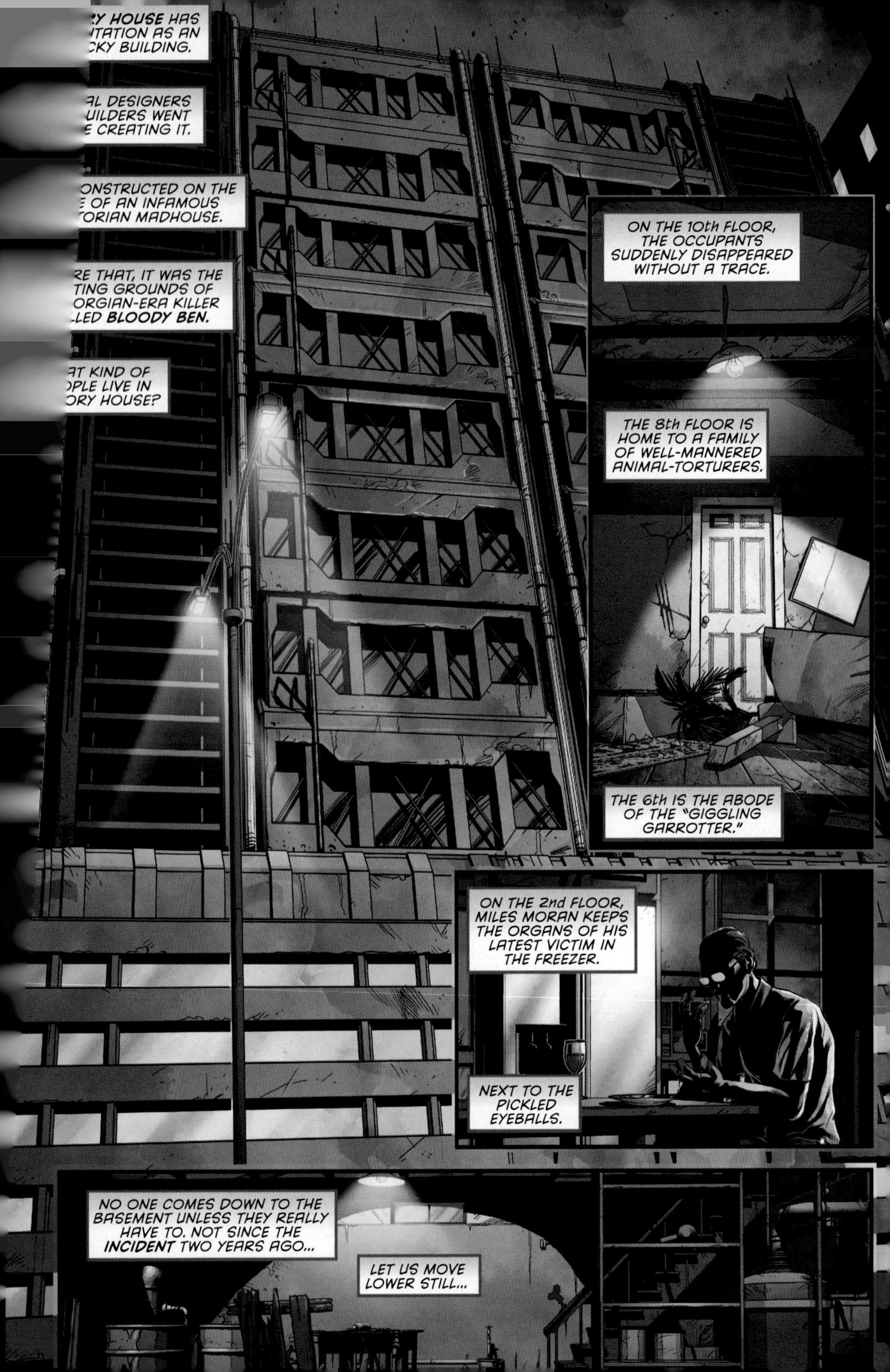

ZY HOUSE HAS
ITATION AS AN
CKY BUILDING.
AL DESIGNERS
UILDERS WENT
E CREATING IT.
ONSTRUCTED ON THE
E OF AN INFAMOUS
TORIAN MADHOUSE.
RE THAT, IT WAS THE
TING GROUNDS OF
ORGIAN-ERA KILLER
LLED BLOODY BEN.
AT KIND OF
OPLE LIVE IN
ORY HOUSE?
ON THE 10th FLOOR, THE OCCUPANTS SUDDENLY DISAPPEARED WITHOUT A TRACE.
THE 8th FLOOR IS HOME TO A FAMILY OF WELL-MANNERED ANIMAL-TORTURERS.
THE 6th IS THE ABODE OF THE "GIGGLING GARROTTER."
ON THE 2nd FLOOR, MILES MORAN KEEPS THE ORGANS OF HIS LATEST VICTIM IN THE FREEZER.
NEXT TO THE PICKLED EYEBALLS.
NO ONE COMES DOWN TO THE BASEMENT UNLESS THEY REALLY HAVE TO. NOT SINCE THE INCIDENT TWO YEARS AGO...
LET US MOVE LOWER STILL...

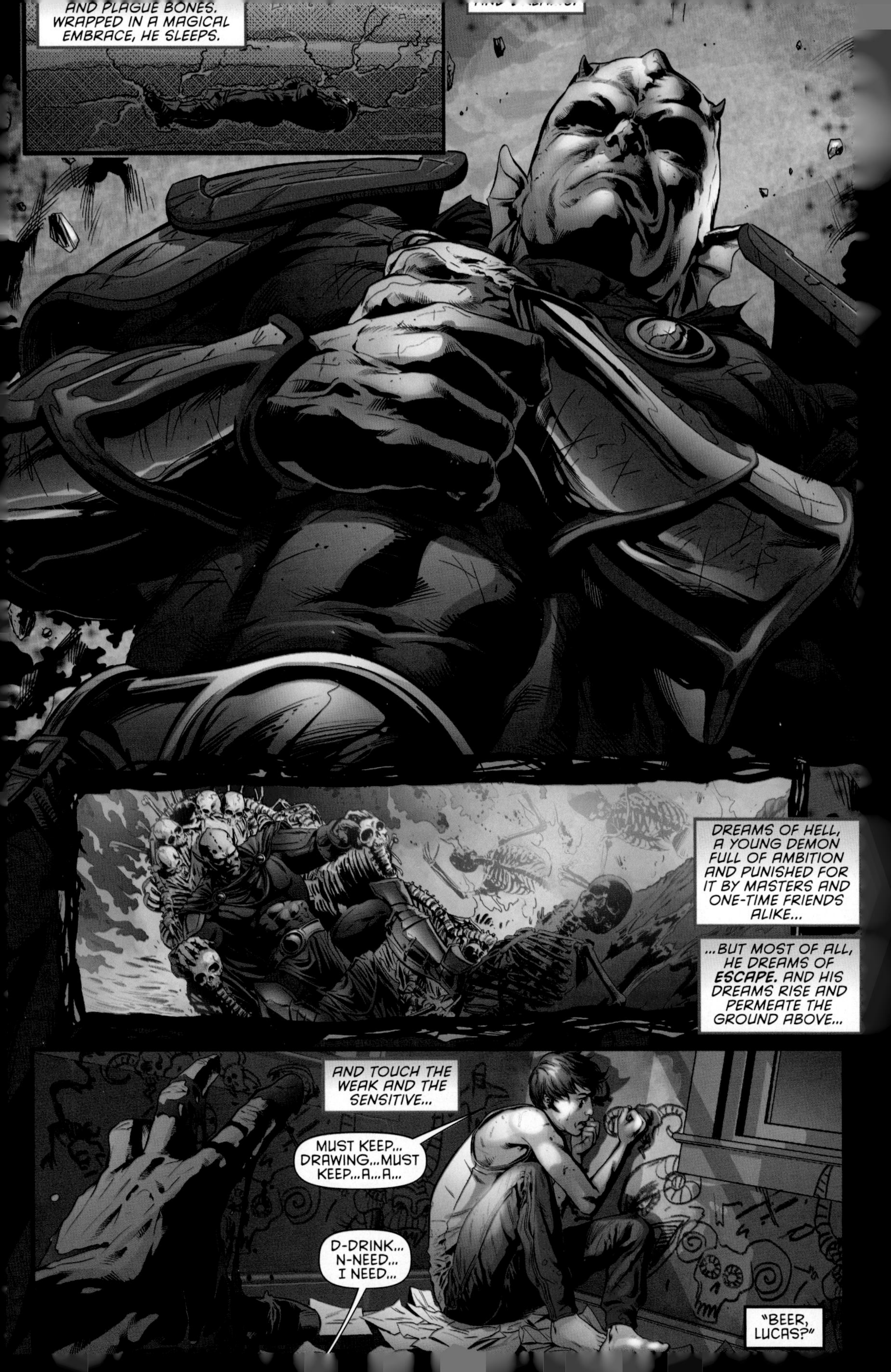

AND PLAGUE BONES. WRAPPED IN A MAGICAL EMBRACE, HE SLEEPS.
DREAMS OF HELL, A YOUNG DEMON FULL OF AMBITION AND PUNISHED FOR IT BY MASTERS AND ONE-TIME FRIENDS ALIKE...
...BUT MOST OF ALL, HE DREAMS OF ESCAPE. AND HIS DREAMS RISE AND PERMEATE THE GROUND ABOVE...
AND TOUCH THE WEAK AND THE SENSITIVE...
MUST KEEP... DRAWING...MUST KEEP...A...A...
D-DRINK... N-NEED... I NEED...
"BEER, LUCAS?"

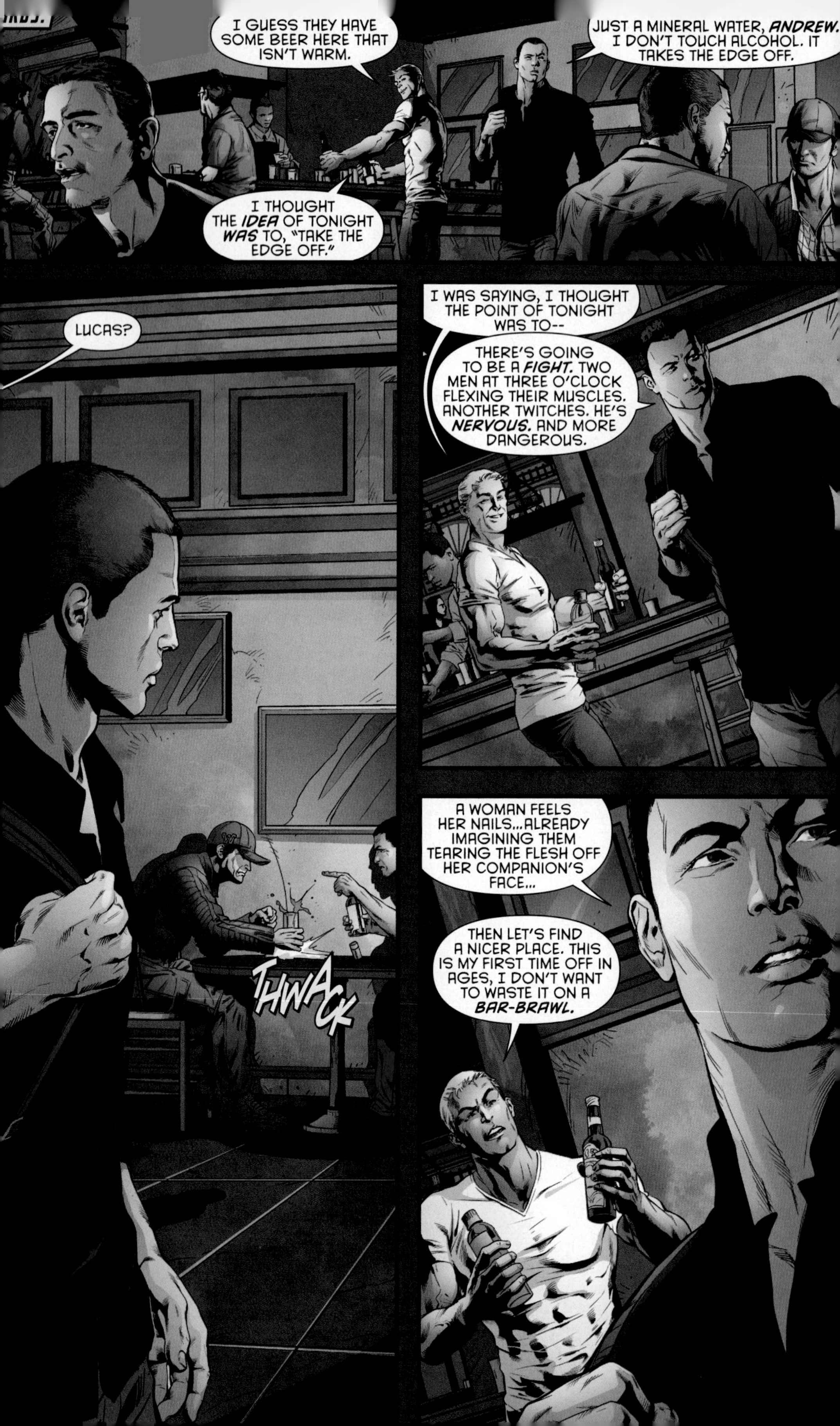
I GUESS THEY HAVE SOME BEER HERE THAT ISN'T WARM.
I THOUGHT THE IDEA OF TONIGHT WAS TO, "TAKE THE EDGE OFF."
JUST A MINERAL WATER, ANDREW. I DON'T TOUCH ALCOHOL. IT TAKES THE EDGE OFF.
LUCAS?
I WAS SAYING, I THOUGHT THE POINT OF TONIGHT WAS TO--
THERE'S GOING TO BE A FIGHT. TWO MEN AT THREE O'CLOCK FLEXING THEIR MUSCLES. ANOTHER TWITCHES. HE'S NERVOUS. AND MORE DANGEROUS.
THWACK
A WOMAN FEELS HER NAILS...ALREADY IMAGINING THEM TEARING THE FLESH OFF HER COMPANION'S FACE...
THEN LET'S FIND A NICER PLACE. THIS IS MY FIRST TIME OFF IN AGES, I DON'T WANT TO WASTE IT ON A BAR-BRAWL.

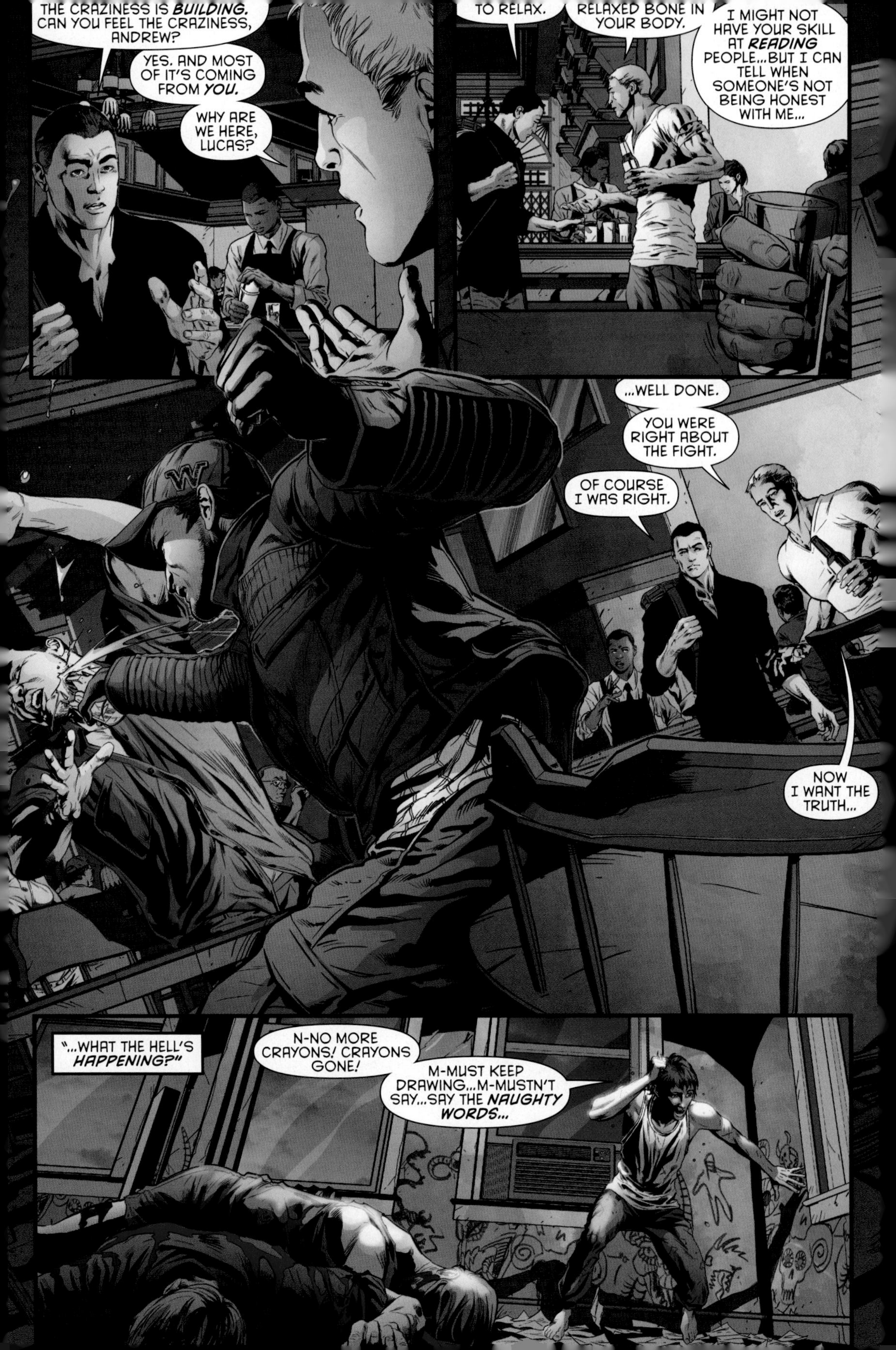
THE CRAZINESS IS BUILDING. CAN YOU FEEL THE CRAZINESS, ANDREW?
YES. AND MOST OF IT'S COMING FROM YOU.
WHY ARE WE HERE, LUCAS?
TO RELAX.
RELAXED BONE IN YOUR BODY.
I MIGHT NOT HAVE YOUR SKILL AT READING PEOPLE...BUT I CAN TELL WHEN SOMEONE'S NOT BEING HONEST WITH ME...
...WELL DONE.
YOU WERE RIGHT ABOUT THE FIGHT.
OF COURSE I WAS RIGHT.
NOW I WANT THE TRUTH...
"...WHAT THE HELL'S HAPPENING?"
N-NO MORE CRAYONS! CRAYONS GONE!
M-MUST KEEP DRAWING...M-MUSTN'T SAY...SAY THE NAUGHTY WORDS...

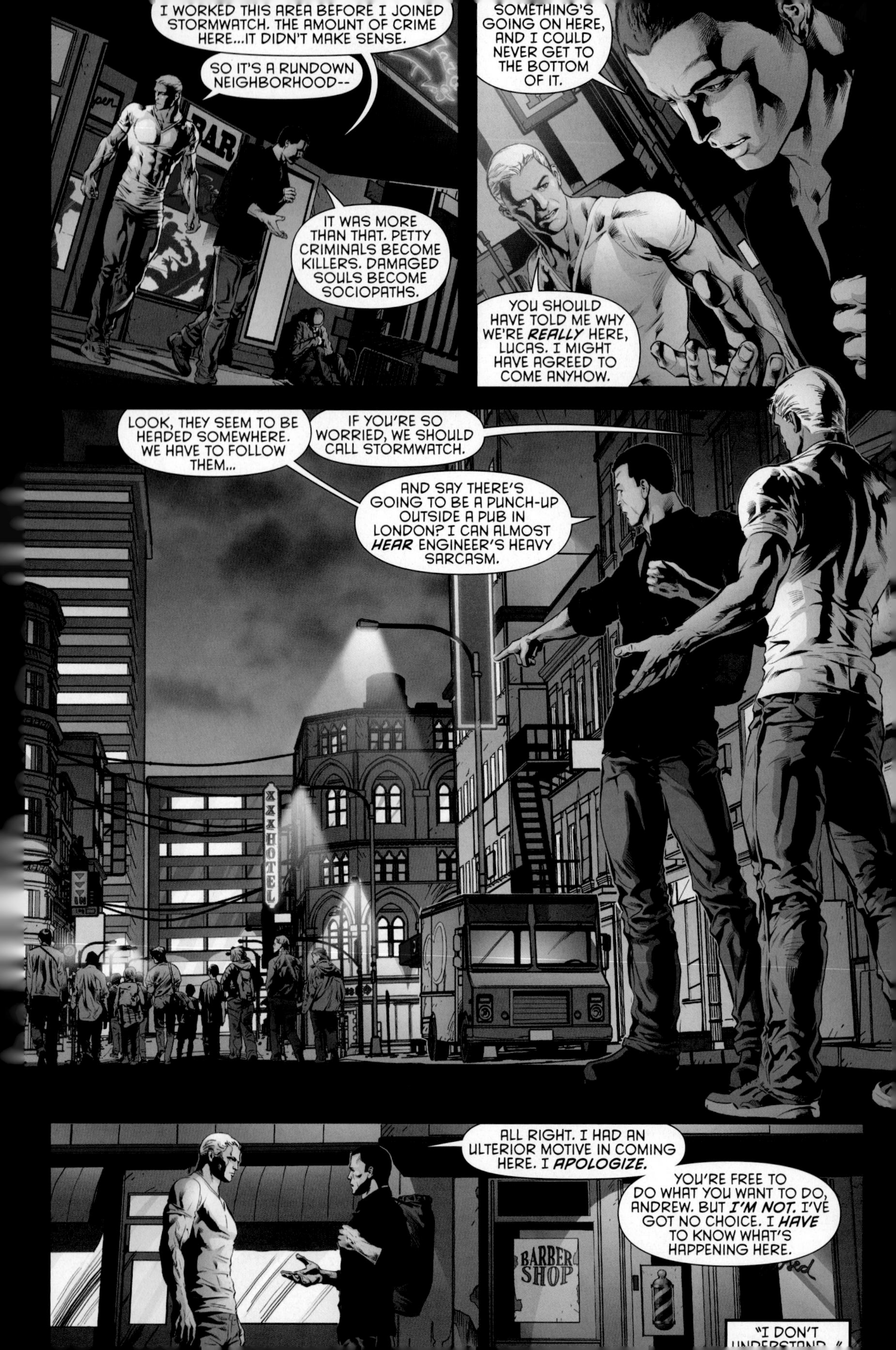
I WORKED THIS AREA BEFORE I JOINED STORMWATCH. THE AMOUNT OF CRIME HERE...IT DIDN'T MAKE SENSE.
SO IT'S A RUNDOWN NEIGHBORHOOD--
BAR
IT WAS MORE THAN THAT. PETTY CRIMINALS BECOME KILLERS. DAMAGED SOULS BECOME SOCIOPATHS.
SOMETHING'S GOING ON HERE, AND I COULD NEVER GET TO THE BOTTOM OF IT.
YOU SHOULD HAVE TOLD ME WHY WE'RE *REALLY* HERE, LUCAS. I MIGHT HAVE AGREED TO COME ANYHOW.
LOOK, THEY SEEM TO BE HEADED SOMEWHERE. WE HAVE TO FOLLOW THEM...
IF YOU'RE SO WORRIED, WE SHOULD CALL STORMWATCH.
AND SAY THERE'S GOING TO BE A PUNCH-UP OUTSIDE A PUB IN LONDON? I CAN ALMOST ***HEAR*** ENGINEER'S HEAVY SARCASM.
HOTEL
ALL RIGHT. I HAD AN ULTERIOR MOTIVE IN COMING HERE. I ***APOLOGIZE.***
YOU'RE FREE TO DO WHAT YOU WANT TO DO, ANDREW. BUT ***I'M NOT.*** I'VE GOT NO CHOICE. I ***HAVE*** TO KNOW WHAT'S HAPPENING HERE.
BARBER SHOP
“I DON'T

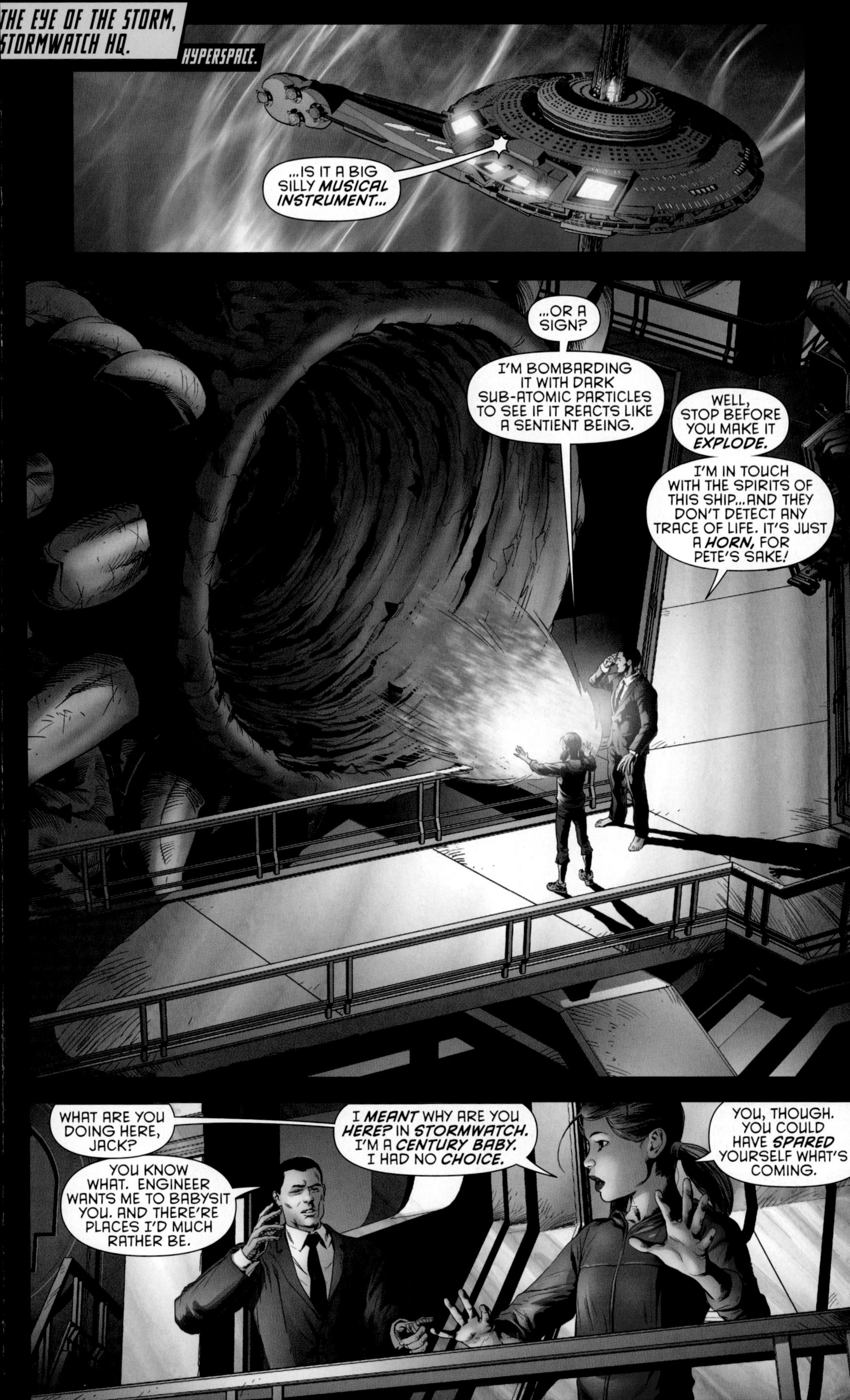
THE EYE OF THE STORM, STORMWATCH HQ.
HYPERSPACE.
...IS IT A BIG SILLY MUSICAL INSTRUMENT...
...OR A SIGN?
I'M BOMBARDING IT WITH DARK SUB-ATOMIC PARTICLES TO SEE IF IT REACTS LIKE A SENTIENT BEING.
WELL, STOP BEFORE YOU MAKE IT EXPLODE.
I'M IN TOUCH WITH THE SPIRITS OF THIS SHIP...AND THEY DON'T DETECT ANY TRACE OF LIFE. IT'S JUST A HORN, FOR PETE'S SAKE!
WHAT ARE YOU DOING HERE, JACK?
YOU KNOW WHAT. ENGINEER WANTS ME TO BABYSIT YOU. AND THERE'RE PLACES I'D MUCH RATHER BE.
I MEANT WHY ARE YOU HERE? IN STORMWATCH. I'M A CENTURY BABY. I HAD NO CHOICE.
YOU, THOUGH. YOU COULD HAVE SPARED YOURSELF WHAT'S COMING.

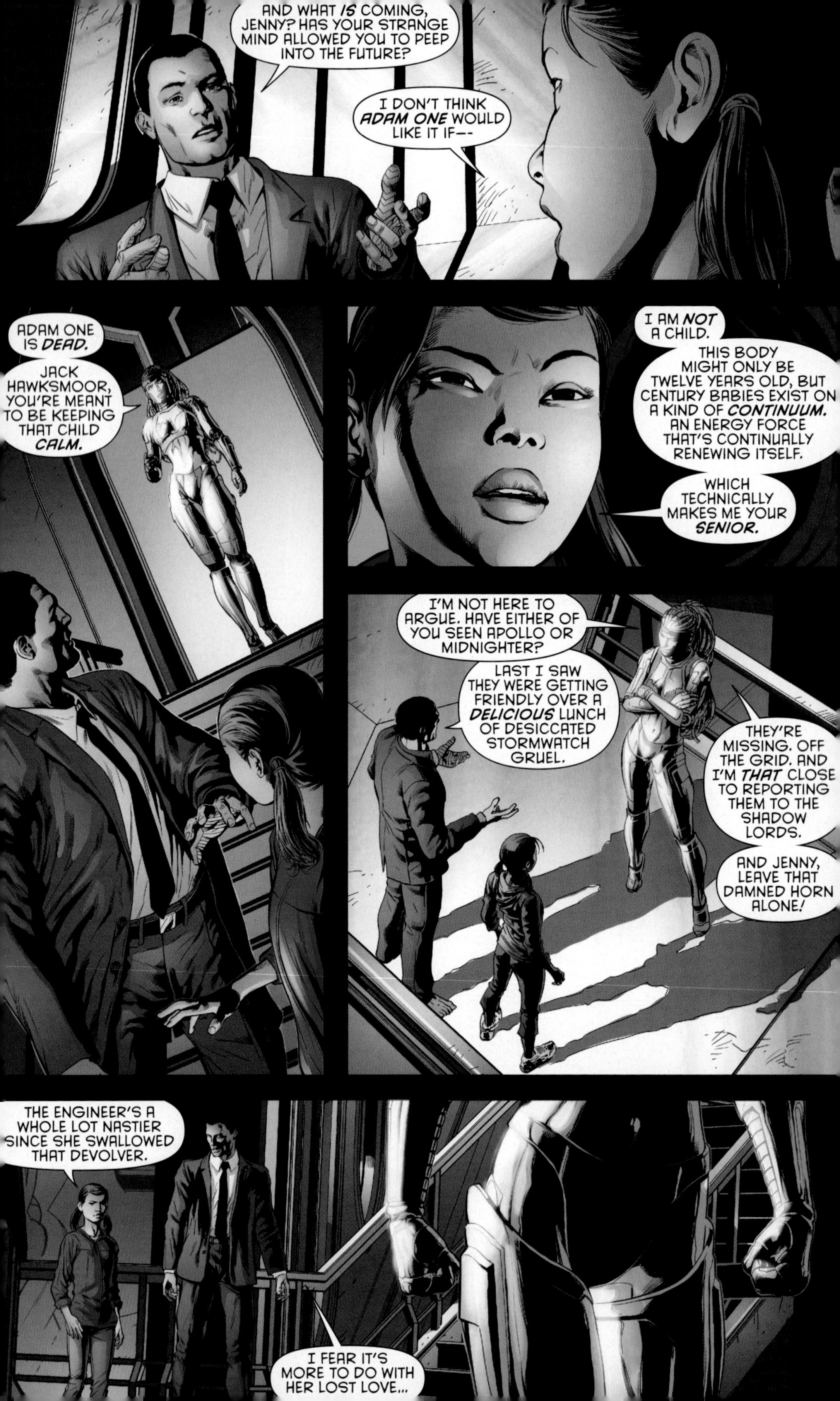
AND WHAT IS COMING, JENNY? HAS YOUR STRANGE MIND ALLOWED YOU TO PEEP INTO THE FUTURE?
I DON'T THINK ADAM ONE WOULD LIKE IT IF--
ADAM ONE IS DEAD.
JACK HAWKSMOOR, YOU'RE MEANT TO BE KEEPING THAT CHILD CALM.
I AM NOT A CHILD.
THIS BODY MIGHT ONLY BE TWELVE YEARS OLD, BUT CENTURY BABIES EXIST ON A KIND OF CONTINUUM. AN ENERGY FORCE THAT'S CONTINUALLY RENEWING ITSELF.
WHICH TECHNICALLY MAKES ME YOUR SENIOR.
I'M NOT HERE TO ARGUE. HAVE EITHER OF YOU SEEN APOLLO OR MIDNIGHTER?
LAST I SAW THEY WERE GETTING FRIENDLY OVER A DELICIOUS LUNCH OF DESICCATED STORMWATCH GRUEL.
THEY'RE MISSING. OFF THE GRID. AND I'M THAT CLOSE TO REPORTING THEM TO THE SHADOW LORDS.
AND JENNY, LEAVE THAT DAMNED HORN ALONE!
THE ENGINEER'S A WHOLE LOT NASTIER SINCE SHE SWALLOWED THAT DEVOLVER.
I FEAR IT'S MORE TO DO WITH HER LOST LOVE...

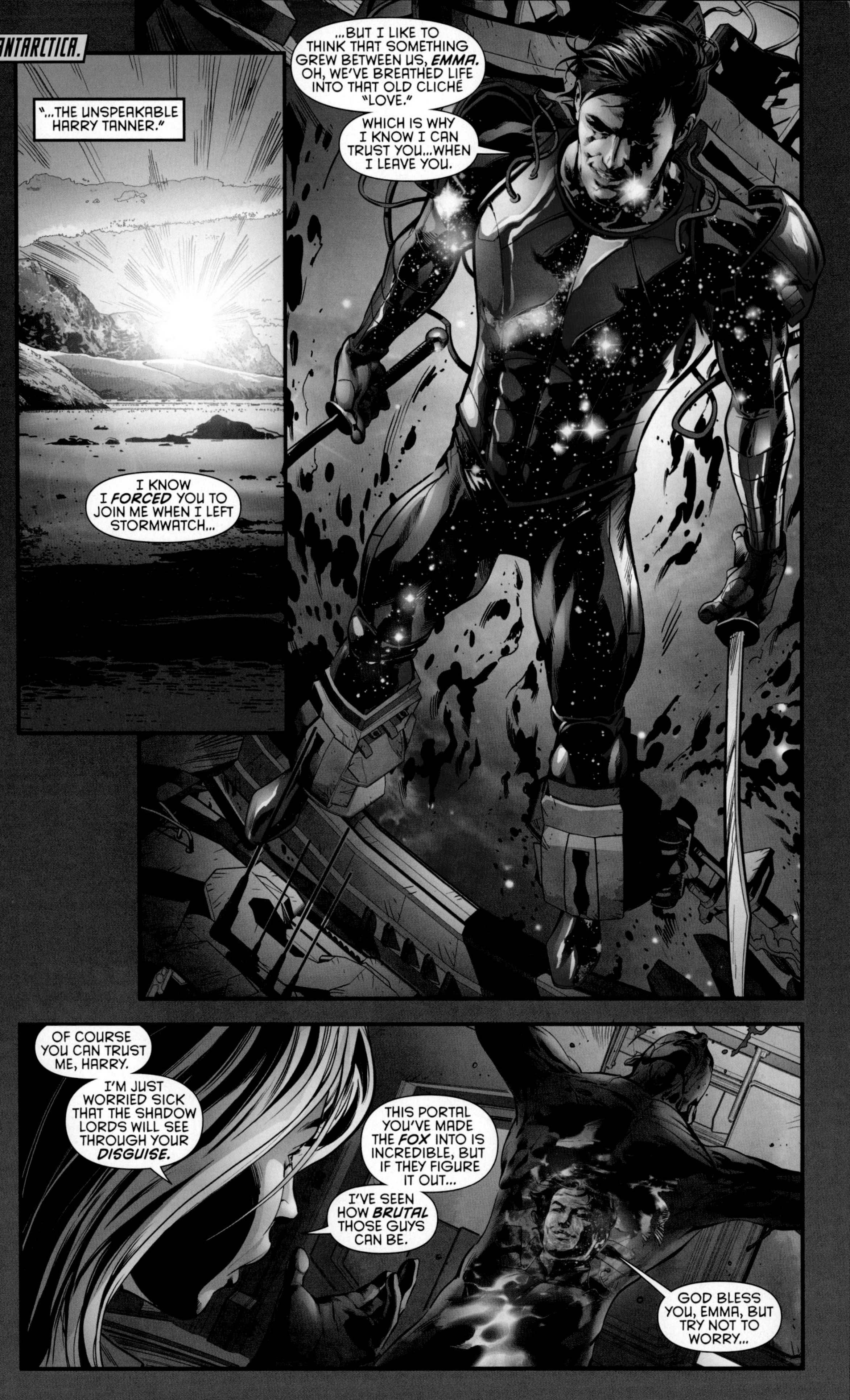
ANTARCTICA.
"...THE UNSPEAKABLE HARRY TANNER."
I KNOW I FORCED YOU TO JOIN ME WHEN I LEFT STORMWATCH...
...BUT I LIKE TO THINK THAT SOMETHING GREW BETWEEN US, EMMA. OH, WE'VE BREATHED LIFE INTO THAT OLD CLICHÉ "LOVE."
WHICH IS WHY I KNOW I CAN TRUST YOU...WHEN I LEAVE YOU.
OF COURSE YOU CAN TRUST ME, HARRY.
I'M JUST WORRIED SICK THAT THE SHADOW LORDS WILL SEE THROUGH YOUR DISGUISE.
THIS PORTAL YOU'VE MADE THE FOX INTO IS INCREDIBLE, BUT IF THEY FIGURE IT OUT...
I'VE SEEN HOW BRUTAL THOSE GUYS CAN BE.
GOD BLESS YOU, EMMA, BUT TRY NOT TO WORRY...

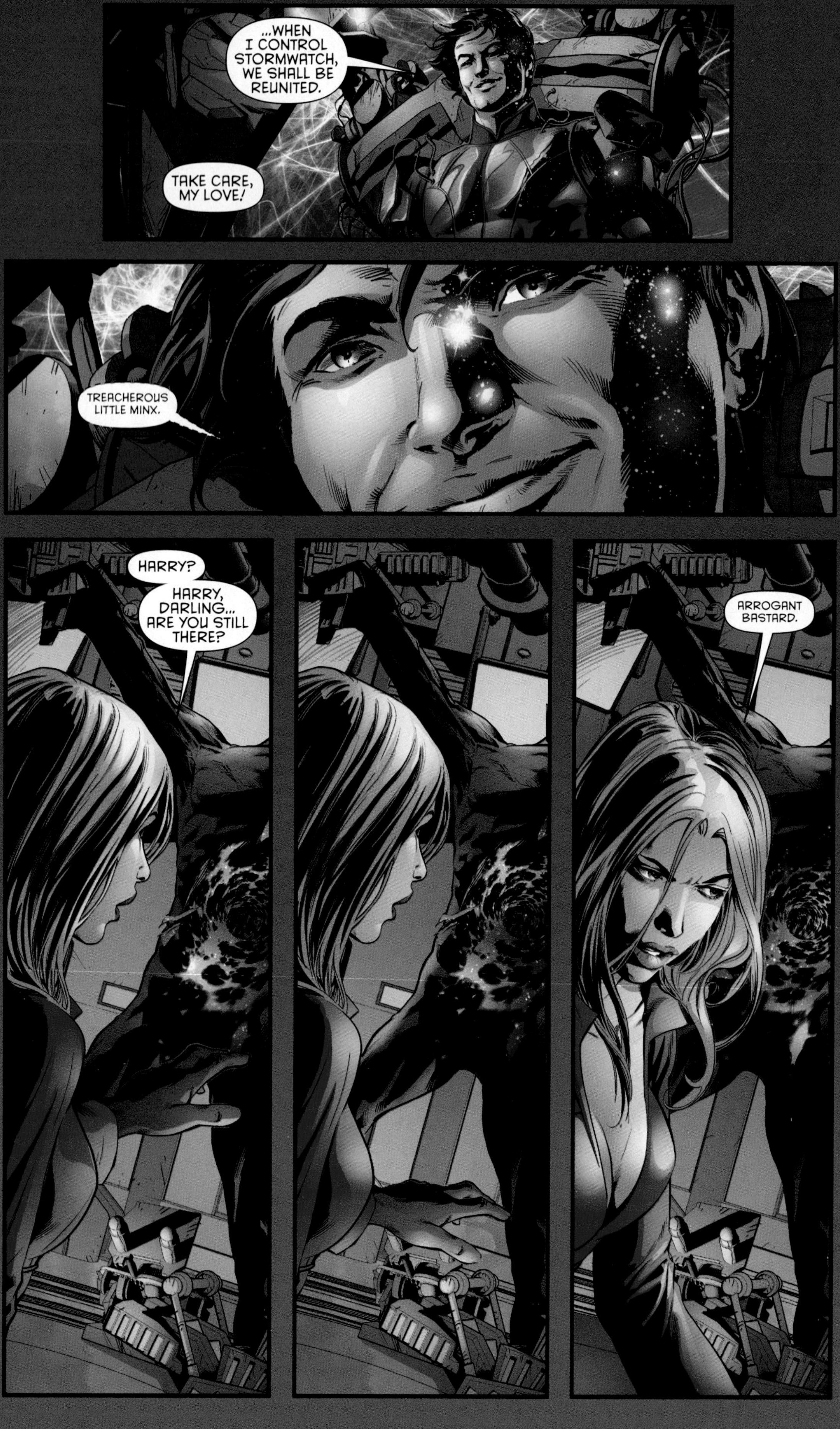
...WHEN I CONTROL STORMWATCH, WE SHALL BE REUNITED.
TAKE CARE, MY LOVE!
TREACHEROUS LITTLE MINX.
HARRY?
HARRY, DARLING... ARE YOU STILL THERE?
ARROGANT BASTARD.

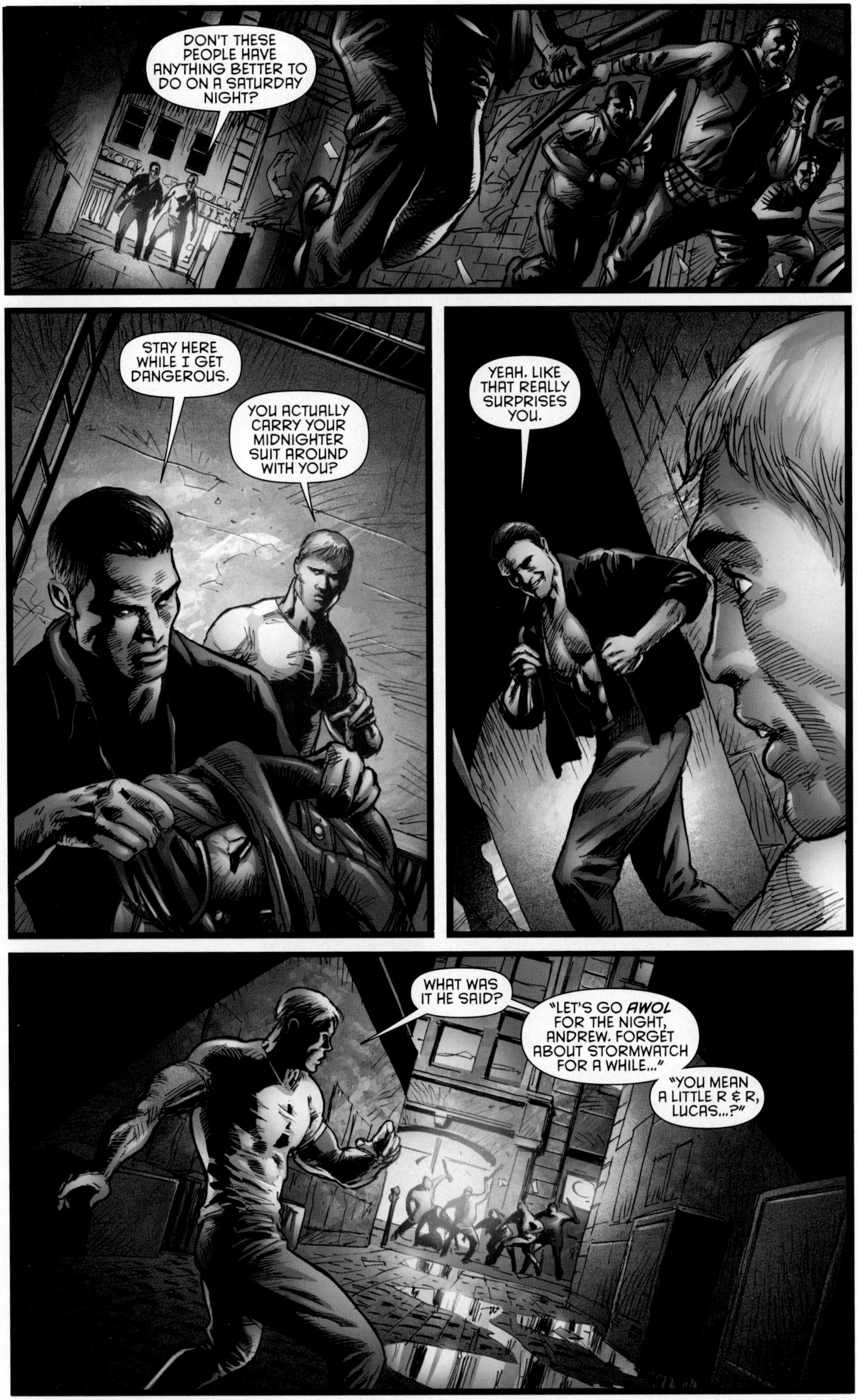
DON'T THESE PEOPLE HAVE ANYTHING BETTER TO DO ON A SATURDAY NIGHT?
STAY HERE WHILE I GET DANGEROUS.
YOU ACTUALLY CARRY YOUR MIDNIGHTER SUIT AROUND WITH YOU?
YEAH. LIKE THAT REALLY SURPRISES YOU.
WHAT WAS IT HE SAID?
"LET'S GO AWOL FOR THE NIGHT, ANDREW. FORGET ABOUT STORMWATCH FOR A WHILE..."
"YOU MEAN A LITTLE R & R, LUCAS...?"

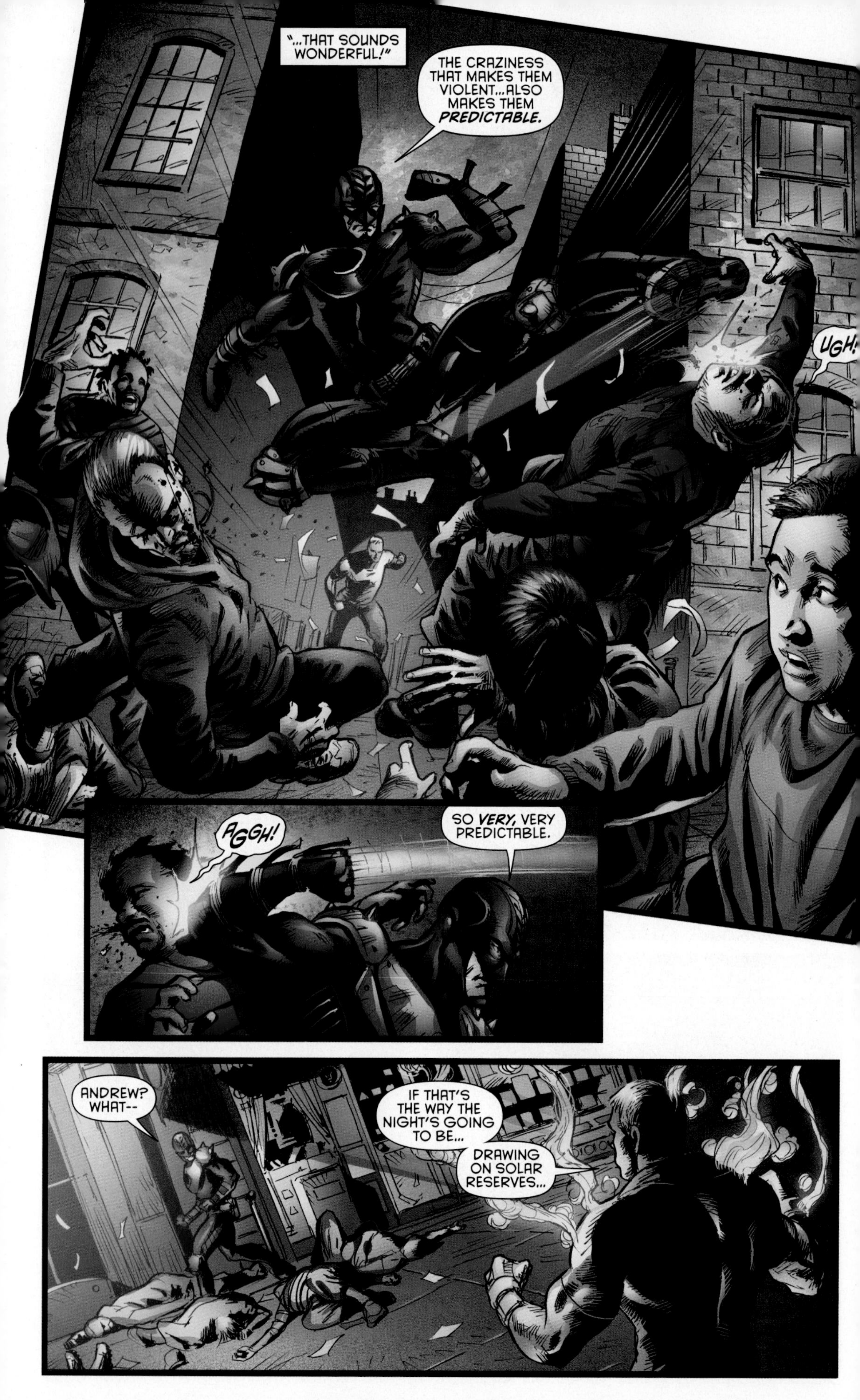
"...THAT SOUNDS WONDERFUL!"
THE CRAZINESS THAT MAKES THEM VIOLENT...ALSO MAKES THEM *PREDICTABLE.*
UGH!
AGGH!
SO *VERY,* VERY PREDICTABLE.
ANDREW? WHAT--
IF THAT'S THE WAY THE NIGHT'S GOING TO BE...
DRAWING ON SOLAR RESERVES...

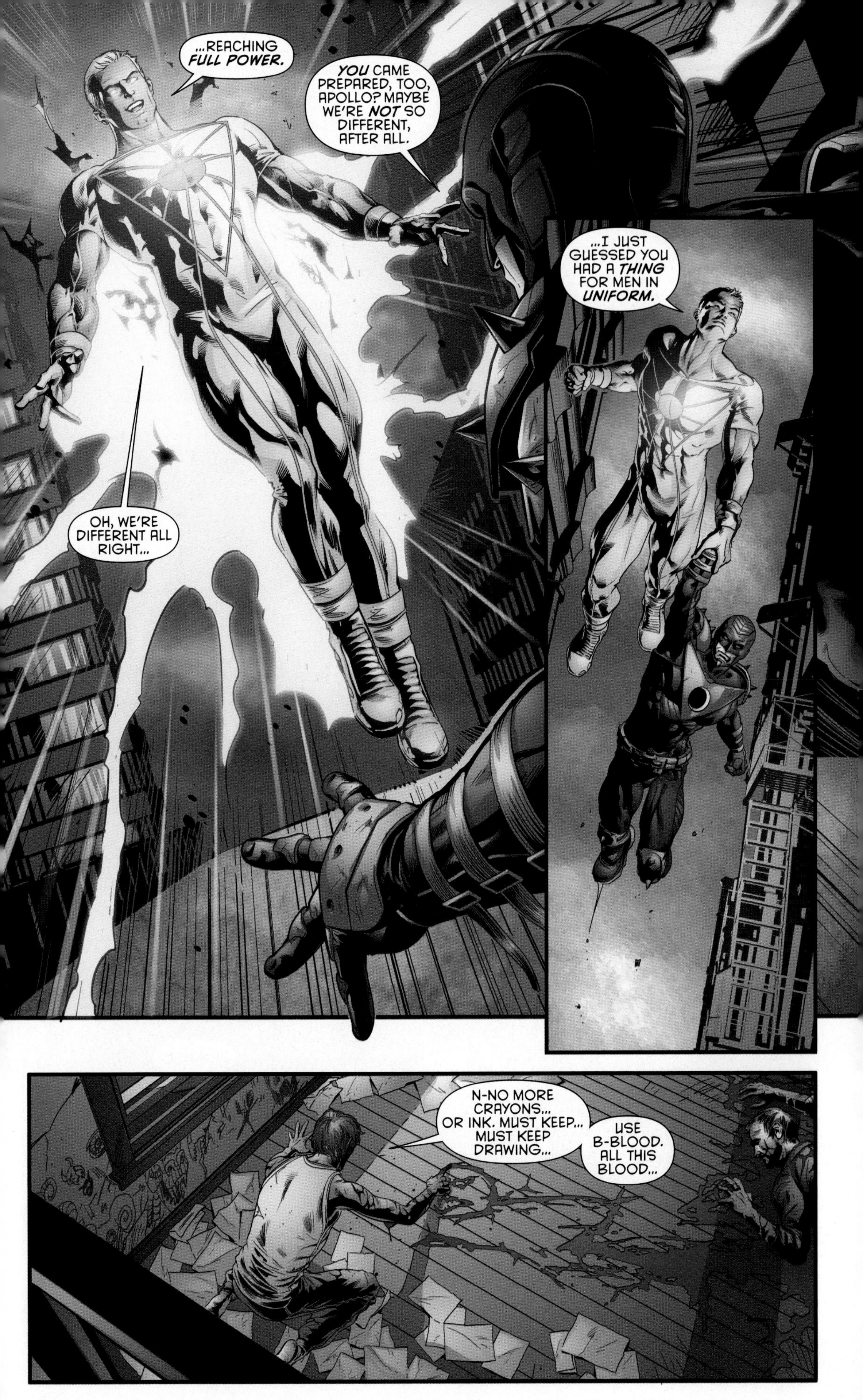

...REACHING FULL POWER.
YOU CAME PREPARED, TOO, APOLLO? MAYBE WE'RE NOT SO DIFFERENT, AFTER ALL.
OH, WE'RE DIFFERENT ALL RIGHT...
...I JUST GUESSED YOU HAD A THING FOR MEN IN UNIFORM.
N-NO MORE CRAYONS... OR INK. MUST KEEP... MUST KEEP DRAWING...
USE B-BLOOD. ALL THIS BLOOD...

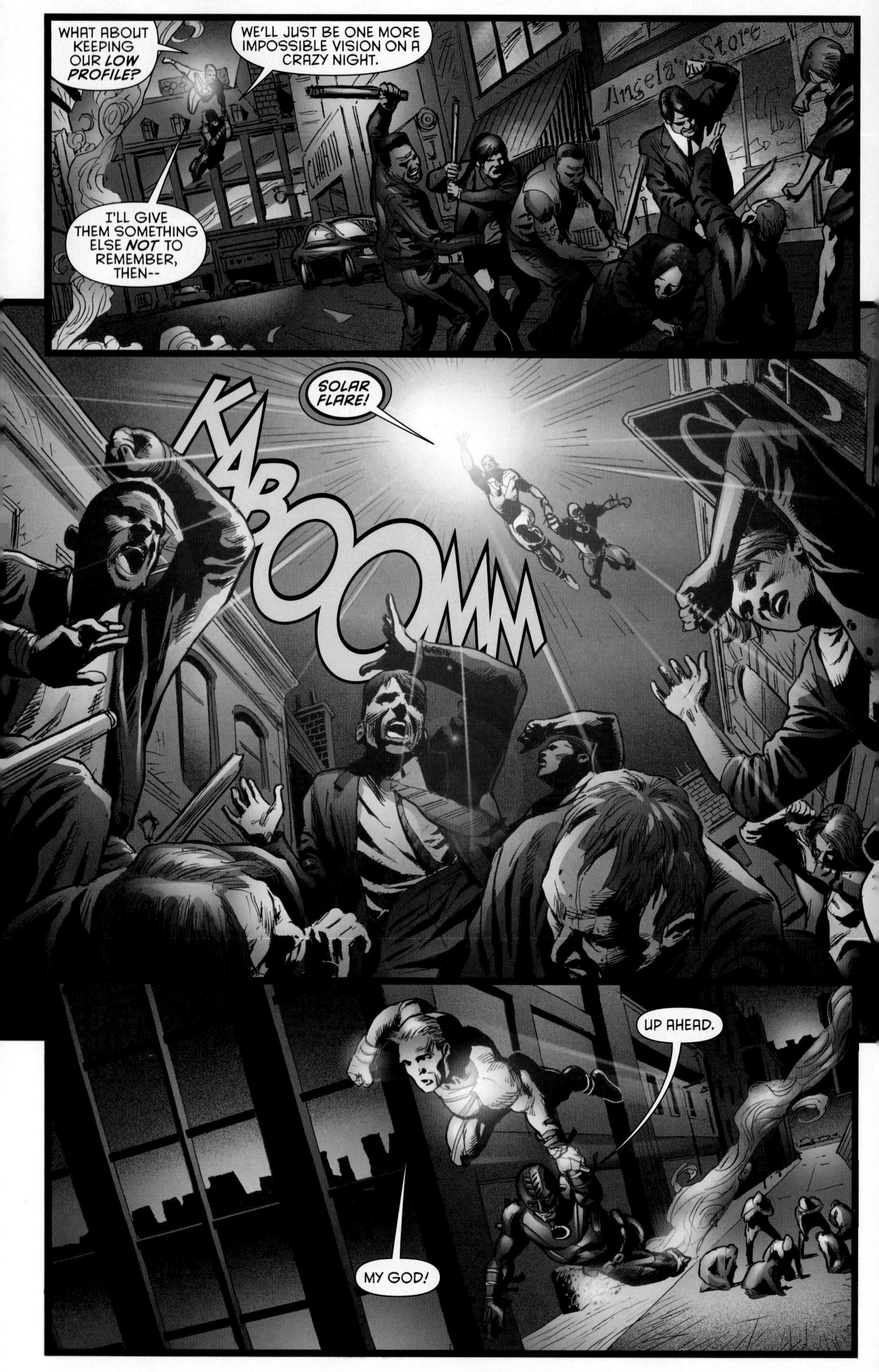
WHAT ABOUT KEEPING OUR *LOW PROFILE?*
WE'LL JUST BE ONE MORE IMPOSSIBLE VISION ON A CRAZY NIGHT.
I'LL GIVE THEM SOMETHING ELSE *NOT* TO REMEMBER, THEN--
Angela's Store
SOLAR FLARE!
KABOOMM
UP AHEAD.
MY GOD!

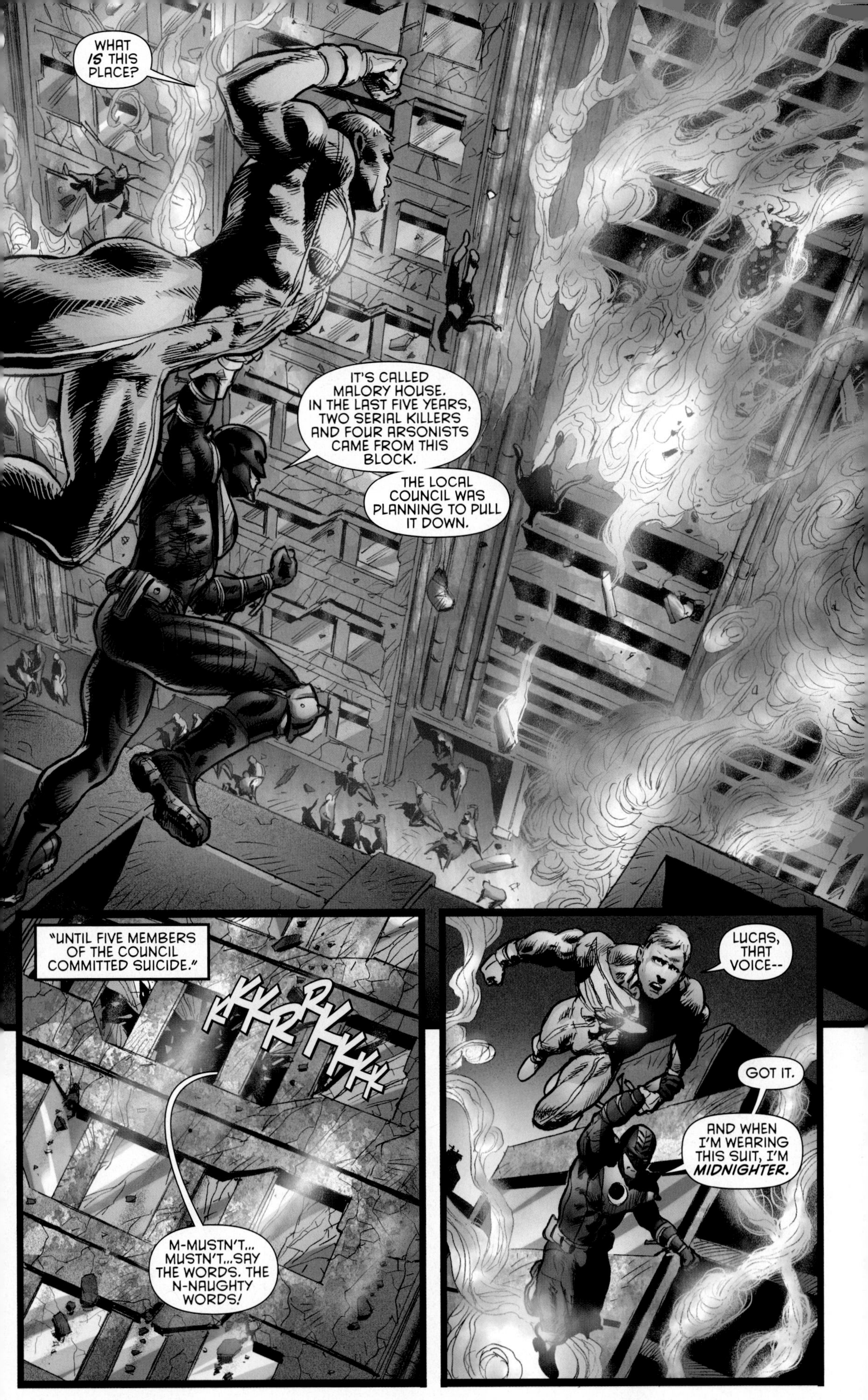
WHAT IS THIS PLACE?
IT'S CALLED MALORY HOUSE. IN THE LAST FIVE YEARS, TWO SERIAL KILLERS AND FOUR ARSONISTS CAME FROM THIS BLOCK.
THE LOCAL COUNCIL WAS PLANNING TO PULL IT DOWN.
"UNTIL FIVE MEMBERS OF THE COUNCIL COMMITTED SUICIDE."
KKKRRKKKK
M-MUSTN'T... MUSTN'T...SAY THE WORDS. THE N-NAUGHTY WORDS!
LUCAS, THAT VOICE--
GOT IT.
AND WHEN I'M WEARING THIS SUIT, I'M MIDNIGHTER.

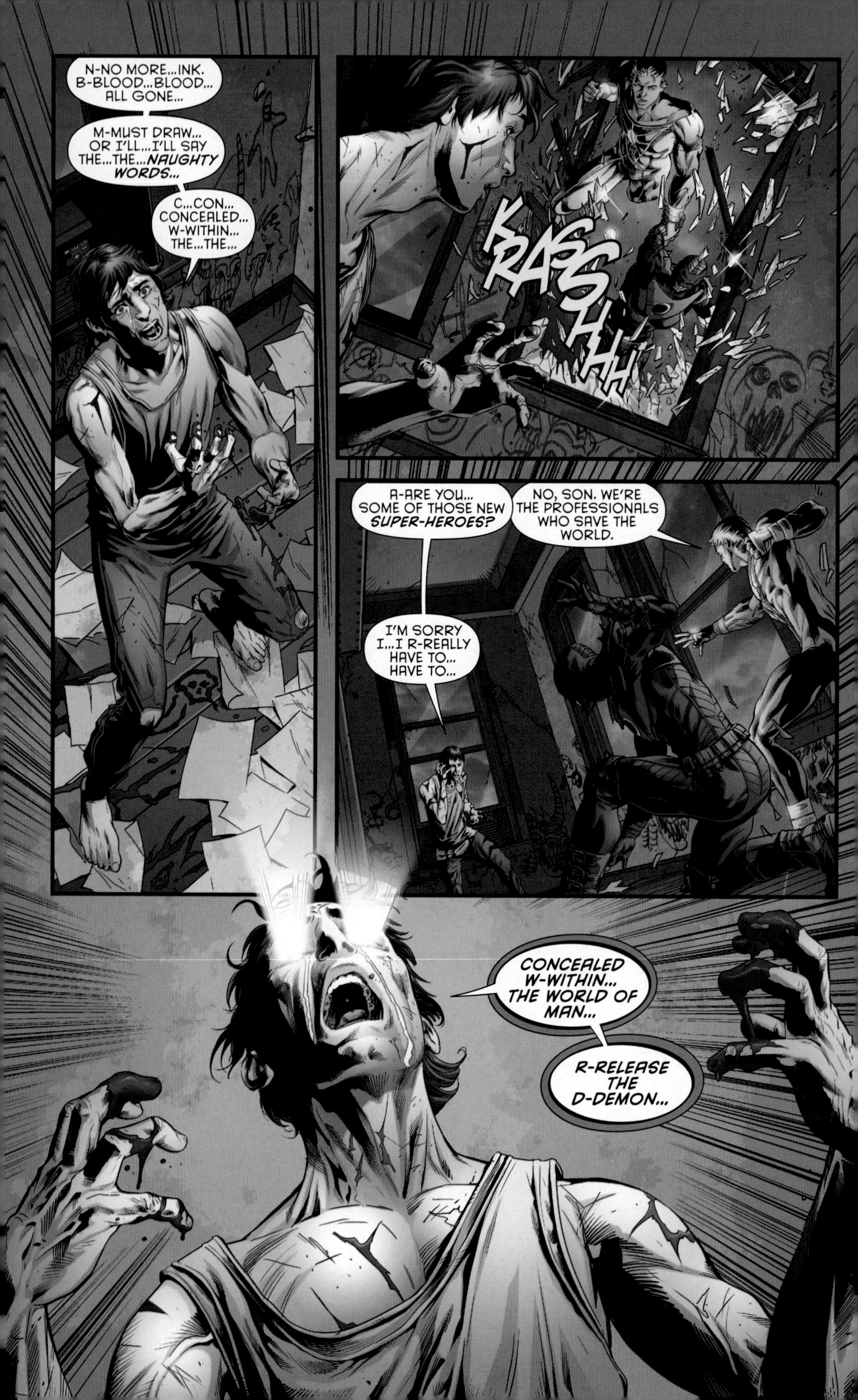
N-NO MORE...INK. B-BLOOD...BLOOD... ALL GONE...
M-MUST DRAW... OR I'LL...I'LL SAY THE...THE...NAUGHTY WORDS...
C...CON... CONCEALED... W-WITHIN... THE...THE...
KRASSHHH
A-ARE YOU... SOME OF THOSE NEW SUPER-HEROES?
NO, SON. WE'RE THE PROFESSIONALS WHO SAVE THE WORLD.
I'M SORRY I...I R-REALLY HAVE TO... HAVE TO...
CONCEALED W-WITHIN... THE WORLD OF MAN...
R-RELEASE THE D-DEMON...

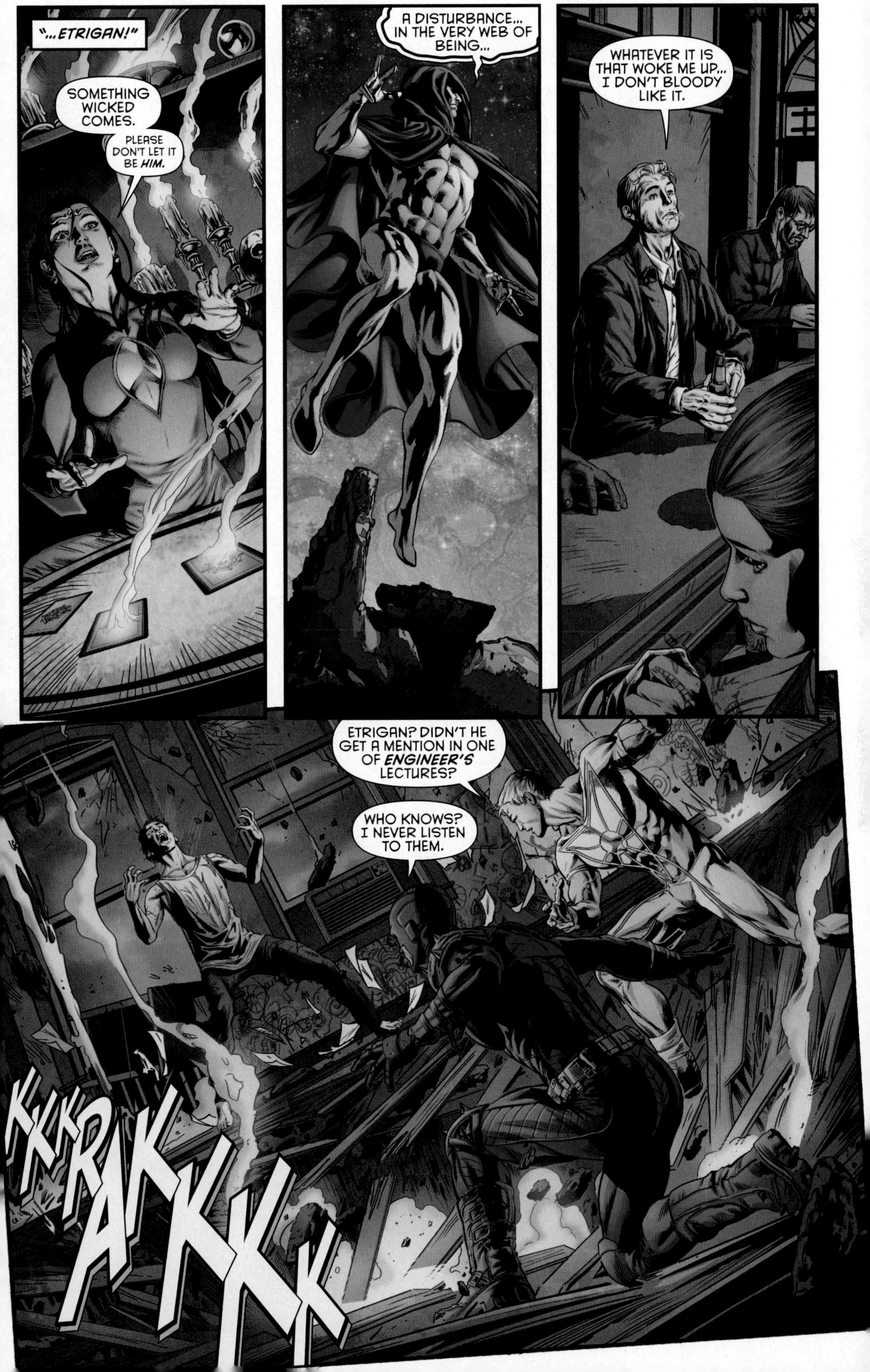
"...ETRIGAN!"
SOMETHING WICKED COMES.
PLEASE DON'T LET IT BE HIM.
A DISTURBANCE... IN THE VERY WEB OF BEING...
WHATEVER IT IS THAT WOKE ME UP... I DON'T BLOODY LIKE IT.
ETRIGAN? DIDN'T HE GET A MENTION IN ONE OF ENGINEER'S LECTURES?
WHO KNOWS? I NEVER LISTEN TO THEM.
KKKRAKKKK

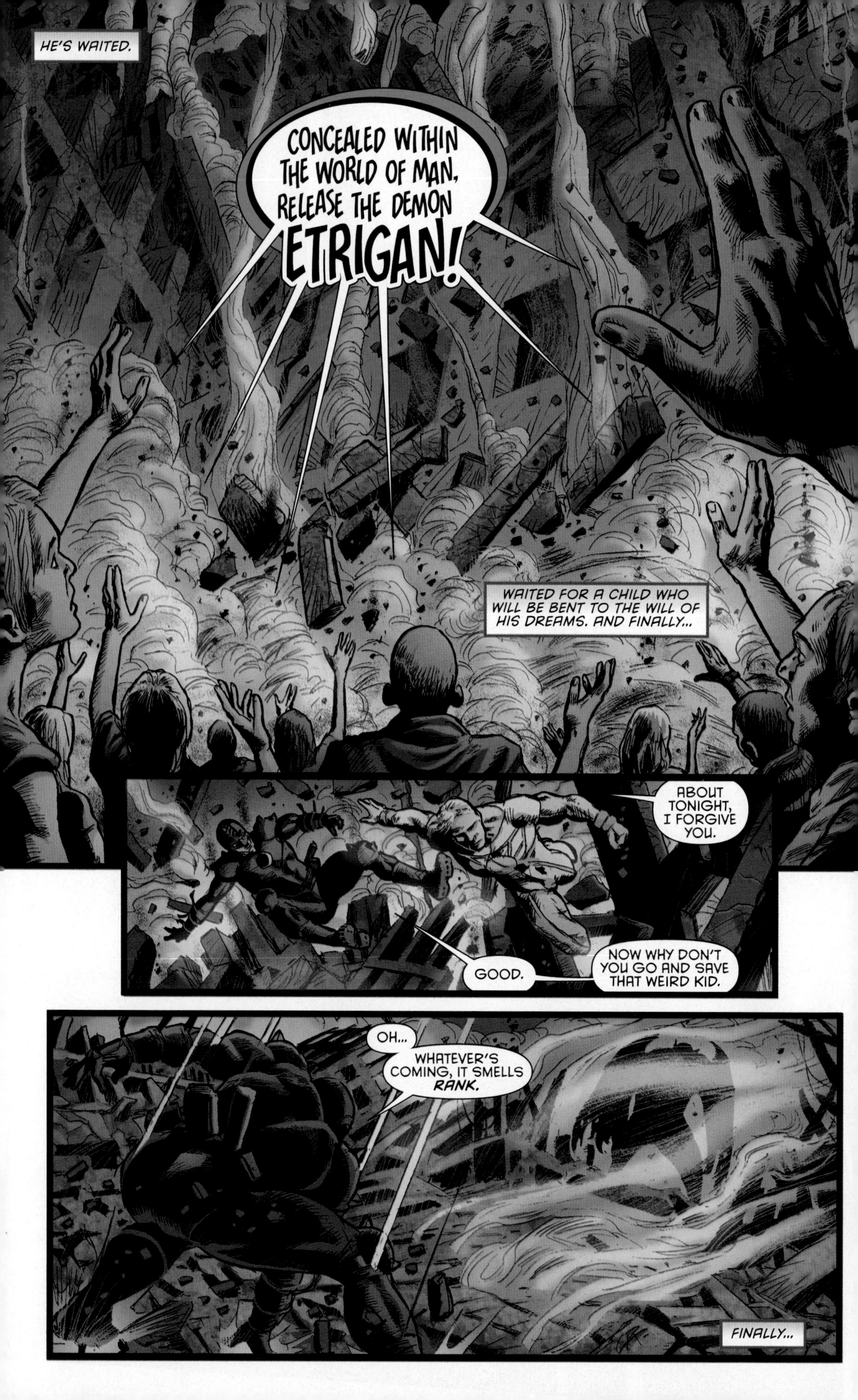
HE'S WAITED.
CONCEALED WITHIN THE WORLD OF MAN, RELEASE THE DEMON ETRIGAN!
WAITED FOR A CHILD WHO WILL BE BENT TO THE WILL OF HIS DREAMS. AND FINALLY...
ABOUT TONIGHT, I FORGIVE YOU.
GOOD.
NOW WHY DON'T YOU GO AND SAVE THAT WEIRD KID.
OH...
WHATEVER'S COMING, IT SMELLS RANK.
FINALLY...

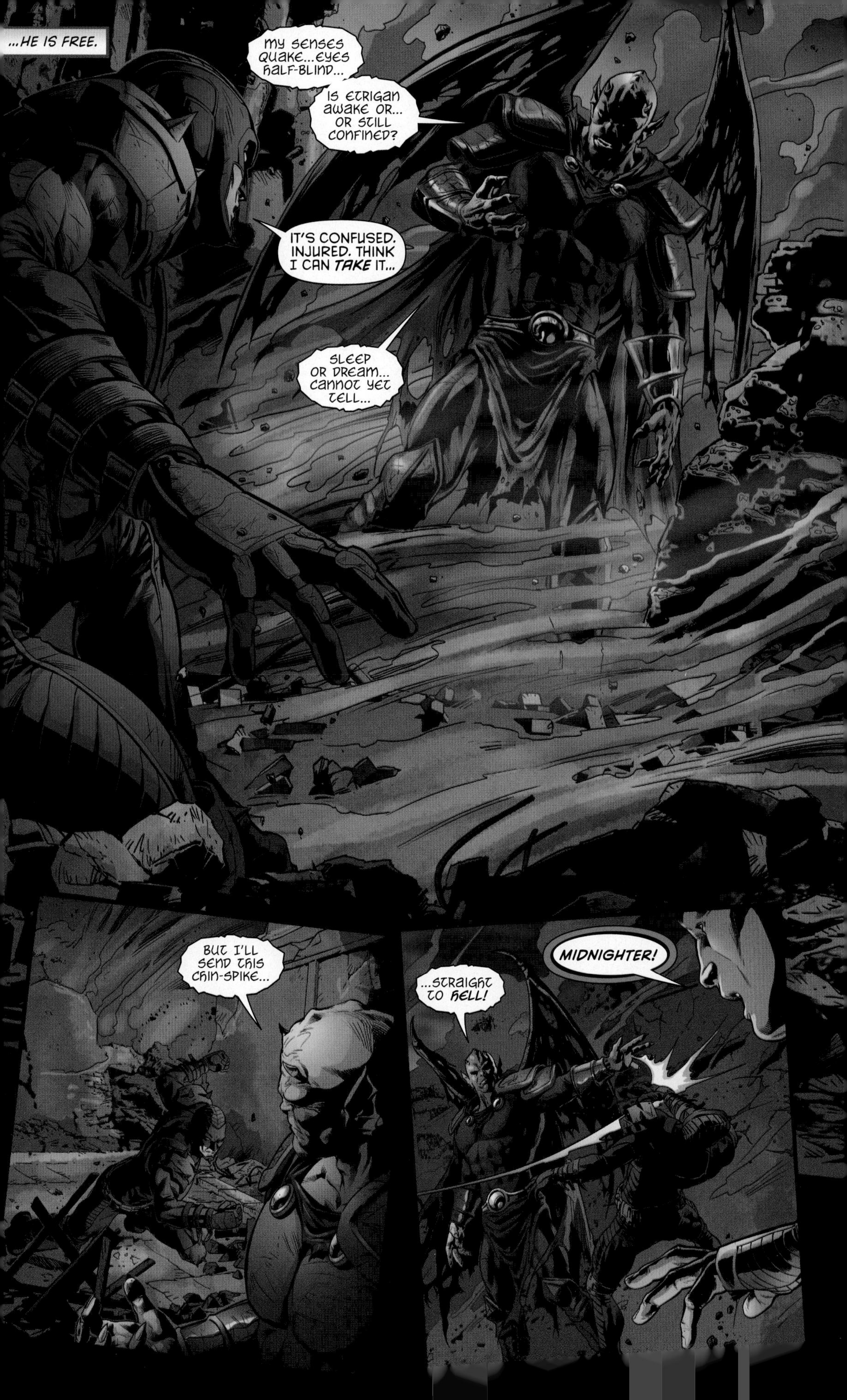
...HE IS FREE.
MY SENSES QUAKE...EYES HALF-BLIND...
IS ETRIGAN AWAKE OR... OR STILL CONFINED?
IT'S CONFUSED. INJURED. THINK I CAN *TAKE* IT...
SLEEP OR DREAM... CANNOT YET TELL...
BUT I'LL SEND THIS CHIN-SPIKE...
...STRAIGHT TO *HELL!*
MIDNIGHTER!

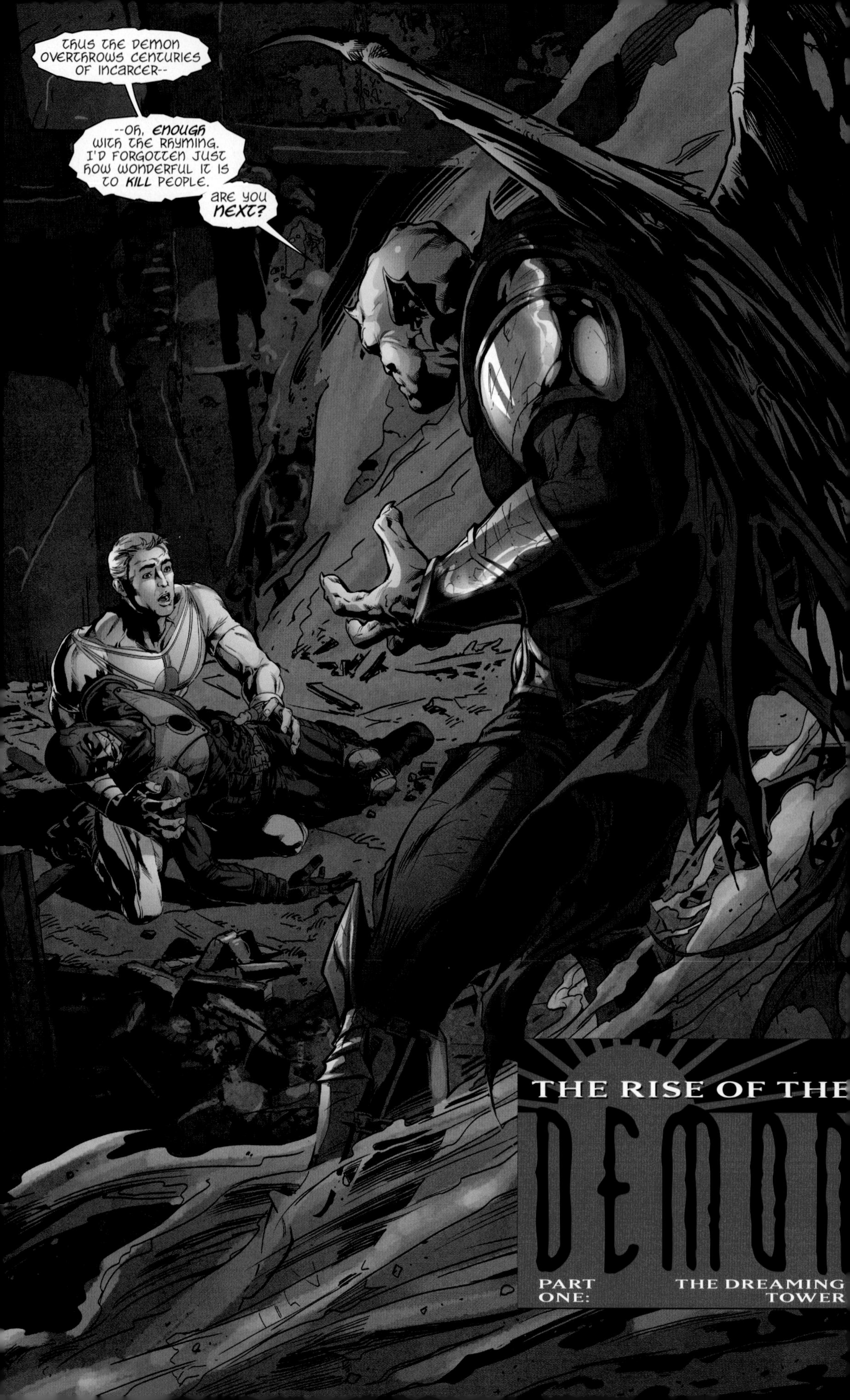
THUS THE DEMON OVERTHROWS CENTURIES OF INCARCER--
--OH, ENOUGH WITH THE RHYMING. I'D FORGOTTEN JUST HOW WONDERFUL IT IS TO KILL PEOPLE.
ARE YOU NEXT?
THE RISE OF THE DEMON
PART ONE: THE DREAMING TOWER

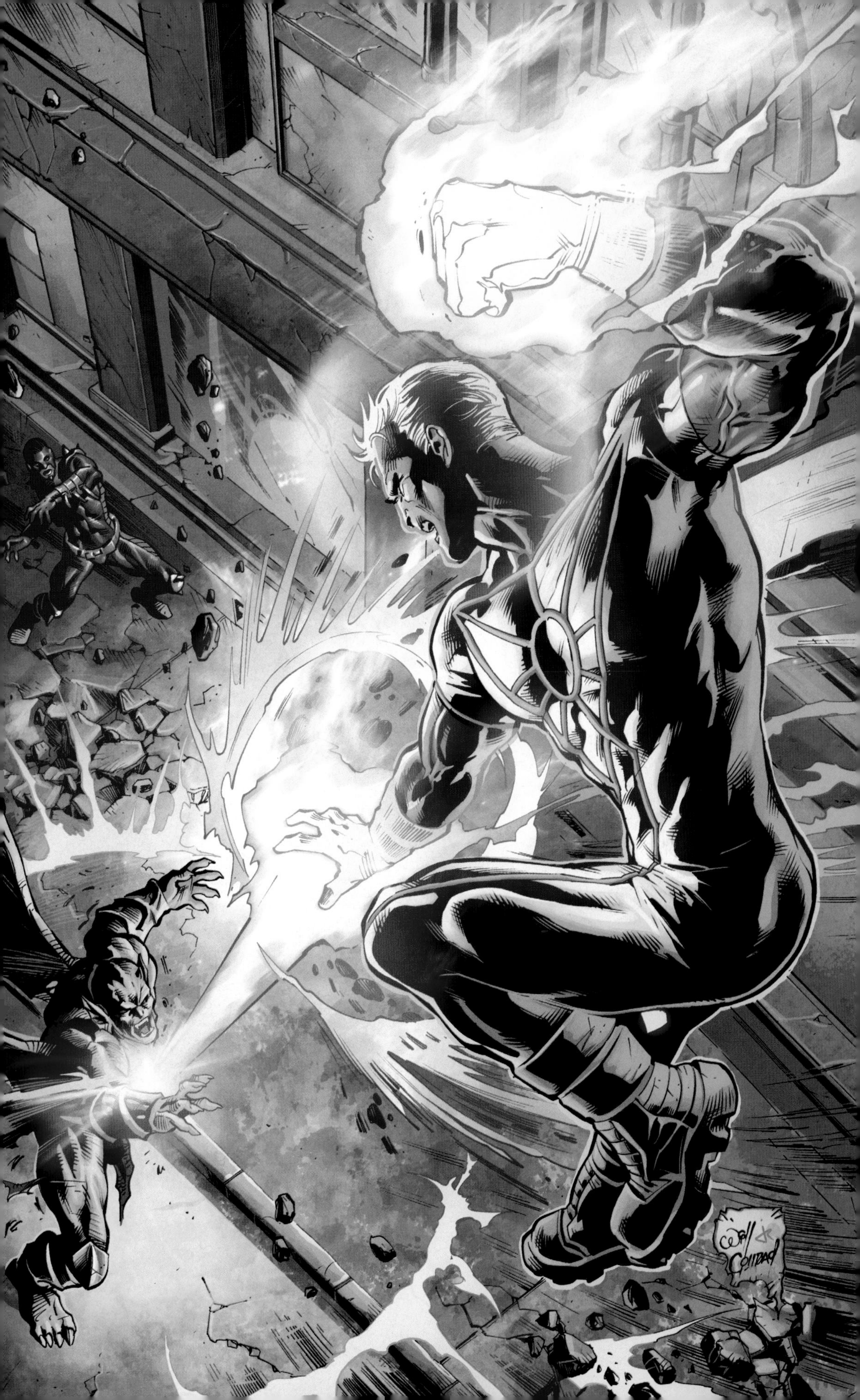

THE RISE OF THE DEMON PART TWO: LONDON'S BURNING

PETER MILLIGAN writer **WILL CONRAD & CLIFF RICHARDS** artists cover art by **WILL CONRAD & JAY DAVID RAMOS**

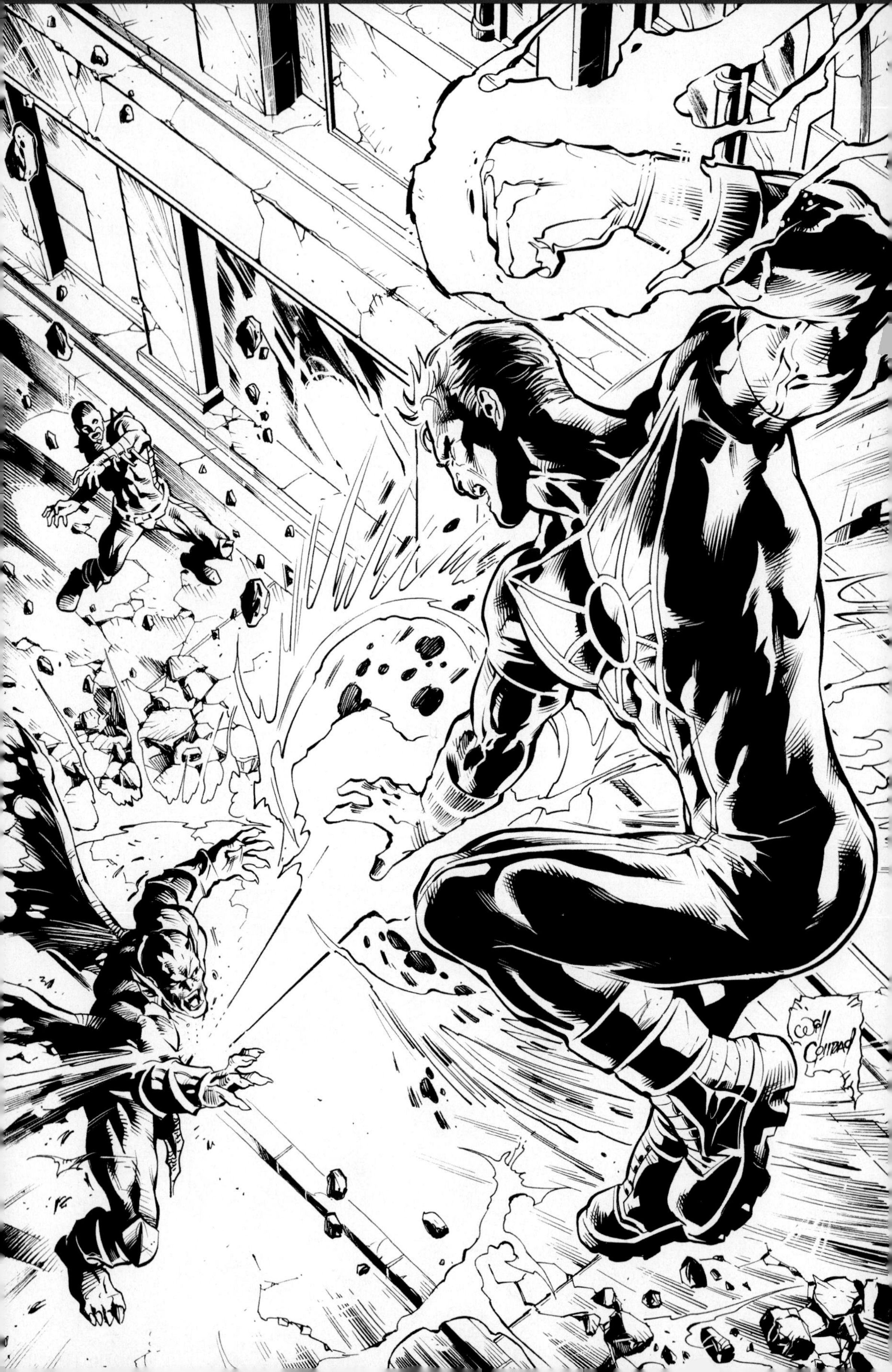

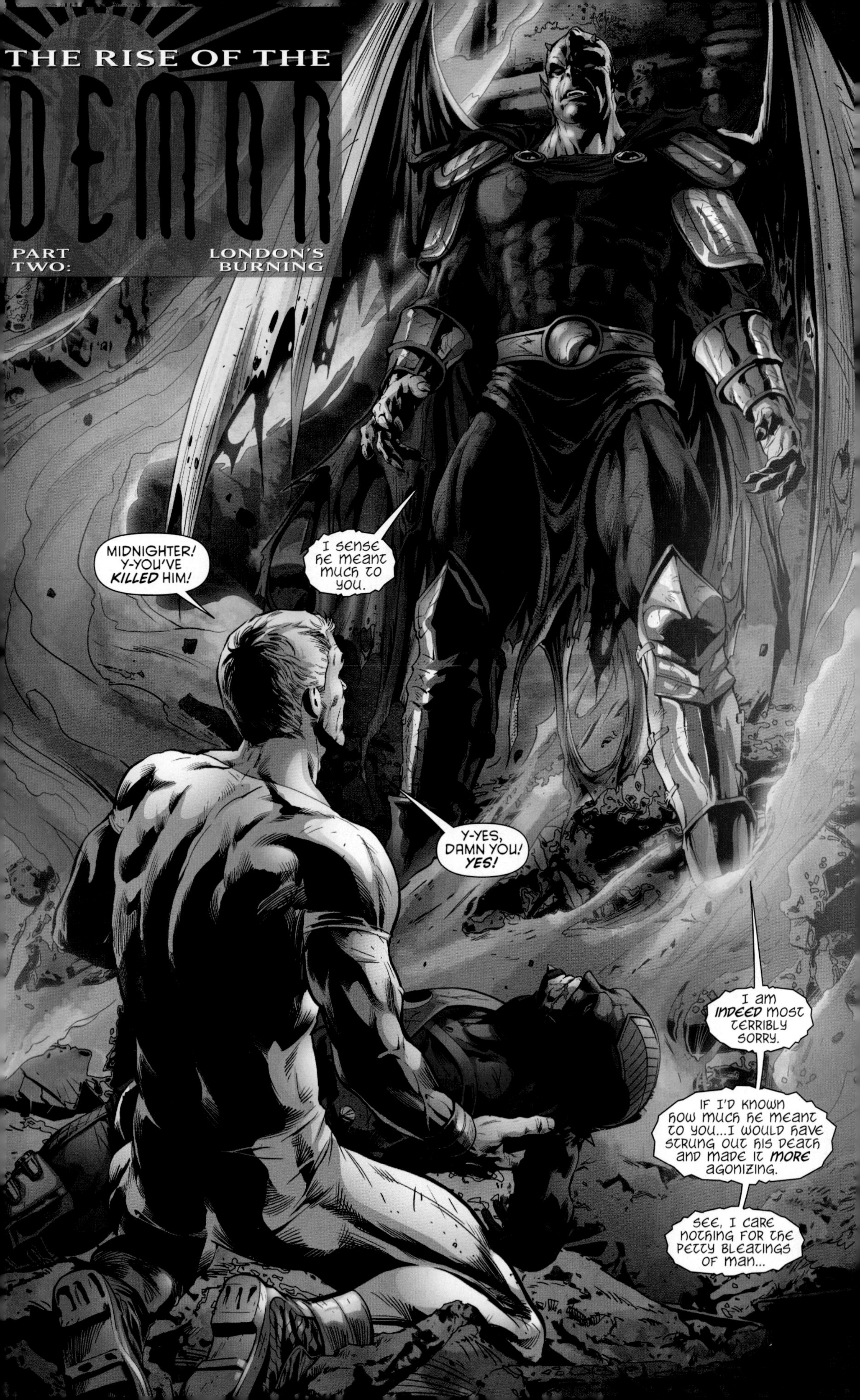
THE RISE OF THE
DEMON
PART TWO:
LONDON'S BURNING
MIDNIGHTER! Y-YOU'VE KILLED HIM!
I SENSE HE MEANT MUCH TO YOU.
Y-YES, DAMN YOU! YES!
I AM INDEED MOST TERRIBLY SORRY.
IF I'D KNOWN HOW MUCH HE MEANT TO YOU...I WOULD HAVE STRUNG OUT HIS DEATH AND MADE IT MORE AGONIZING.
SEE, I CARE NOTHING FOR THE PETTY BLEATINGS OF MAN...

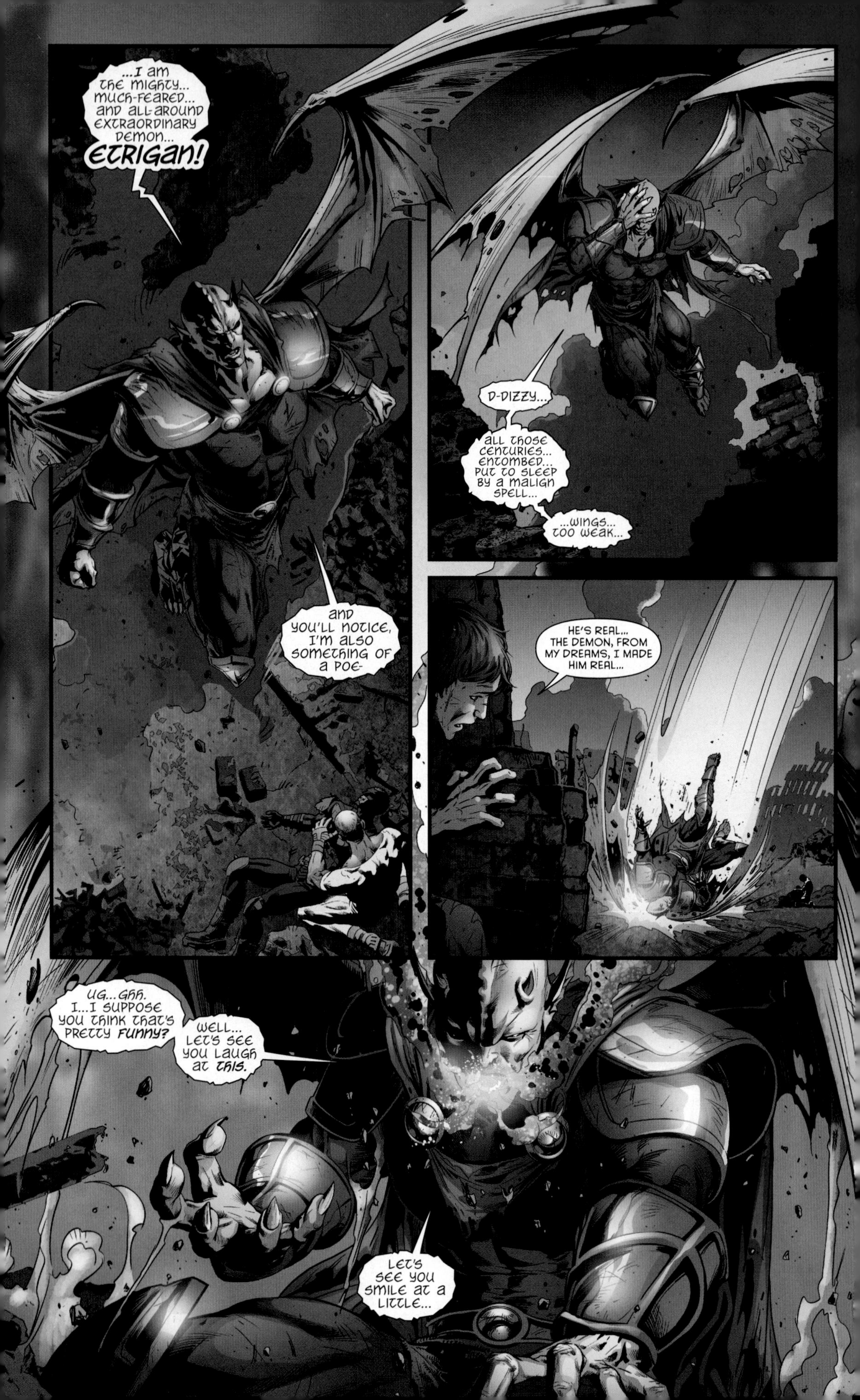
...I AM THE MIGHTY... MUCH-FEARED... AND ALL-AROUND EXTRAORDINARY DEMON... ETRIGAN!
AND YOU'LL NOTICE, I'M ALSO SOMETHING OF A POE-
D-DIZZY...
ALL THOSE CENTURIES... ENTOMBED... PUT TO SLEEP BY A MALIGN SPELL...
...WINGS... TOO WEAK...
HE'S REAL... THE DEMON, FROM MY DREAMS, I MADE HIM REAL...
UG...GHH. I...I SUPPOSE YOU THINK THAT'S PRETTY FUNNY?
WELL... LET'S SEE YOU LAUGH AT THIS.
LET'S SEE YOU SMILE AT A LITTLE...

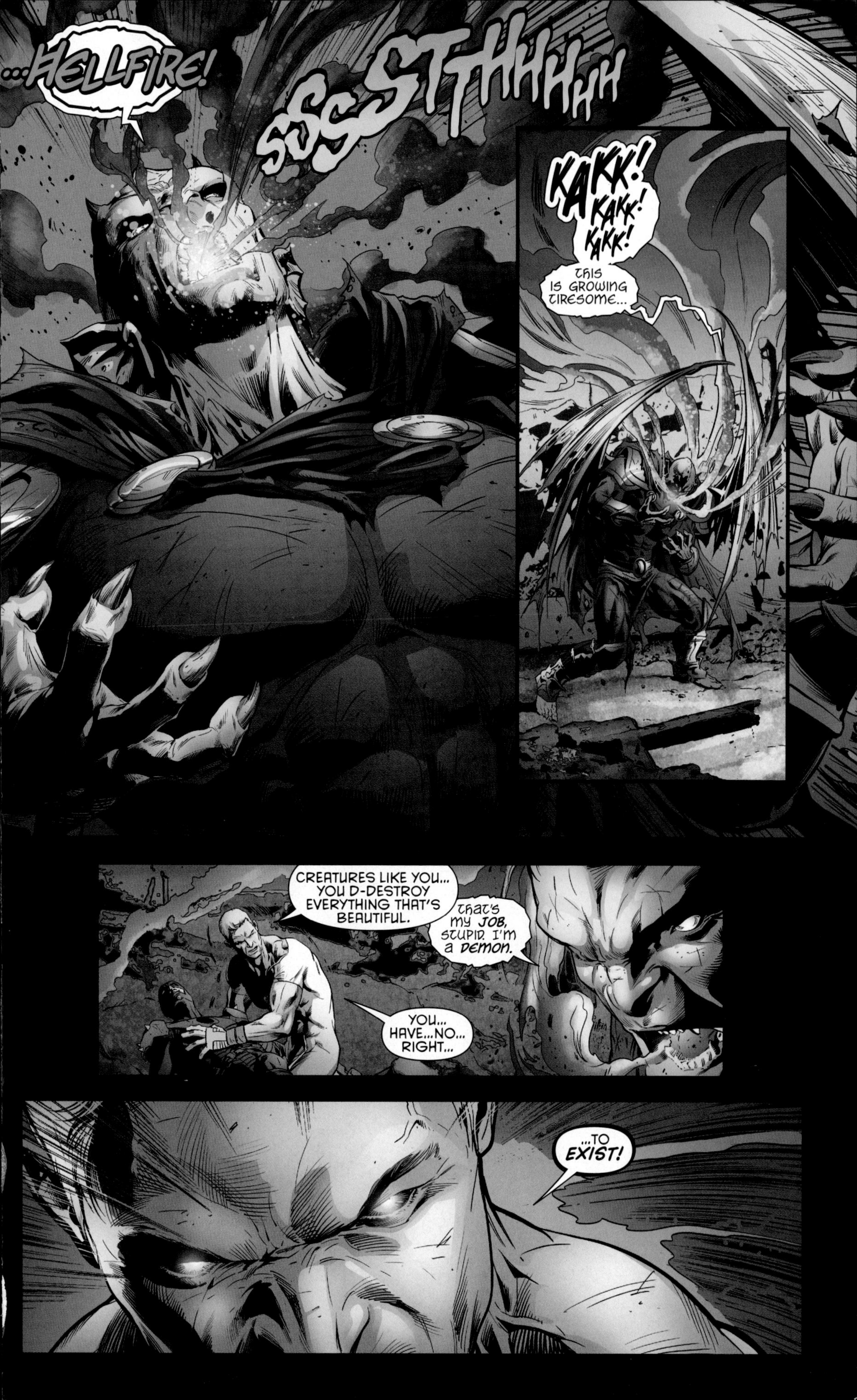

...HELLFIRE!
SSSSTTHHHHHH
KAKK! KAKK! KAKK!
THIS IS GROWING TIRESOME...
CREATURES LIKE YOU... YOU D-DESTROY EVERYTHING THAT'S BEAUTIFUL.
THAT'S MY JOB, STUPID. I'M A DEMON.
YOU... HAVE...NO... RIGHT...
...TO EXIST!

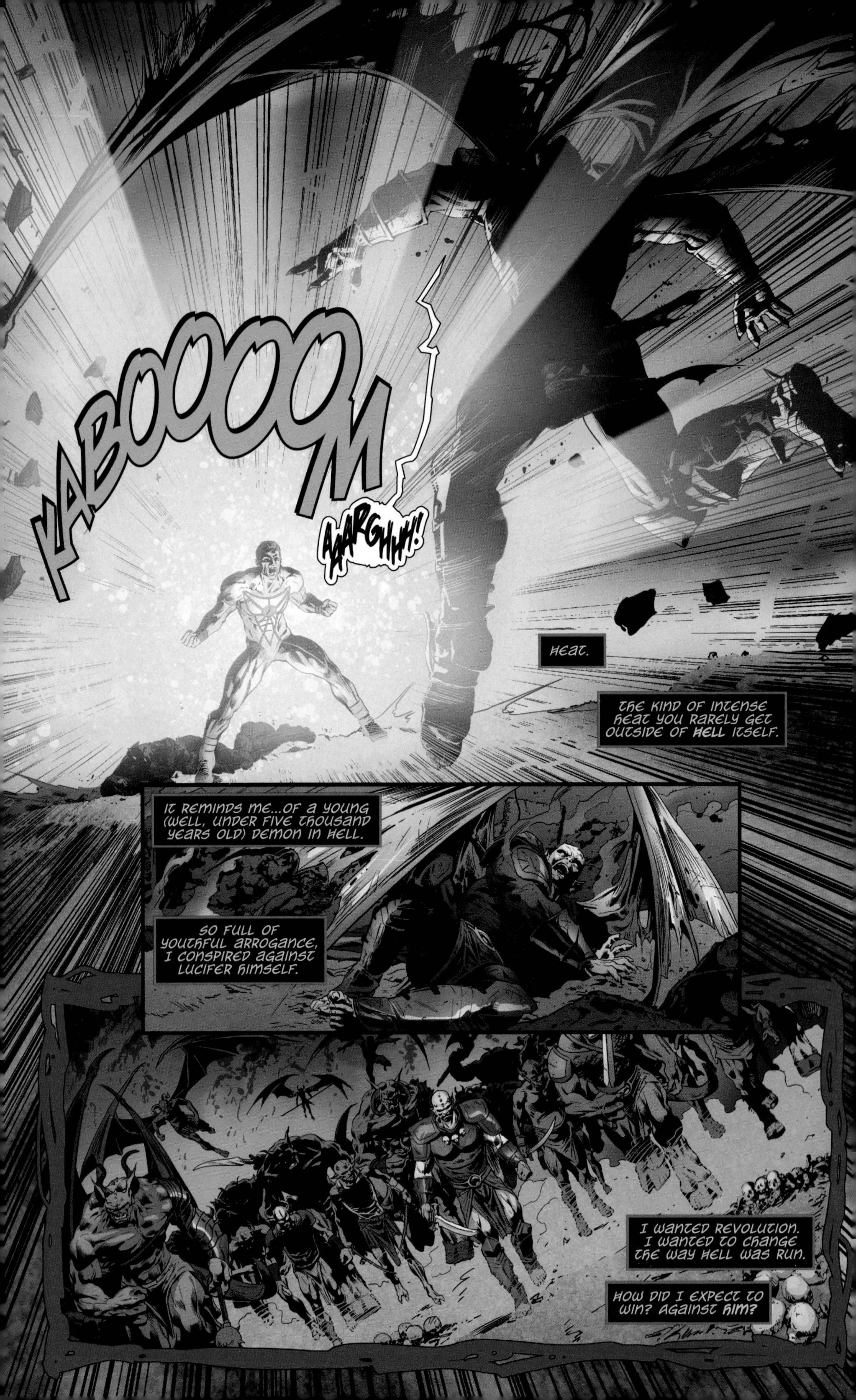
KABOOOOM
AAARGHHH!
HEAT.
THE KIND OF INTENSE HEAT YOU RARELY GET OUTSIDE OF HELL ITSELF.
IT REMINDS ME...OF A YOUNG (WELL, UNDER FIVE THOUSAND YEARS OLD) DEMON IN HELL.
SO FULL OF YOUTHFUL ARROGANCE, I CONSPIRED AGAINST LUCIFER HIMSELF.
I WANTED REVOLUTION. I WANTED TO CHANGE THE WAY HELL WAS RUN.
HOW DID I EXPECT TO WIN? AGAINST HIM?

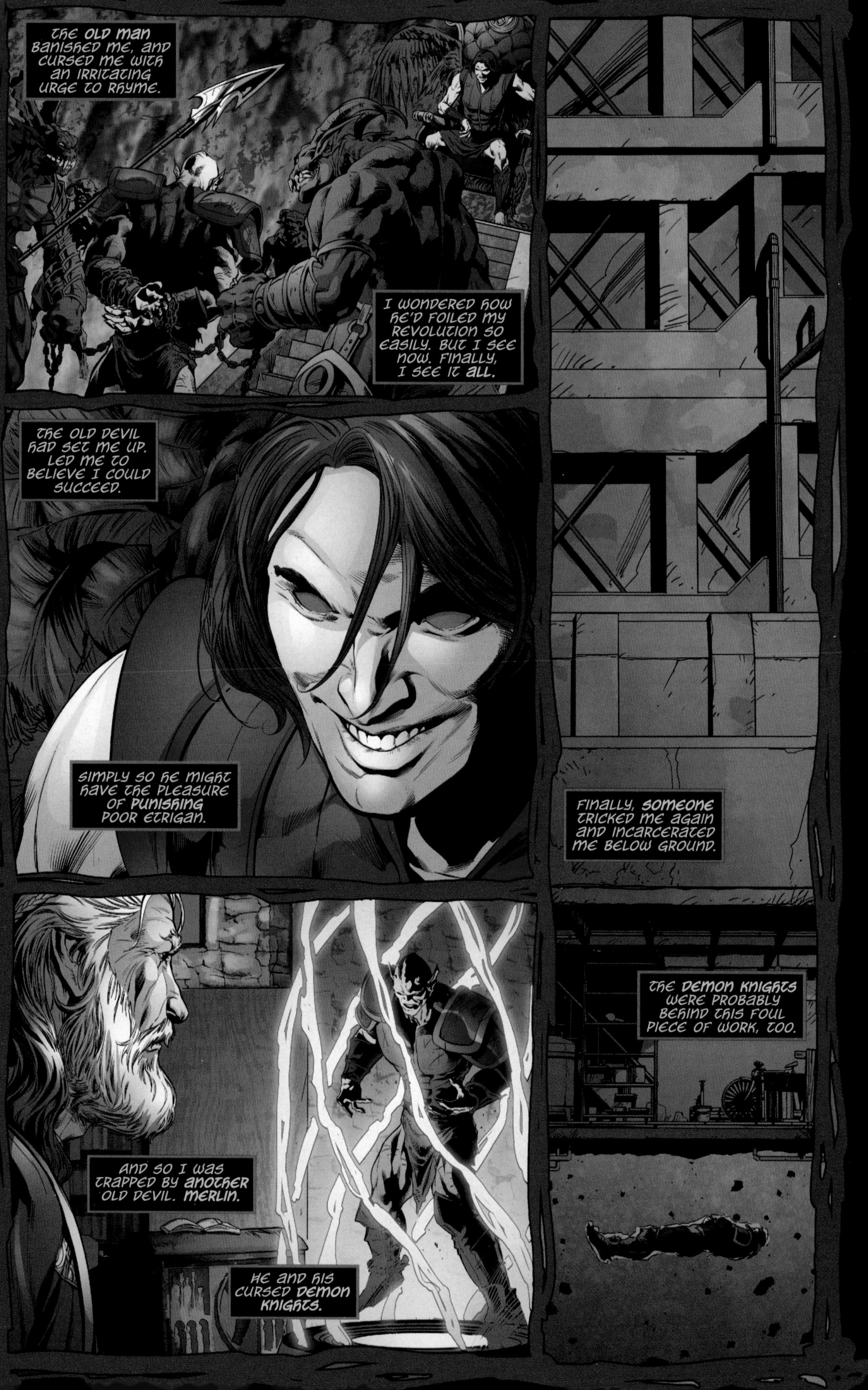
THE OLD MAN BANISHED ME, AND CURSED ME WITH AN IRRITATING URGE TO RHYME.
I WONDERED HOW HE'D FOILED MY REVOLUTION SO EASILY. BUT I SEE NOW. FINALLY, I SEE IT ALL.
THE OLD DEVIL HAD SET ME UP. LED ME TO BELIEVE I COULD SUCCEED.
SIMPLY SO HE MIGHT HAVE THE PLEASURE OF PUNISHING POOR ETRIGAN.
AND SO I WAS TRAPPED BY ANOTHER OLD DEVIL. MERLIN.
HE AND HIS CURSED DEMON KNIGHTS.
FINALLY, SOMEONE TRICKED ME AGAIN AND INCARCERATED ME BELOW GROUND.
THE DEMON KNIGHTS WERE PROBABLY BEHIND THIS FOUL PIECE OF WORK, TOO.

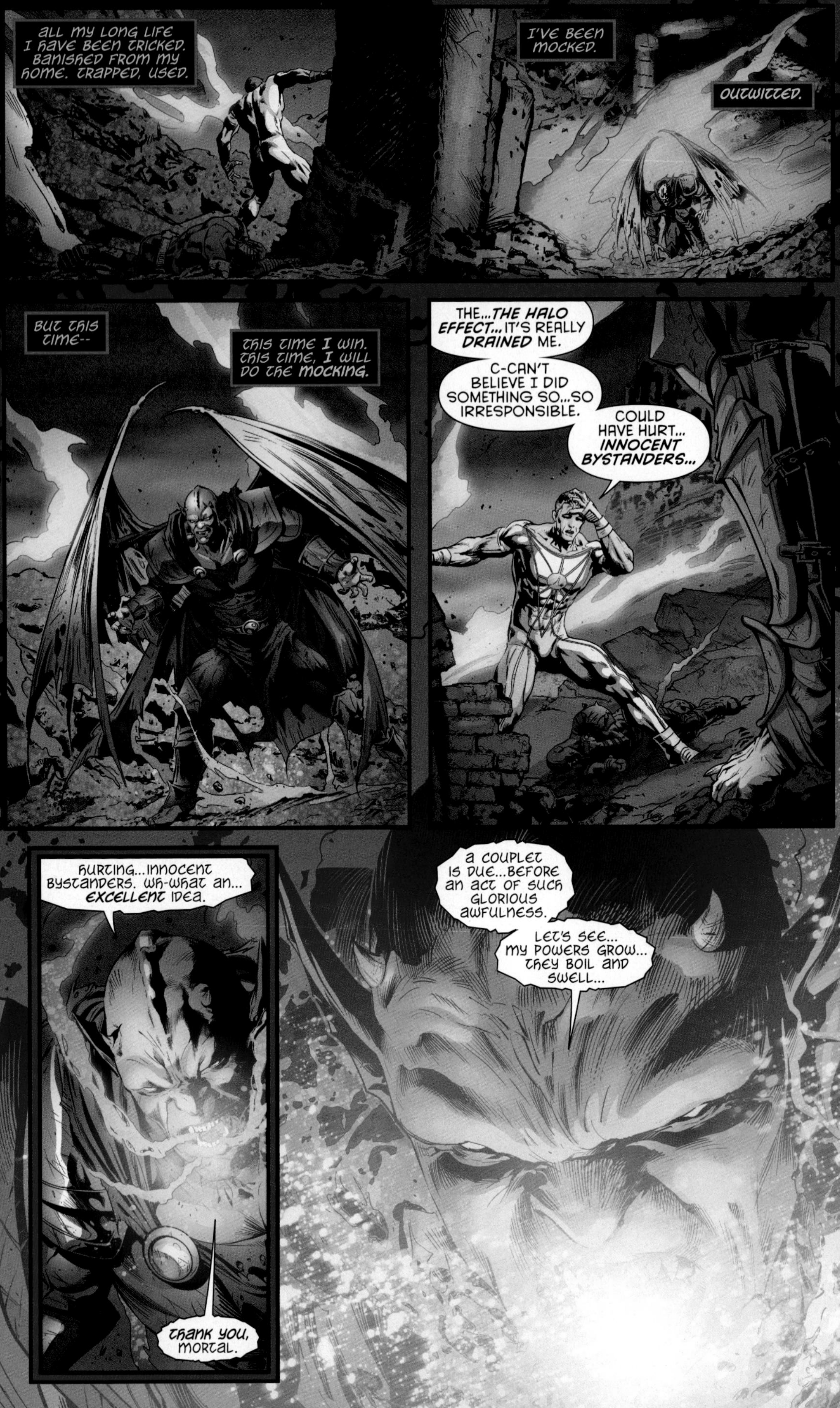
All my long life I have been tricked. Banished from my home. Trapped, used.
I've been mocked.
Outwitted.
But this time--
This time I win. This time, I will do the mocking.
The...the halo effect...it's really drained me.
C-can't believe I did something so...so irresponsible.
Could have hurt... innocent bystanders...
Hurting...innocent bystanders. Wh-what an... excellent idea.
Thank you, mortal.
A couplet is due...before an act of such glorious awfulness.
Let's see... my powers grow... they boil and swell...

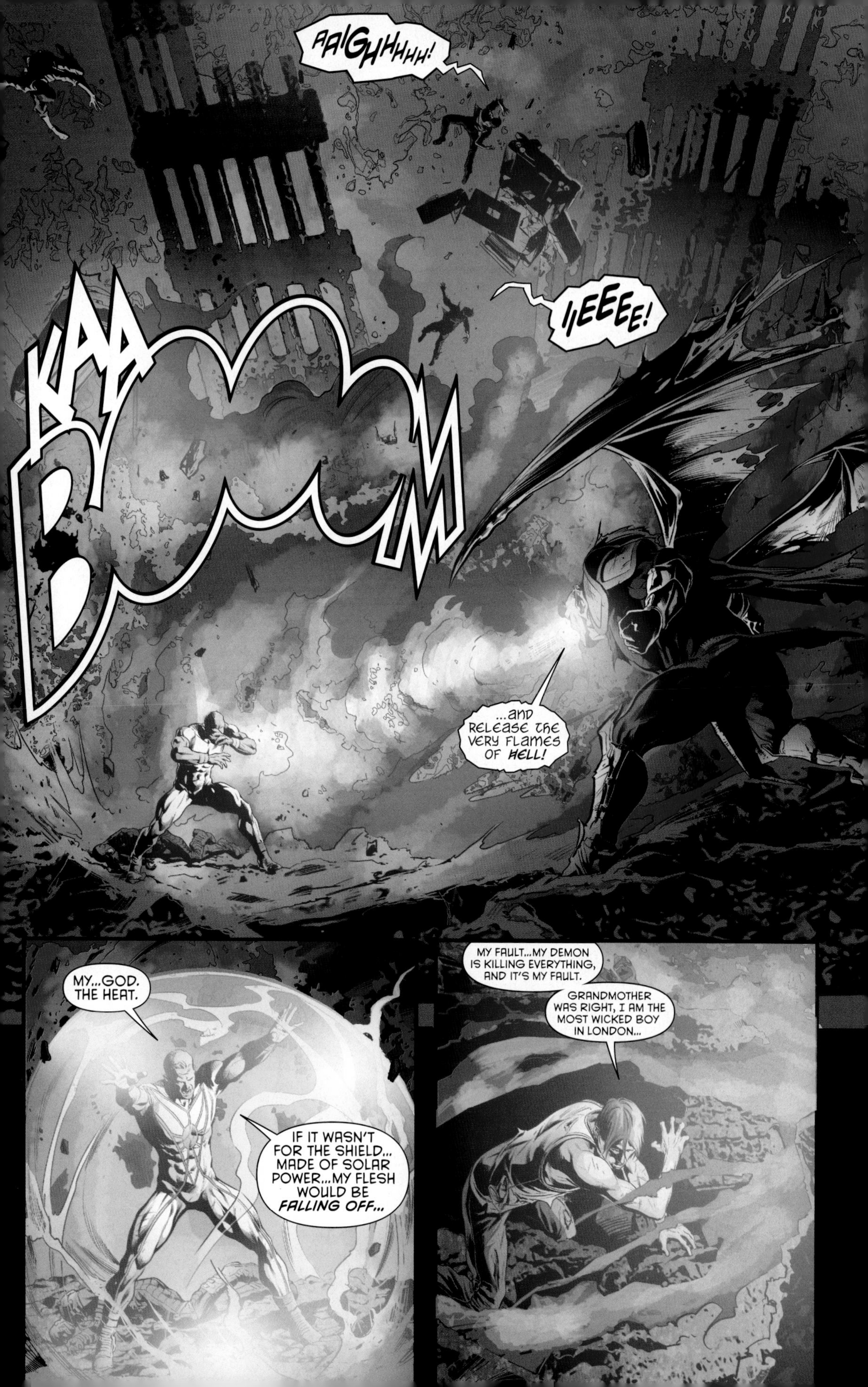
AAIGHHHHH!
IIEEEE!
KABOOM
...AND RELEASE THE VERY FLAMES OF HELL!
MY...GOD. THE HEAT.
IF IT WASN'T FOR THE SHIELD... MADE OF SOLAR POWER...MY FLESH WOULD BE FALLING OFF...
MY FAULT...MY DEMON IS KILLING EVERYTHING, AND IT'S MY FAULT.
GRANDMOTHER WAS RIGHT, I AM THE MOST WICKED BOY IN LONDON...

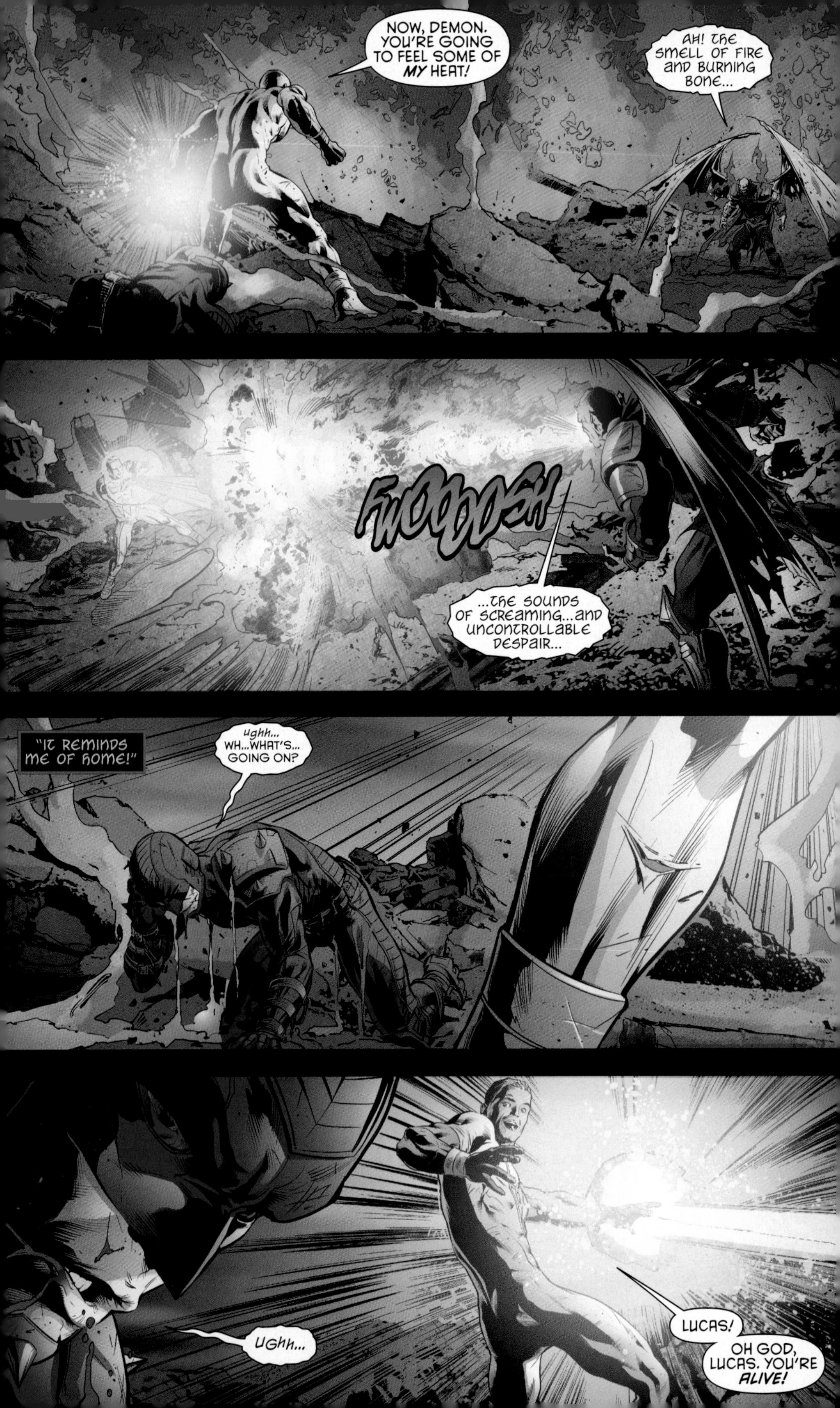
NOW, DEMON. YOU'RE GOING TO FEEL SOME OF MY HEAT!
AH! THE SMELL OF FIRE AND BURNING BONE...
FWOOOOSH
...THE SOUNDS OF SCREAMING...AND UNCONTROLLABLE DESPAIR...
"IT REMINDS ME OF HOME!"
UGHH... WH...WHAT'S... GOING ON?
UGHH...
LUCAS!
OH GOD, LUCAS. YOU'RE ALIVE!

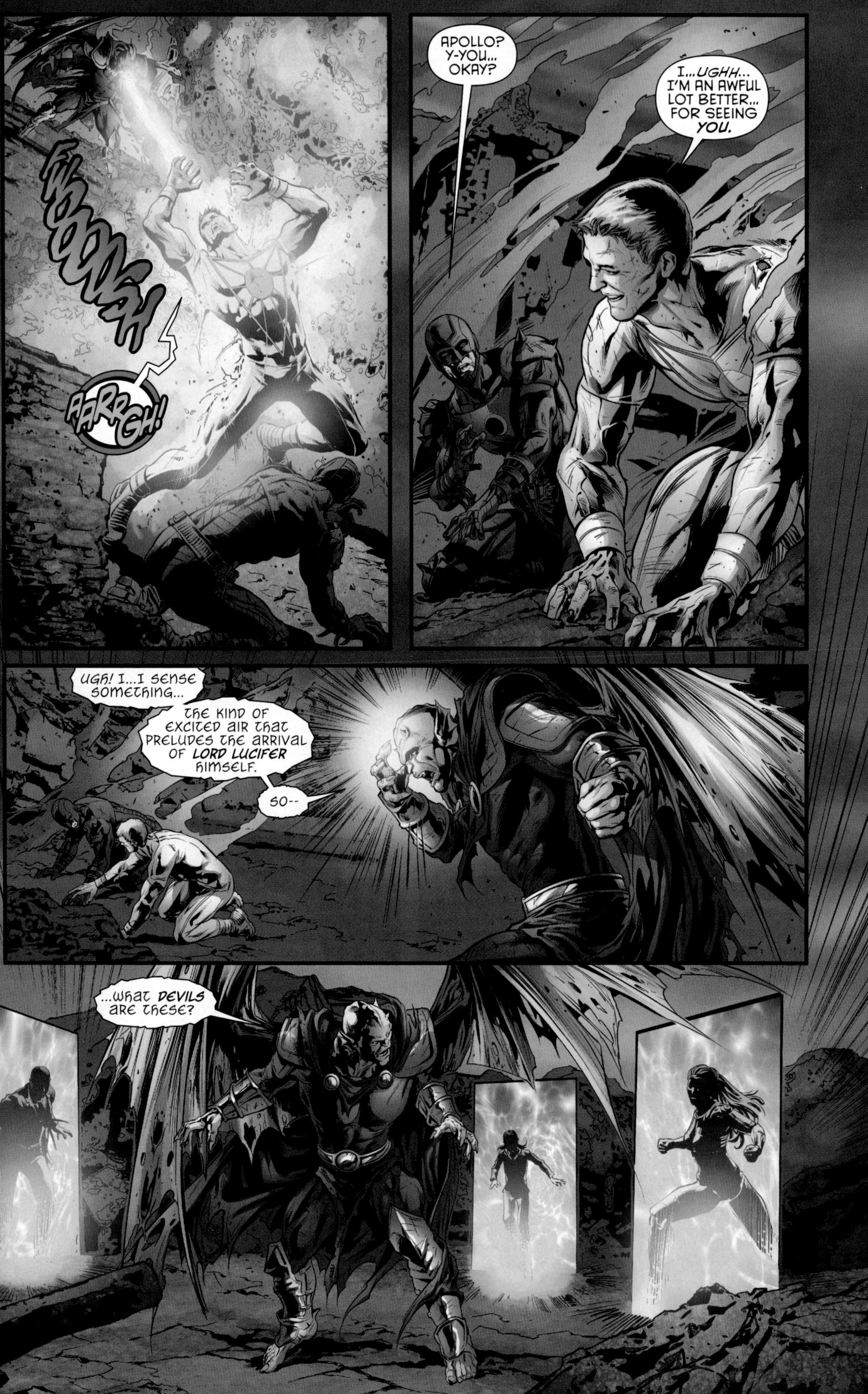
FWOOOOOSH
AARRGH!
APOLLO? Y-YOU... OKAY?
I...UGHH... I'M AN AWFUL LOT BETTER... FOR SEEING YOU.
UGH! I...I SENSE SOMETHING...
THE KIND OF EXCITED AIR THAT PRELUDES THE ARRIVAL OF LORD LUCIFER HIMSELF.
SO--
...WHAT DEVILS ARE THESE?

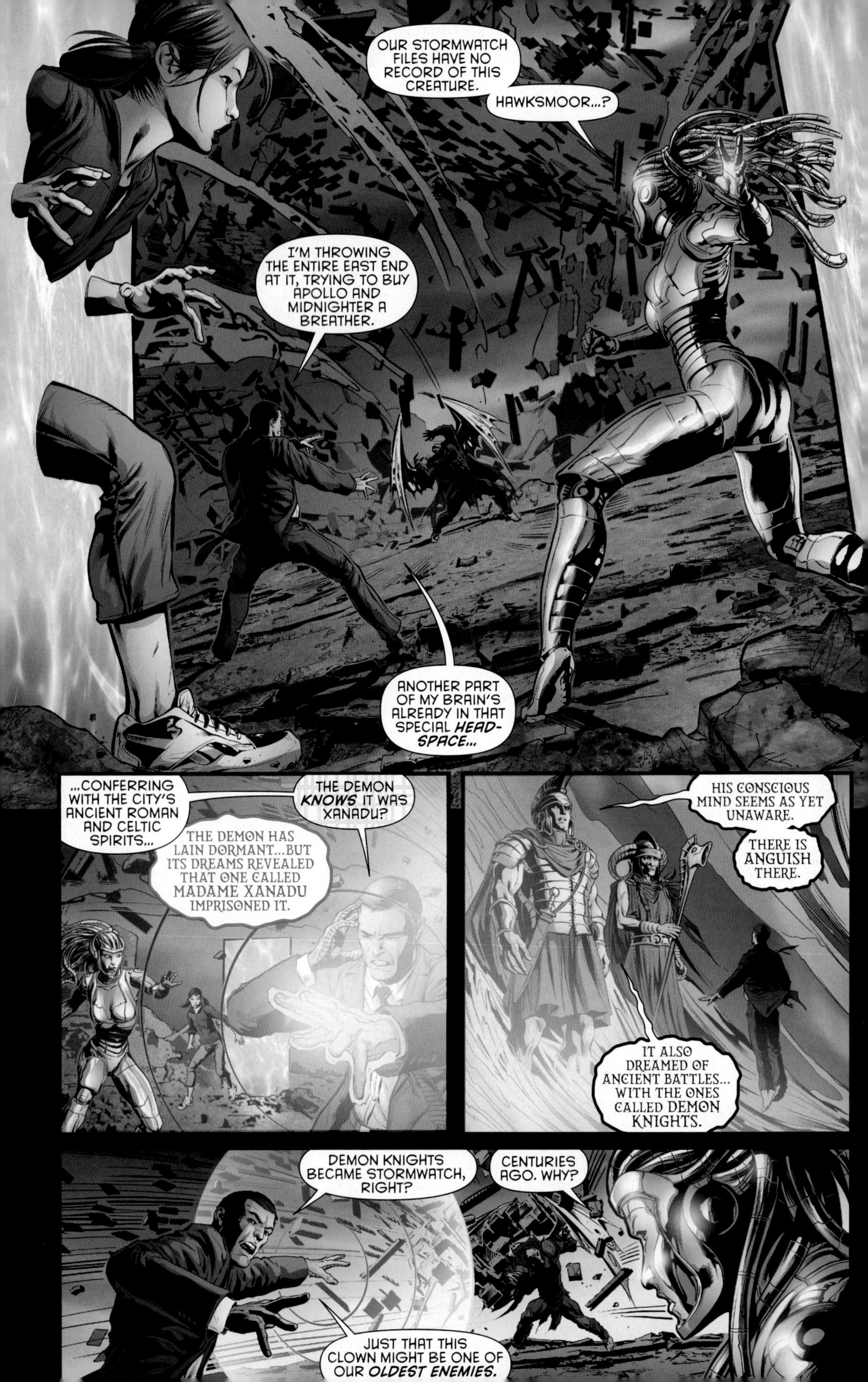
OUR STORMWATCH FILES HAVE NO RECORD OF THIS CREATURE.
HAWKSMOOR...?
I'M THROWING THE ENTIRE EAST END AT IT, TRYING TO BUY APOLLO AND MIDNIGHTER A BREATHER.
ANOTHER PART OF MY BRAIN'S ALREADY IN THAT SPECIAL HEAD-SPACE...
...CONFERRING WITH THE CITY'S ANCIENT ROMAN AND CELTIC SPIRITS...
THE DEMON HAS LAIN DORMANT...BUT ITS DREAMS REVEALED THAT ONE CALLED MADAME XANADU IMPRISONED IT.
THE DEMON KNOWS IT WAS XANADU?
HIS CONSCIOUS MIND SEEMS AS YET UNAWARE.
THERE IS ANGUISH THERE.
IT ALSO DREAMED OF ANCIENT BATTLES... WITH THE ONES CALLED DEMON KNIGHTS.
DEMON KNIGHTS BECAME STORMWATCH, RIGHT?
CENTURIES AGO. WHY?
JUST THAT THIS CLOWN MIGHT BE ONE OF OUR OLDEST ENEMIES.

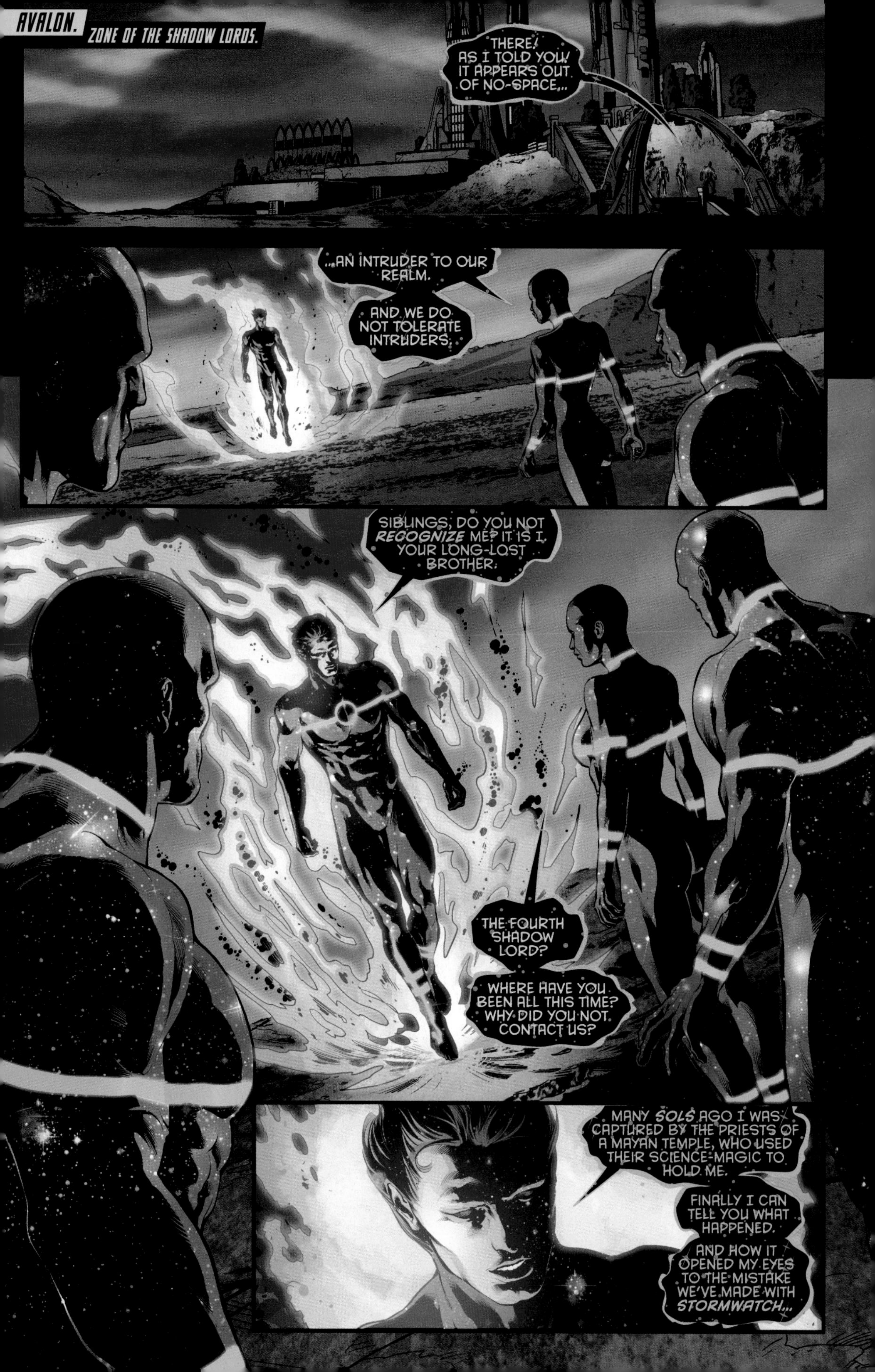
AVALON.
ZONE OF THE SHADOW LORDS.
THERE! AS I TOLD YOU! IT APPEARS OUT OF NO-SPACE...
...AN INTRUDER TO OUR REALM.
AND WE DO NOT TOLERATE INTRUDERS.
SIBLINGS, DO YOU NOT RECOGNIZE ME? IT IS I, YOUR LONG-LOST BROTHER.
THE FOURTH SHADOW LORD?
WHERE HAVE YOU BEEN ALL THIS TIME? WHY DID YOU NOT CONTACT US?
MANY SOLS AGO I WAS CAPTURED BY THE PRIESTS OF A MAYAN TEMPLE, WHO USED THEIR SCIENCE-MAGIC TO HOLD ME.
FINALLY I CAN TELL YOU WHAT HAPPENED.
AND HOW IT OPENED MY EYES TO THE MISTAKE WE'VE MADE WITH STORMWATCH...

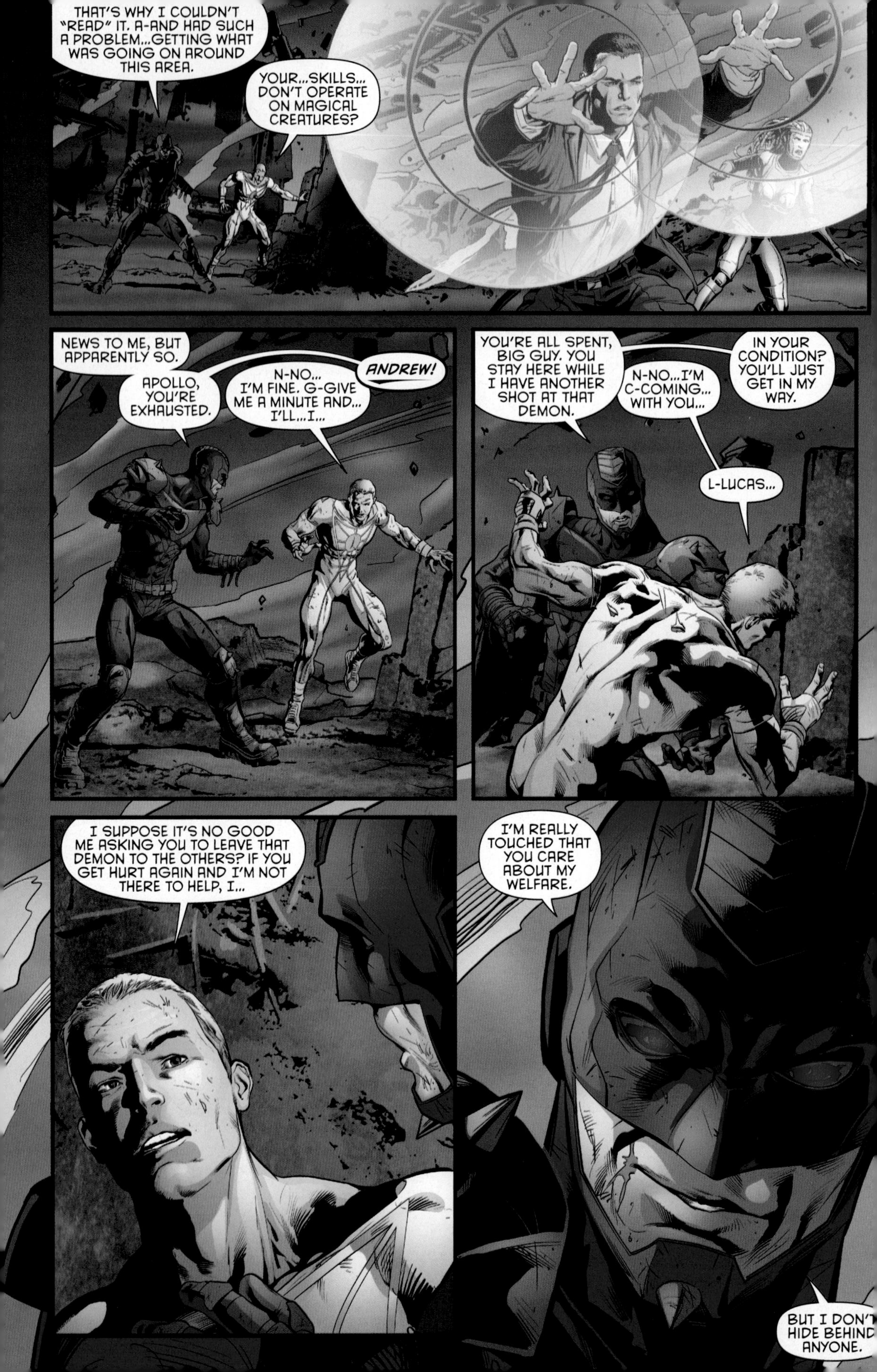

THAT'S WHY I COULDN'T "READ" IT. A-AND HAD SUCH A PROBLEM...GETTING WHAT WAS GOING ON AROUND THIS AREA.
YOUR...SKILLS... DON'T OPERATE ON MAGICAL CREATURES?
NEWS TO ME, BUT APPARENTLY SO.
ANDREW!
APOLLO, YOU'RE EXHAUSTED.
N-NO... I'M FINE. G-GIVE ME A MINUTE AND... I'LL...I...
YOU'RE ALL SPENT, BIG GUY. YOU STAY HERE WHILE I HAVE ANOTHER SHOT AT THAT DEMON.
N-NO...I'M C-COMING... WITH YOU...
IN YOUR CONDITION? YOU'LL JUST GET IN MY WAY.
L-LUCAS...
I SUPPOSE IT'S NO GOOD ME ASKING YOU TO LEAVE THAT DEMON TO THE OTHERS? IF YOU GET HURT AGAIN AND I'M NOT THERE TO HELP, I...
I'M REALLY TOUCHED THAT YOU CARE ABOUT MY WELFARE.
BUT I DON'T HIDE BEHIND ANYONE.

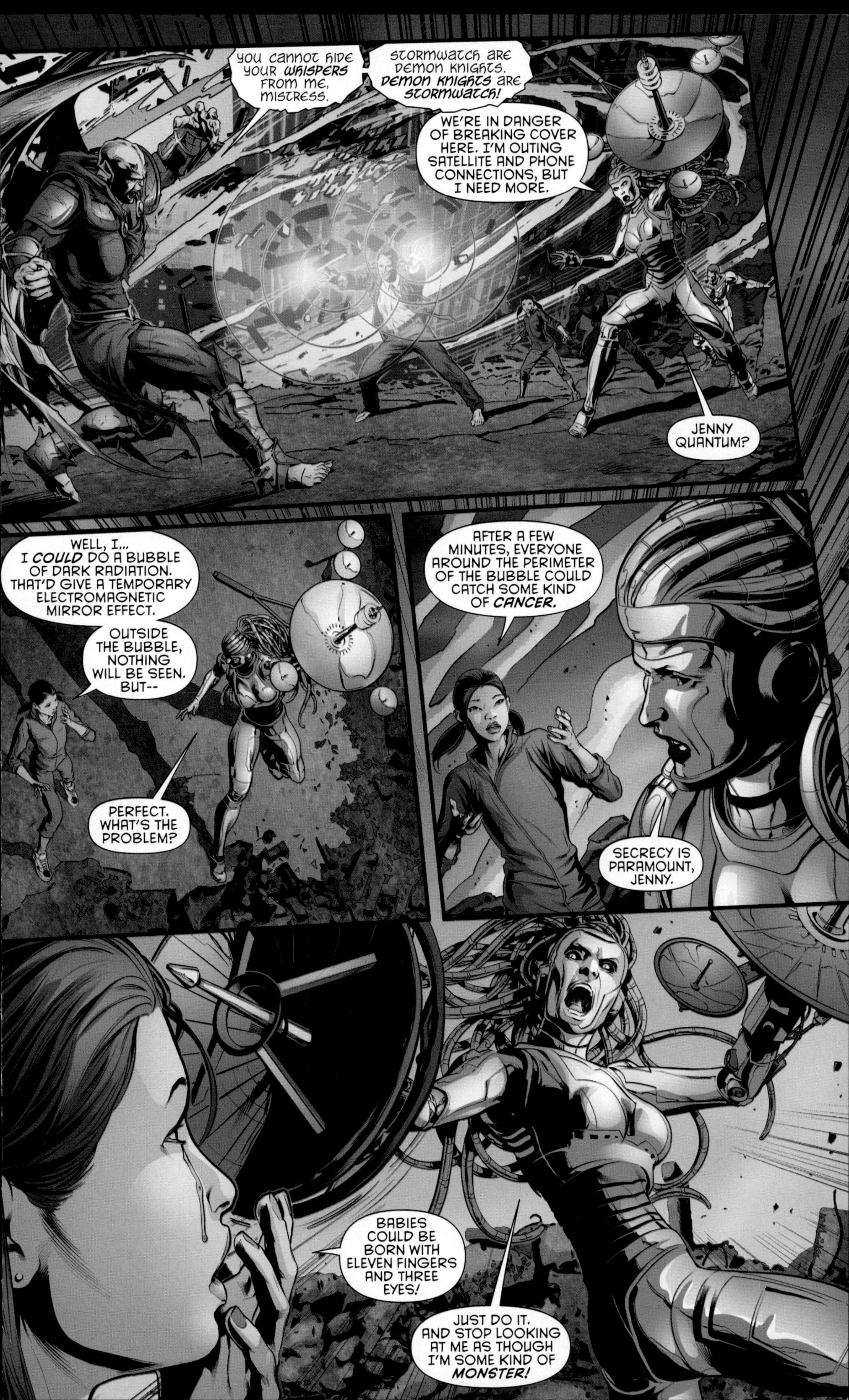

YOU CANNOT HIDE YOUR WHISPERS FROM ME, MISTRESS.
STORMWATCH ARE DEMON KNIGHTS. DEMON KNIGHTS ARE STORMWATCH!
WE'RE IN DANGER OF BREAKING COVER HERE. I'M OUTING SATELLITE AND PHONE CONNECTIONS, BUT I NEED MORE.
JENNY QUANTUM?
WELL, I... I COULD DO A BUBBLE OF DARK RADIATION. THAT'D GIVE A TEMPORARY ELECTROMAGNETIC MIRROR EFFECT.
OUTSIDE THE BUBBLE, NOTHING WILL BE SEEN. BUT--
PERFECT. WHAT'S THE PROBLEM?
AFTER A FEW MINUTES, EVERYONE AROUND THE PERIMETER OF THE BUBBLE COULD CATCH SOME KIND OF CANCER.
SECRECY IS PARAMOUNT, JENNY.
BABIES COULD BE BORN WITH ELEVEN FINGERS AND THREE EYES!
JUST DO IT. AND STOP LOOKING AT ME AS THOUGH I'M SOME KIND OF MONSTER!

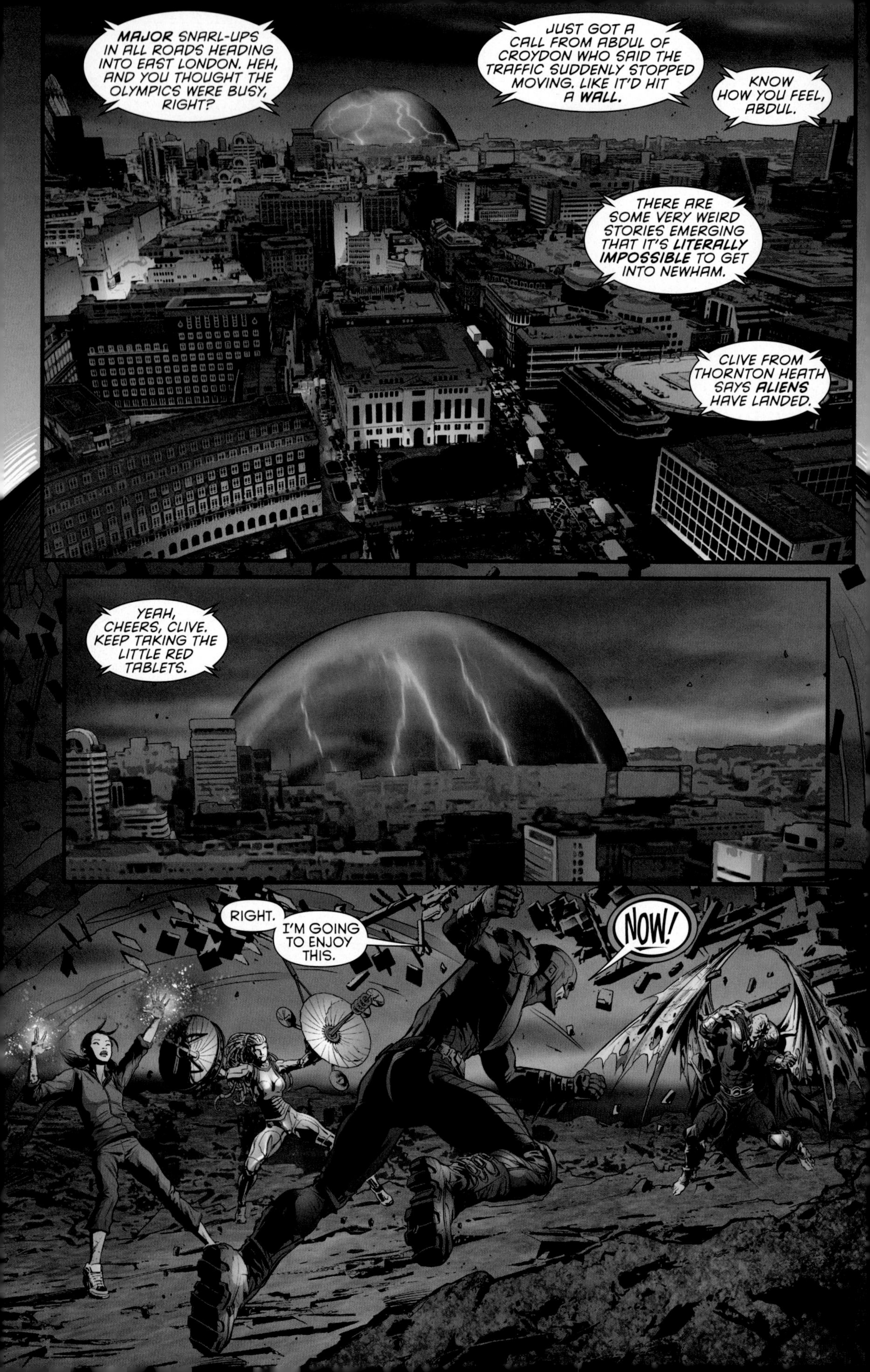
MAJOR SNARL-UPS IN ALL ROADS HEADING INTO EAST LONDON. HEH, AND YOU THOUGHT THE OLYMPICS WERE BUSY, RIGHT?
JUST GOT A CALL FROM ABDUL OF CROYDON WHO SAID THE TRAFFIC SUDDENLY STOPPED MOVING. LIKE IT'D HIT A WALL.
KNOW HOW YOU FEEL, ABDUL.
THERE ARE SOME VERY WEIRD STORIES EMERGING THAT IT'S LITERALLY IMPOSSIBLE TO GET INTO NEWHAM.
CLIVE FROM THORNTON HEATH SAYS ALIENS HAVE LANDED.
YEAH, CHEERS, CLIVE. KEEP TAKING THE LITTLE RED TABLETS.
RIGHT.
I'M GOING TO ENJOY THIS.
NOW!

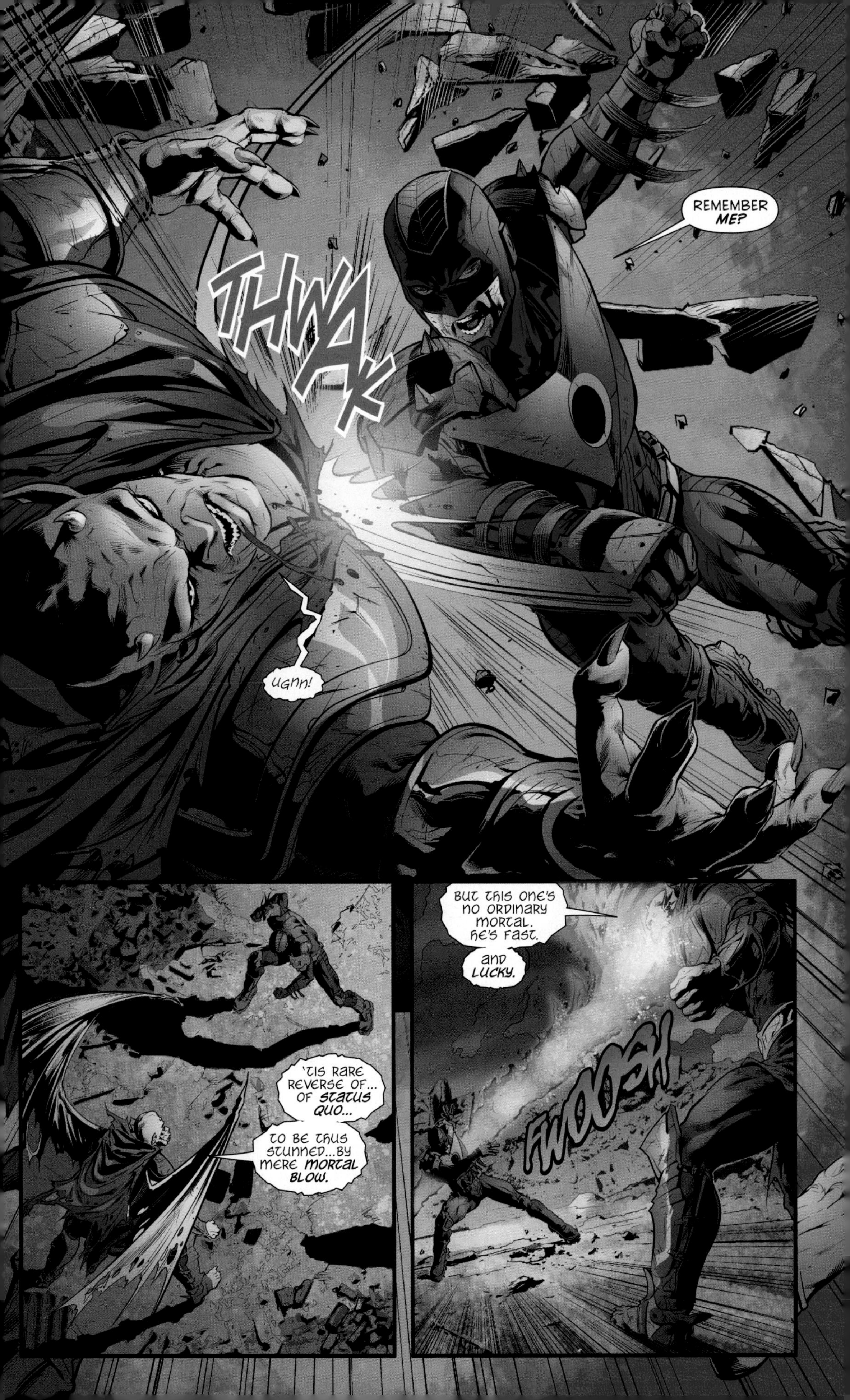
REMEMBER *ME?*
THWAK
UGHN!
'TIS RARE REVERSE OF... OF *STATUS QUO...*
TO BE THUS STUNNED...BY MERE *MORTAL BLOW.*
BUT THIS ONE'S NO ORDINARY MORTAL. HE'S FAST.
AND *LUCKY.*
FWOOSH

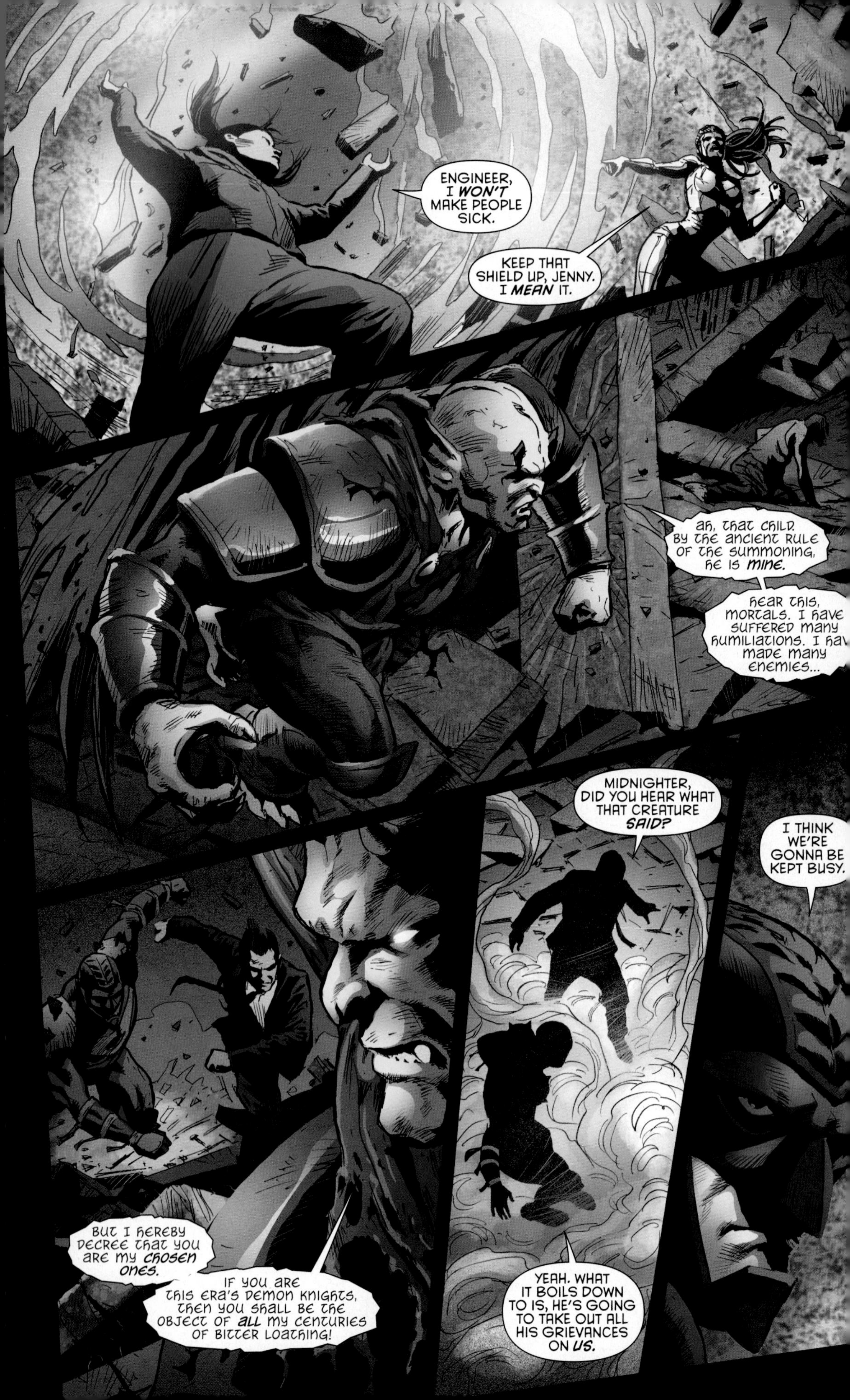
ENGINEER, I WON'T MAKE PEOPLE SICK.
KEEP THAT SHIELD UP, JENNY. I MEAN IT.
AH, THAT CHILD. BY THE ANCIENT RULE OF THE SUMMONING, HE IS MINE.
HEAR THIS, MORTALS. I HAVE SUFFERED MANY HUMILIATIONS. I HAV MADE MANY ENEMIES...
BUT I HEREBY DECREE THAT YOU ARE MY CHOSEN ONES.
IF YOU ARE THIS ERA'S DEMON KNIGHTS, THEN YOU SHALL BE THE OBJECT OF ALL MY CENTURIES OF BITTER LOATHING!
MIDNIGHTER, DID YOU HEAR WHAT THAT CREATURE SAID?
YEAH. WHAT IT BOILS DOWN TO IS, HE'S GOING TO TAKE OUT ALL HIS GRIEVANCES ON US.
I THINK WE'RE GONNA BE KEPT BUSY.

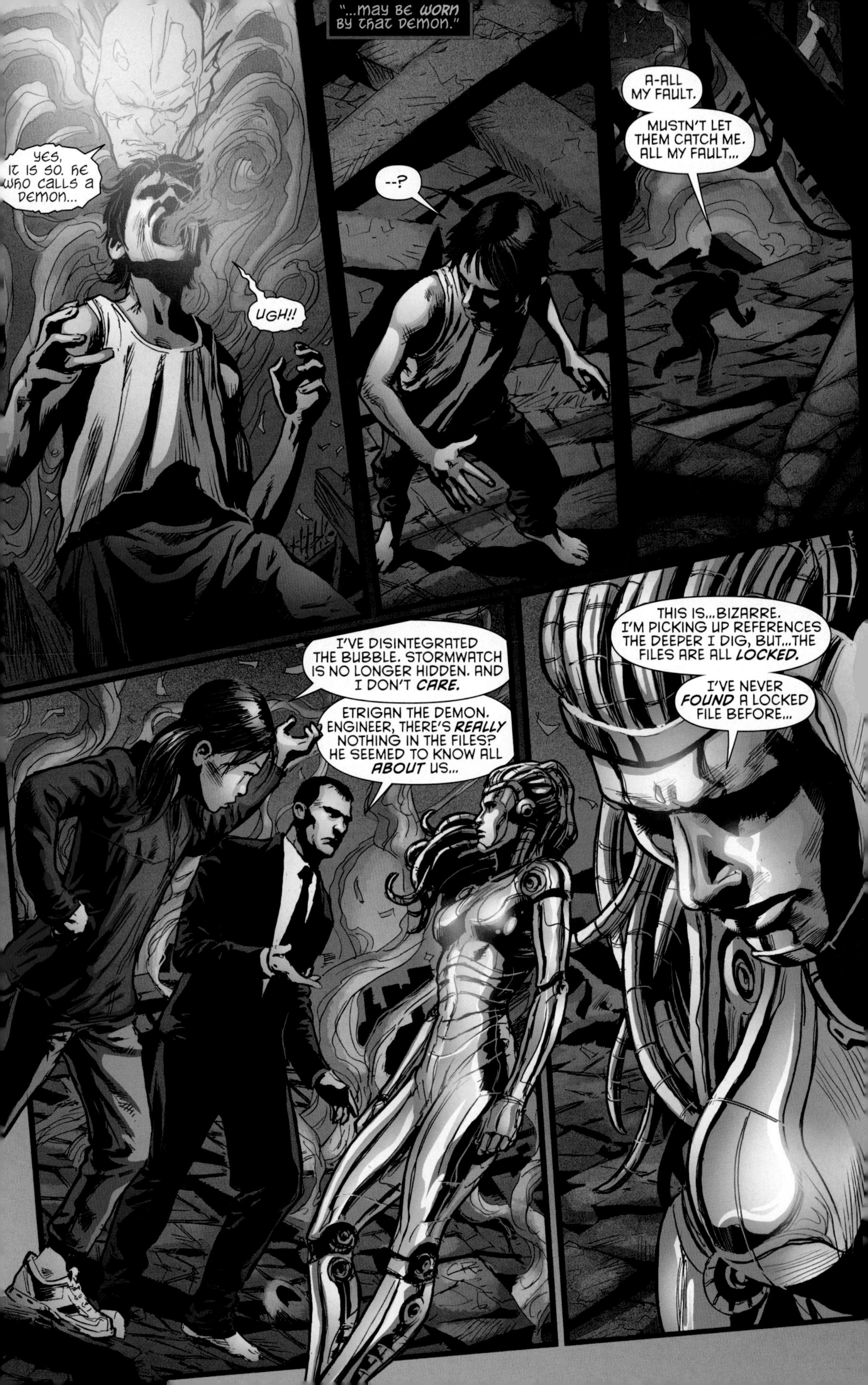
"...may be WORN by that demon."
Yes, it is so. He who calls a demon...
UGH!!
--?
A-ALL MY FAULT.
MUSTN'T LET THEM CATCH ME. ALL MY FAULT...
I'VE DISINTEGRATED THE BUBBLE. STORMWATCH IS NO LONGER HIDDEN. AND I DON'T CARE.
ETRIGAN THE DEMON. ENGINEER, THERE'S REALLY NOTHING IN THE FILES? HE SEEMED TO KNOW ALL ABOUT US...
THIS IS...BIZARRE. I'M PICKING UP REFERENCES THE DEEPER I DIG, BUT...THE FILES ARE ALL LOCKED.
I'VE NEVER FOUND A LOCKED FILE BEFORE...

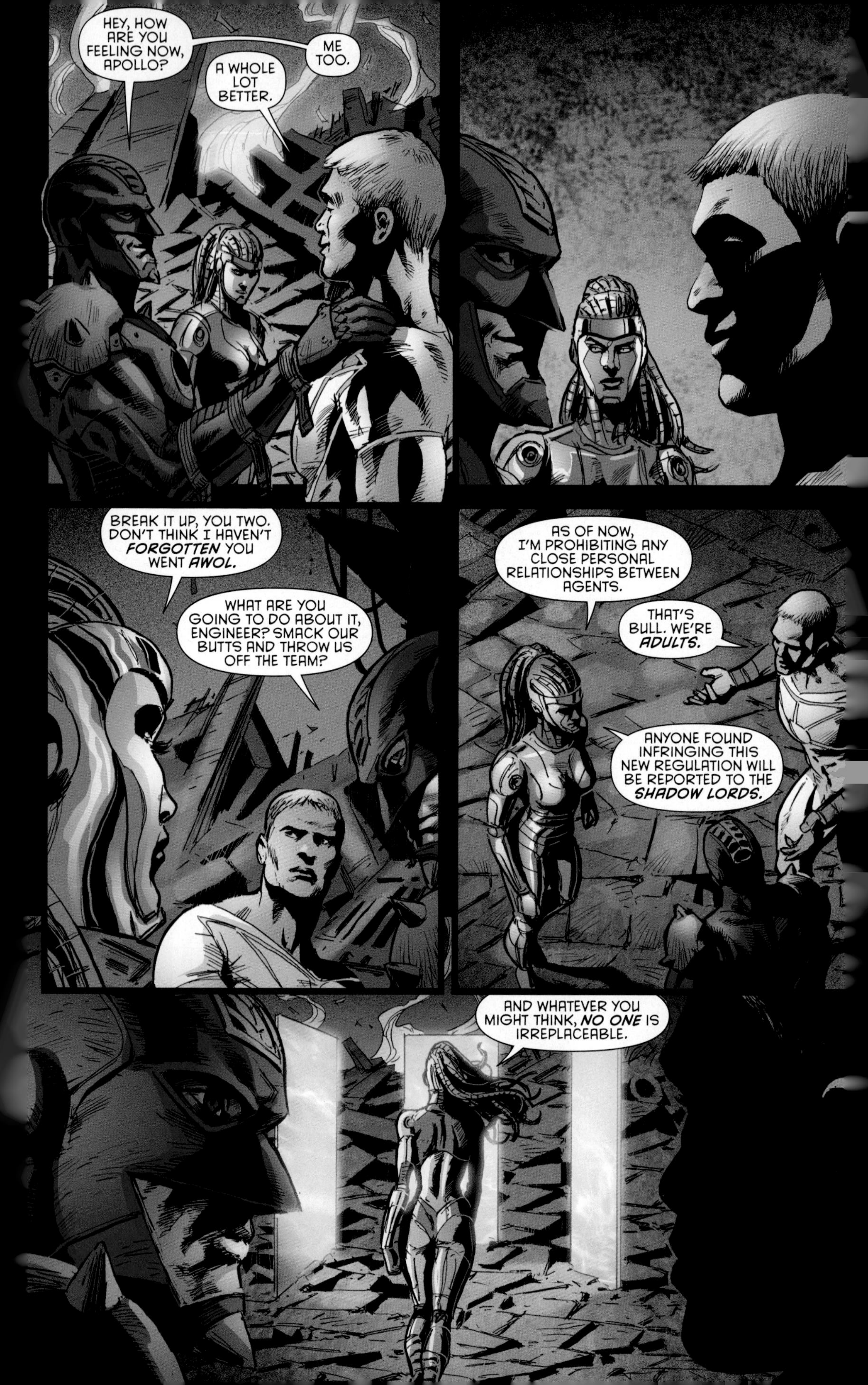
HEY, HOW ARE YOU FEELING NOW, APOLLO?
A WHOLE LOT BETTER.
ME TOO.
BREAK IT UP, YOU TWO. DON'T THINK I HAVEN'T *FORGOTTEN* YOU WENT *AWOL.*
WHAT ARE YOU GOING TO DO ABOUT IT, ENGINEER? SMACK OUR BUTTS AND THROW US OFF THE TEAM?
AS OF NOW, I'M PROHIBITING ANY CLOSE PERSONAL RELATIONSHIPS BETWEEN AGENTS.
THAT'S BULL. WE'RE *ADULTS.*
ANYONE FOUND INFRINGING THIS NEW REGULATION WILL BE REPORTED TO THE *SHADOW LORDS.*
AND WHATEVER YOU MIGHT THINK, *NO ONE* IS IRREPLACEABLE.

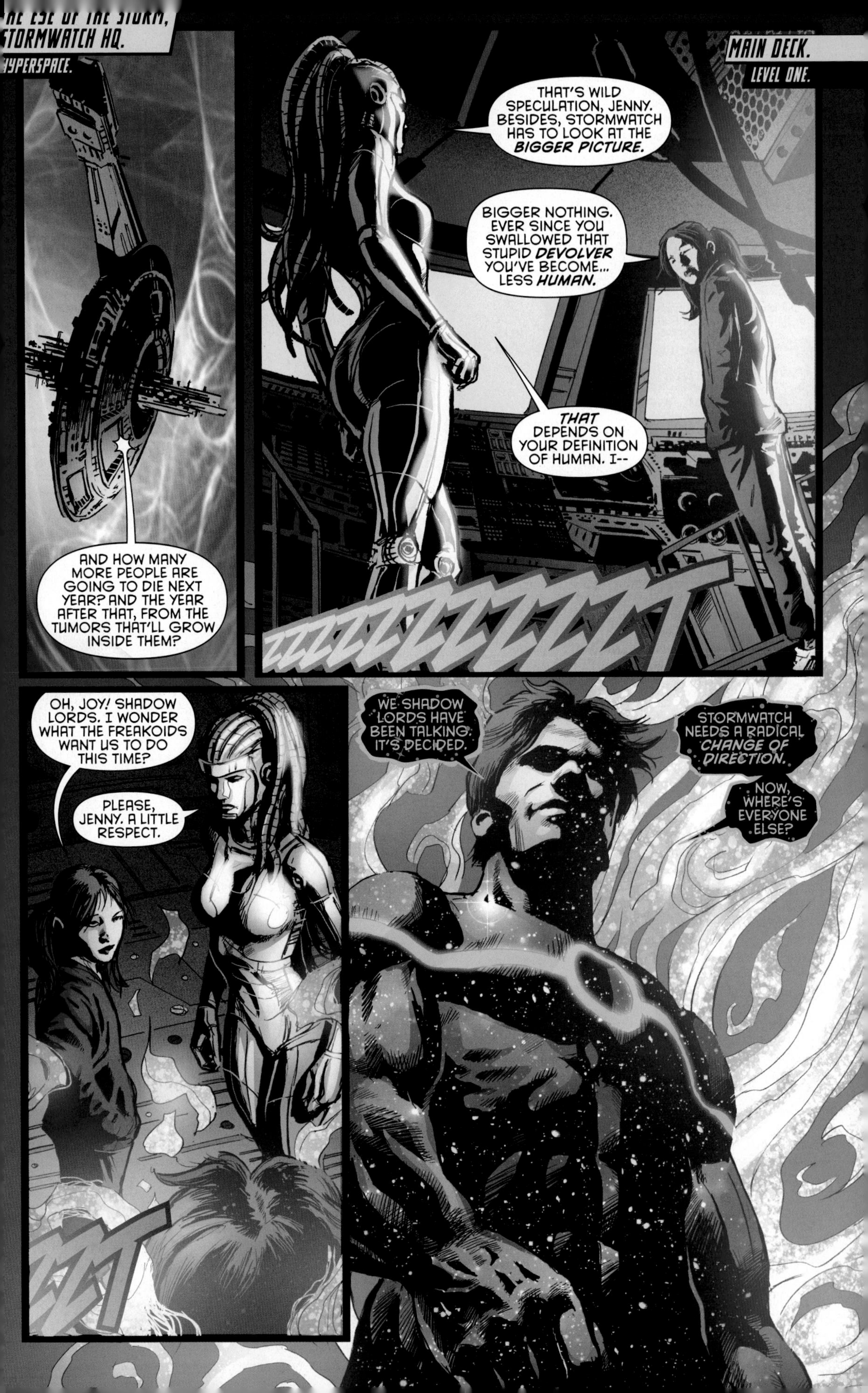

EYE OF THE STORM,
STORMWATCH HQ.
HYPERSPACE.
AND HOW MANY MORE PEOPLE ARE GOING TO DIE NEXT YEAR? AND THE YEAR AFTER THAT, FROM THE TUMORS THAT'LL GROW INSIDE THEM?
MAIN DECK.
LEVEL ONE.
THAT'S WILD SPECULATION, JENNY. BESIDES, STORMWATCH HAS TO LOOK AT THE *BIGGER PICTURE.*
BIGGER NOTHING. EVER SINCE YOU SWALLOWED THAT STUPID *DEVOLVER* YOU'VE BECOME... LESS *HUMAN.*
THAT DEPENDS ON YOUR DEFINITION OF HUMAN. I--
ZZZZZZZZZZZT
OH, JOY! SHADOW LORDS. I WONDER WHAT THE FREAKOIDS WANT US TO DO THIS TIME?
PLEASE, JENNY. A LITTLE RESPECT.
WE SHADOW LORDS HAVE BEEN TALKING. IT'S DECIDED.
STORMWATCH NEEDS A RADICAL *CHANGE OF DIRECTION.*
NOW, WHERE'S EVERYONE ELSE?

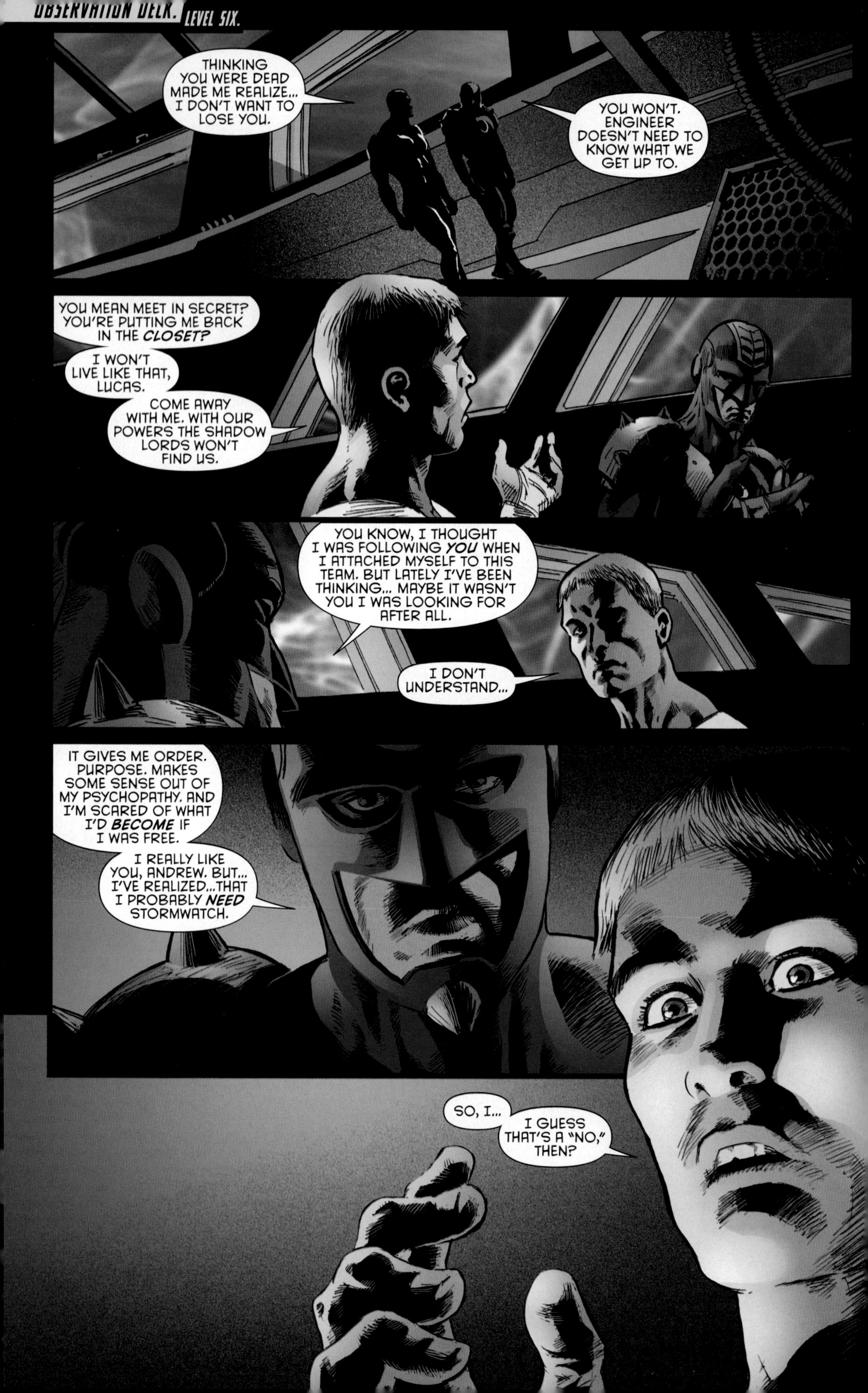
OBSERVATION DECK. LEVEL SIX.
THINKING YOU WERE DEAD MADE ME REALIZE... I DON'T WANT TO LOSE YOU.
YOU WON'T. ENGINEER DOESN'T NEED TO KNOW WHAT WE GET UP TO.
YOU MEAN MEET IN SECRET? YOU'RE PUTTING ME BACK IN THE CLOSET?
I WON'T LIVE LIKE THAT, LUCAS.
COME AWAY WITH ME. WITH OUR POWERS THE SHADOW LORDS WON'T FIND US.
YOU KNOW, I THOUGHT I WAS FOLLOWING YOU WHEN I ATTACHED MYSELF TO THIS TEAM. BUT LATELY I'VE BEEN THINKING... MAYBE IT WASN'T YOU I WAS LOOKING FOR AFTER ALL.
I DON'T UNDERSTAND...
IT GIVES ME ORDER. PURPOSE. MAKES SOME SENSE OUT OF MY PSYCHOPATHY. AND I'M SCARED OF WHAT I'D BECOME IF I WAS FREE.
I REALLY LIKE YOU, ANDREW. BUT... I'VE REALIZED...THAT I PROBABLY NEED STORMWATCH.
SO, I...
I GUESS THAT'S A "NO," THEN?

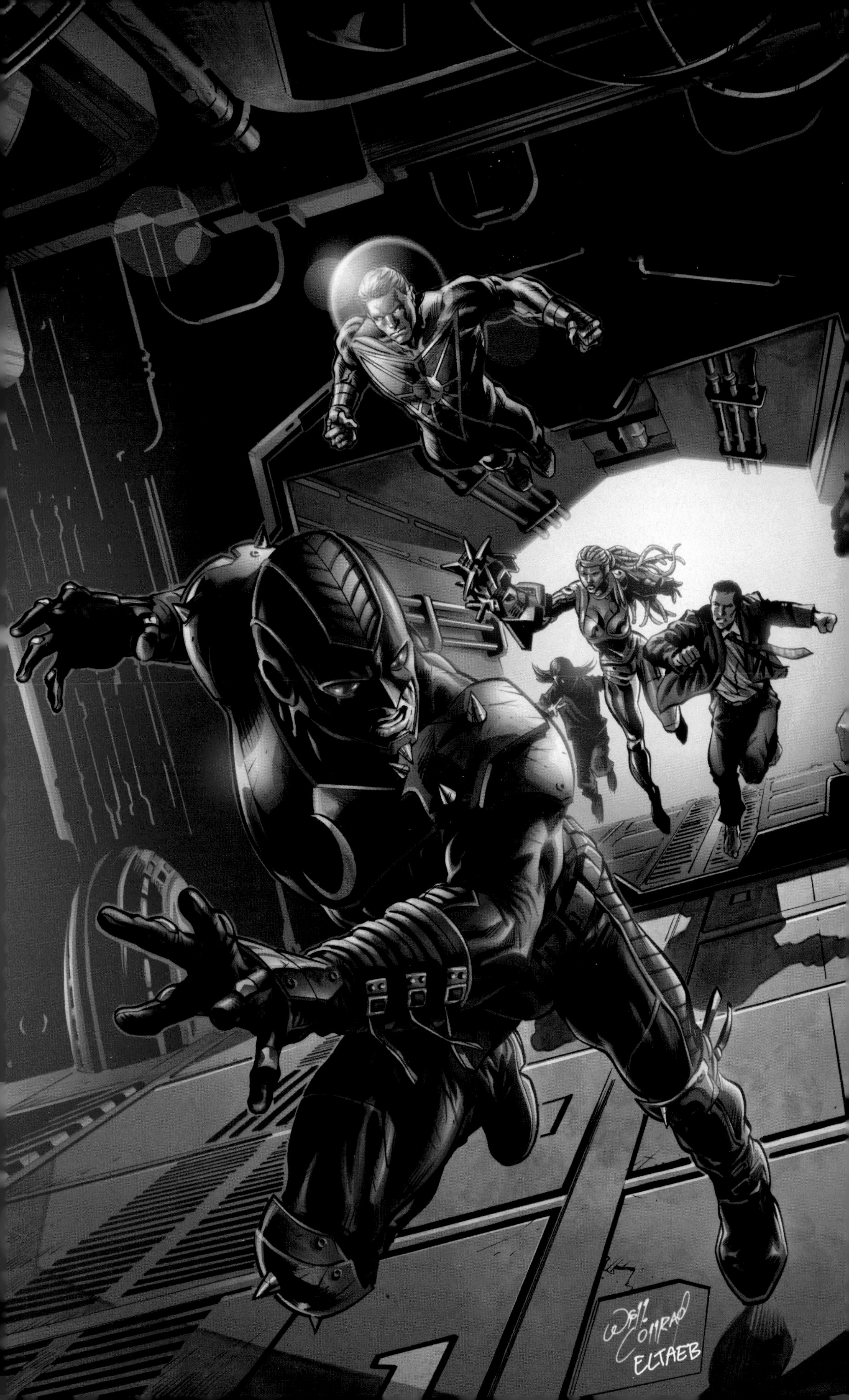
ELTAEB

BETRAYAL PART ONE: BROKEN HEARTS AND COLD FEET

PETER MILLIGAN writer **WILL CONRAD & CLIFF RICHARDS** artists cover art by **WILL CONRAD & GABE ELTAEB**

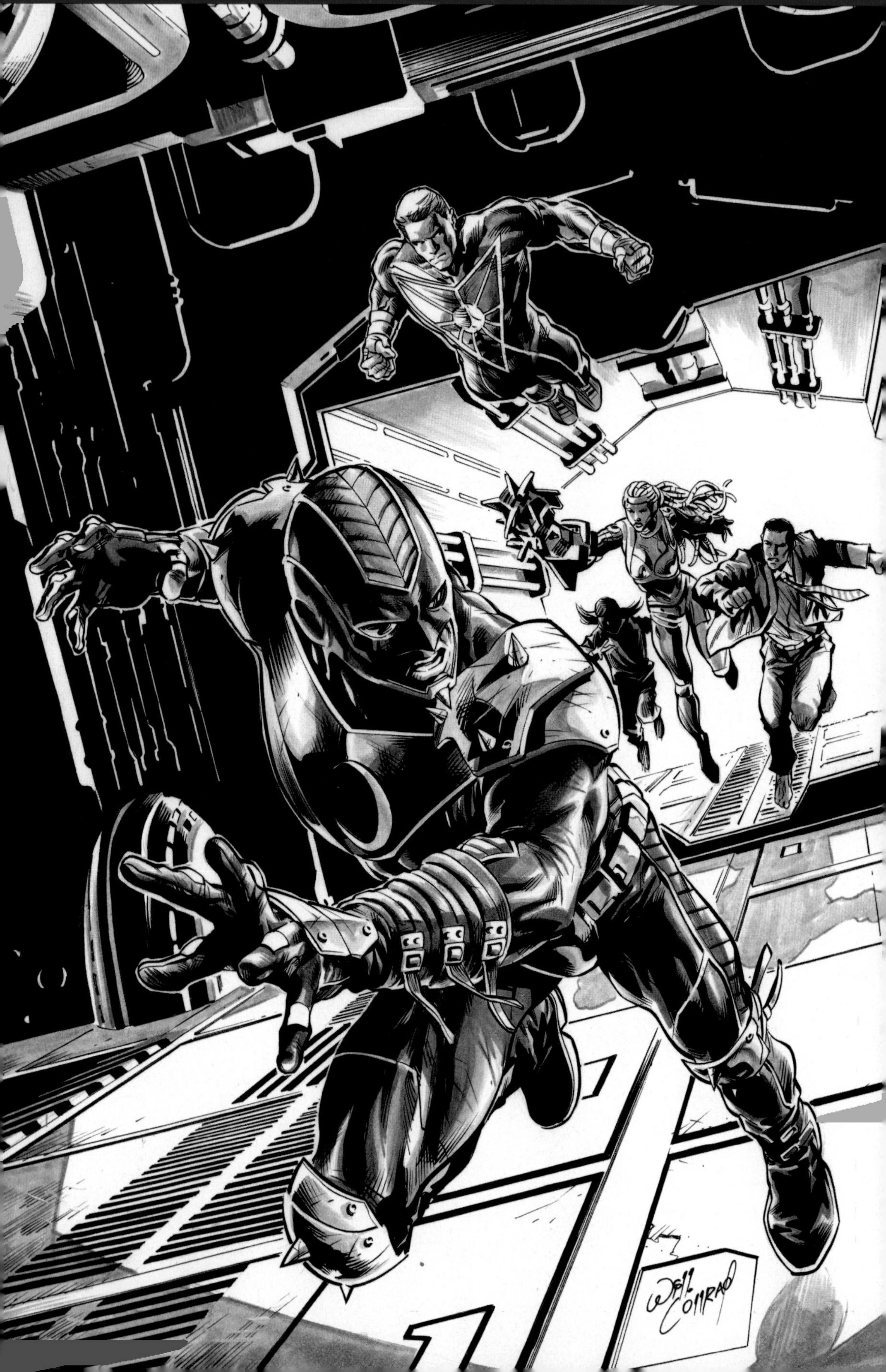

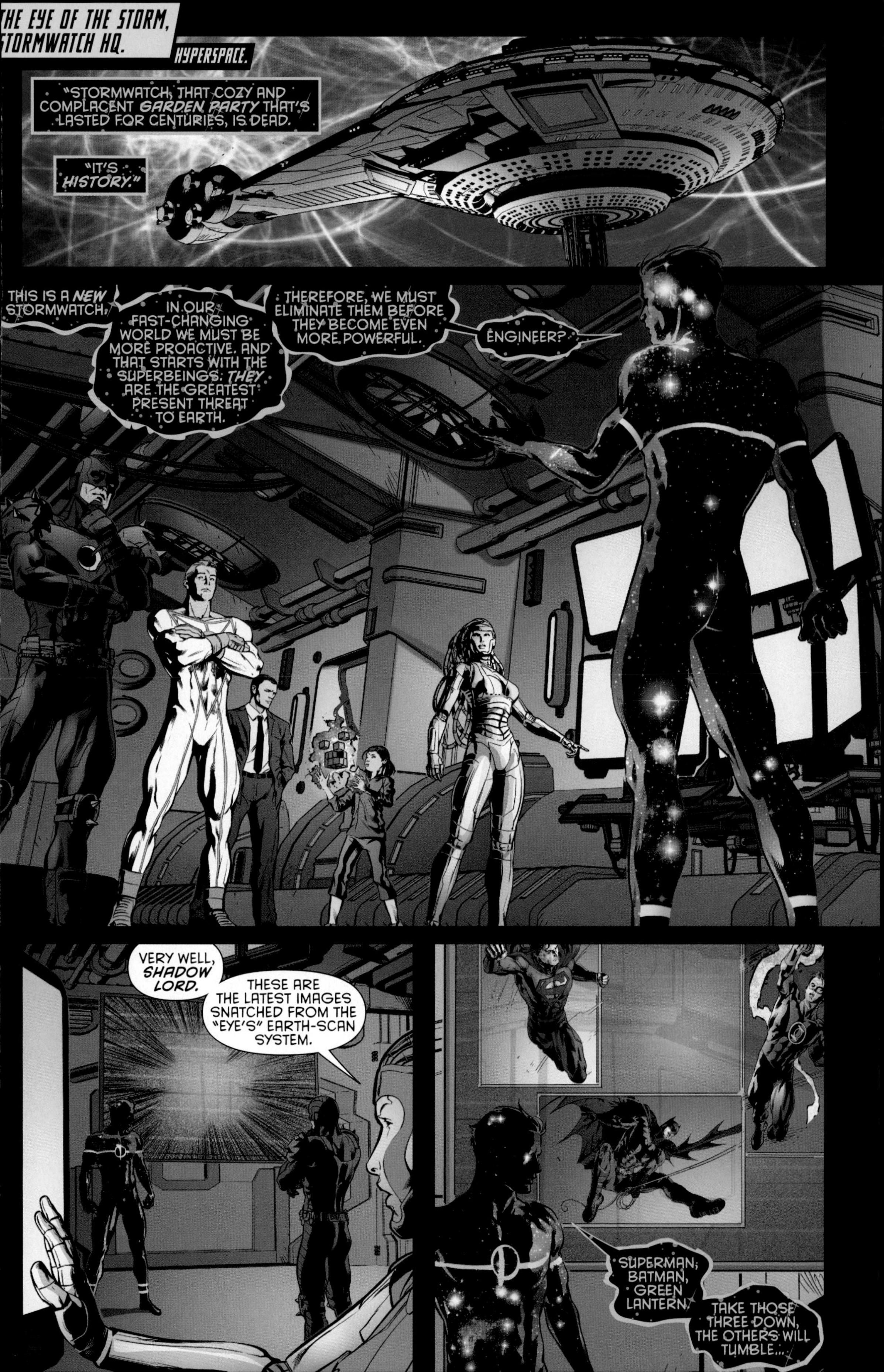
THE EYE OF THE STORM, STORMWATCH HQ.
HYPERSPACE.
"STORMWATCH, THAT COZY AND COMPLACENT GARDEN PARTY THAT'S LASTED FOR CENTURIES, IS DEAD.
"IT'S HISTORY."
THIS IS A NEW STORMWATCH.
IN OUR FAST-CHANGING WORLD WE MUST BE MORE PROACTIVE. AND THAT STARTS WITH THE SUPERBEINGS: THEY ARE THE GREATEST PRESENT THREAT TO EARTH.
THEREFORE, WE MUST ELIMINATE THEM BEFORE THEY BECOME EVEN MORE POWERFUL.
ENGINEER?
VERY WELL, SHADOW LORD.
THESE ARE THE LATEST IMAGES SNATCHED FROM THE "EYE'S" EARTH-SCAN SYSTEM.
SUPERMAN, BATMAN, GREEN LANTERN.
TAKE THOSE THREE DOWN, THE OTHERS WILL TUMBLE...

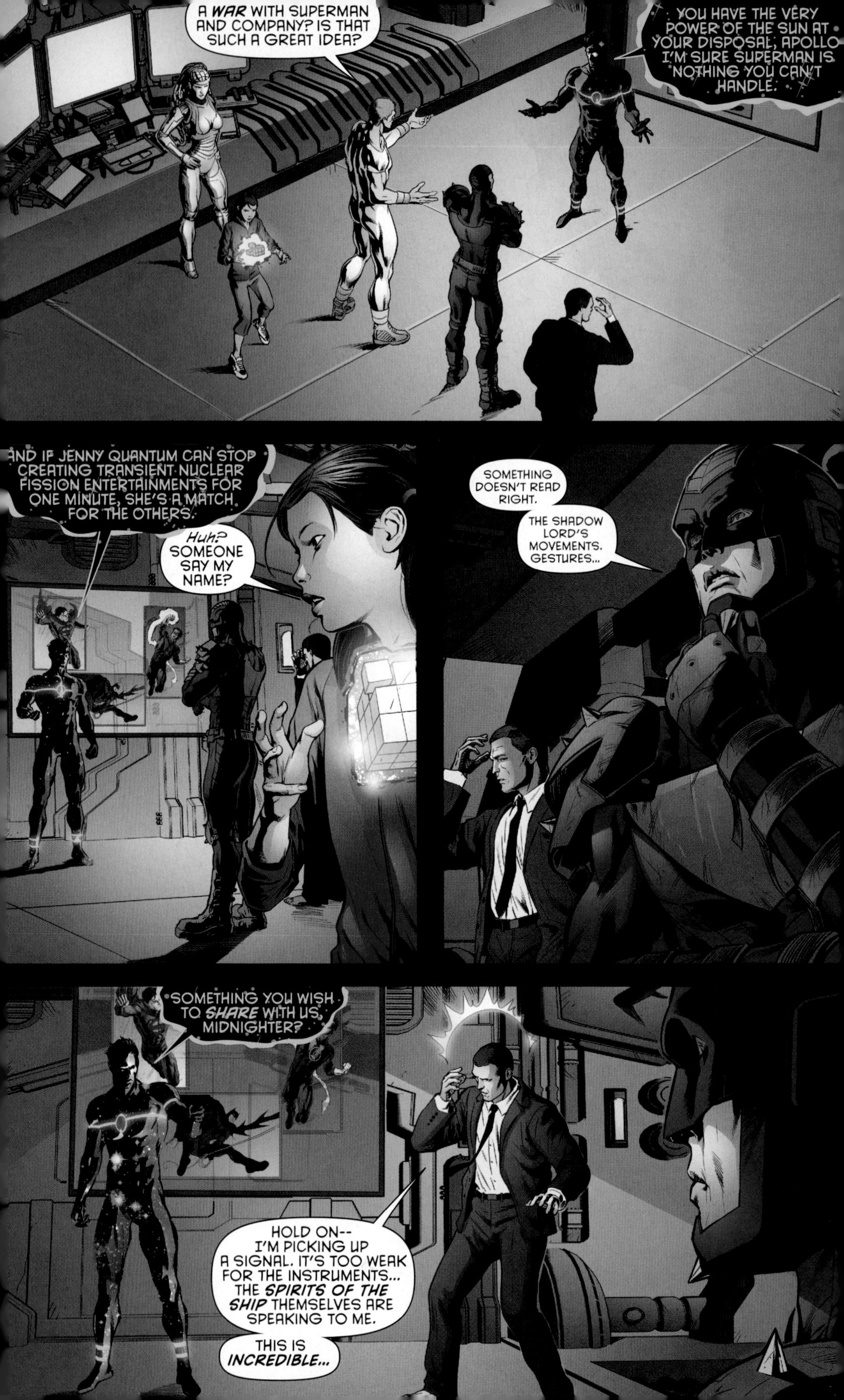
A WAR WITH SUPERMAN AND COMPANY? IS THAT SUCH A GREAT IDEA?
YOU HAVE THE VERY POWER OF THE SUN AT YOUR DISPOSAL, APOLLO. I'M SURE SUPERMAN IS NOTHING YOU CAN'T HANDLE.
AND IF JENNY QUANTUM CAN STOP CREATING TRANSIENT NUCLEAR FISSION ENTERTAINMENTS FOR ONE MINUTE, SHE'S A MATCH FOR THE OTHERS.
Huh? SOMEONE SAY MY NAME?
SOMETHING DOESN'T READ RIGHT.
THE SHADOW LORD'S MOVEMENTS. GESTURES...
SOMETHING YOU WISH TO SHARE WITH US, MIDNIGHTER?
HOLD ON-- I'M PICKING UP A SIGNAL. IT'S TOO WEAK FOR THE INSTRUMENTS... THE SPIRITS OF THE SHIP THEMSELVES ARE SPEAKING TO ME.
THIS IS INCREDIBLE...

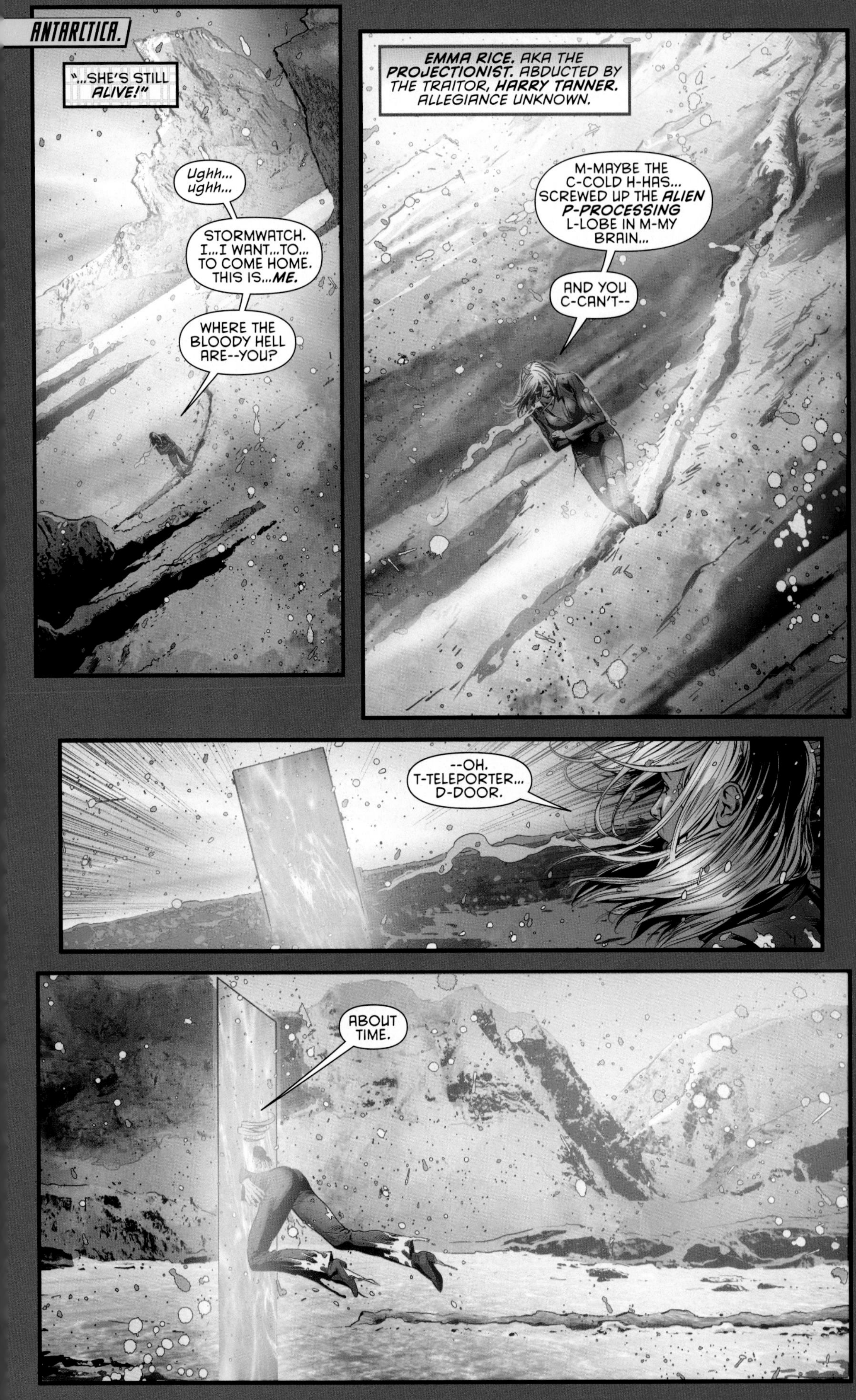
ANTARCTICA.
"...SHE'S STILL ALIVE!"
Ughh... ughh...
STORMWATCH. I...I WANT...TO... TO COME HOME. THIS IS...ME.
WHERE THE BLOODY HELL ARE--YOU?
EMMA RICE. AKA THE PROJECTIONIST. ABDUCTED BY THE TRAITOR, HARRY TANNER. ALLEGIANCE UNKNOWN.
M-MAYBE THE C-COLD H-HAS... SCREWED UP THE ALIEN P-PROCESSING L-LOBE IN M-MY BRAIN...
AND YOU C-CAN'T--
--OH. T-TELEPORTER... D-DOOR.
ABOUT TIME.

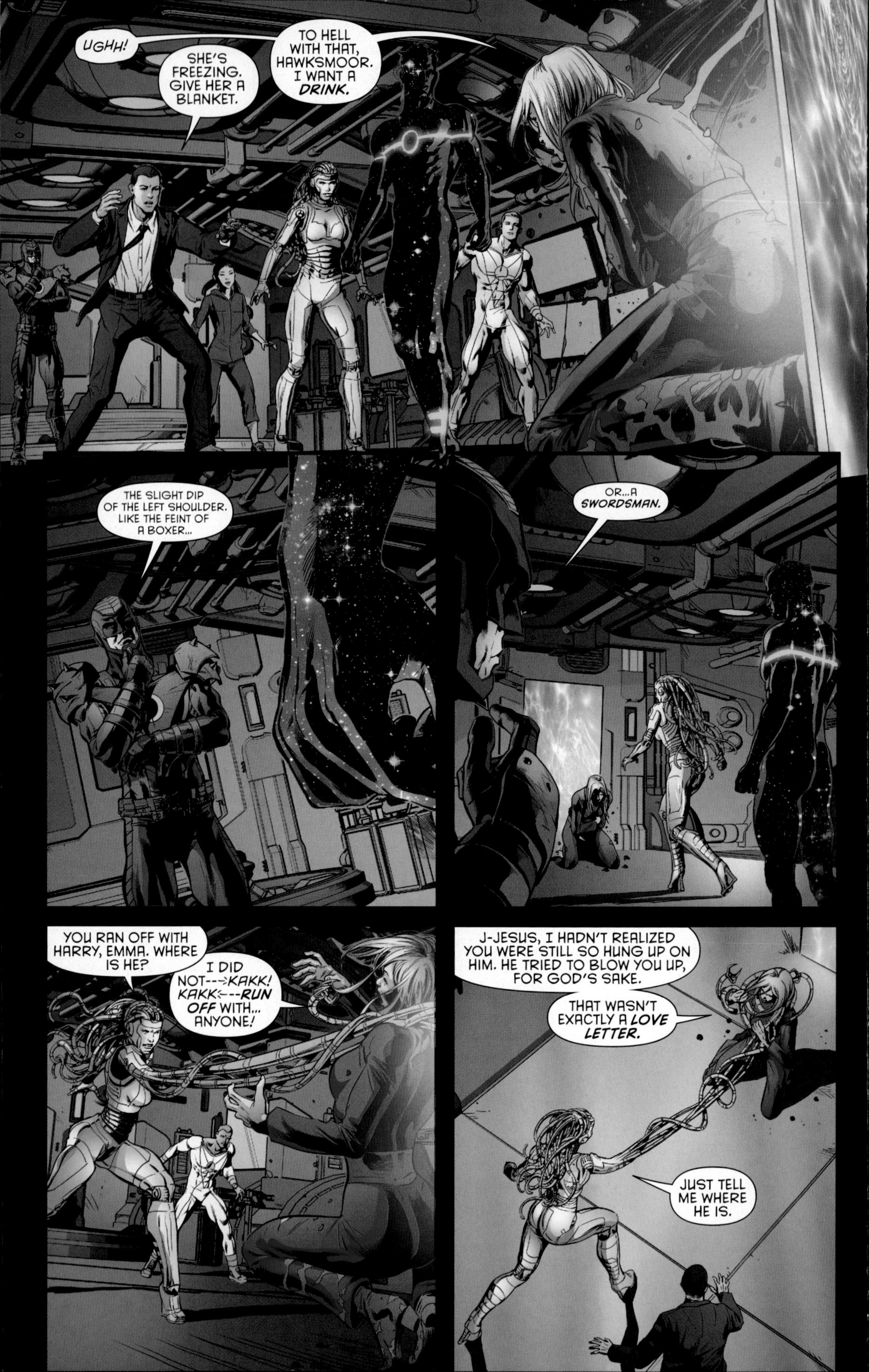

UGHH!
SHE'S FREEZING. GIVE HER A BLANKET.
TO HELL WITH THAT, HAWKSMOOR. I WANT A DRINK.
THE SLIGHT DIP OF THE LEFT SHOULDER. LIKE THE FEINT OF A BOXER...
OR...A SWORDSMAN.
YOU RAN OFF WITH HARRY, EMMA. WHERE IS HE?
I DID NOT--→KAKK! KAKK←--RUN OFF WITH... ANYONE!
J-JESUS, I HADN'T REALIZED YOU WERE STILL SO HUNG UP ON HIM. HE TRIED TO BLOW YOU UP, FOR GOD'S SAKE.
THAT WASN'T EXACTLY A LOVE LETTER.
JUST TELL ME WHERE HE IS.

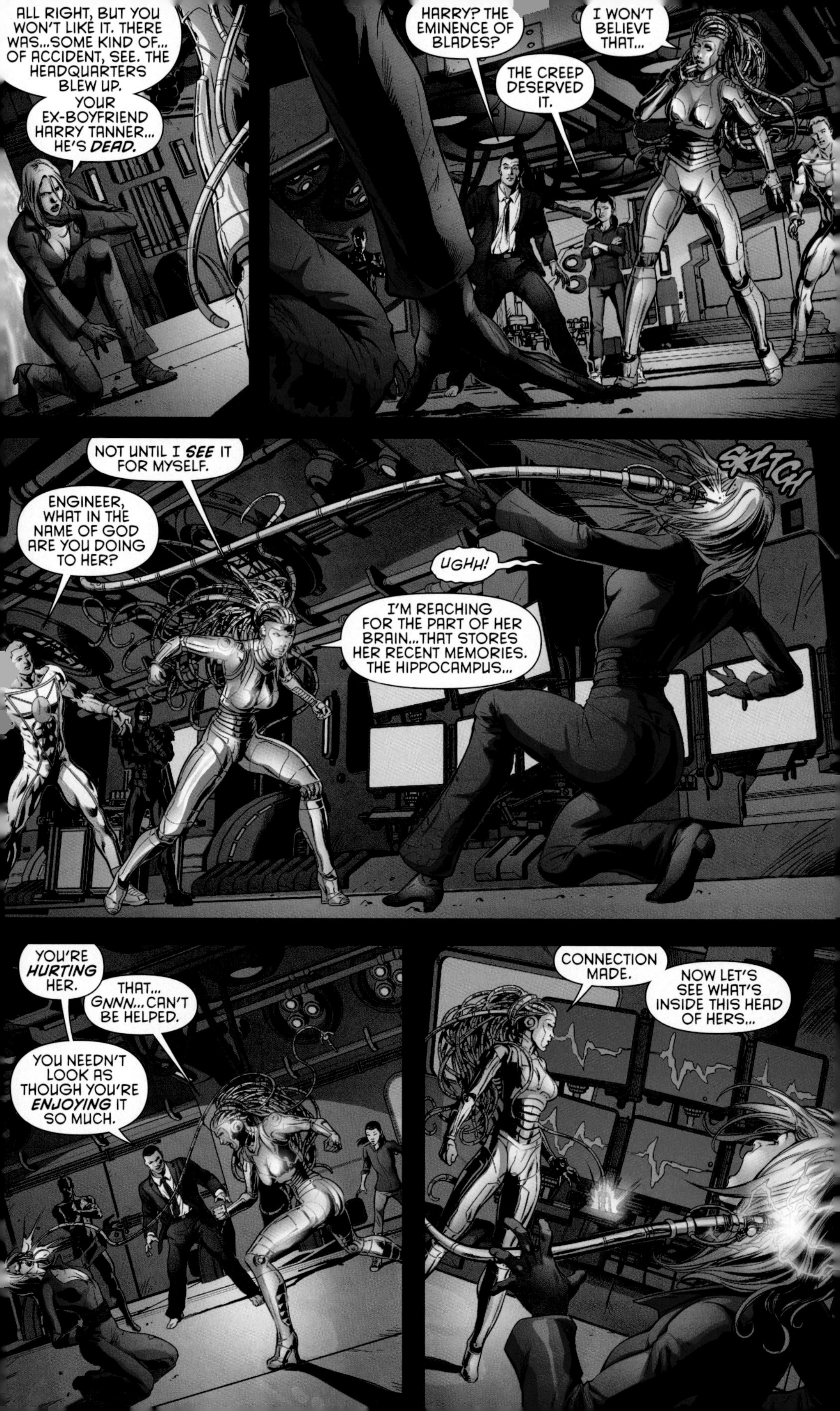

ALL RIGHT, BUT YOU WON'T LIKE IT. THERE WAS...SOME KIND OF... OF ACCIDENT, SEE. THE HEADQUARTERS BLEW UP.
YOUR EX-BOYFRIEND HARRY TANNER... HE'S DEAD.
HARRY? THE EMINENCE OF BLADES?
THE CREEP DESERVED IT.
I WON'T BELIEVE THAT...
NOT UNTIL I SEE IT FOR MYSELF.
SKLTCH
ENGINEER, WHAT IN THE NAME OF GOD ARE YOU DOING TO HER?
UGHH!
I'M REACHING FOR THE PART OF HER BRAIN...THAT STORES HER RECENT MEMORIES. THE HIPPOCAMPUS...
YOU'RE HURTING HER.
THAT... GNNN...CAN'T BE HELPED.
YOU NEEDN'T LOOK AS THOUGH YOU'RE ENJOYING IT SO MUCH.
CONNECTION MADE.
NOW LET'S SEE WHAT'S INSIDE THIS HEAD OF HERS...

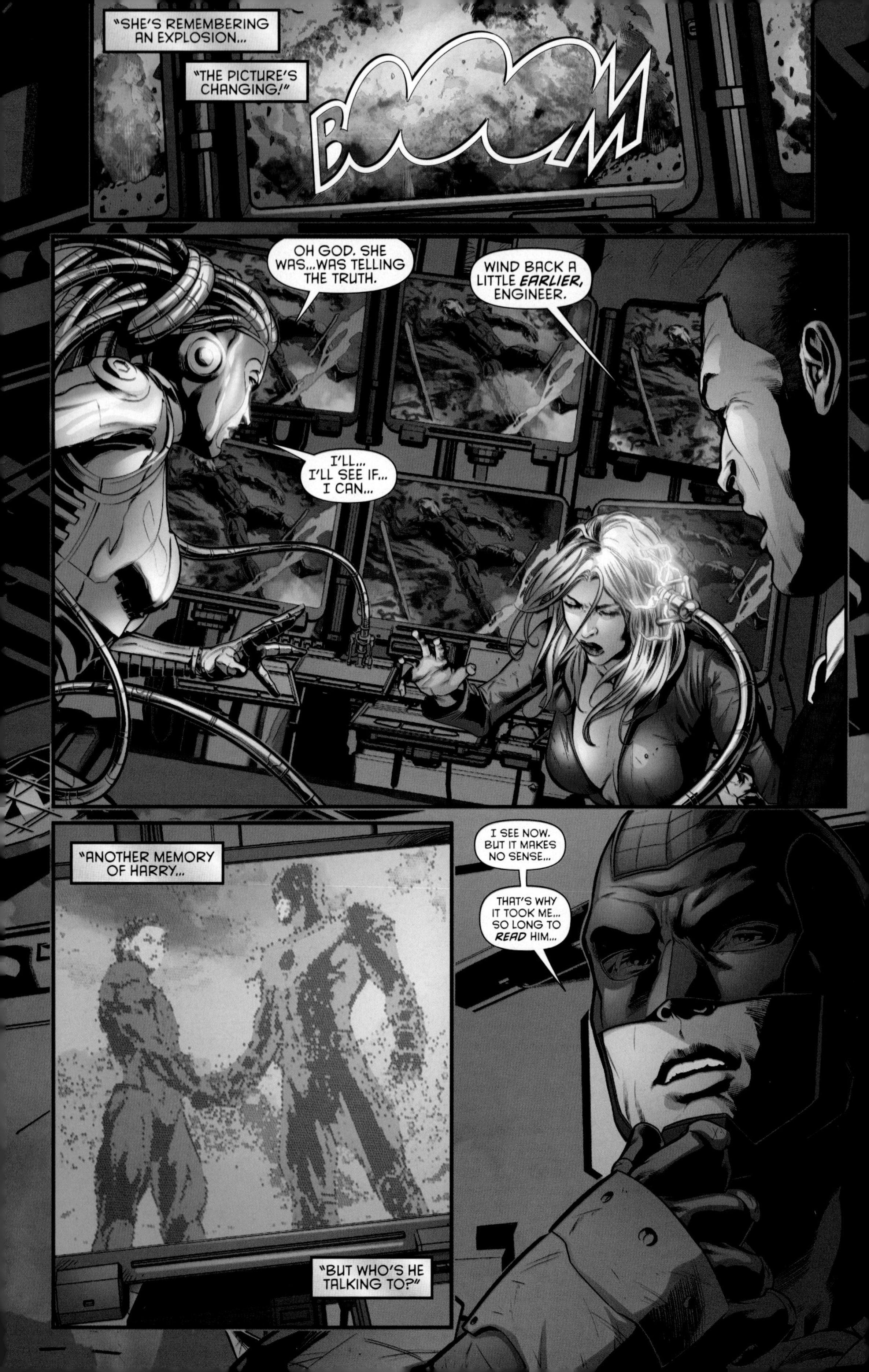
"SHE'S REMEMBERING AN EXPLOSION...
"THE PICTURE'S CHANGING!"
BOOOM
OH GOD. SHE WAS...WAS TELLING THE TRUTH.
WIND BACK A LITTLE EARLIER, ENGINEER.
I'LL... I'LL SEE IF... I CAN...
"ANOTHER MEMORY OF HARRY...
I SEE NOW. BUT IT MAKES NO SENSE...
THAT'S WHY IT TOOK ME... SO LONG TO READ HIM...
"BUT WHO'S HE TALKING TO?"

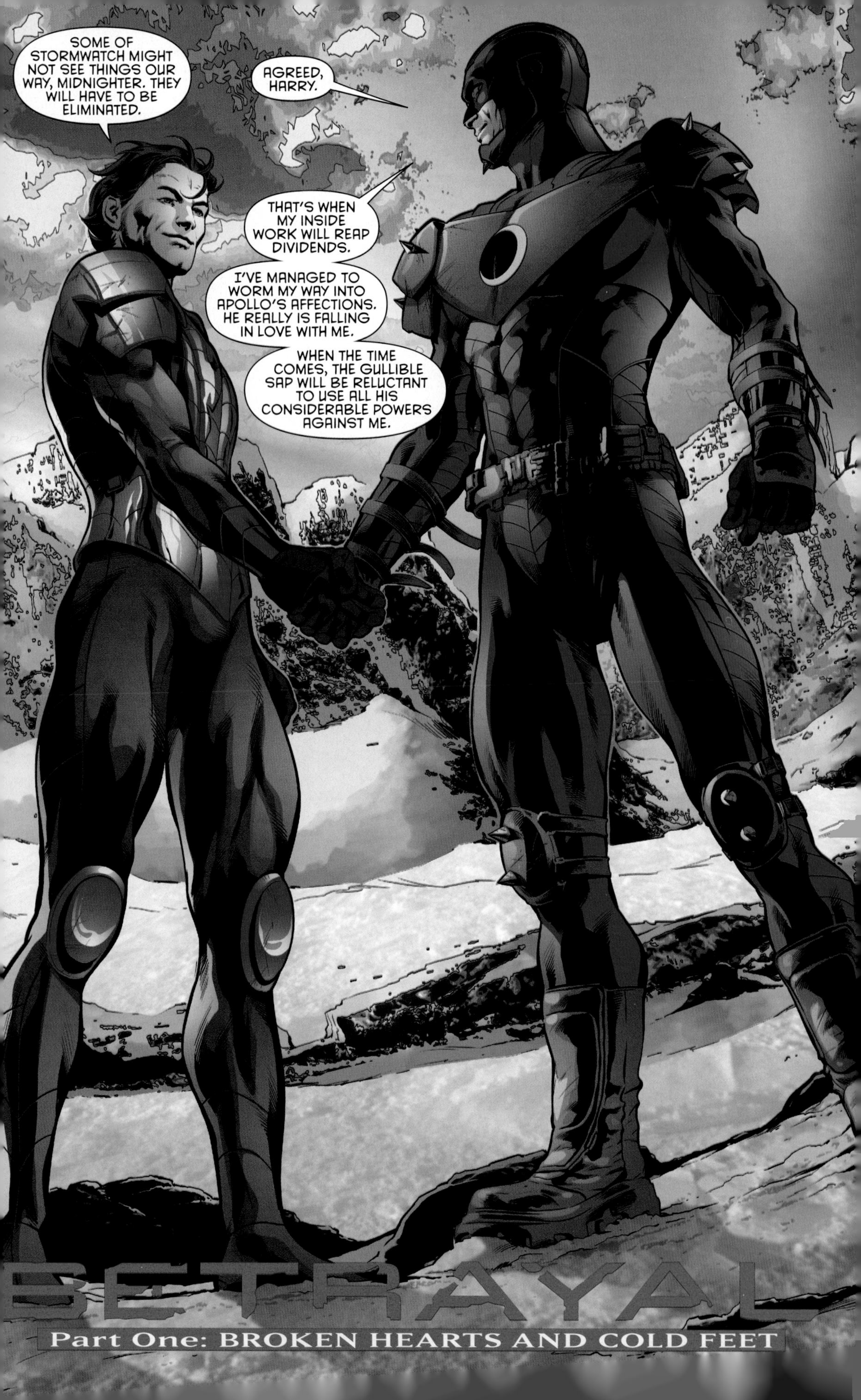
SOME OF STORMWATCH MIGHT NOT SEE THINGS OUR WAY, MIDNIGHTER. THEY WILL HAVE TO BE ELIMINATED.
AGREED, HARRY.
THAT'S WHEN MY INSIDE WORK WILL REAP DIVIDENDS.
I'VE MANAGED TO WORM MY WAY INTO APOLLO'S AFFECTIONS. HE REALLY IS FALLING IN LOVE WITH ME.
WHEN THE TIME COMES, THE GULLIBLE SAP WILL BE RELUCTANT TO USE ALL HIS CONSIDERABLE POWERS AGAINST ME.
BETRAYAL
Part One: BROKEN HEARTS AND COLD FEET

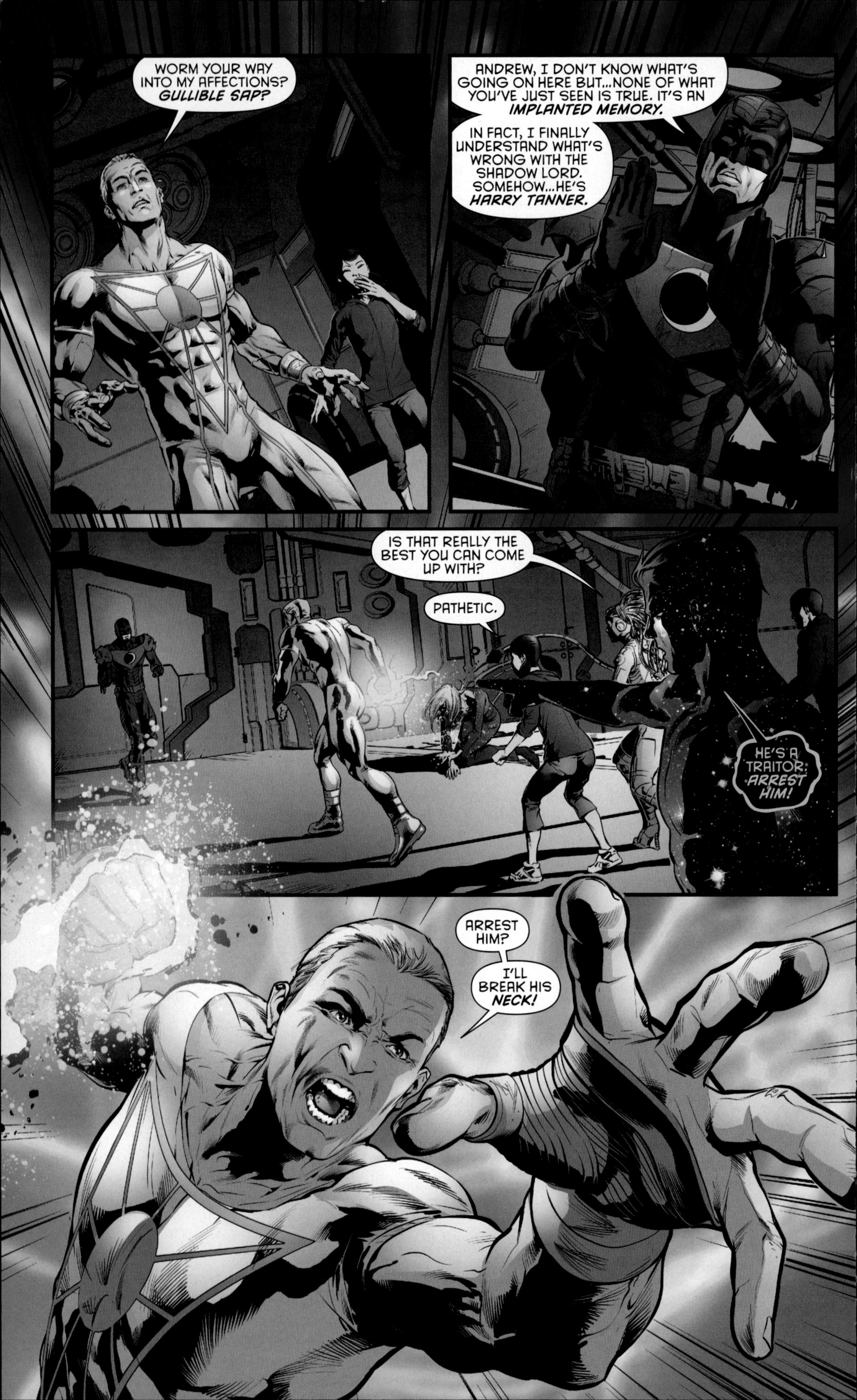
WORM YOUR WAY INTO MY AFFECTIONS? GULLIBLE SAP?
ANDREW, I DON'T KNOW WHAT'S GOING ON HERE BUT...NONE OF WHAT YOU'VE JUST SEEN IS TRUE. IT'S AN IMPLANTED MEMORY.
IN FACT, I FINALLY UNDERSTAND WHAT'S WRONG WITH THE SHADOW LORD. SOMEHOW...HE'S HARRY TANNER.
IS THAT REALLY THE BEST YOU CAN COME UP WITH?
PATHETIC.
HE'S A TRAITOR. ARREST HIM!
ARREST HIM?
I'LL BREAK HIS NECK!

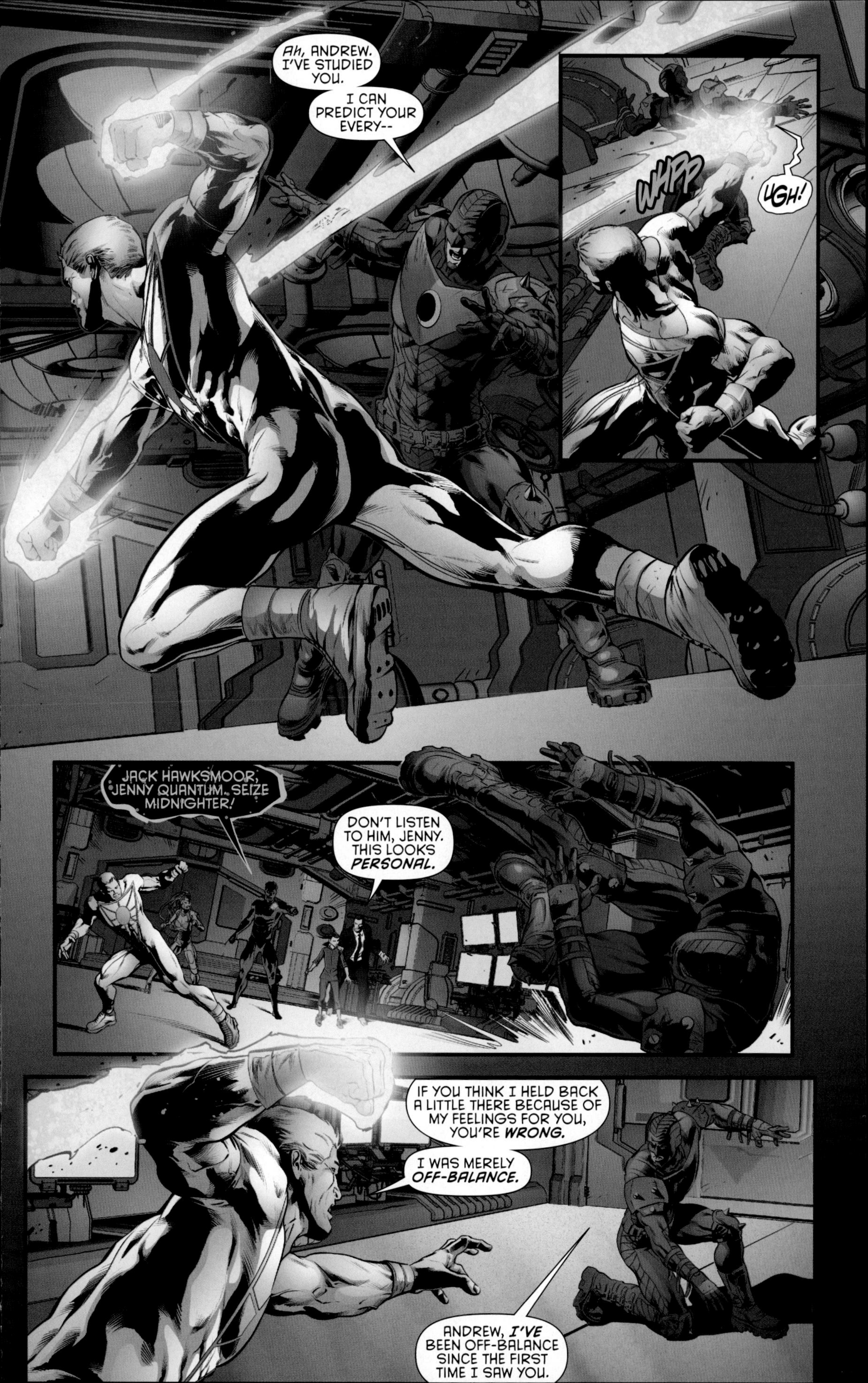
AH, ANDREW. I'VE STUDIED YOU.
I CAN PREDICT YOUR EVERY--
WHPP
UGH!
JACK HAWKSMOOR, JENNY QUANTUM...SEIZE MIDNIGHTER!
DON'T LISTEN TO HIM, JENNY. THIS LOOKS PERSONAL.
IF YOU THINK I HELD BACK A LITTLE THERE BECAUSE OF MY FEELINGS FOR YOU, YOU'RE WRONG.
I WAS MERELY OFF-BALANCE.
ANDREW, I'VE BEEN OFF-BALANCE SINCE THE FIRST TIME I SAW YOU.

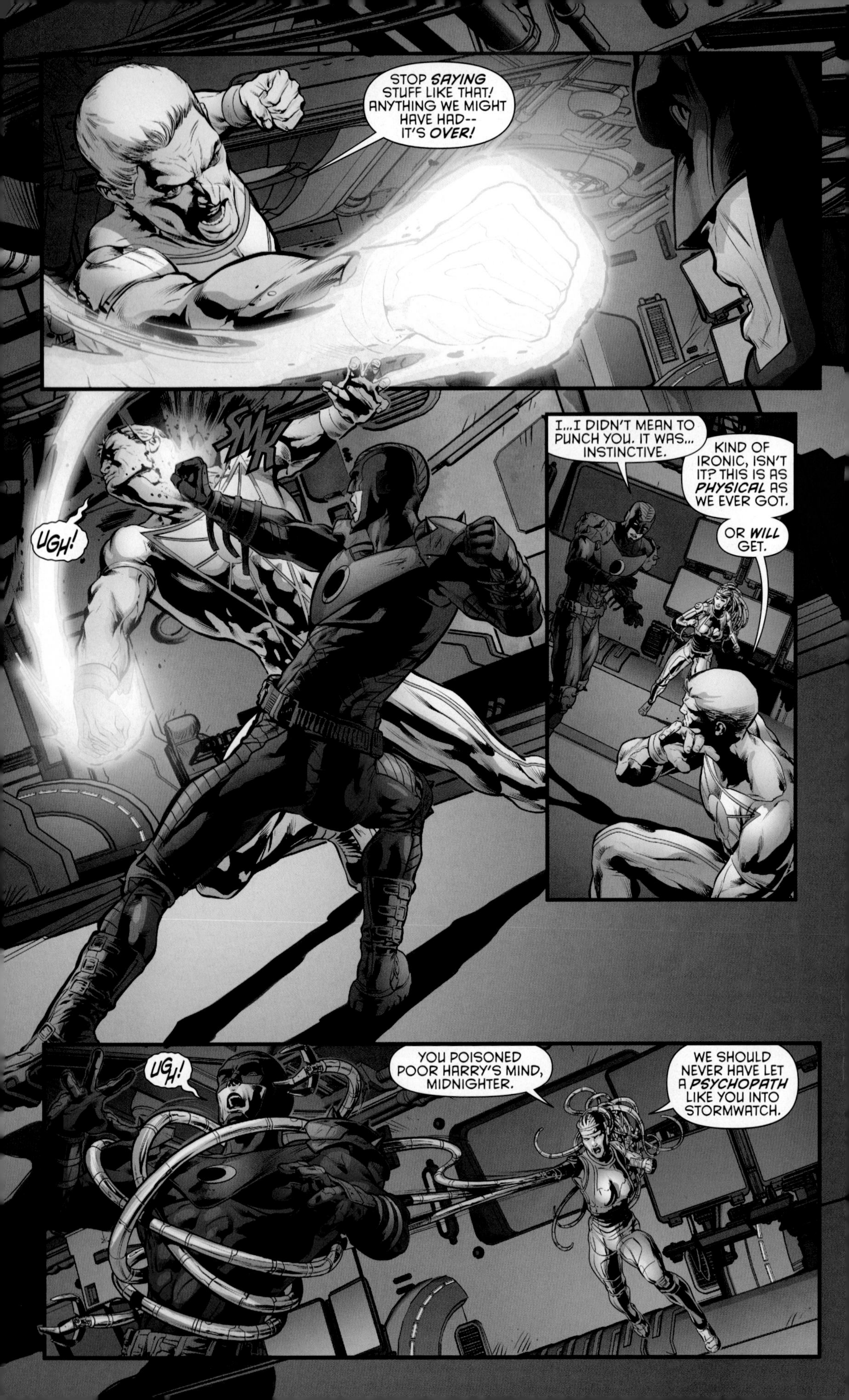
STOP SAYING STUFF LIKE THAT! ANYTHING WE MIGHT HAVE HAD-- IT'S OVER!
SMK
UGH!
I...I DIDN'T MEAN TO PUNCH YOU. IT WAS... INSTINCTIVE.
KIND OF IRONIC, ISN'T IT? THIS IS AS PHYSICAL AS WE EVER GOT.
OR WILL GET.
UGH!
YOU POISONED POOR HARRY'S MIND, MIDNIGHTER.
WE SHOULD NEVER HAVE LET A PSYCHOPATH LIKE YOU INTO STORMWATCH.

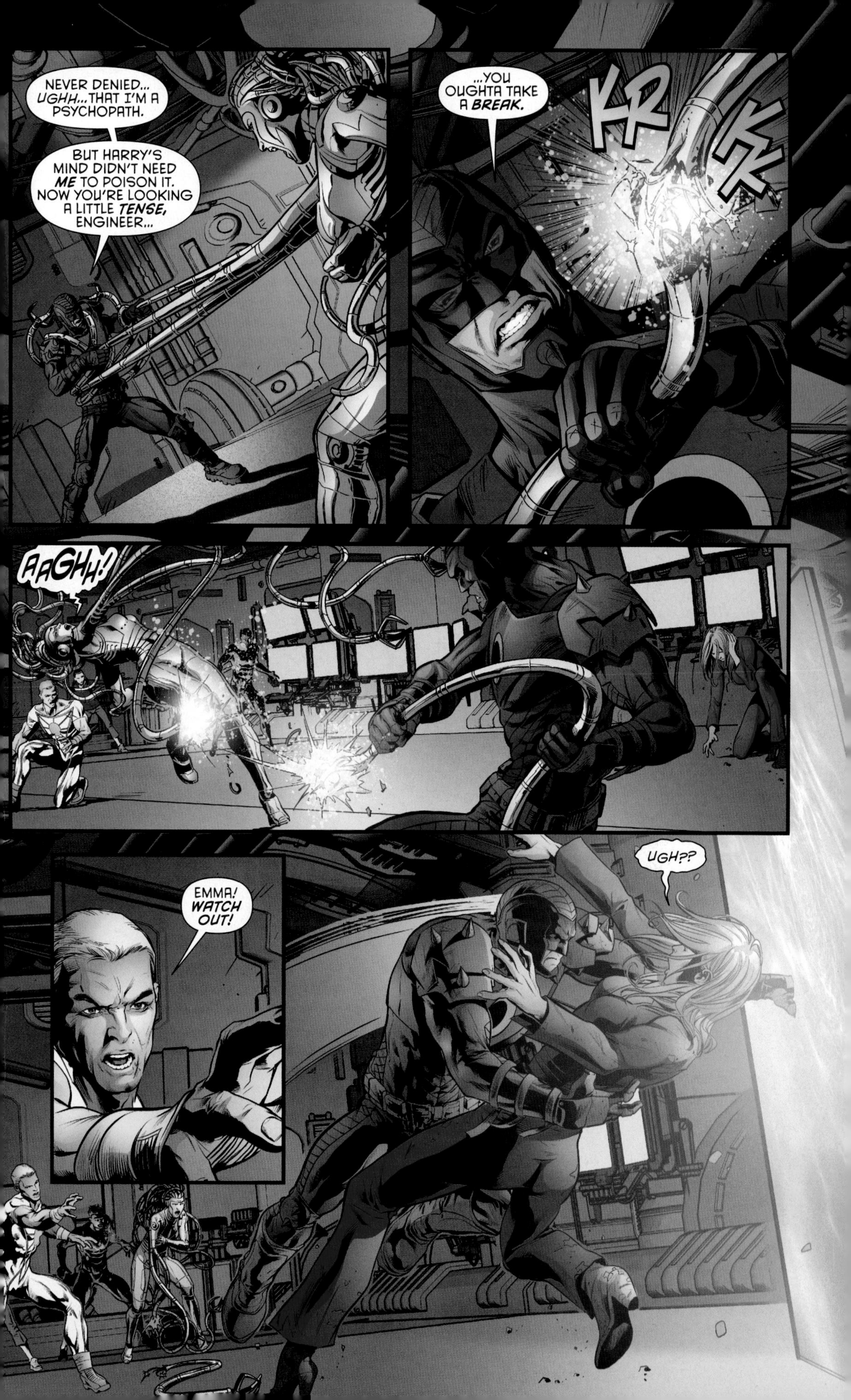
NEVER DENIED... UGHH...THAT I'M A PSYCHOPATH.
BUT HARRY'S MIND DIDN'T NEED ME TO POISON IT. NOW YOU'RE LOOKING A LITTLE TENSE, ENGINEER...
...YOU OUGHTA TAKE A BREAK.
KRKK
AAGHH!
EMMA! WATCH OUT!
UGH??

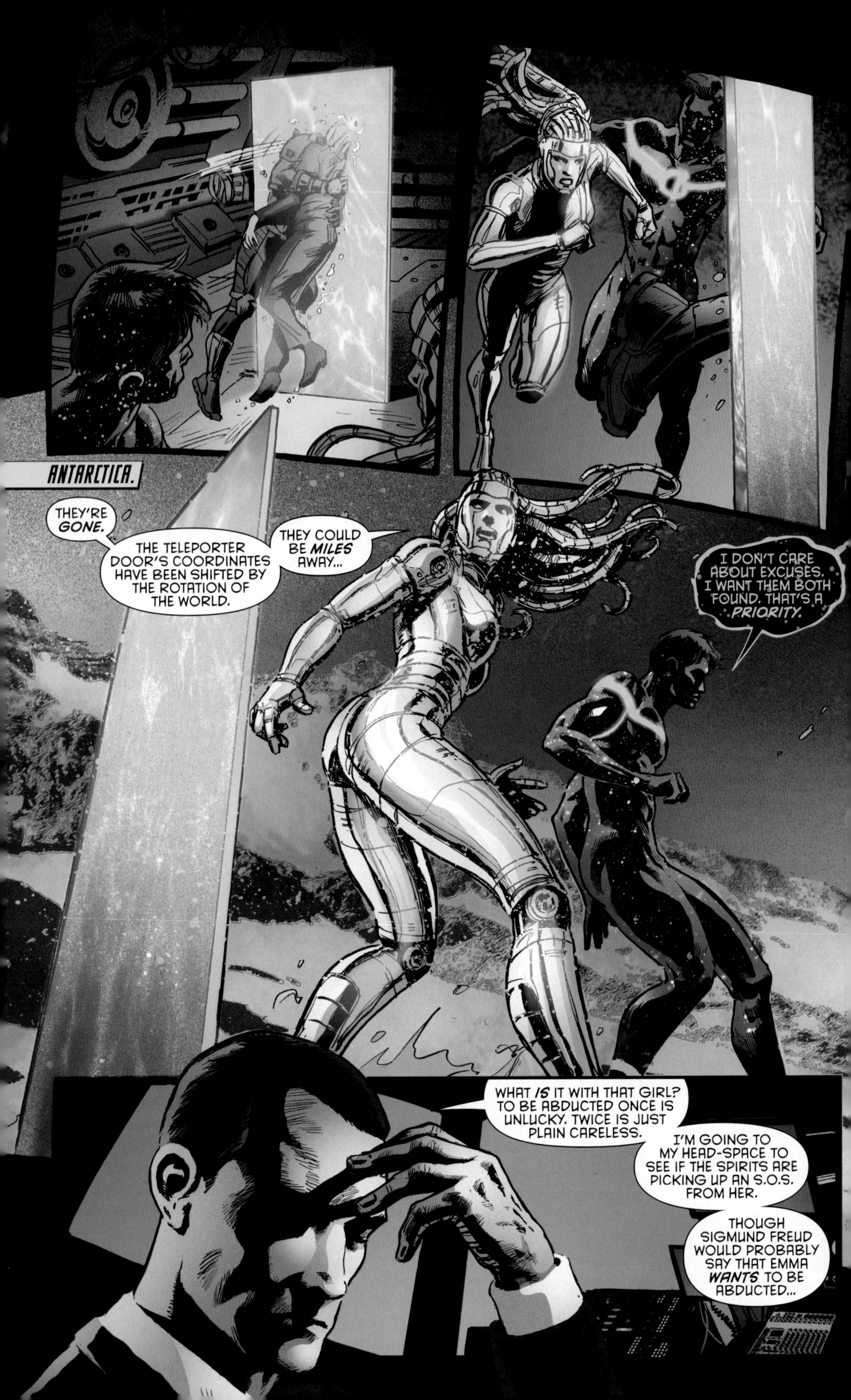
ANTARCTICA.
THEY'RE GONE.
THE TELEPORTER DOOR'S COORDINATES HAVE BEEN SHIFTED BY THE ROTATION OF THE WORLD.
THEY COULD BE MILES AWAY...
I DON'T CARE ABOUT EXCUSES. I WANT THEM BOTH FOUND. THAT'S A PRIORITY.
WHAT IS IT WITH THAT GIRL? TO BE ABDUCTED ONCE IS UNLUCKY. TWICE IS JUST PLAIN CARELESS.
I'M GOING TO MY HEAD-SPACE TO SEE IF THE SPIRITS ARE PICKING UP AN S.O.S. FROM HER.
THOUGH SIGMUND FREUD WOULD PROBABLY SAY THAT EMMA WANTS TO BE ABDUCTED...

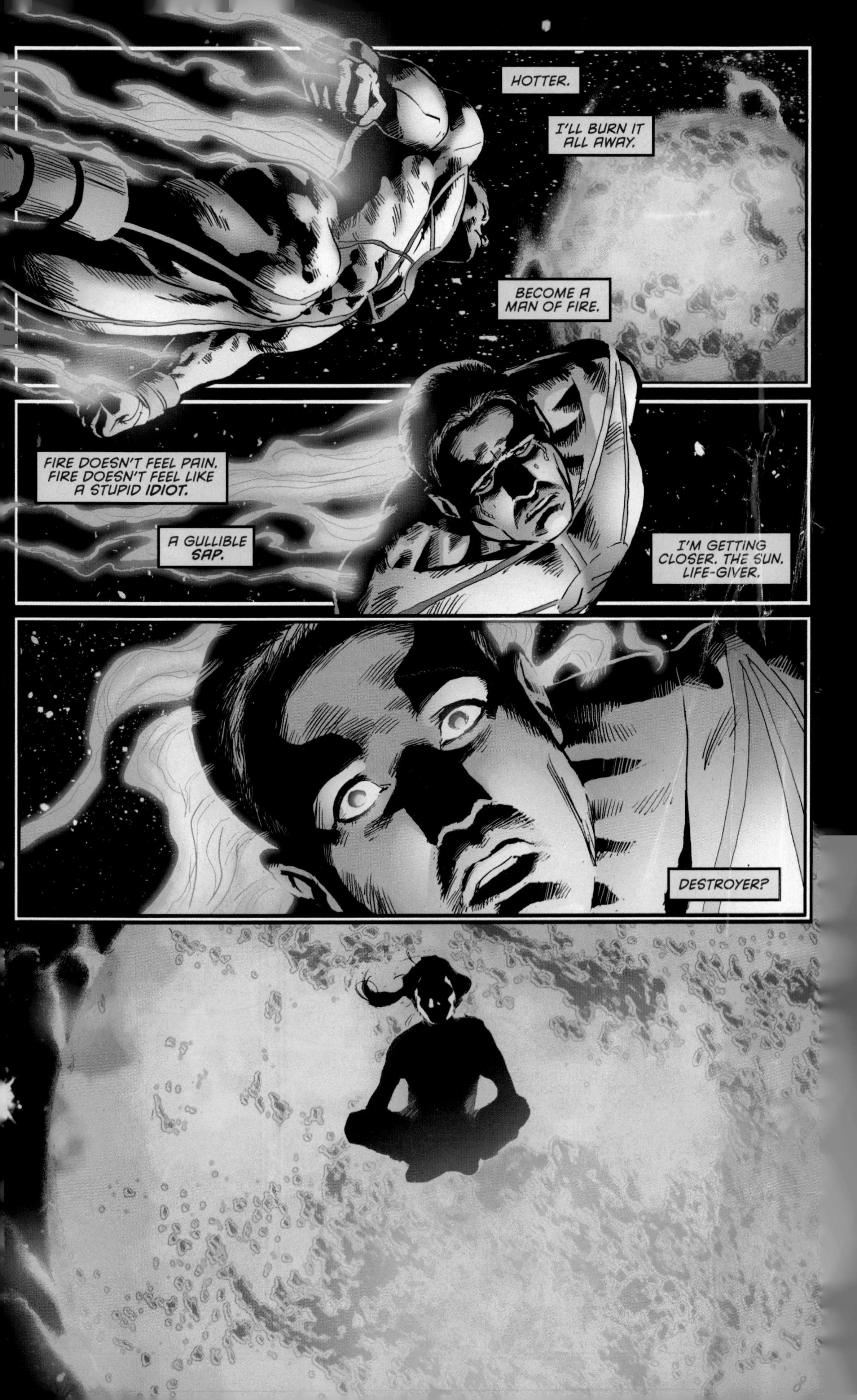
HOTTER.
I'LL BURN IT ALL AWAY.
BECOME A MAN OF FIRE.
FIRE DOESN'T FEEL PAIN. FIRE DOESN'T FEEL LIKE A STUPID IDIOT.
A GULLIBLE SAP.
I'M GETTING CLOSER. THE SUN. LIFE-GIVER.
DESTROYER?

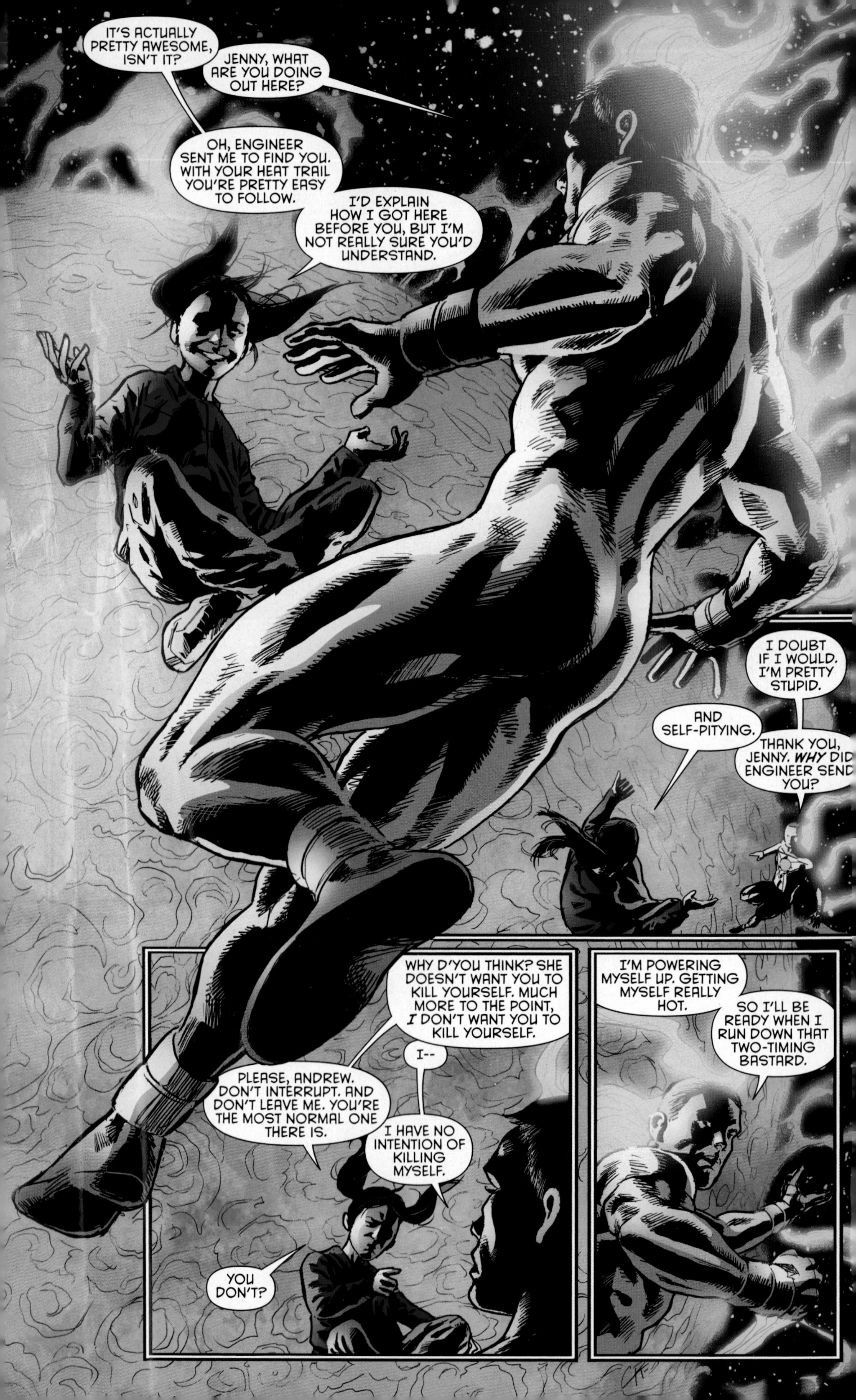
IT'S ACTUALLY PRETTY AWESOME, ISN'T IT?
JENNY, WHAT ARE YOU DOING OUT HERE?
OH, ENGINEER SENT ME TO FIND YOU. WITH YOUR HEAT TRAIL YOU'RE PRETTY EASY TO FOLLOW.
I'D EXPLAIN HOW I GOT HERE BEFORE YOU, BUT I'M NOT REALLY SURE YOU'D UNDERSTAND.
I DOUBT IF I WOULD. I'M PRETTY STUPID.
AND SELF-PITYING.
THANK YOU, JENNY. *WHY* DID ENGINEER SEND YOU?
WHY D'YOU THINK? SHE DOESN'T WANT YOU TO KILL YOURSELF. MUCH MORE TO THE POINT, *I* DON'T WANT YOU TO KILL YOURSELF.
I--
PLEASE, ANDREW. DON'T INTERRUPT. AND DON'T LEAVE ME. YOU'RE THE MOST NORMAL ONE THERE IS.
I HAVE NO INTENTION OF KILLING MYSELF.
YOU DON'T?
I'M POWERING MYSELF UP. GETTING MYSELF REALLY HOT.
SO I'LL BE READY WHEN I RUN DOWN THAT TWO-TIMING BASTARD.

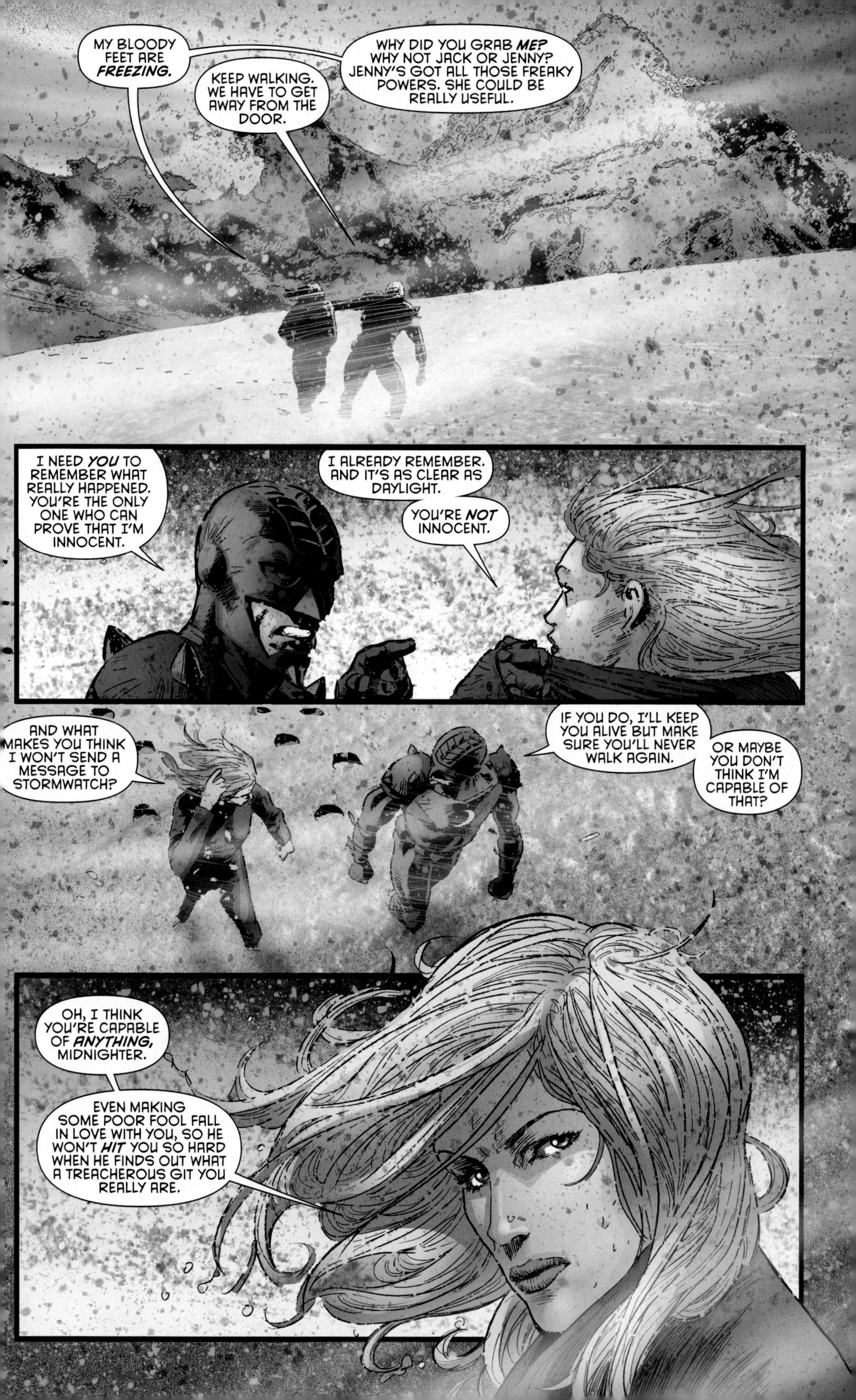
MY BLOODY FEET ARE FREEZING.
WHY DID YOU GRAB ME? WHY NOT JACK OR JENNY? JENNY'S GOT ALL THOSE FREAKY POWERS. SHE COULD BE REALLY USEFUL.
KEEP WALKING. WE HAVE TO GET AWAY FROM THE DOOR.
I NEED YOU TO REMEMBER WHAT REALLY HAPPENED. YOU'RE THE ONLY ONE WHO CAN PROVE THAT I'M INNOCENT.
I ALREADY REMEMBER. AND IT'S AS CLEAR AS DAYLIGHT.
YOU'RE NOT INNOCENT.
AND WHAT MAKES YOU THINK I WON'T SEND A MESSAGE TO STORMWATCH?
IF YOU DO, I'LL KEEP YOU ALIVE BUT MAKE SURE YOU'LL NEVER WALK AGAIN.
OR MAYBE YOU DON'T THINK I'M CAPABLE OF THAT?
OH, I THINK YOU'RE CAPABLE OF ANYTHING, MIDNIGHTER.
EVEN MAKING SOME POOR FOOL FALL IN LOVE WITH YOU, SO HE WON'T HIT YOU SO HARD WHEN HE FINDS OUT WHAT A TREACHEROUS GIT YOU REALLY ARE.

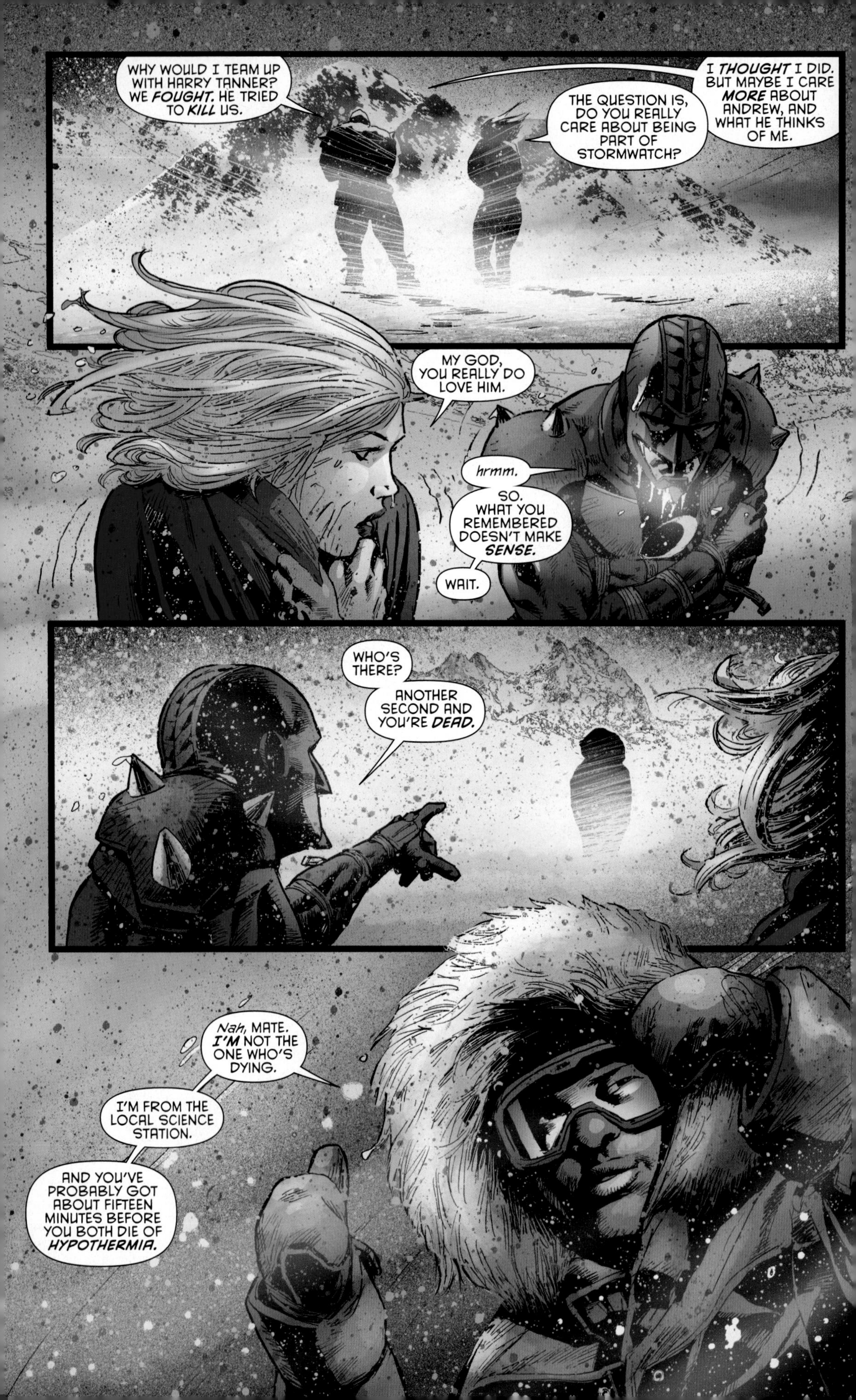
WHY WOULD I TEAM UP WITH HARRY TANNER? WE FOUGHT. HE TRIED TO KILL US.
THE QUESTION IS, DO YOU REALLY CARE ABOUT BEING PART OF STORMWATCH?
I THOUGHT I DID. BUT MAYBE I CARE MORE ABOUT ANDREW, AND WHAT HE THINKS OF ME.
MY GOD, YOU REALLY DO LOVE HIM.
hrmm.
SO. WHAT YOU REMEMBERED DOESN'T MAKE SENSE.
WAIT.
WHO'S THERE?
ANOTHER SECOND AND YOU'RE DEAD.
Nah, MATE. I'M NOT THE ONE WHO'S DYING.
I'M FROM THE LOCAL SCIENCE STATION.
AND YOU'VE PROBABLY GOT ABOUT FIFTEEN MINUTES BEFORE YOU BOTH DIE OF HYPOTHERMIA.

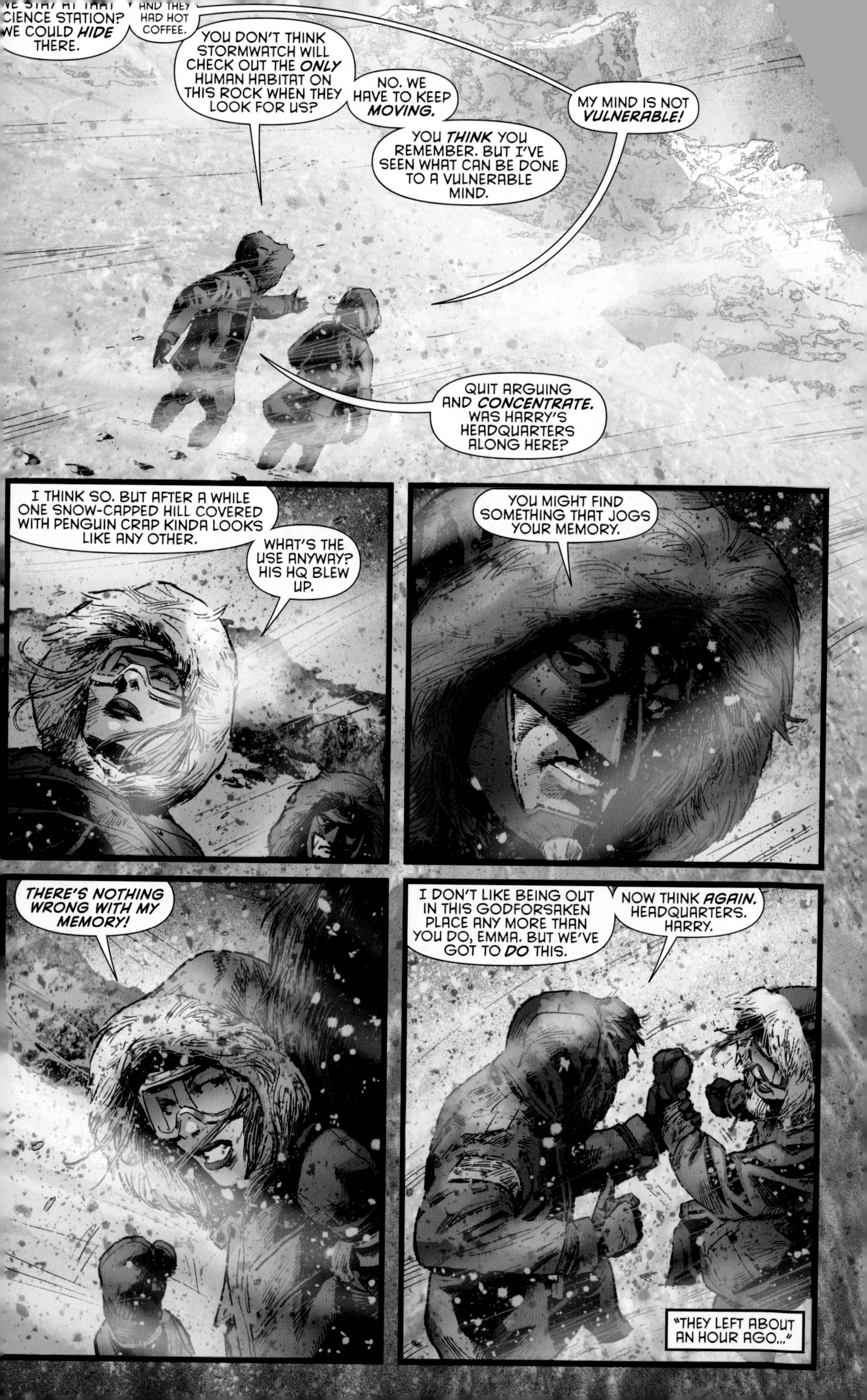

CIENCE STATION? WE COULD HIDE THERE.
AND THEY HAD HOT COFFEE.
YOU DON'T THINK STORMWATCH WILL CHECK OUT THE ONLY HUMAN HABITAT ON THIS ROCK WHEN THEY LOOK FOR US?
NO. WE HAVE TO KEEP MOVING.
MY MIND IS NOT VULNERABLE!
YOU THINK YOU REMEMBER. BUT I'VE SEEN WHAT CAN BE DONE TO A VULNERABLE MIND.
QUIT ARGUING AND CONCENTRATE. WAS HARRY'S HEADQUARTERS ALONG HERE?
I THINK SO. BUT AFTER A WHILE ONE SNOW-CAPPED HILL COVERED WITH PENGUIN CRAP KINDA LOOKS LIKE ANY OTHER.
WHAT'S THE USE ANYWAY? HIS HQ BLEW UP.
YOU MIGHT FIND SOMETHING THAT JOGS YOUR MEMORY.
THERE'S NOTHING WRONG WITH MY MEMORY!
I DON'T LIKE BEING OUT IN THIS GODFORSAKEN PLACE ANY MORE THAN YOU DO, EMMA. BUT WE'VE GOT TO DO THIS.
NOW THINK AGAIN. HEADQUARTERS. HARRY.
"THEY LEFT ABOUT AN HOUR AGO..."

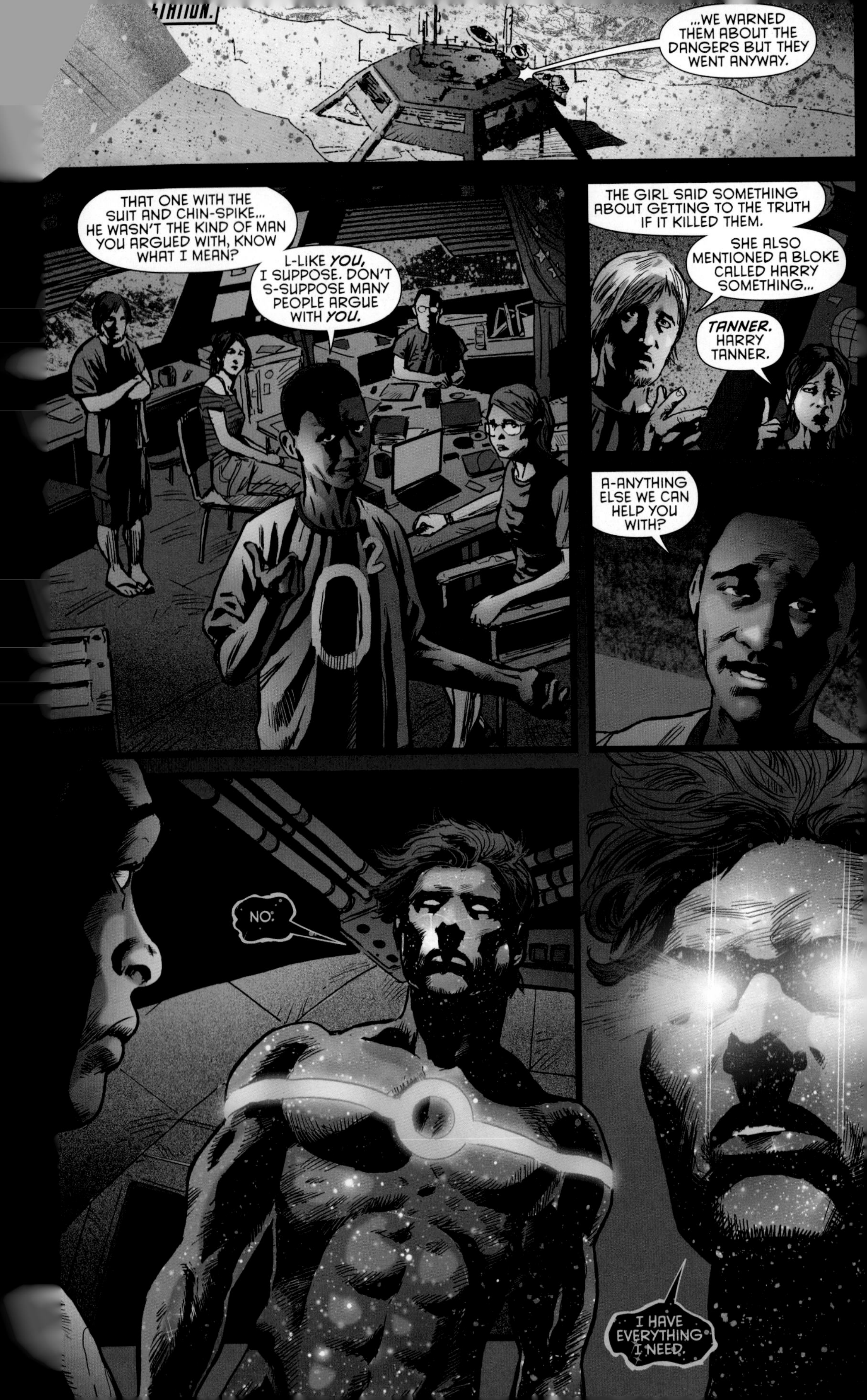

STATION.
...WE WARNED THEM ABOUT THE DANGERS BUT THEY WENT ANYWAY.
THAT ONE WITH THE SUIT AND CHIN-SPIKE... HE WASN'T THE KIND OF MAN YOU ARGUED WITH, KNOW WHAT I MEAN?
L-LIKE *YOU,* I SUPPOSE. DON'T S-SUPPOSE MANY PEOPLE ARGUE WITH *YOU.*
THE GIRL SAID SOMETHING ABOUT GETTING TO THE TRUTH IF IT KILLED THEM.
SHE ALSO MENTIONED A BLOKE CALLED HARRY SOMETHING...
TANNER. HARRY TANNER.
A-ANYTHING ELSE WE CAN HELP YOU WITH?
NO.
I HAVE EVERYTHING I NEED.

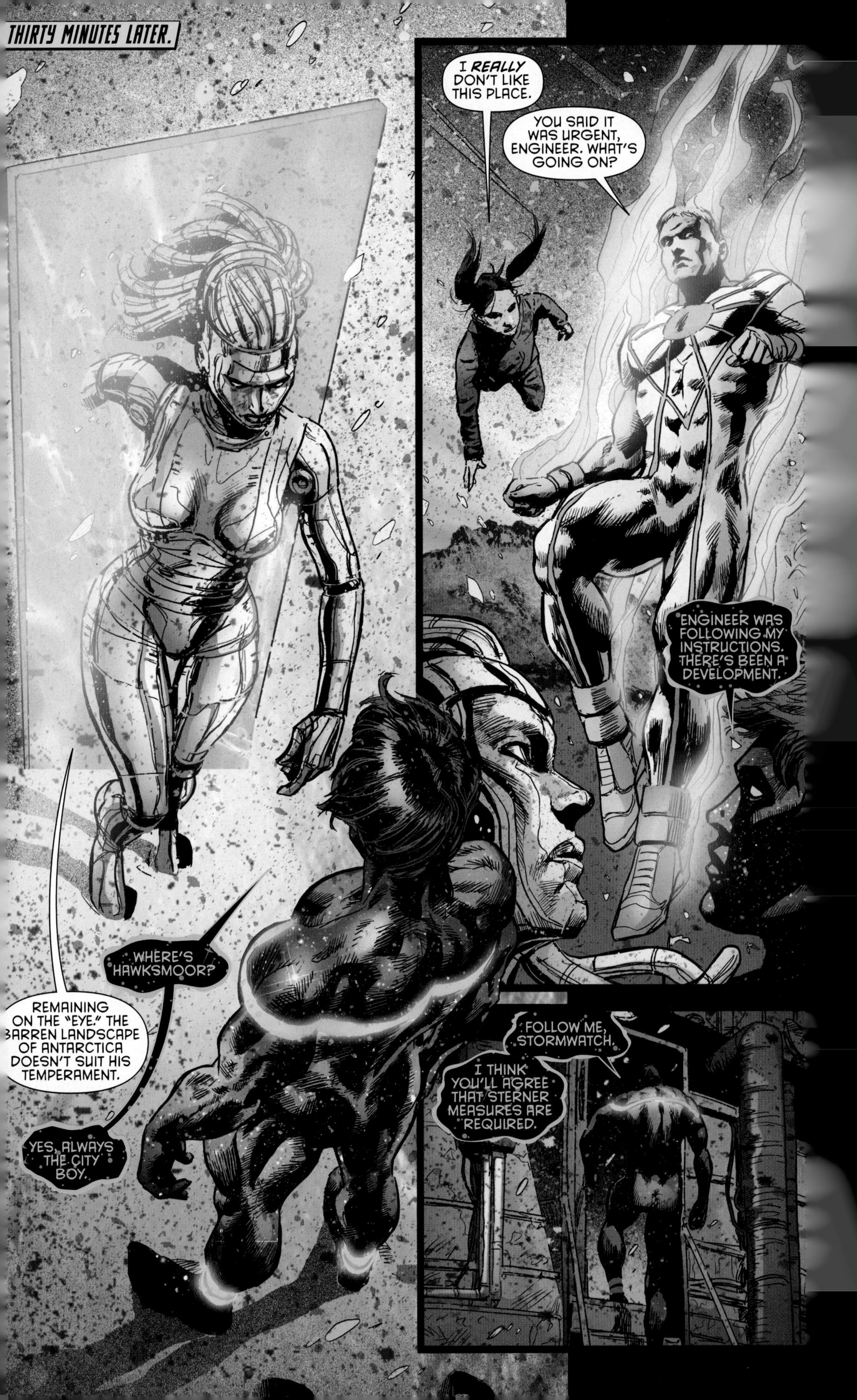
THIRTY MINUTES LATER.
I REALLY DON'T LIKE THIS PLACE.
YOU SAID IT WAS URGENT, ENGINEER. WHAT'S GOING ON?
ENGINEER WAS FOLLOWING MY INSTRUCTIONS. THERE'S BEEN A DEVELOPMENT.
WHERE'S HAWKSMOOR?
REMAINING ON THE "EYE." THE BARREN LANDSCAPE OF ANTARCTICA DOESN'T SUIT HIS TEMPERAMENT.
YES, ALWAYS THE CITY BOY.
FOLLOW ME, STORMWATCH.
I THINK YOU'LL AGREE THAT STERNER MEASURES ARE REQUIRED.

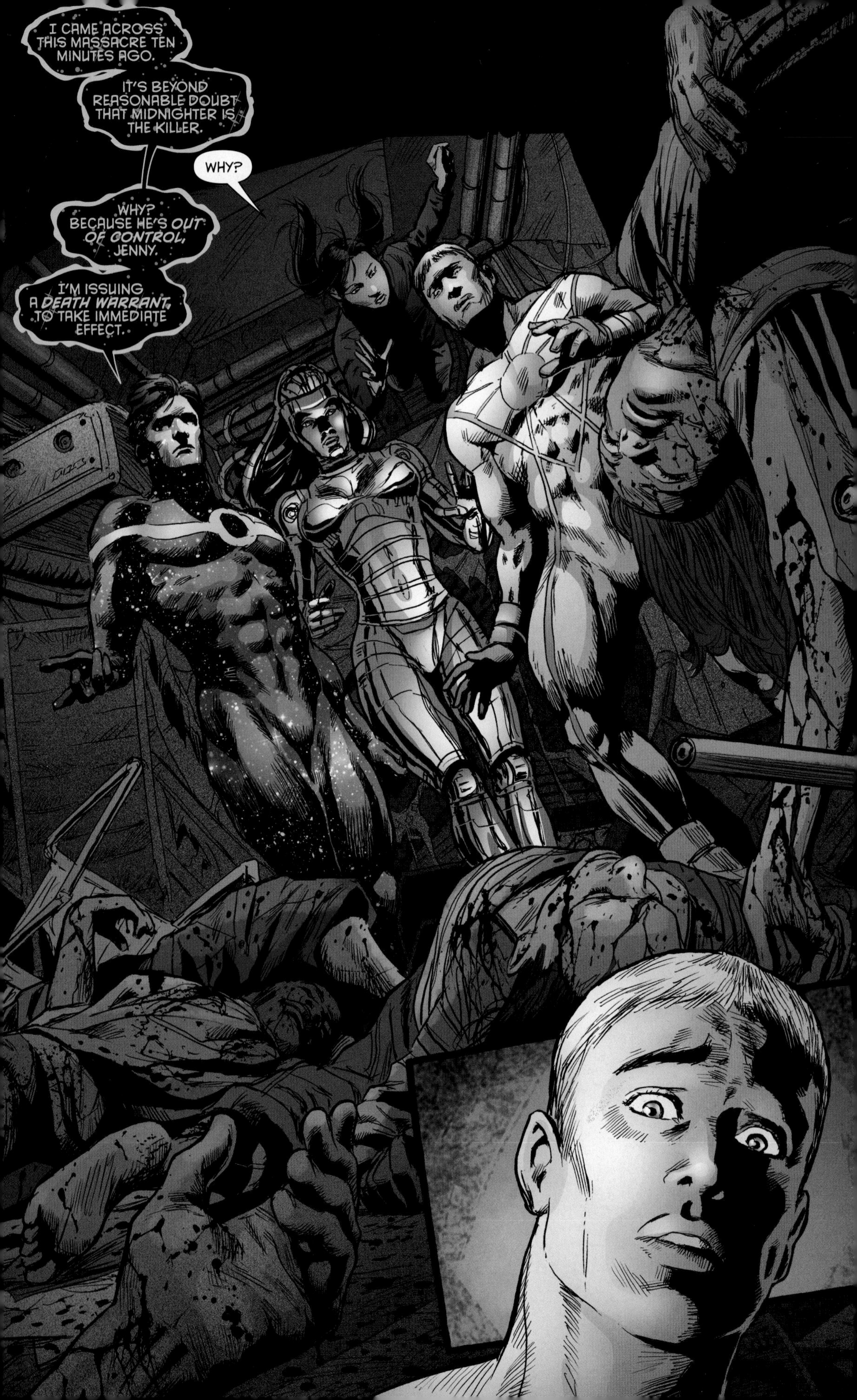
I CAME ACROSS THIS MASSACRE TEN MINUTES AGO.
IT'S BEYOND REASONABLE DOUBT THAT MIDNIGHTER IS THE KILLER.
WHY?
WHY? BECAUSE HE'S *OUT OF CONTROL,* JENNY.
I'M ISSUING A *DEATH WARRANT,* TO TAKE IMMEDIATE EFFECT.

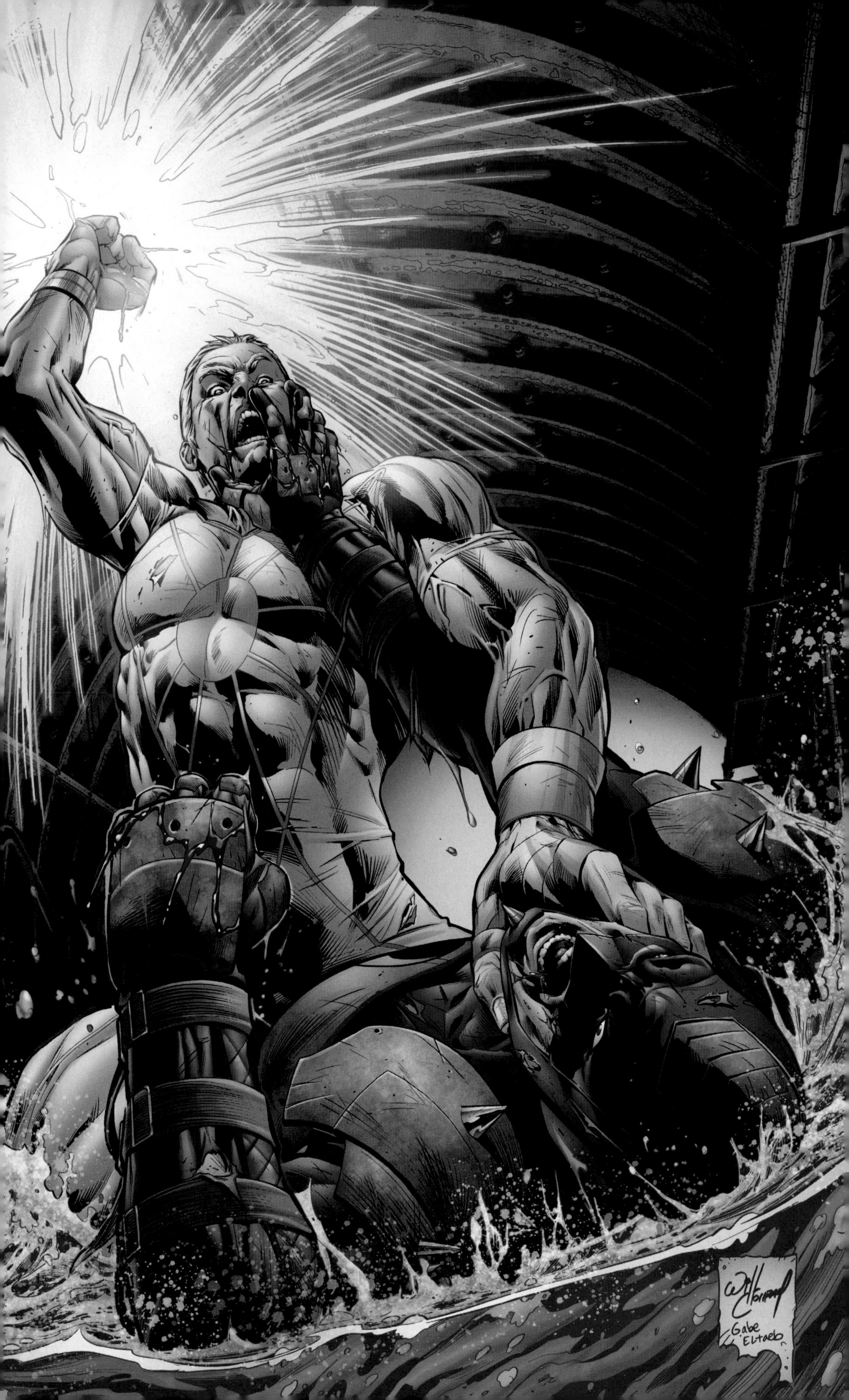
Gabe
Eltaeb

BETRAYAL PART TWO: THE HUNT FOR MIDNIGHTER

PETER MILLIGAN writer **WILL CONRAD, EDUARDO PANSICA & JULIO FERRIERA** artists cover art by **WILL CONRAD & GABE ELTAEB**

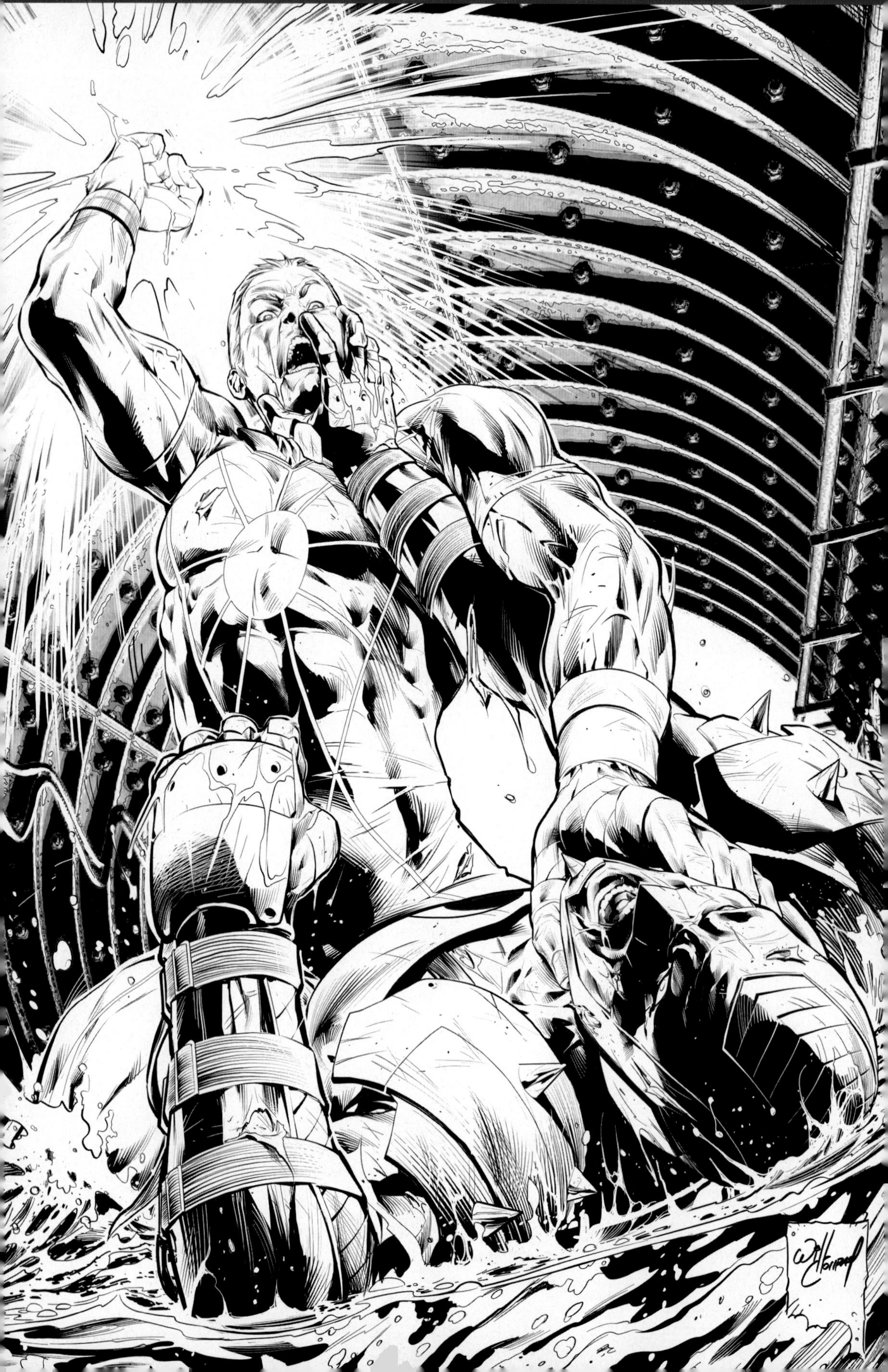

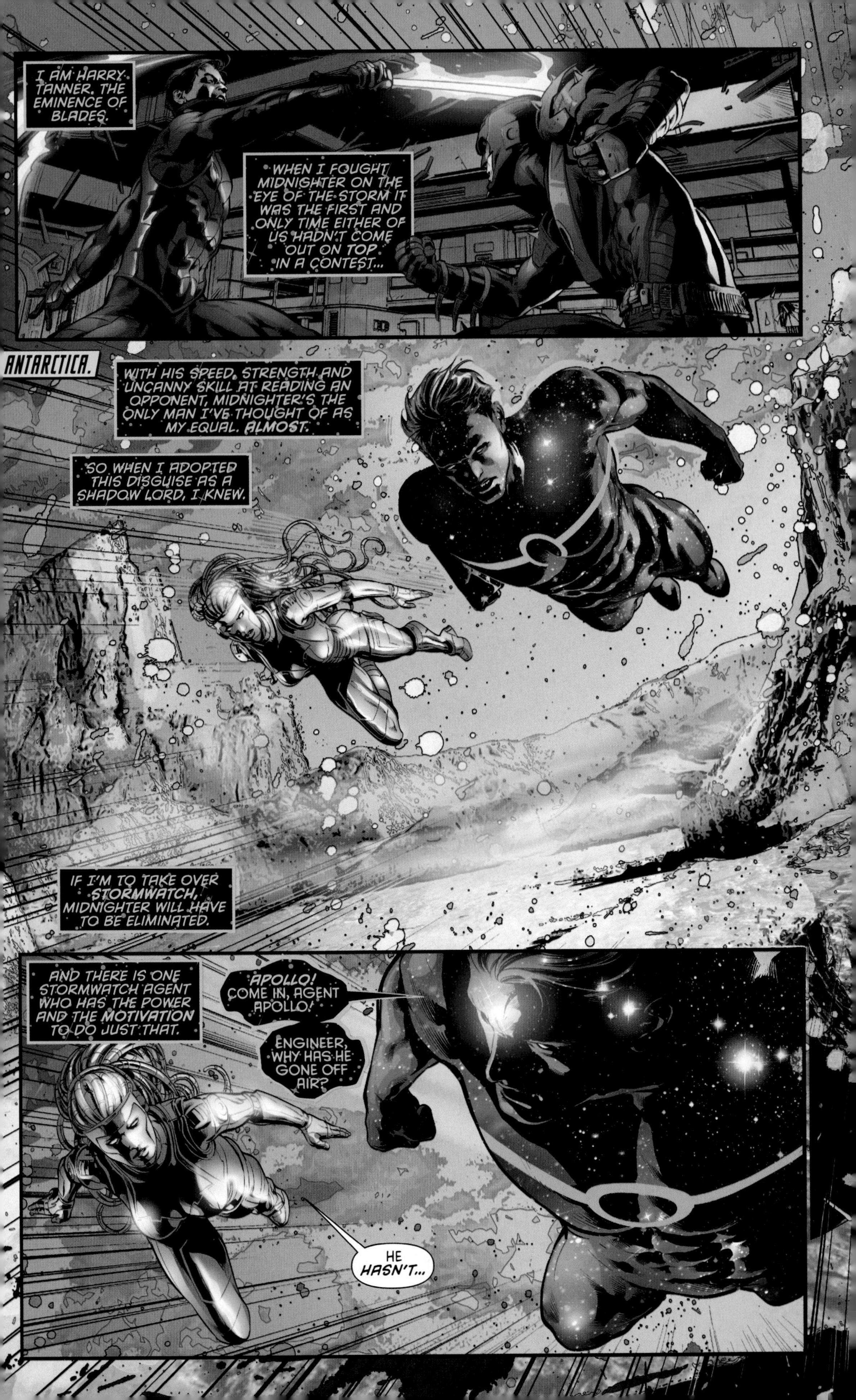
I AM HARRY TANNER. THE EMINENCE OF BLADES.
WHEN I FOUGHT MIDNIGHTER ON THE EYE OF THE STORM IT WAS THE FIRST AND ONLY TIME EITHER OF US HADN'T COME OUT ON TOP IN A CONTEST...
ANTARCTICA.
WITH HIS SPEED, STRENGTH AND UNCANNY SKILL AT READING AN OPPONENT, MIDNIGHTER'S THE ONLY MAN I'VE THOUGHT OF AS MY EQUAL. ALMOST.
SO WHEN I ADOPTED THIS DISGUISE AS A SHADOW LORD, I KNEW.
IF I'M TO TAKE OVER STORMWATCH, MIDNIGHTER WILL HAVE TO BE ELIMINATED.
AND THERE IS ONE STORMWATCH AGENT WHO HAS THE POWER AND THE MOTIVATION TO DO JUST THAT.
APOLLO! COME IN, AGENT APOLLO!
ENGINEER, WHY HAS HE GONE OFF AIR?
HE HASN'T...

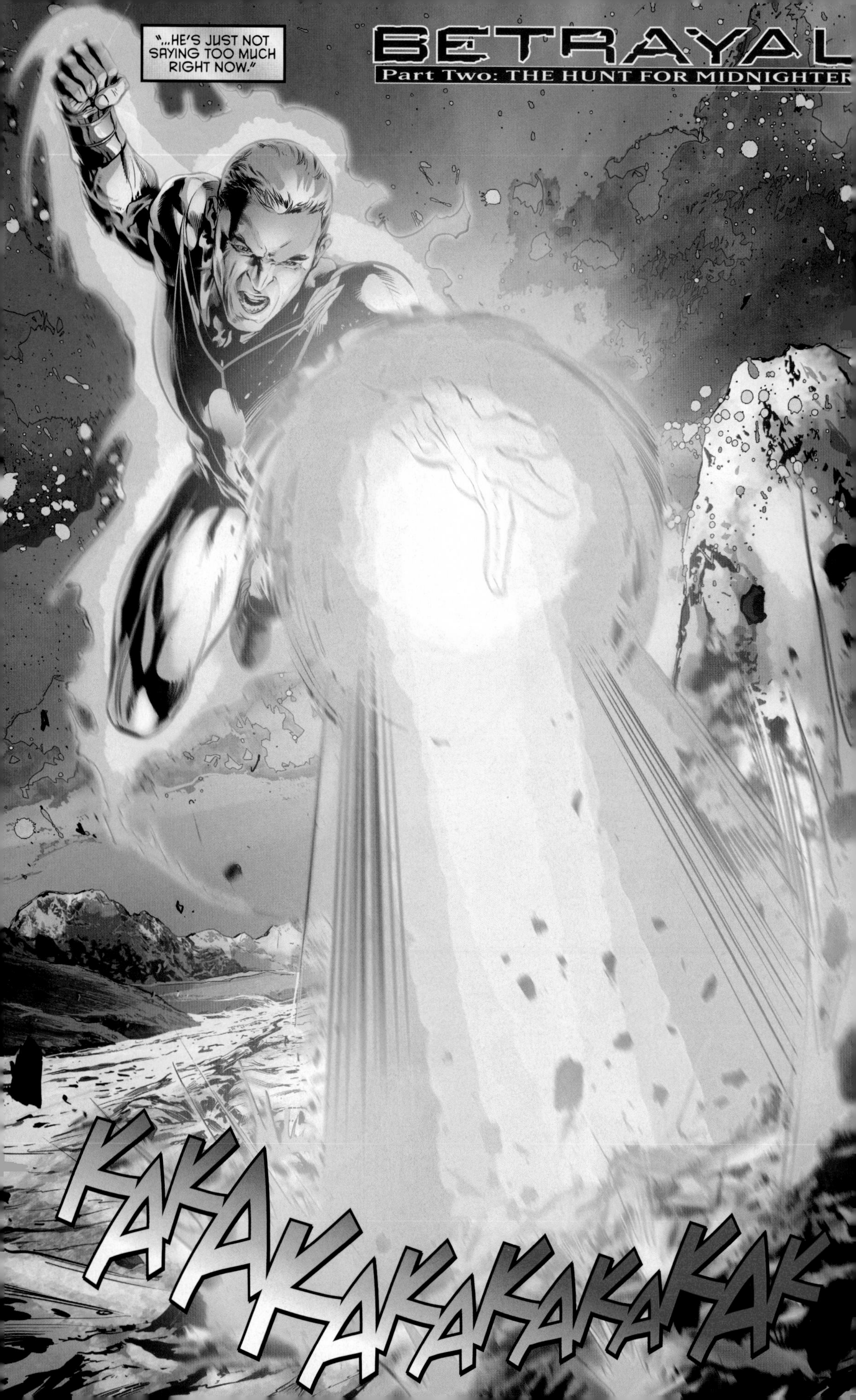
"...HE'S JUST NOT SAYING TOO MUCH RIGHT NOW."
BETRAYAL
Part Two: THE HUNT FOR MIDNIGHTER
KAKAKAKAKAKAKAKAK

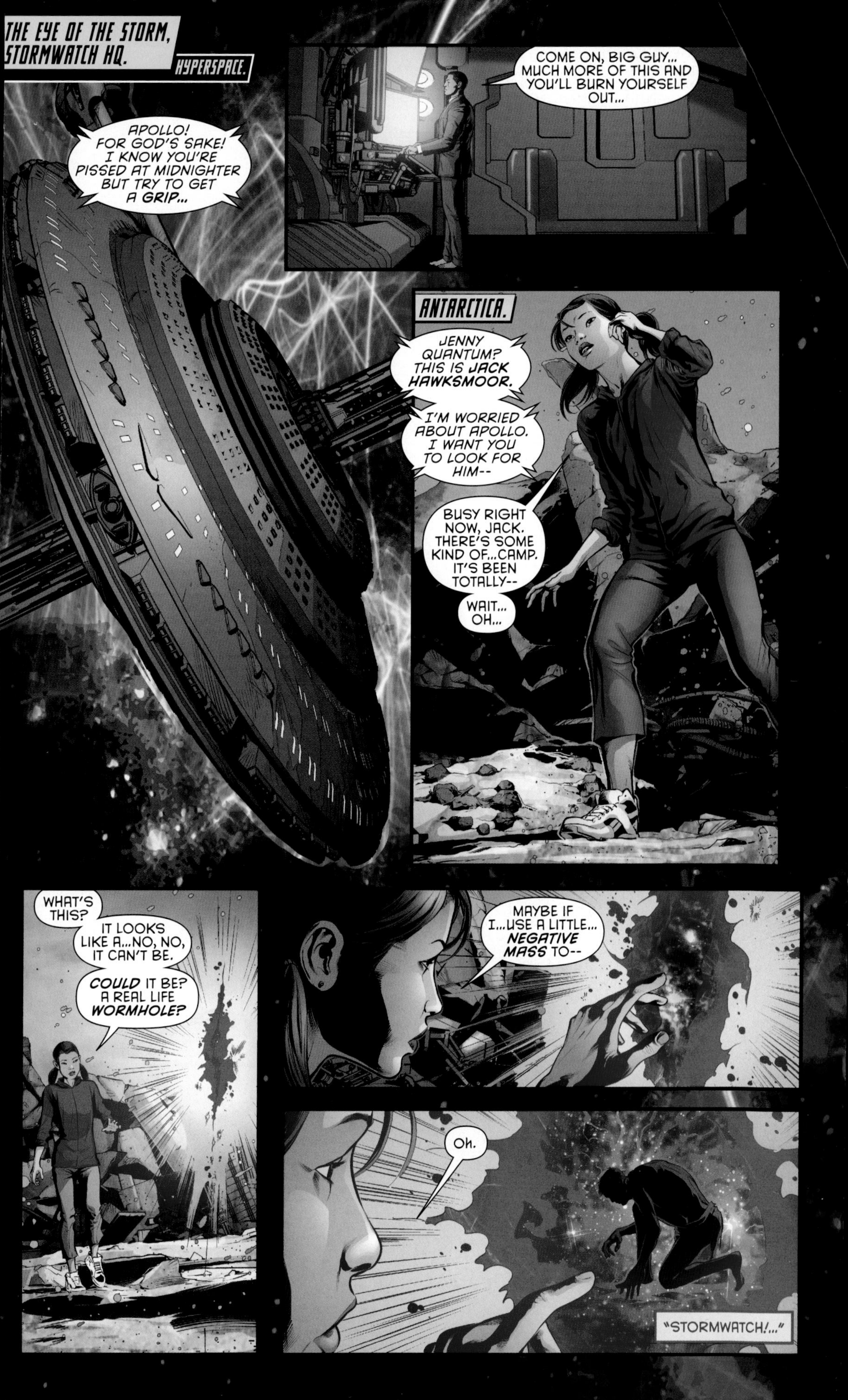
THE EYE OF THE STORM, STORMWATCH HQ.
HYPERSPACE.
COME ON, BIG GUY... MUCH MORE OF THIS AND YOU'LL BURN YOURSELF OUT...
APOLLO! FOR GOD'S SAKE! I KNOW YOU'RE PISSED AT MIDNIGHTER BUT TRY TO GET A GRIP...
ANTARCTICA.
JENNY QUANTUM? THIS IS JACK HAWKSMOOR.
I'M WORRIED ABOUT APOLLO. I WANT YOU TO LOOK FOR HIM--
BUSY RIGHT NOW, JACK. THERE'S SOME KIND OF...CAMP. IT'S BEEN TOTALLY--
WAIT... OH...
WHAT'S THIS?
IT LOOKS LIKE A...NO, NO, IT CAN'T BE.
COULD IT BE? A REAL LIFE WORMHOLE?
MAYBE IF I...USE A LITTLE... NEGATIVE MASS TO--
Oh.
"STORMWATCH!..."

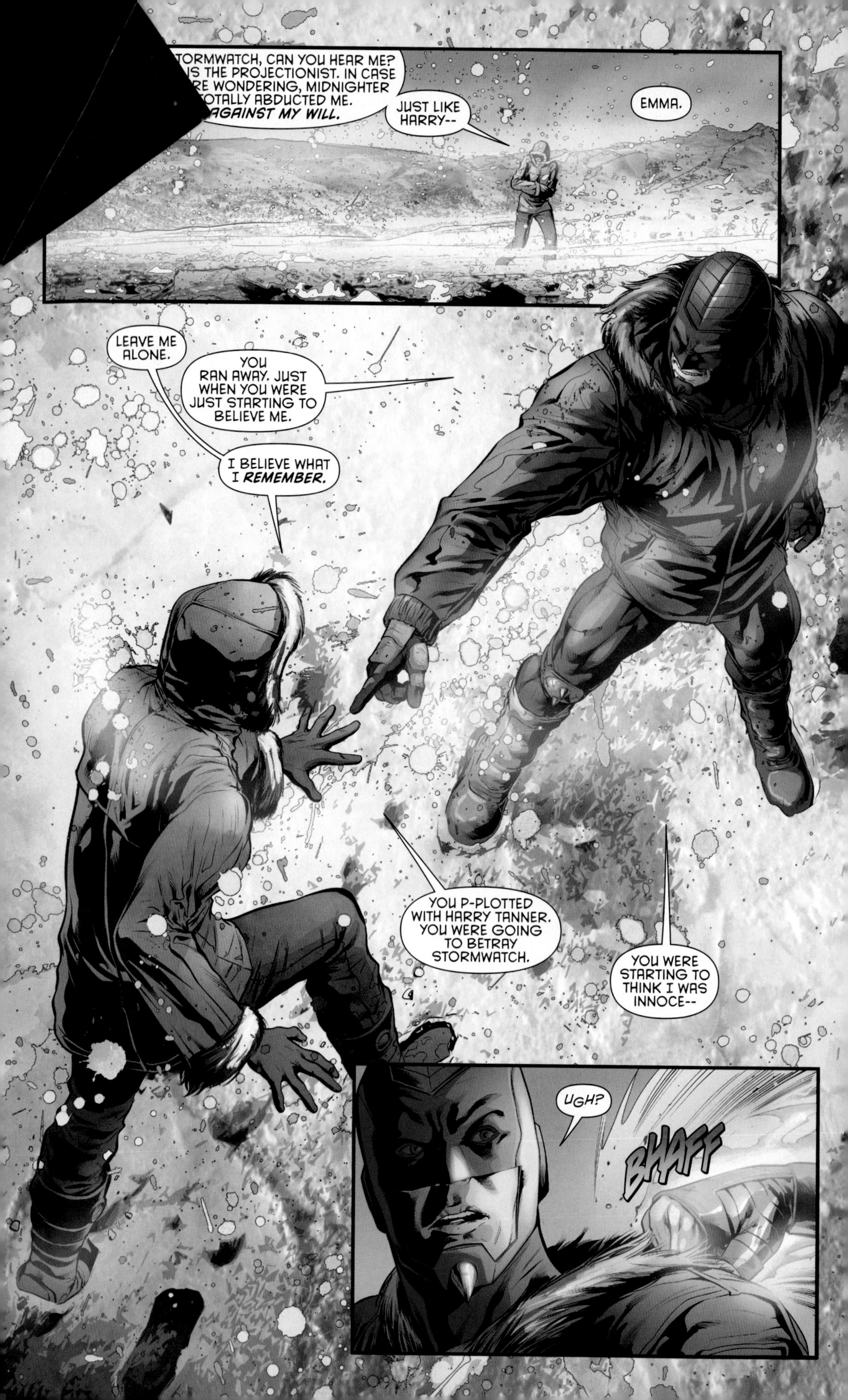

TORMWATCH, CAN YOU HEAR ME? IS THE PROJECTIONIST. IN CASE RE WONDERING, MIDNIGHTER TOTALLY ABDUCTED ME. AGAINST MY WILL.
JUST LIKE HARRY--
EMMA.
LEAVE ME ALONE.
YOU RAN AWAY. JUST WHEN YOU WERE JUST STARTING TO BELIEVE ME.
I BELIEVE WHAT I REMEMBER.
YOU P-PLOTTED WITH HARRY TANNER. YOU WERE GOING TO BETRAY STORMWATCH.
YOU WERE STARTING TO THINK I WAS INNOCE--
UGH?
BHAFF

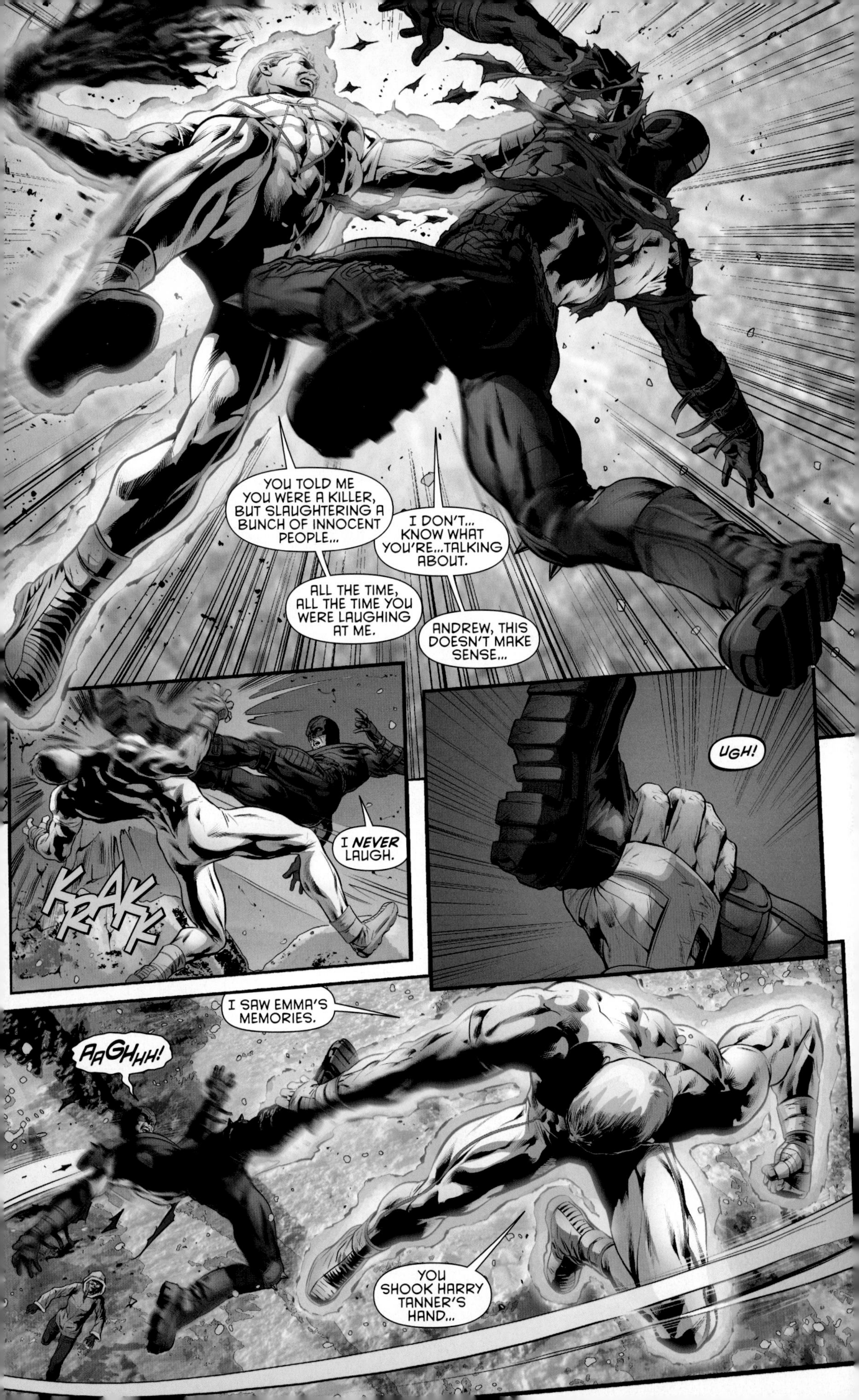

YOU TOLD ME YOU WERE A KILLER, BUT SLAUGHTERING A BUNCH OF INNOCENT PEOPLE...
I DON'T... KNOW WHAT YOU'RE...TALKING ABOUT.
ALL THE TIME, ALL THE TIME YOU WERE LAUGHING AT ME.
ANDREW, THIS DOESN'T MAKE SENSE...
I *NEVER* LAUGH.
KRAK KRUNK
UGH!
I SAW EMMA'S MEMORIES.
AAGHHH!
YOU SHOOK HARRY TANNER'S HAND...

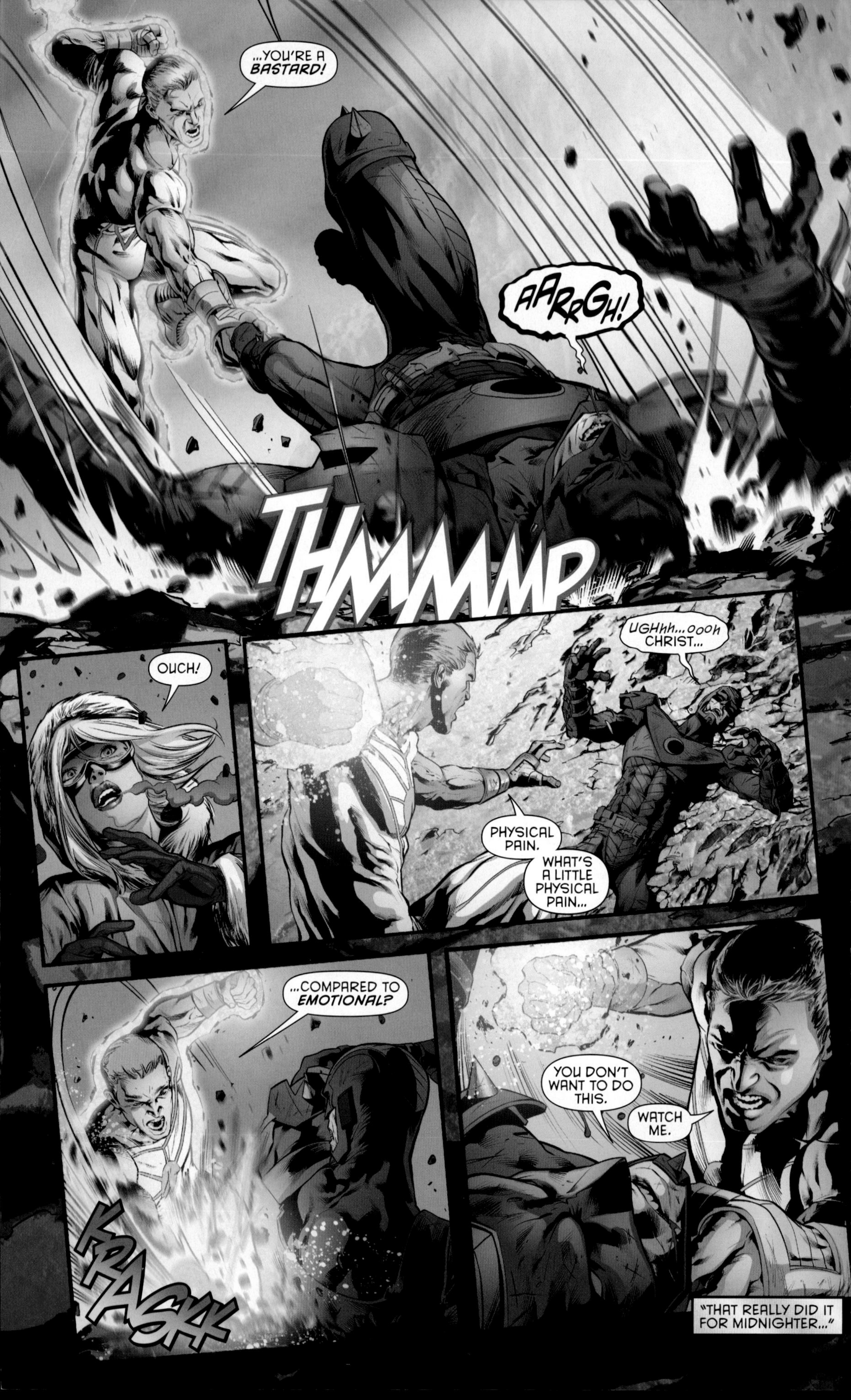
...YOU'RE A BASTARD!
AARRGH!
THMMMP
OUCH!
UGHhh...oooh CHRIST...
PHYSICAL PAIN.
WHAT'S A LITTLE PHYSICAL PAIN...
...COMPARED TO EMOTIONAL?
KRASKK
YOU DON'T WANT TO DO THIS.
WATCH ME.
"THAT REALLY DID IT FOR MIDNIGHTER..."

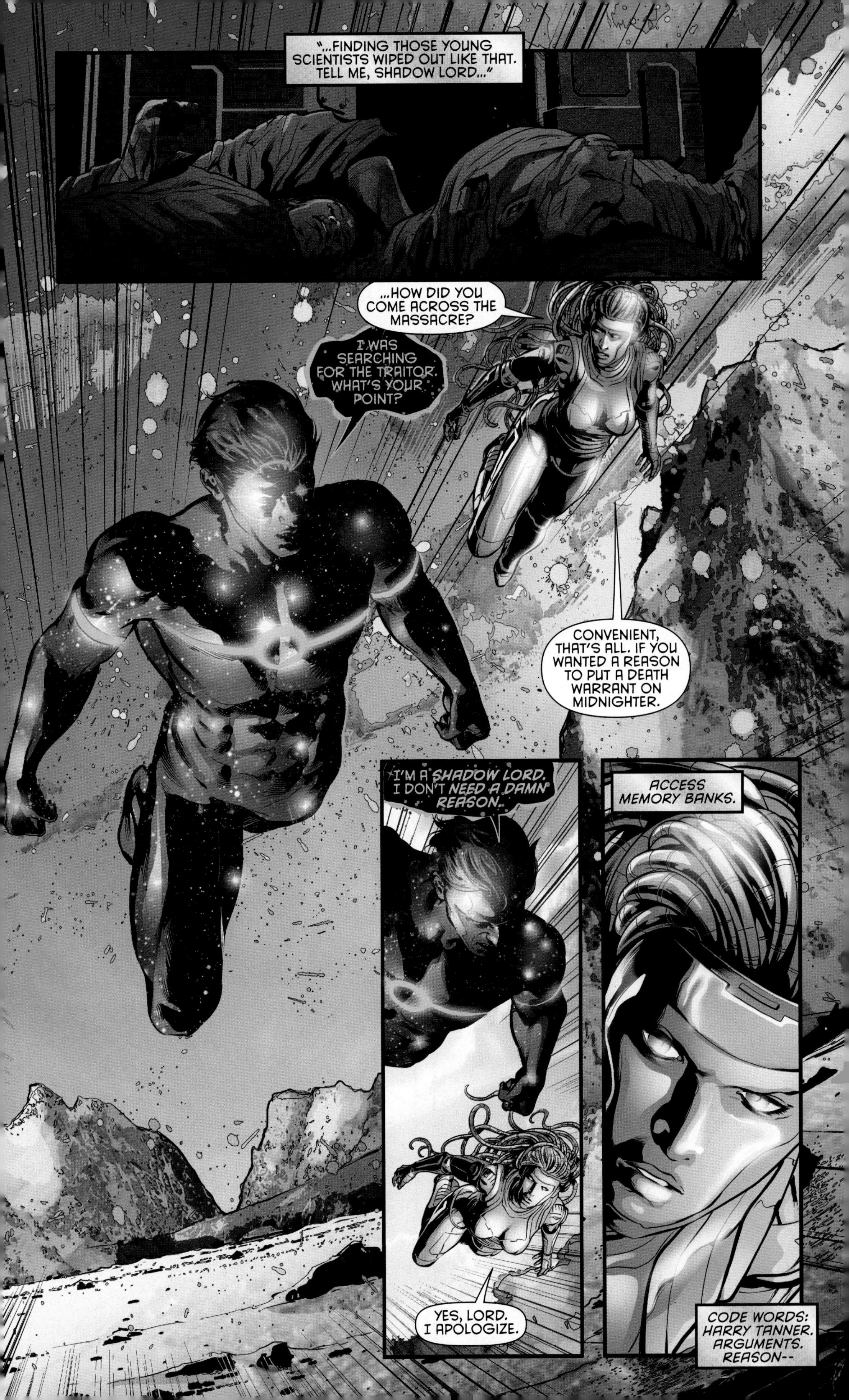

"...FINDING THOSE YOUNG SCIENTISTS WIPED OUT LIKE THAT. TELL ME, SHADOW LORD..."
...HOW DID YOU COME ACROSS THE MASSACRE?
I WAS SEARCHING FOR THE TRAITOR. WHAT'S YOUR POINT?
CONVENIENT, THAT'S ALL. IF YOU WANTED A REASON TO PUT A DEATH WARRANT ON MIDNIGHTER.
I'M A SHADOW LORD. I DON'T NEED A DAMN REASON.
YES, LORD. I APOLOGIZE.
ACCESS MEMORY BANKS.
CODE WORDS: HARRY TANNER. ARGUMENTS. REASON--

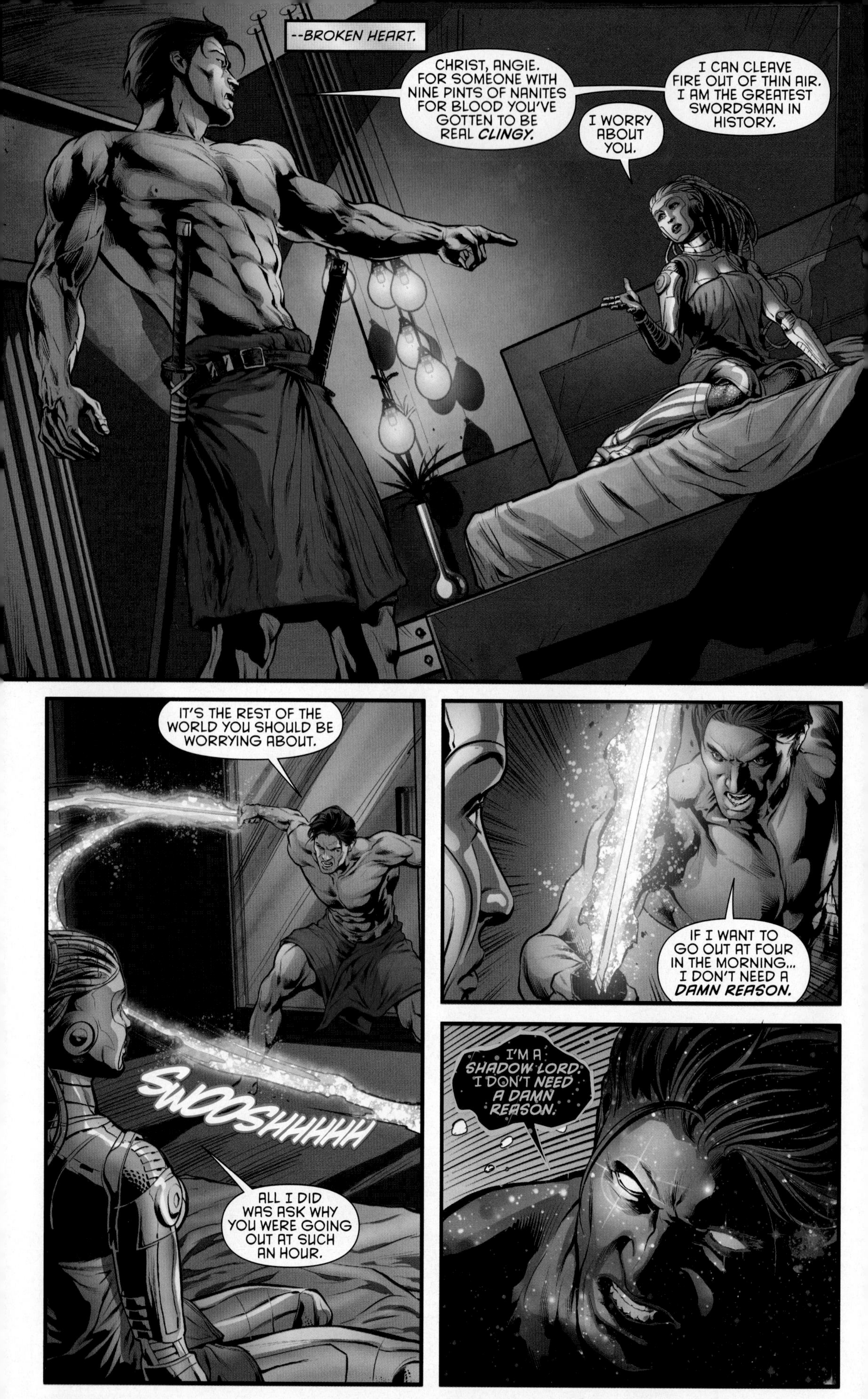
--BROKEN HEART.
CHRIST, ANGIE. FOR SOMEONE WITH NINE PINTS OF NANITES FOR BLOOD YOU'VE GOTTEN TO BE REAL CLINGY.
I WORRY ABOUT YOU.
I CAN CLEAVE FIRE OUT OF THIN AIR. I AM THE GREATEST SWORDSMAN IN HISTORY.
IT'S THE REST OF THE WORLD YOU SHOULD BE WORRYING ABOUT.
SWOOSHHHHH
ALL I DID WAS ASK WHY YOU WERE GOING OUT AT SUCH AN HOUR.
IF I WANT TO GO OUT AT FOUR IN THE MORNING... I DON'T NEED A DAMN REASON.
I'M A SHADOW LORD. I DON'T NEED A DAMN REASON.

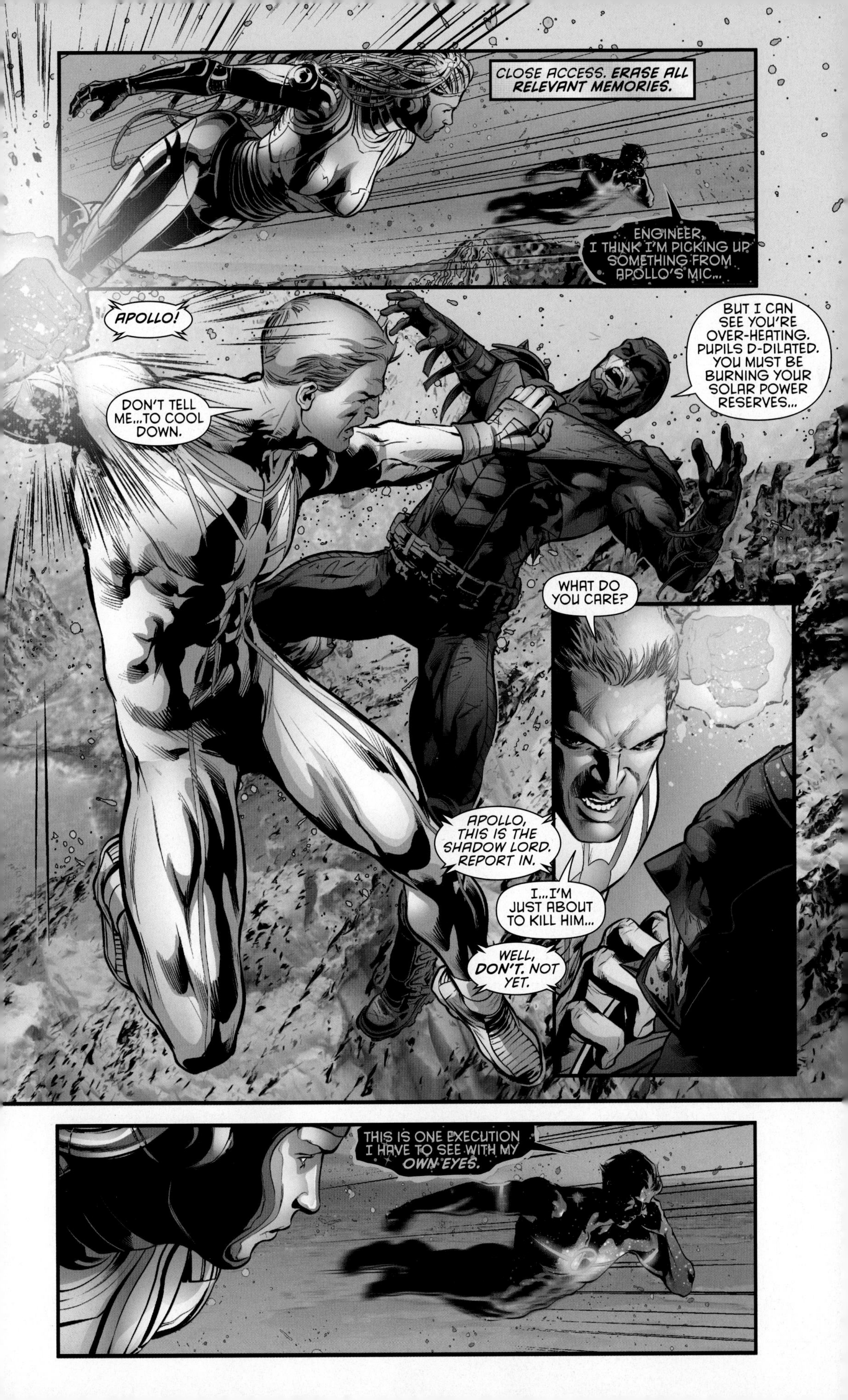
CLOSE ACCESS. ERASE ALL RELEVANT MEMORIES.
ENGINEER, I THINK I'M PICKING UP SOMETHING FROM APOLLO'S MIC...
APOLLO!
DON'T TELL ME...TO COOL DOWN.
BUT I CAN SEE YOU'RE OVER-HEATING. PUPILS D-DILATED. YOU MUST BE BURNING YOUR SOLAR POWER RESERVES...
WHAT DO YOU CARE?
APOLLO, THIS IS THE SHADOW LORD. REPORT IN.
I...I'M JUST ABOUT TO KILL HIM...
WELL, DON'T. NOT YET.
THIS IS ONE EXECUTION I HAVE TO SEE WITH MY OWN EYES.

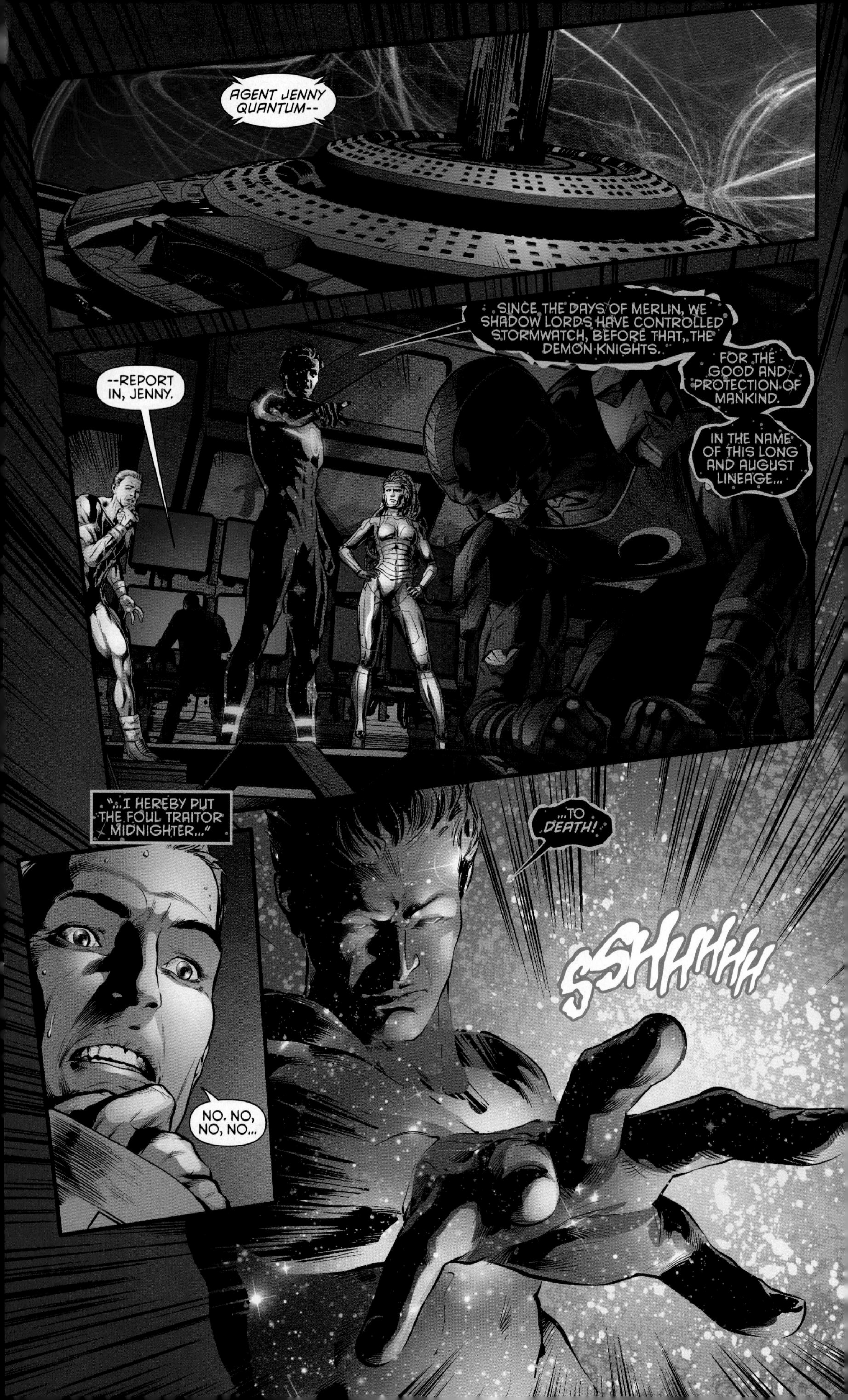
AGENT JENNY QUANTUM--
--REPORT IN, JENNY.
SINCE THE DAYS OF MERLIN, WE SHADOW LORDS HAVE CONTROLLED STORMWATCH. BEFORE THAT, THE DEMON KNIGHTS.
FOR THE GOOD AND PROTECTION OF MANKIND.
IN THE NAME OF THIS LONG AND AUGUST LINEAGE...
"...I HEREBY PUT THE FOUL TRAITOR MIDNIGHTER..."
...TO DEATH!
SSHHHHH
NO. NO, NO, NO...

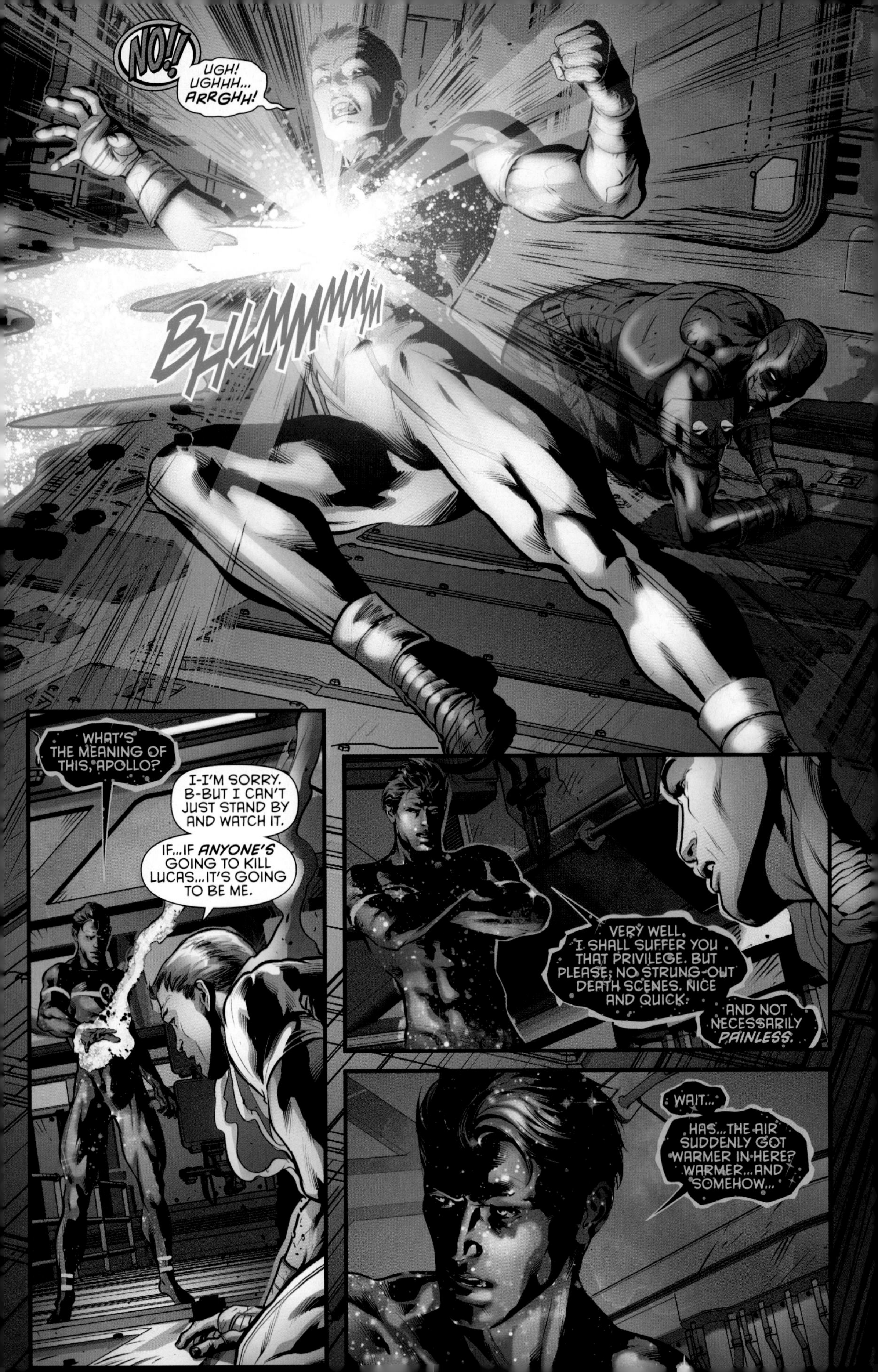
NO!!
UGH! UGHHH... ARRGHH!
BHUMMMMM
WHAT'S THE MEANING OF THIS, APOLLO?
I-I'M SORRY. B-BUT I CAN'T JUST STAND BY AND WATCH IT.
IF...IF ANYONE'S GOING TO KILL LUCAS...IT'S GOING TO BE ME.
VERY WELL. I SHALL SUFFER YOU THAT PRIVILEGE. BUT PLEASE, NO STRUNG-OUT DEATH SCENES. NICE AND QUICK.
AND NOT NECESSARILY PAINLESS.
WAIT...
HAS...THE AIR SUDDENLY GOT WARMER IN HERE? WARMER...AND SOMEHOW...

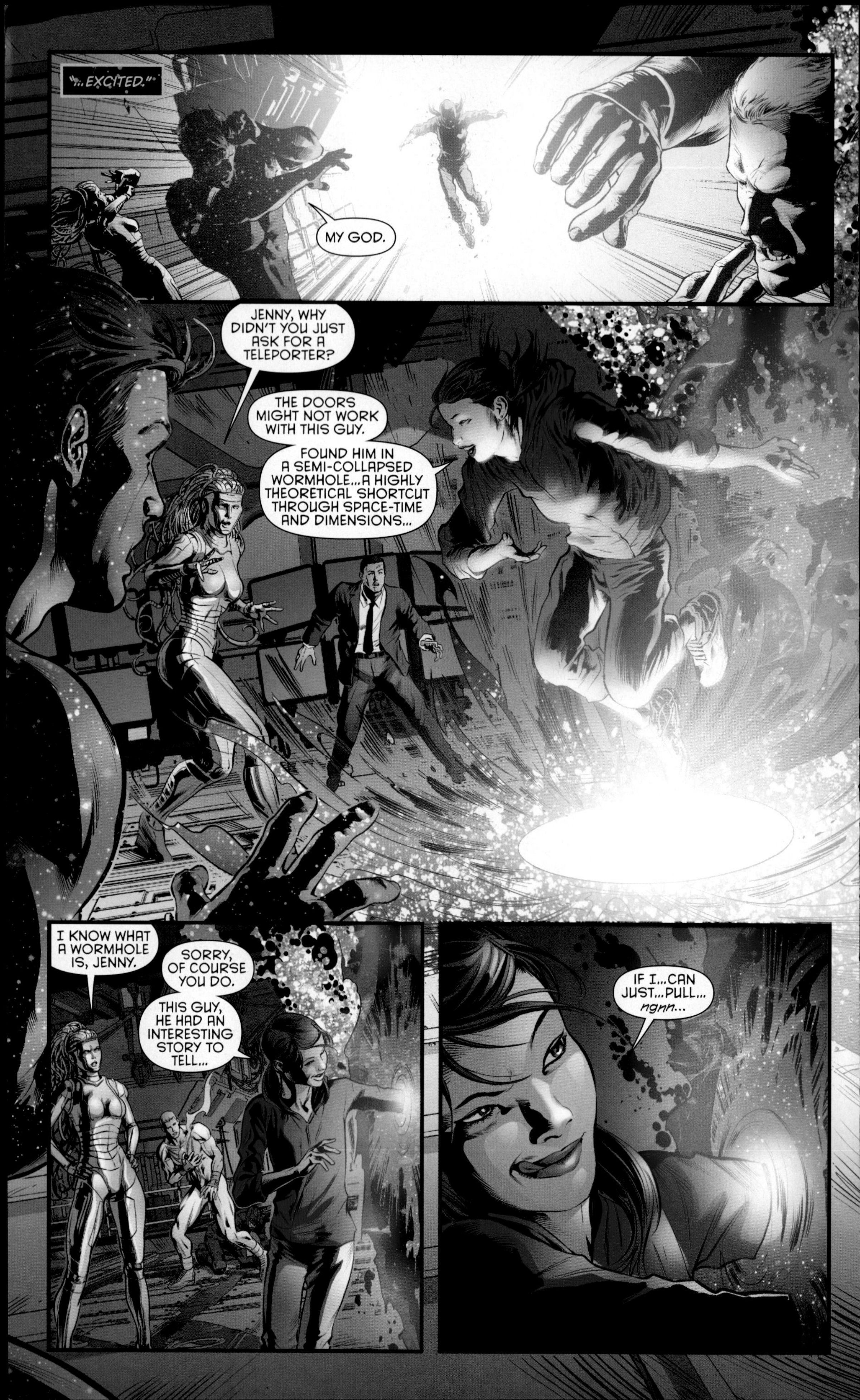
"...EXCITED."
MY GOD.
JENNY, WHY DIDN'T YOU JUST ASK FOR A TELEPORTER?
THE DOORS MIGHT NOT WORK WITH THIS GUY.
FOUND HIM IN A SEMI-COLLAPSED WORMHOLE...A HIGHLY THEORETICAL SHORTCUT THROUGH SPACE-TIME AND DIMENSIONS...
I KNOW WHAT A WORMHOLE IS, JENNY.
SORRY, OF COURSE YOU DO.
THIS GUY, HE HAD AN INTERESTING STORY TO TELL...
IF I...CAN JUST...PULL... *ngnn...*

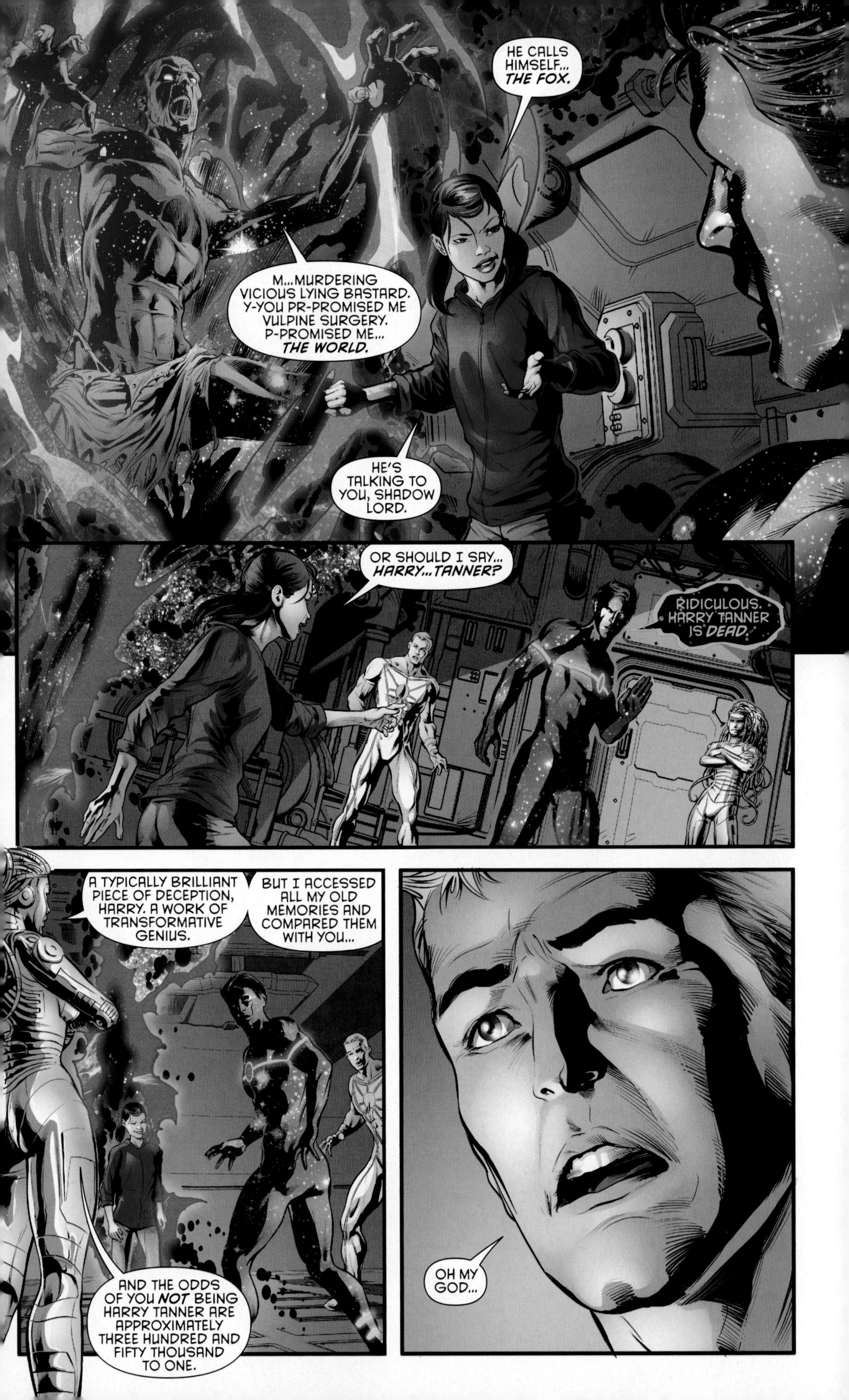
HE CALLS HIMSELF... THE FOX.
M...MURDERING VICIOUS LYING BASTARD. Y-YOU PR-PROMISED ME VULPINE SURGERY. P-PROMISED ME... THE WORLD.
HE'S TALKING TO YOU, SHADOW LORD.
OR SHOULD I SAY... HARRY...TANNER?
RIDICULOUS. HARRY TANNER IS DEAD.
A TYPICALLY BRILLIANT PIECE OF DECEPTION, HARRY. A WORK OF TRANSFORMATIVE GENIUS.
BUT I ACCESSED ALL MY OLD MEMORIES AND COMPARED THEM WITH YOU...
AND THE ODDS OF YOU NOT BEING HARRY TANNER ARE APPROXIMATELY THREE HUNDRED AND FIFTY THOUSAND TO ONE.
OH MY GOD...

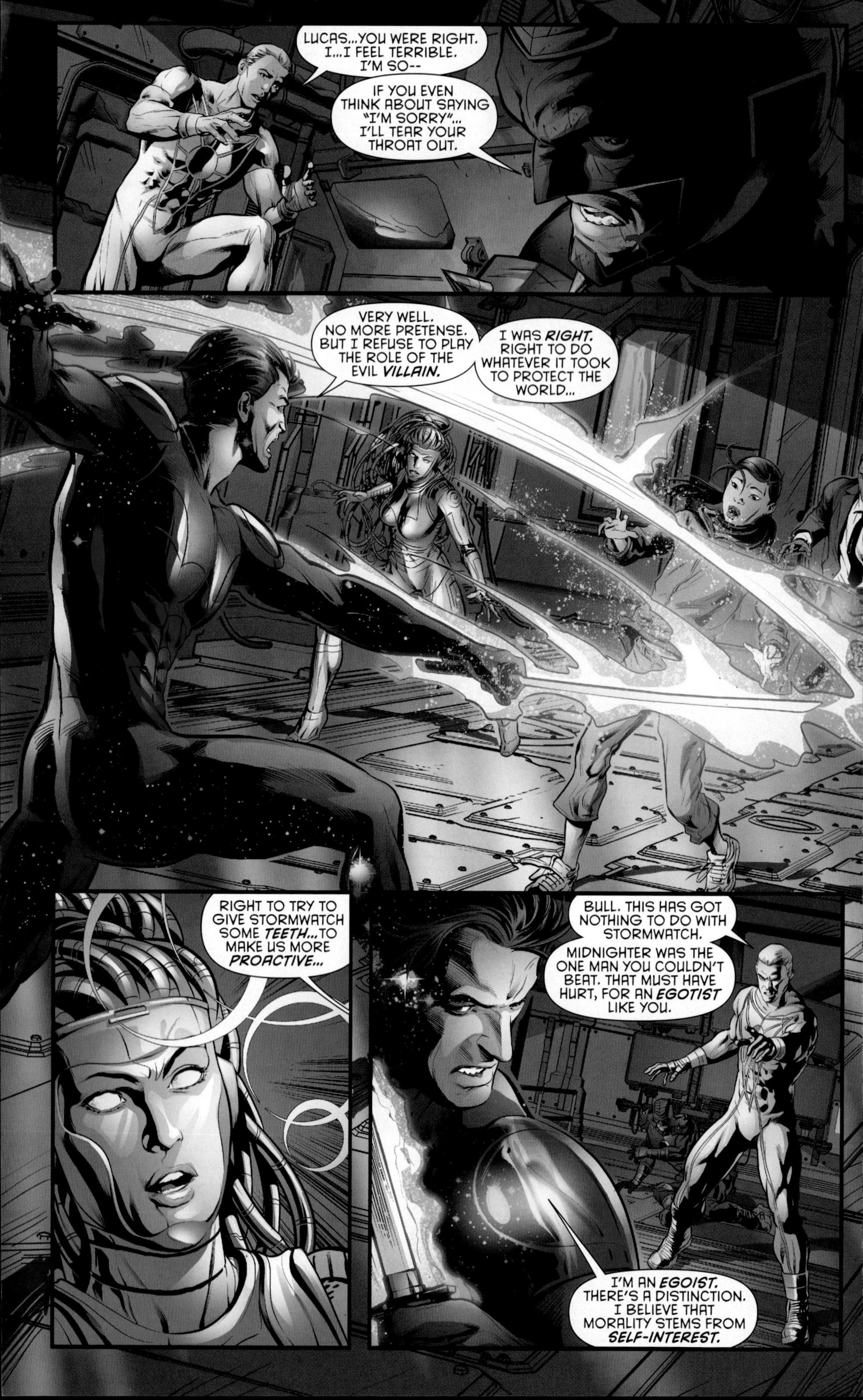
LUCAS...YOU WERE RIGHT. I...I FEEL TERRIBLE. I'M SO--
IF YOU EVEN THINK ABOUT SAYING "I'M SORRY"... I'LL TEAR YOUR THROAT OUT.
VERY WELL. NO MORE PRETENSE. BUT I REFUSE TO PLAY THE ROLE OF THE EVIL VILLAIN.
I WAS RIGHT. RIGHT TO DO WHATEVER IT TOOK TO PROTECT THE WORLD...
RIGHT TO TRY TO GIVE STORMWATCH SOME TEETH...TO MAKE US MORE PROACTIVE...
BULL. THIS HAS GOT NOTHING TO DO WITH STORMWATCH.
MIDNIGHTER WAS THE ONE MAN YOU COULDN'T BEAT. THAT MUST HAVE HURT, FOR AN EGOTIST LIKE YOU.
I'M AN EGOIST. THERE'S A DISTINCTION. I BELIEVE THAT MORALITY STEMS FROM SELF-INTEREST.

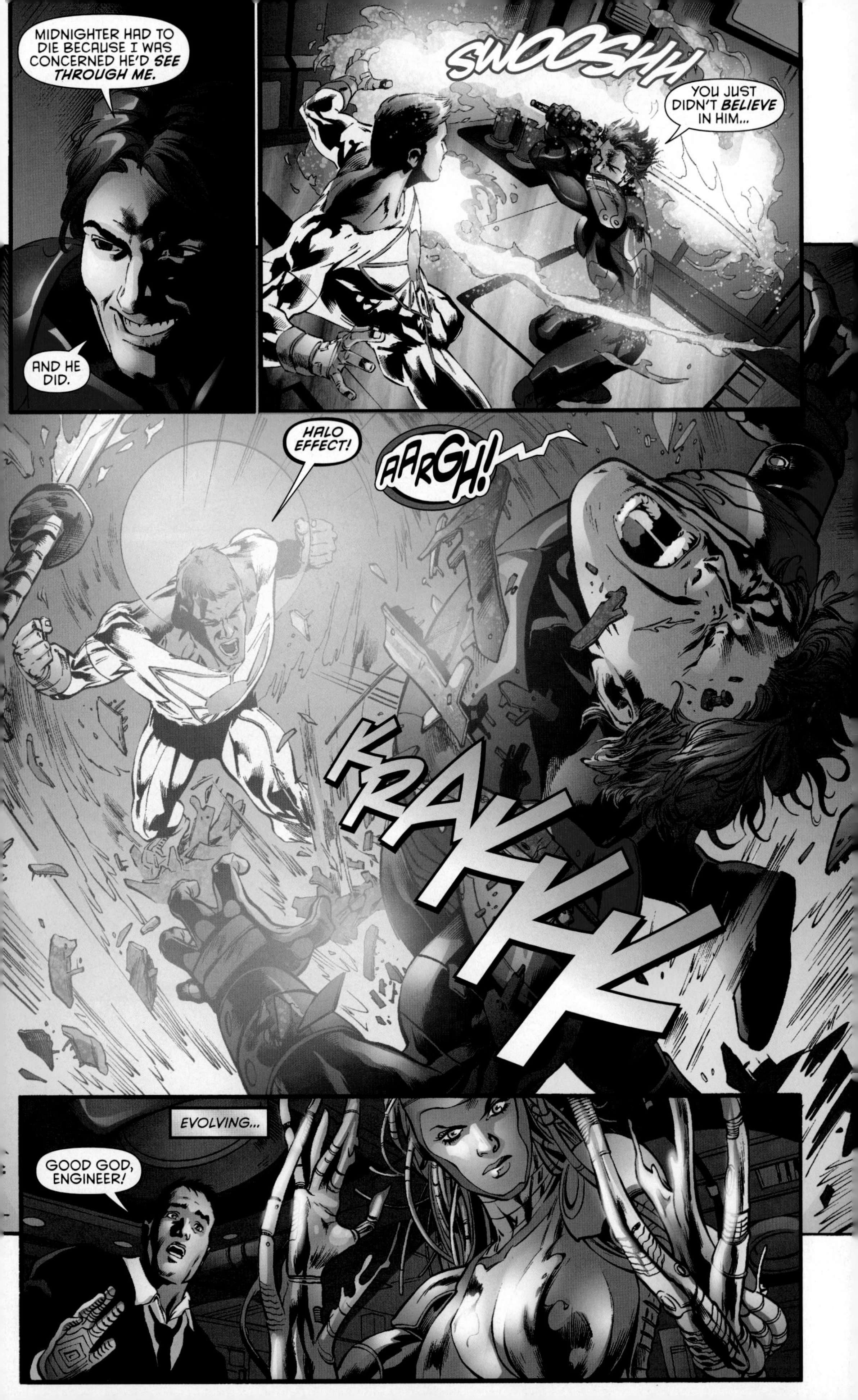
MIDNIGHTER HAD TO DIE BECAUSE I WAS CONCERNED HE'D SEE THROUGH ME.
AND HE DID.
SWOOSHH
YOU JUST DIDN'T BELIEVE IN HIM...
HALO EFFECT!
AARGH!
KRAKK
EVOLVING...
GOOD GOD, ENGINEER!

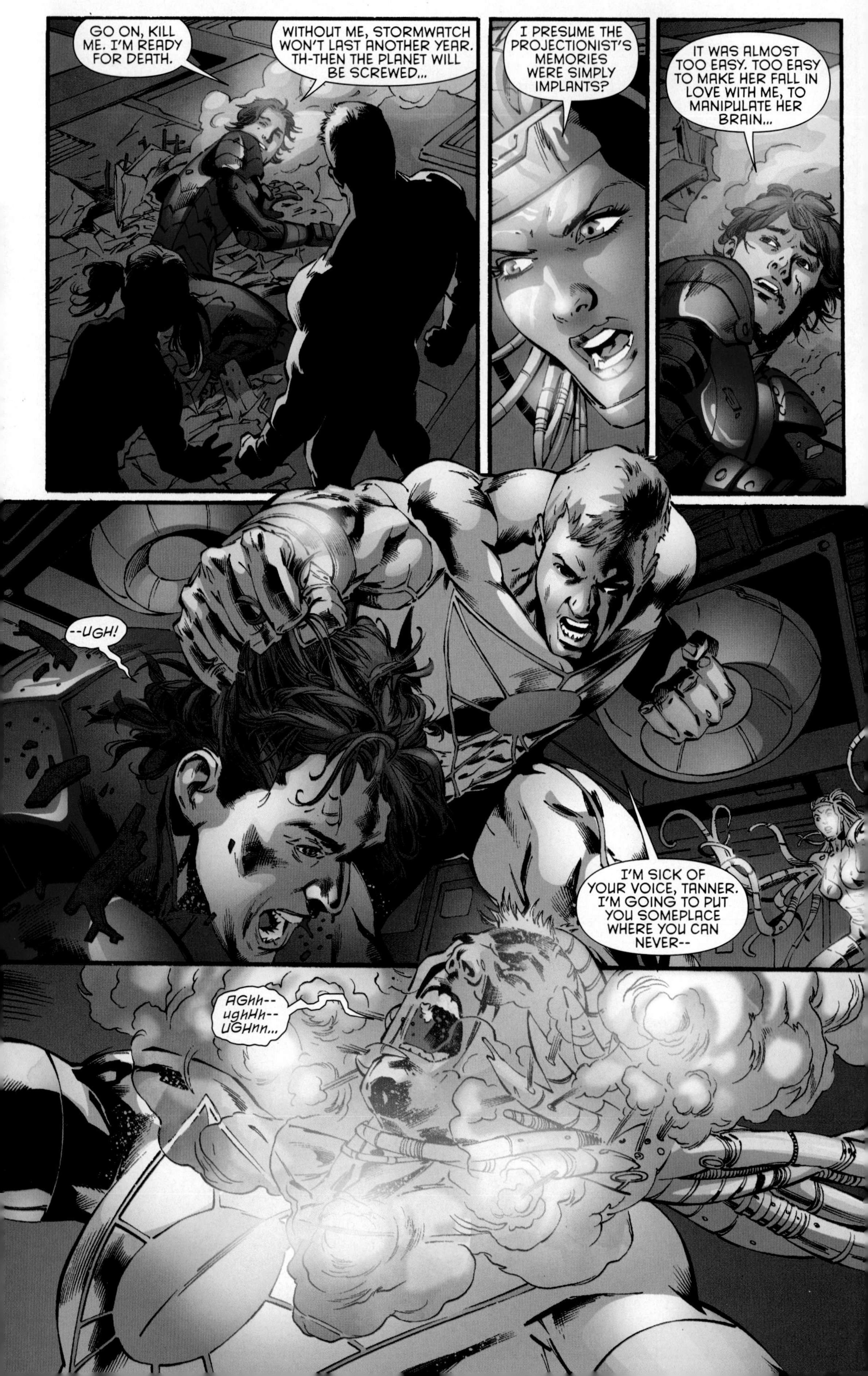
GO ON, KILL ME. I'M READY FOR DEATH.
WITHOUT ME, STORMWATCH WON'T LAST ANOTHER YEAR. TH-THEN THE PLANET WILL BE SCREWED...
I PRESUME THE PROJECTIONIST'S MEMORIES WERE SIMPLY IMPLANTS?
IT WAS ALMOST TOO EASY. TOO EASY TO MAKE HER FALL IN LOVE WITH ME, TO MANIPULATE HER BRAIN...
--UGH!
I'M SICK OF YOUR VOICE, TANNER. I'M GOING TO PUT YOU SOMEPLACE WHERE YOU CAN NEVER--
AGhh-- ughHh-- UGHnn...

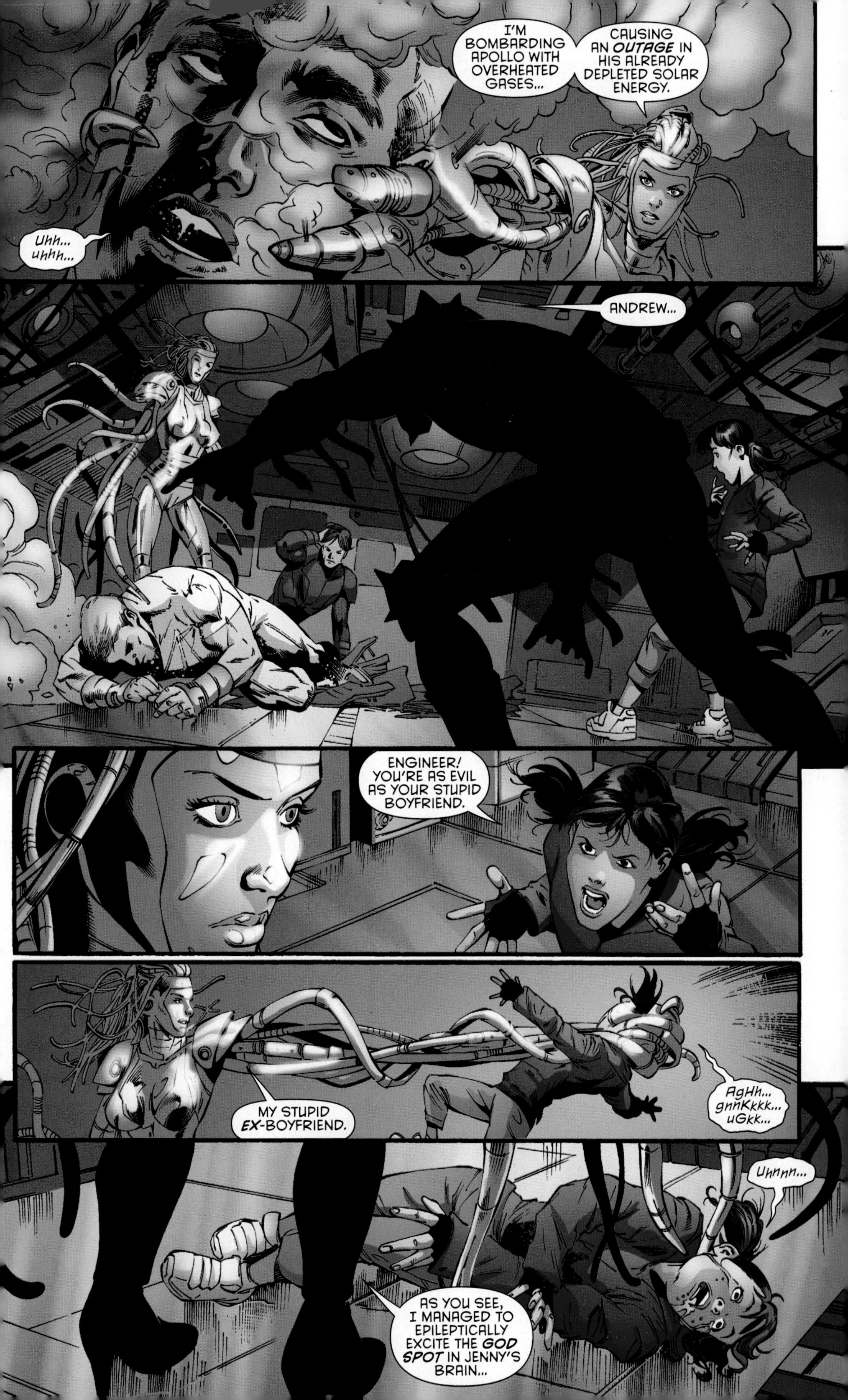
I'M BOMBARDING APOLLO WITH OVERHEATED GASES...
CAUSING AN *OUTAGE* IN HIS ALREADY DEPLETED SOLAR ENERGY.
Uhh... uhhh...
ANDREW...
ENGINEER! YOU'RE AS EVIL AS YOUR STUPID BOYFRIEND.
MY STUPID *EX*-BOYFRIEND.
AgHh... gnnKkkk... uGkk...
Uhnnn...
AS YOU SEE, I MANAGED TO EPILEPTICALLY EXCITE THE *GOD SPOT* IN JENNY'S BRAIN...

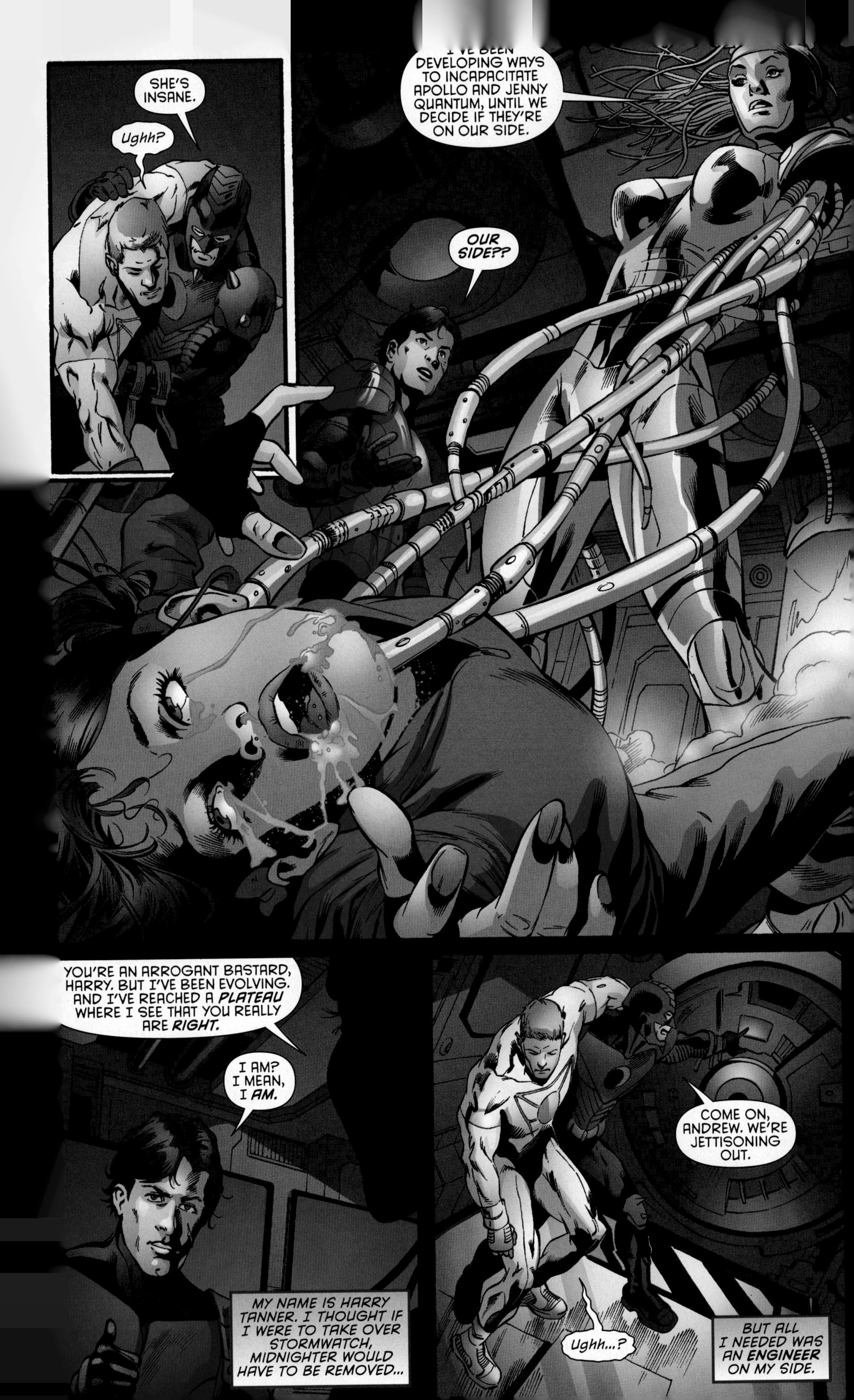

SHE'S INSANE.
Ughh?
DEVELOPING WAYS TO INCAPACITATE APOLLO AND JENNY QUANTUM, UNTIL WE DECIDE IF THEY'RE ON OUR SIDE.
OUR SIDE??
YOU'RE AN ARROGANT BASTARD, HARRY. BUT I'VE BEEN EVOLVING. AND I'VE REACHED A PLATEAU WHERE I SEE THAT YOU REALLY ARE RIGHT.
I AM? I MEAN, I AM.
MY NAME IS HARRY TANNER. I THOUGHT IF I WERE TO TAKE OVER STORMWATCH, MIDNIGHTER WOULD HAVE TO BE REMOVED...
COME ON, ANDREW. WE'RE JETTISONING OUT.
Ughh...?
BUT ALL I NEEDED WAS AN ENGINEER ON MY SIDE.

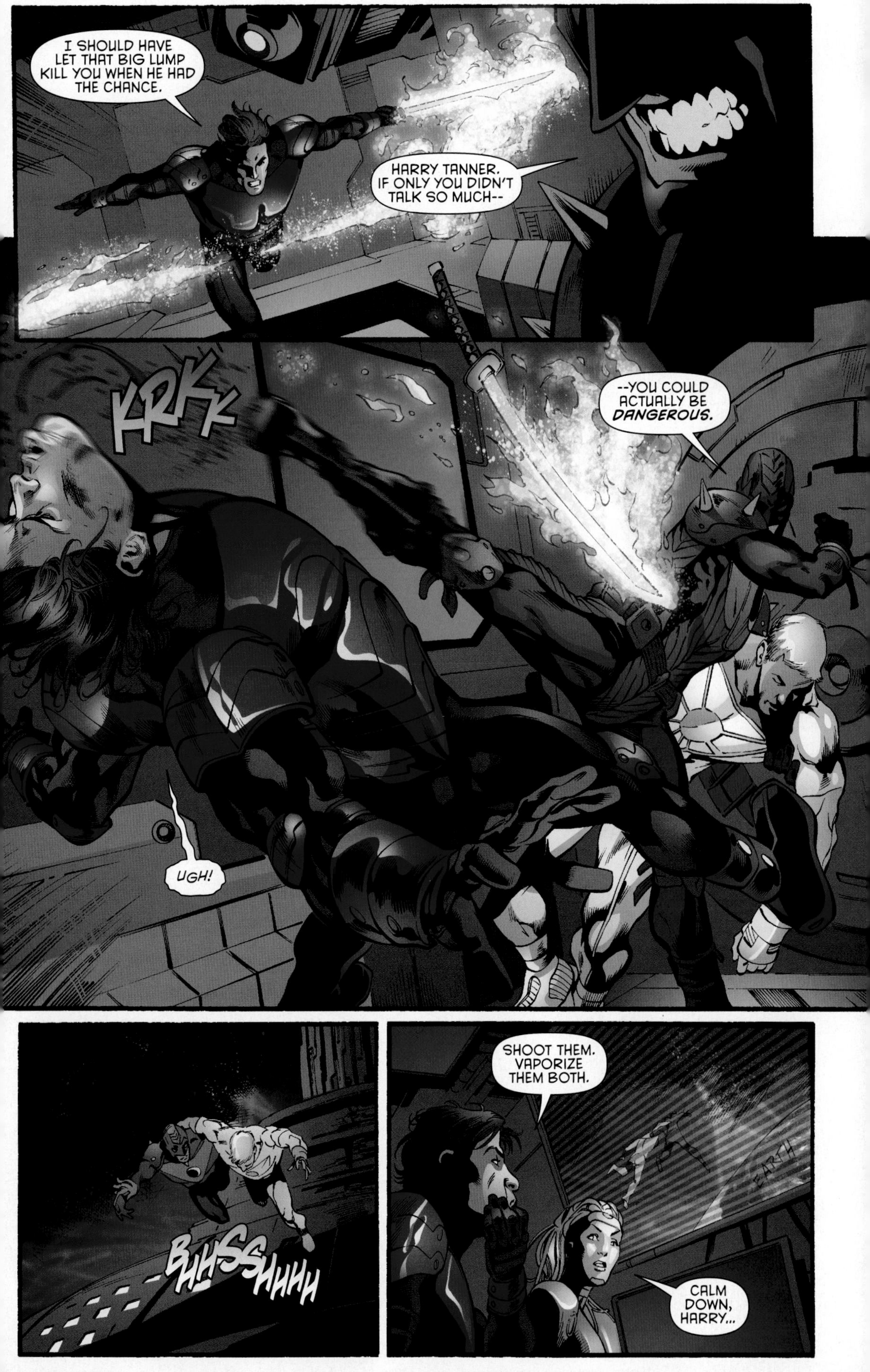
I SHOULD HAVE LET THAT BIG LUMP KILL YOU WHEN HE HAD THE CHANCE.
HARRY TANNER. IF ONLY YOU DIDN'T TALK SO MUCH--
KRKK
--YOU COULD ACTUALLY BE *DANGEROUS.*
UGH!
BHHSSHHHH
SHOOT THEM. VAPORIZE THEM BOTH.
EARTH
CALM DOWN, HARRY...

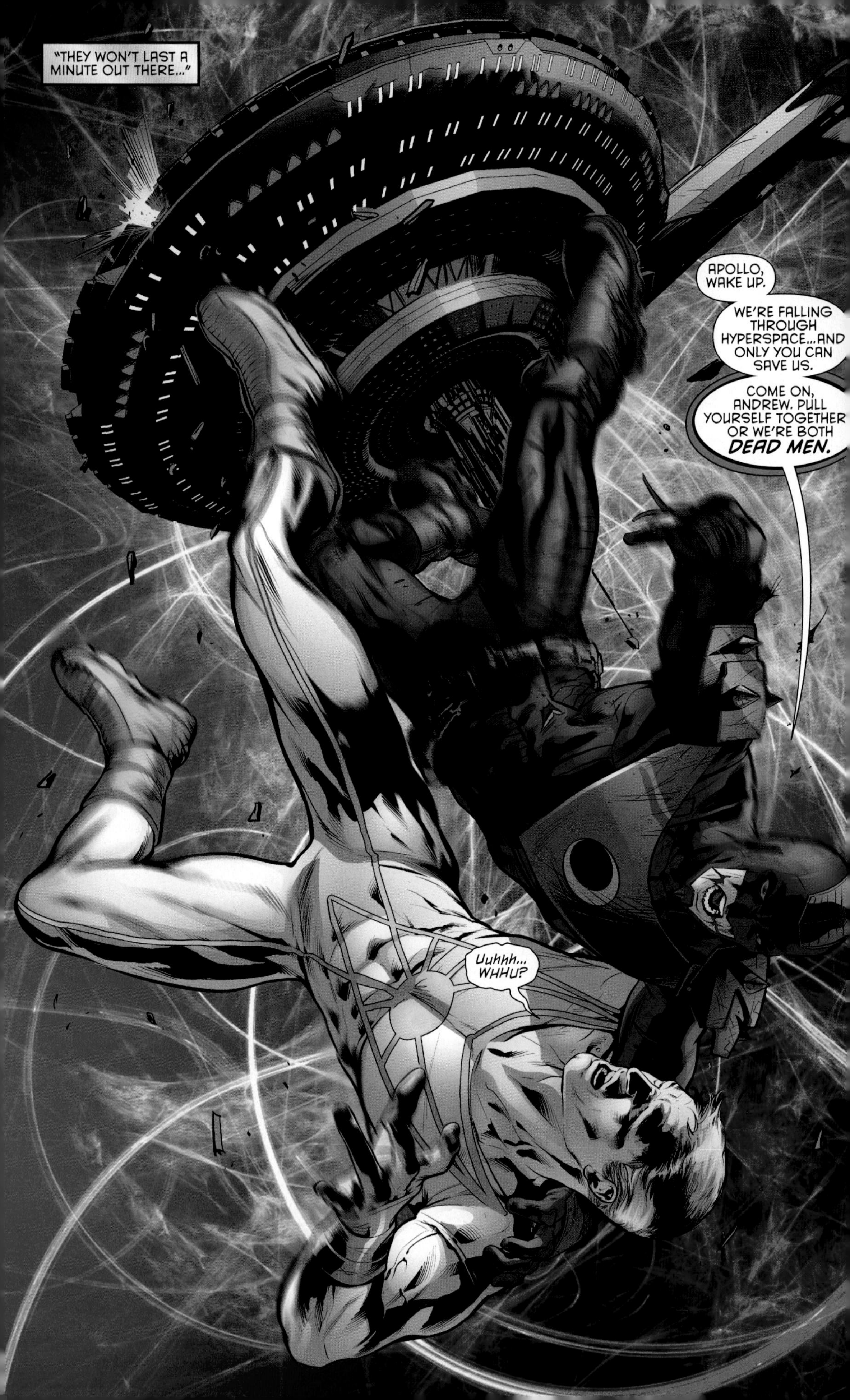
"THEY WON'T LAST A MINUTE OUT THERE..."
APOLLO, WAKE UP.
WE'RE FALLING THROUGH HYPERSPACE...AND ONLY YOU CAN SAVE US.
COME ON, ANDREW. PULL YOURSELF TOGETHER OR WE'RE BOTH DEAD MEN.
Uuhhh... WHHU?

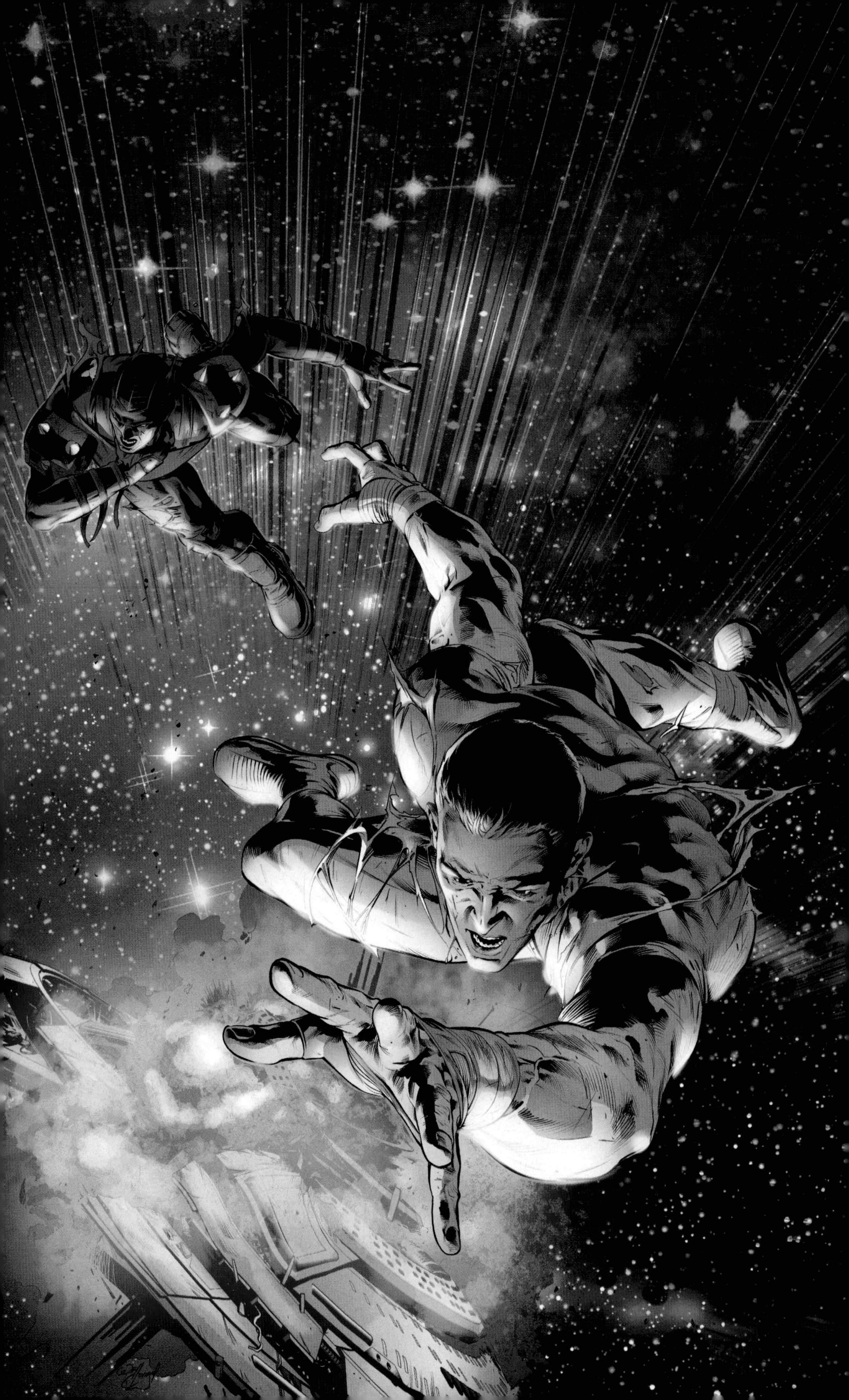

THE MEN WHO FELL TO EARTH

PETER MILLIGAN writer **WILL CONRAD** artist cover art by **WILL CONRAD & GUY MAJOR**

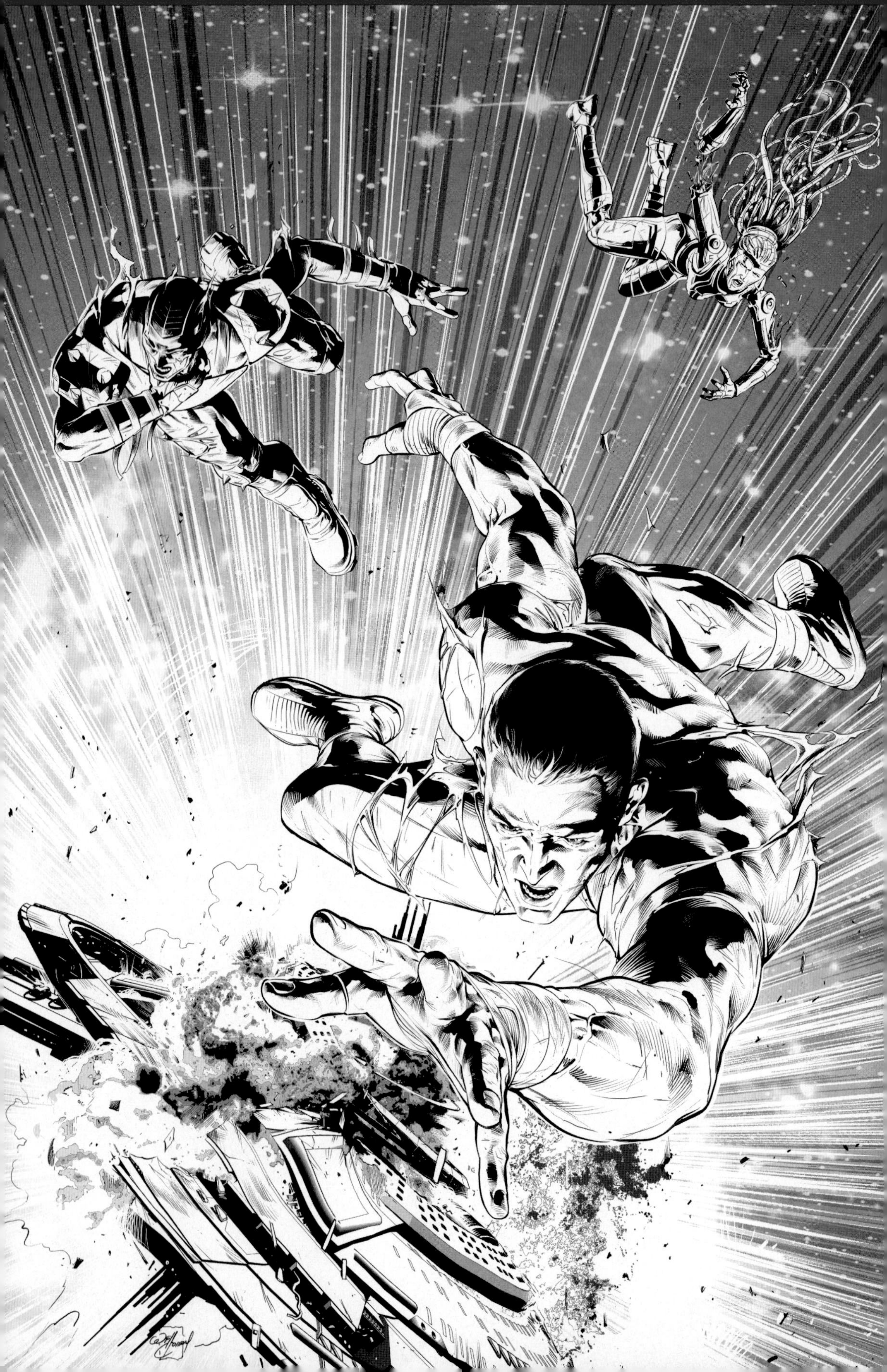

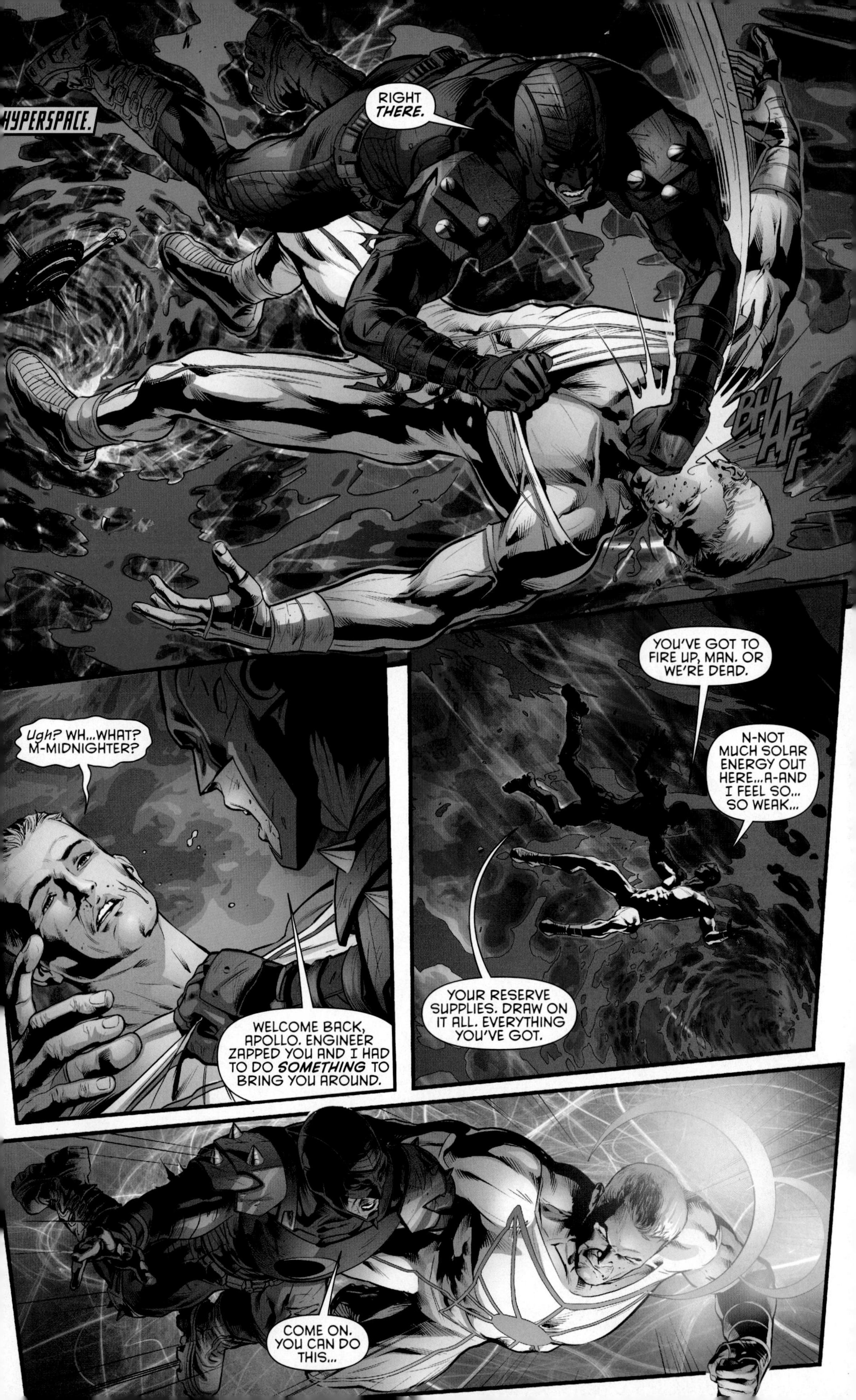
HYPERSPACE.
RIGHT THERE.
BHAFF
Ugh? WH...WHAT? M-MIDNIGHTER?
WELCOME BACK, APOLLO. ENGINEER ZAPPED YOU AND I HAD TO DO SOMETHING TO BRING YOU AROUND.
YOU'VE GOT TO FIRE UP, MAN. OR WE'RE DEAD.
N-NOT MUCH SOLAR ENERGY OUT HERE...A-AND I FEEL SO... SO WEAK...
YOUR RESERVE SUPPLIES. DRAW ON IT ALL. EVERYTHING YOU'VE GOT.
COME ON. YOU CAN DO THIS...

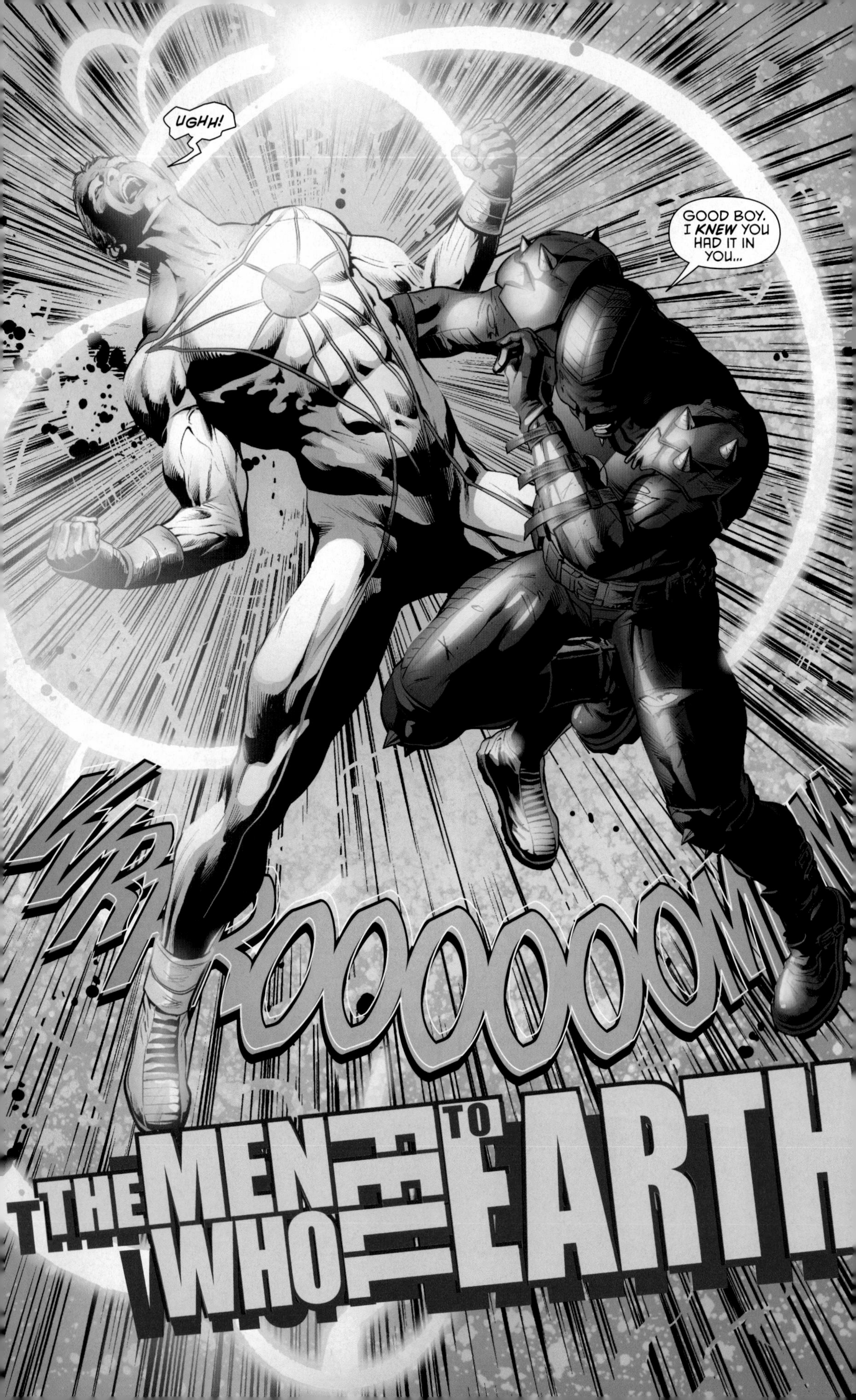

UGHH!
GOOD BOY. I **KNEW** YOU HAD IT IN YOU...
VROOOOOOM
THE MEN WHO FELL TO EARTH

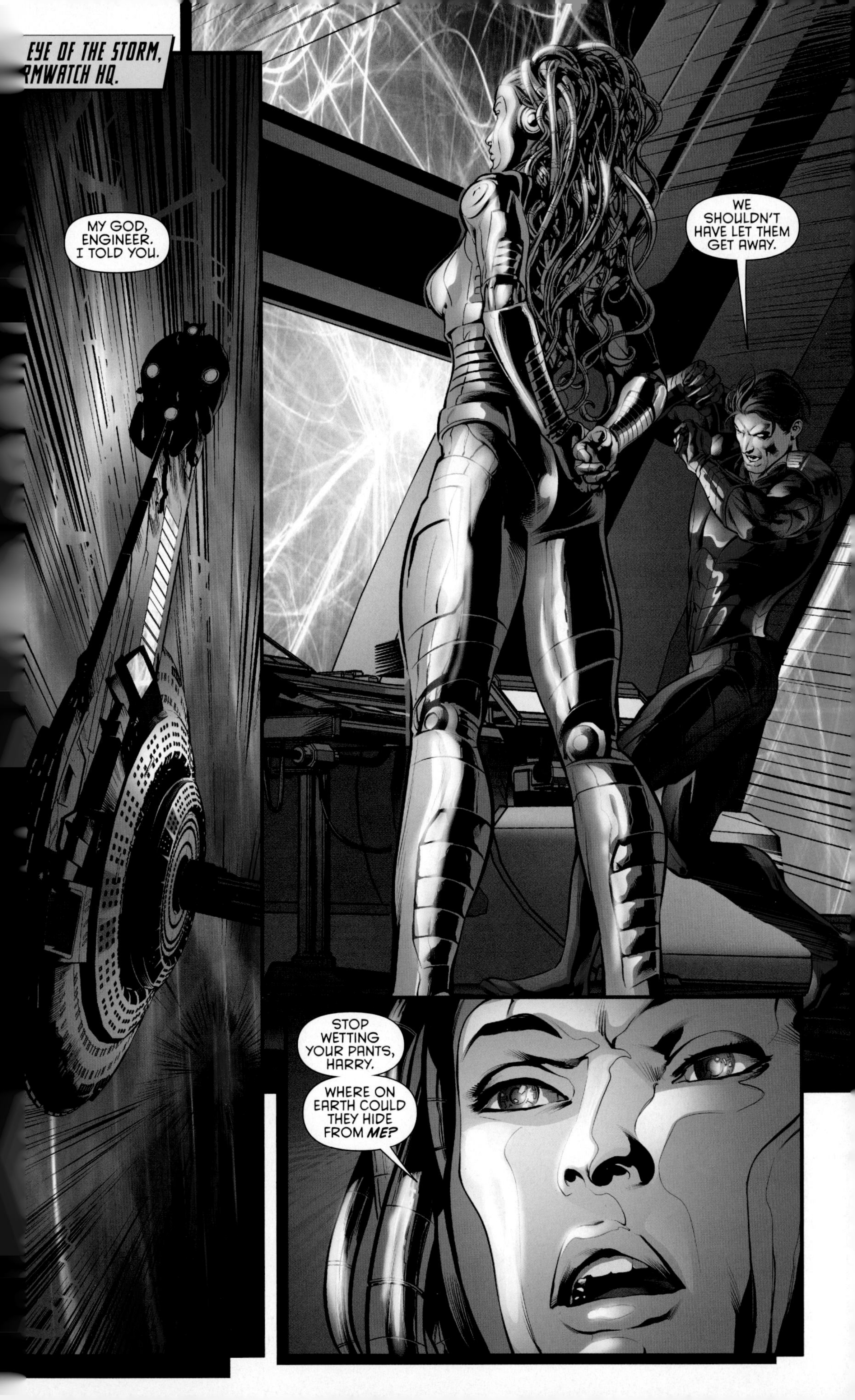
EYE OF THE STORM,
RMWATCH HQ.
MY GOD, ENGINEER. I TOLD YOU.
WE SHOULDN'T HAVE LET THEM GET AWAY.
STOP WETTING YOUR PANTS, HARRY.
WHERE ON EARTH COULD THEY HIDE FROM *ME?*

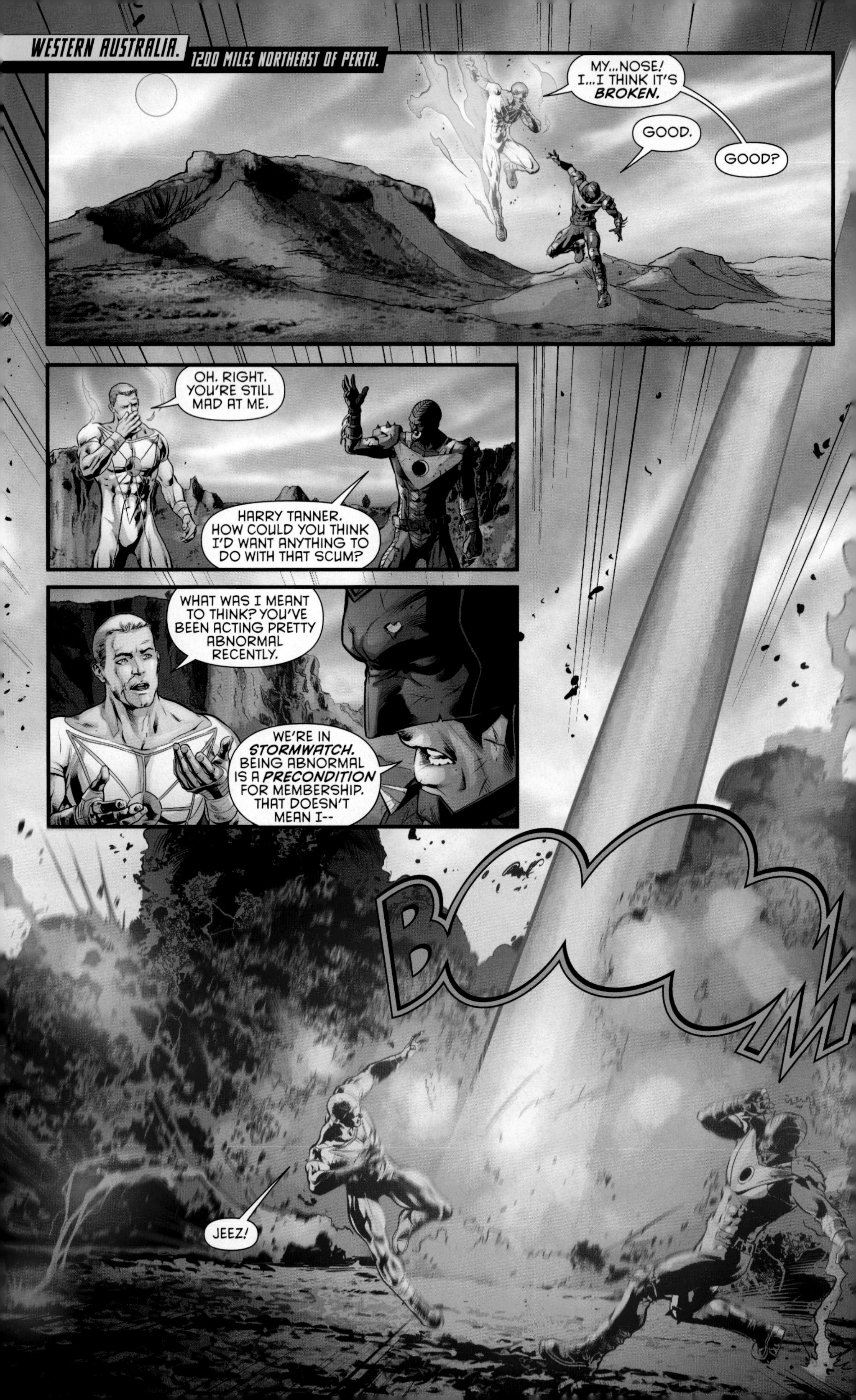
WESTERN AUSTRALIA.
1200 MILES NORTHEAST OF PERTH.
MY...NOSE! I...I THINK IT'S BROKEN.
GOOD.
GOOD?
OH. RIGHT. YOU'RE STILL MAD AT ME.
HARRY TANNER. HOW COULD YOU THINK I'D WANT ANYTHING TO DO WITH THAT SCUM?
WHAT WAS I MEANT TO THINK? YOU'VE BEEN ACTING PRETTY ABNORMAL RECENTLY.
WE'RE IN STORMWATCH. BEING ABNORMAL IS A PRECONDITION FOR MEMBERSHIP. THAT DOESN'T MEAN I--
BOOM
JEEZ!

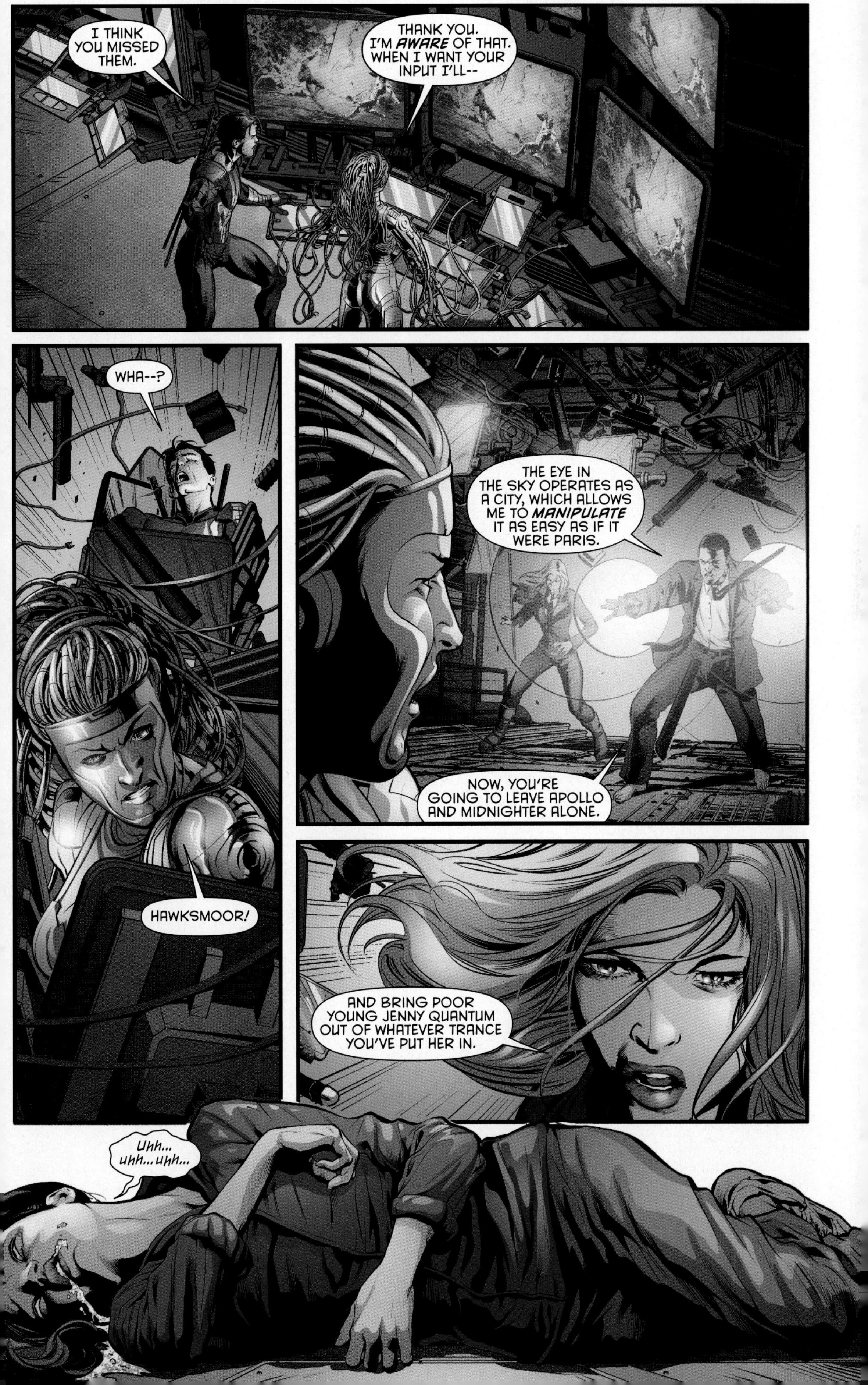
I THINK YOU MISSED THEM.
THANK YOU. I'M *AWARE* OF THAT. WHEN I WANT YOUR INPUT I'LL--
WHA--?
THE EYE IN THE SKY OPERATES AS A CITY, WHICH ALLOWS ME TO *MANIPULATE* IT AS EASY AS IF IT WERE PARIS.
NOW, YOU'RE GOING TO LEAVE APOLLO AND MIDNIGHTER ALONE.
HAWKSMOOR!
AND BRING POOR YOUNG JENNY QUANTUM OUT OF WHATEVER TRANCE YOU'VE PUT HER IN.
Uhh... uhh...uhh...

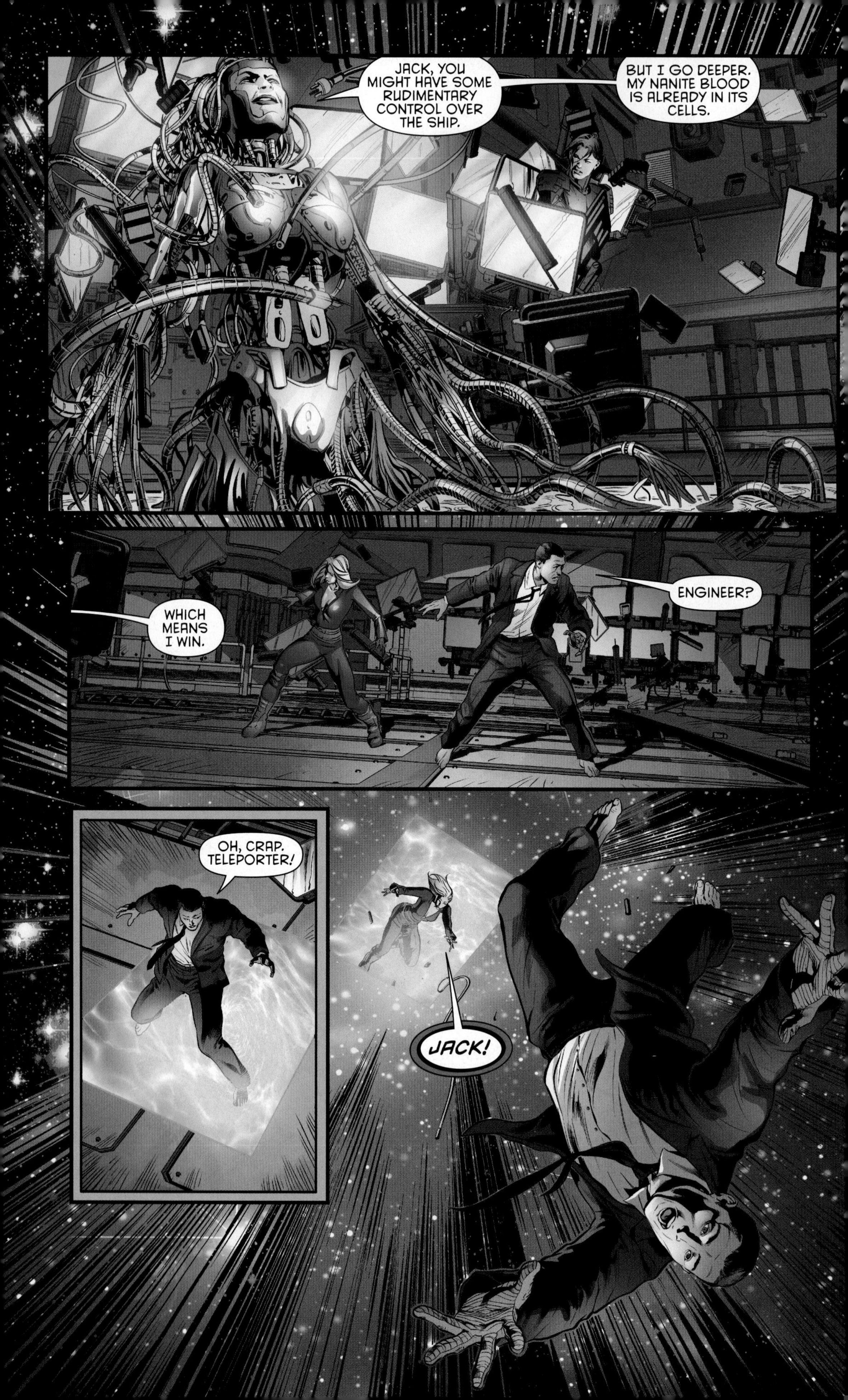
JACK, YOU MIGHT HAVE SOME RUDIMENTARY CONTROL OVER THE SHIP.
BUT I GO DEEPER. MY NANITE BLOOD IS ALREADY IN ITS CELLS.
WHICH MEANS I WIN.
ENGINEER?
OH, CRAP. TELEPORTER!
JACK!

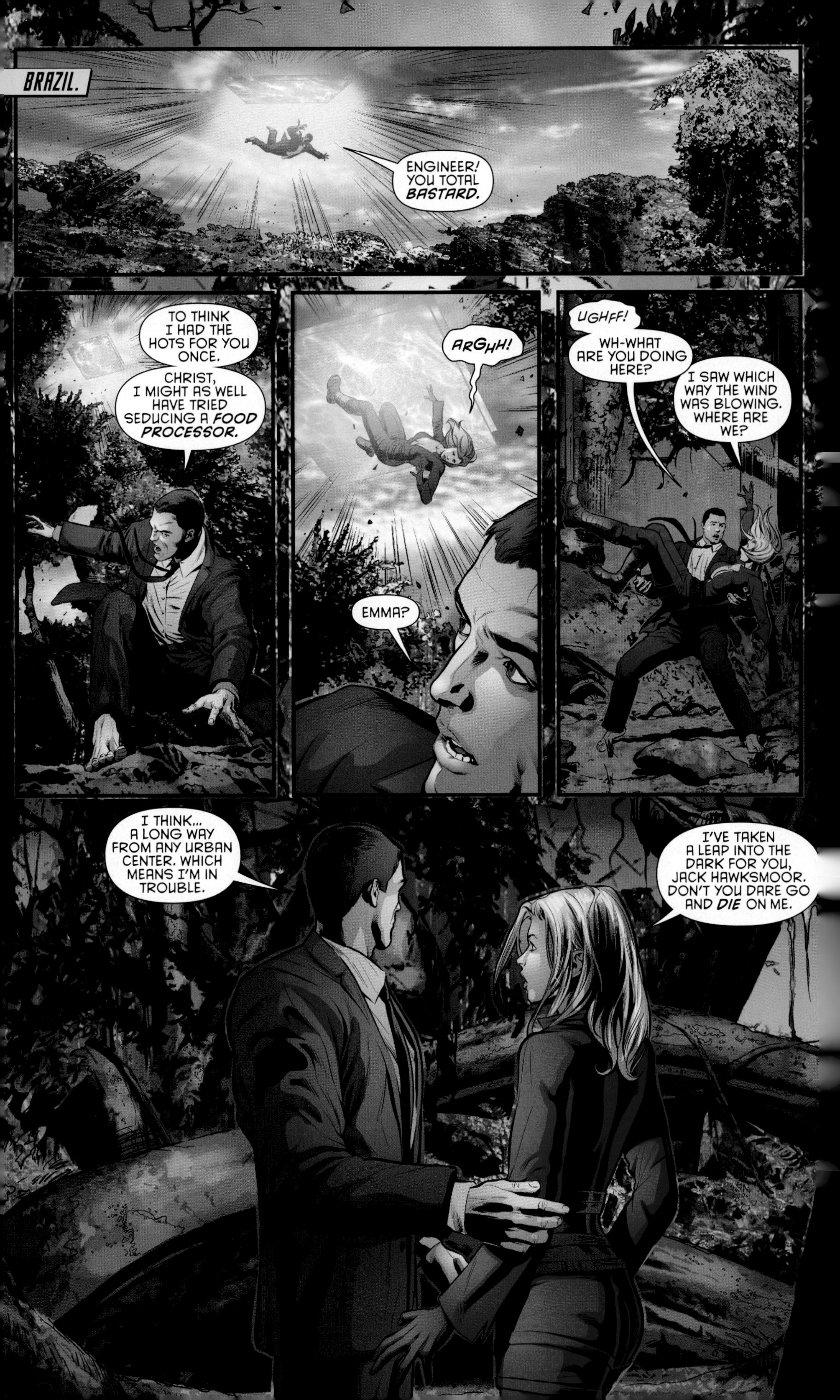
BRAZIL.
ENGINEER! YOU TOTAL BASTARD.
TO THINK I HAD THE HOTS FOR YOU ONCE.
CHRIST, I MIGHT AS WELL HAVE TRIED SEDUCING A FOOD PROCESSOR.
ARGHH!
EMMA?
UGHFF!
WH-WHAT ARE YOU DOING HERE?
I SAW WHICH WAY THE WIND WAS BLOWING. WHERE ARE WE?
I THINK... A LONG WAY FROM ANY URBAN CENTER. WHICH MEANS I'M IN TROUBLE.
I'VE TAKEN A LEAP INTO THE DARK FOR YOU, JACK HAWKSMOOR. DON'T YOU DARE GO AND DIE ON ME.

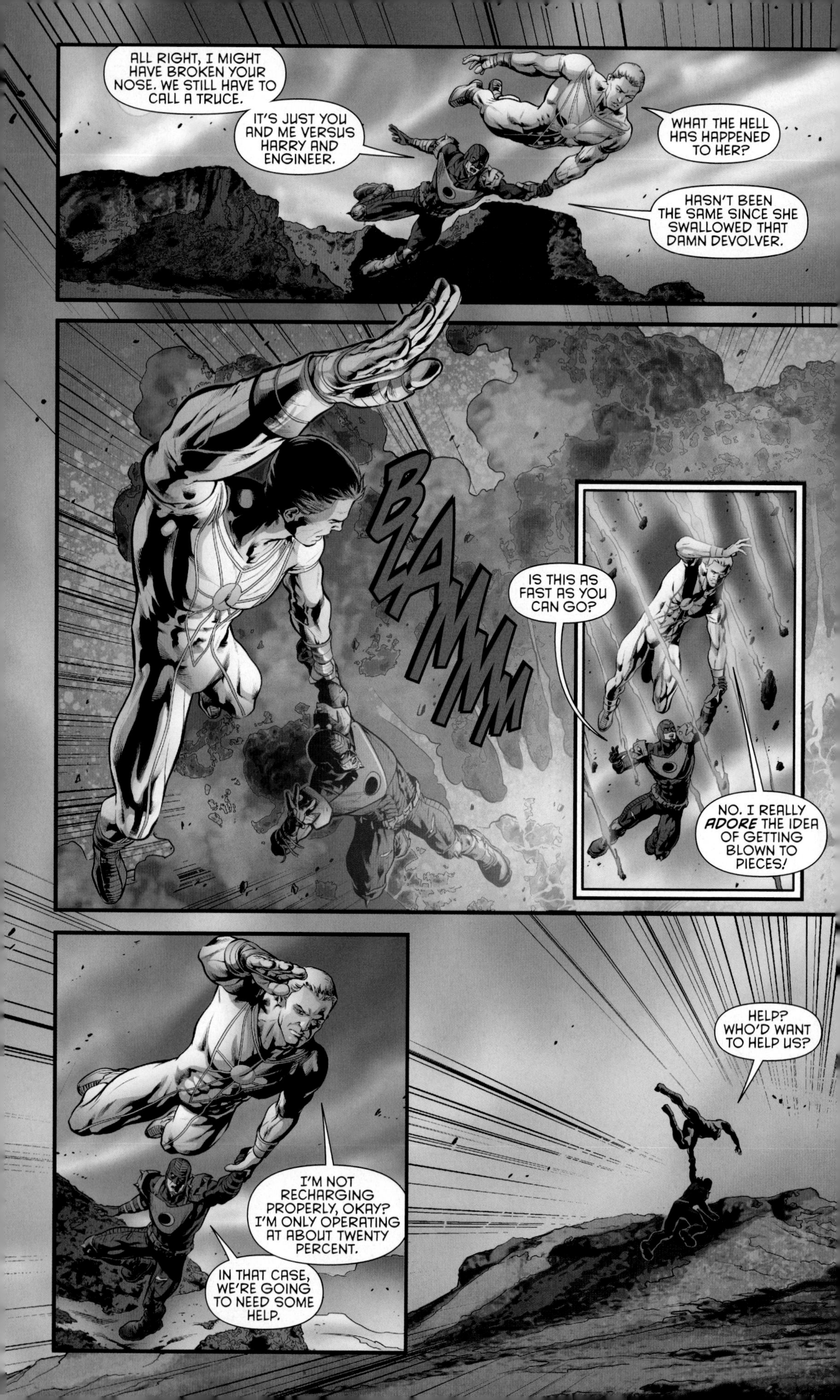

ALL RIGHT, I MIGHT HAVE BROKEN YOUR NOSE. WE STILL HAVE TO CALL A TRUCE.
IT'S JUST YOU AND ME VERSUS HARRY AND ENGINEER.
WHAT THE HELL HAS HAPPENED TO HER?
HASN'T BEEN THE SAME SINCE SHE SWALLOWED THAT DAMN DEVOLVER.
BLAMMM
IS THIS AS FAST AS YOU CAN GO?
NO. I REALLY *ADORE* THE IDEA OF GETTING BLOWN TO PIECES!
I'M NOT RECHARGING PROPERLY, OKAY? I'M ONLY OPERATING AT ABOUT TWENTY PERCENT.
IN THAT CASE, WE'RE GOING TO NEED SOME HELP.
HELP? WHO'D WANT TO HELP US?

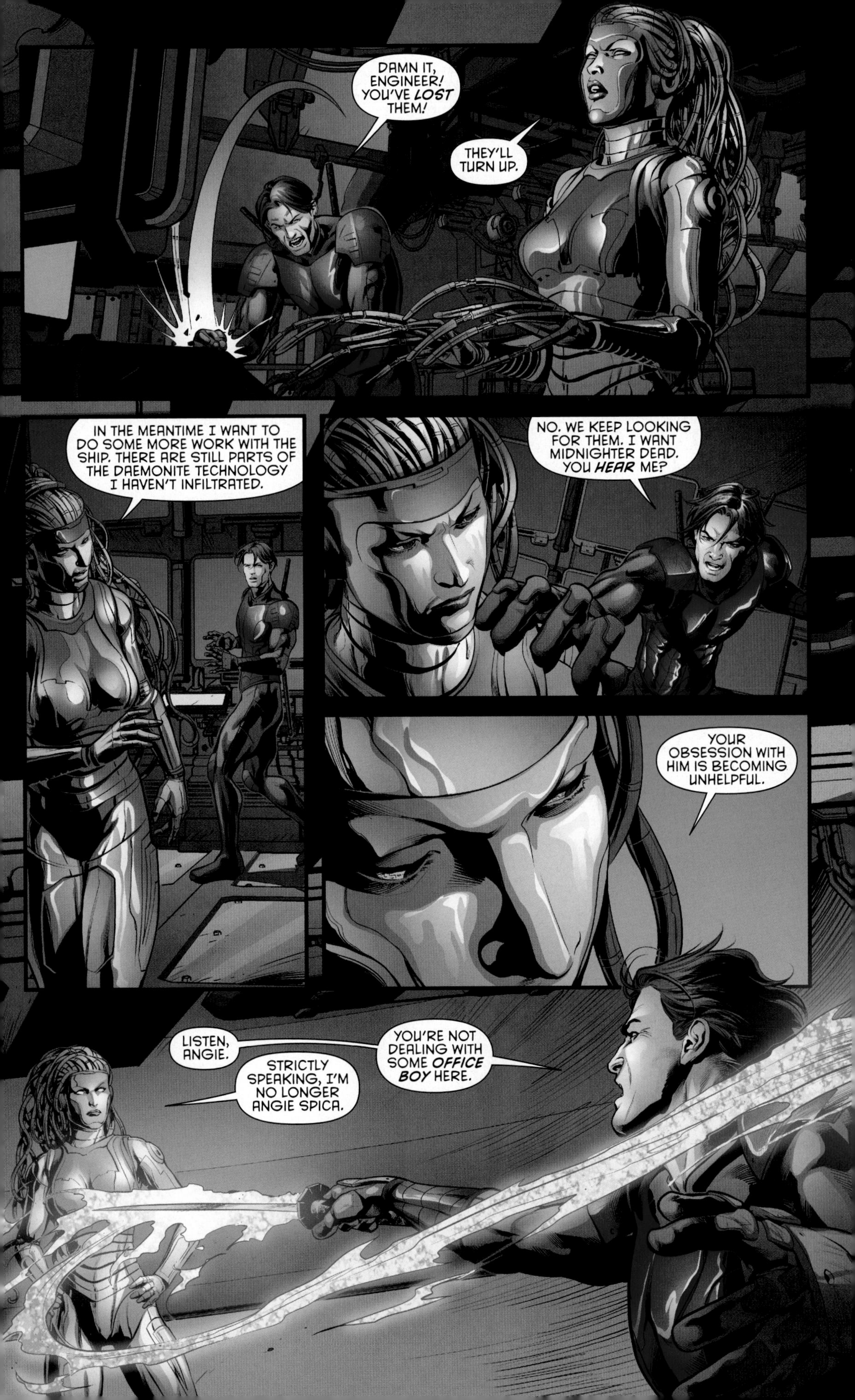
DAMN IT, ENGINEER! YOU'VE LOST THEM!
THEY'LL TURN UP.
IN THE MEANTIME I WANT TO DO SOME MORE WORK WITH THE SHIP. THERE ARE STILL PARTS OF THE DAEMONITE TECHNOLOGY I HAVEN'T INFILTRATED.
NO. WE KEEP LOOKING FOR THEM. I WANT MIDNIGHTER DEAD. YOU HEAR ME?
YOUR OBSESSION WITH HIM IS BECOMING UNHELPFUL.
LISTEN, ANGIE.
YOU'RE NOT DEALING WITH SOME OFFICE BOY HERE.
STRICTLY SPEAKING, I'M NO LONGER ANGIE SPICA.

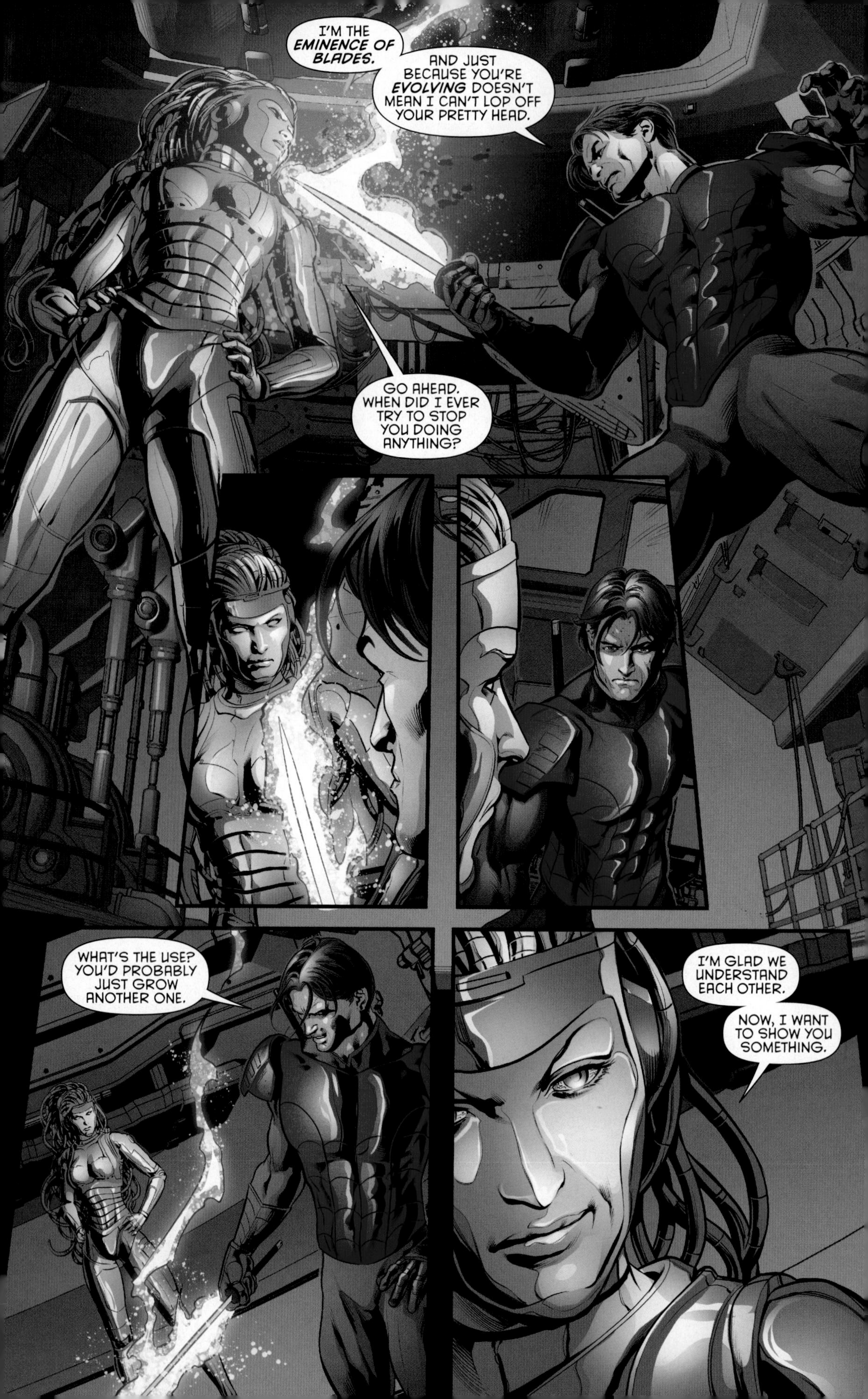
I'M THE *EMINENCE OF BLADES.*
AND JUST BECAUSE YOU'RE *EVOLVING* DOESN'T MEAN I CAN'T LOP OFF YOUR PRETTY HEAD.
GO AHEAD. WHEN DID I EVER TRY TO STOP YOU DOING ANYTHING?
WHAT'S THE USE? YOU'D PROBABLY JUST GROW ANOTHER ONE.
I'M GLAD WE UNDERSTAND EACH OTHER.
NOW, I WANT TO SHOW YOU SOMETHING.

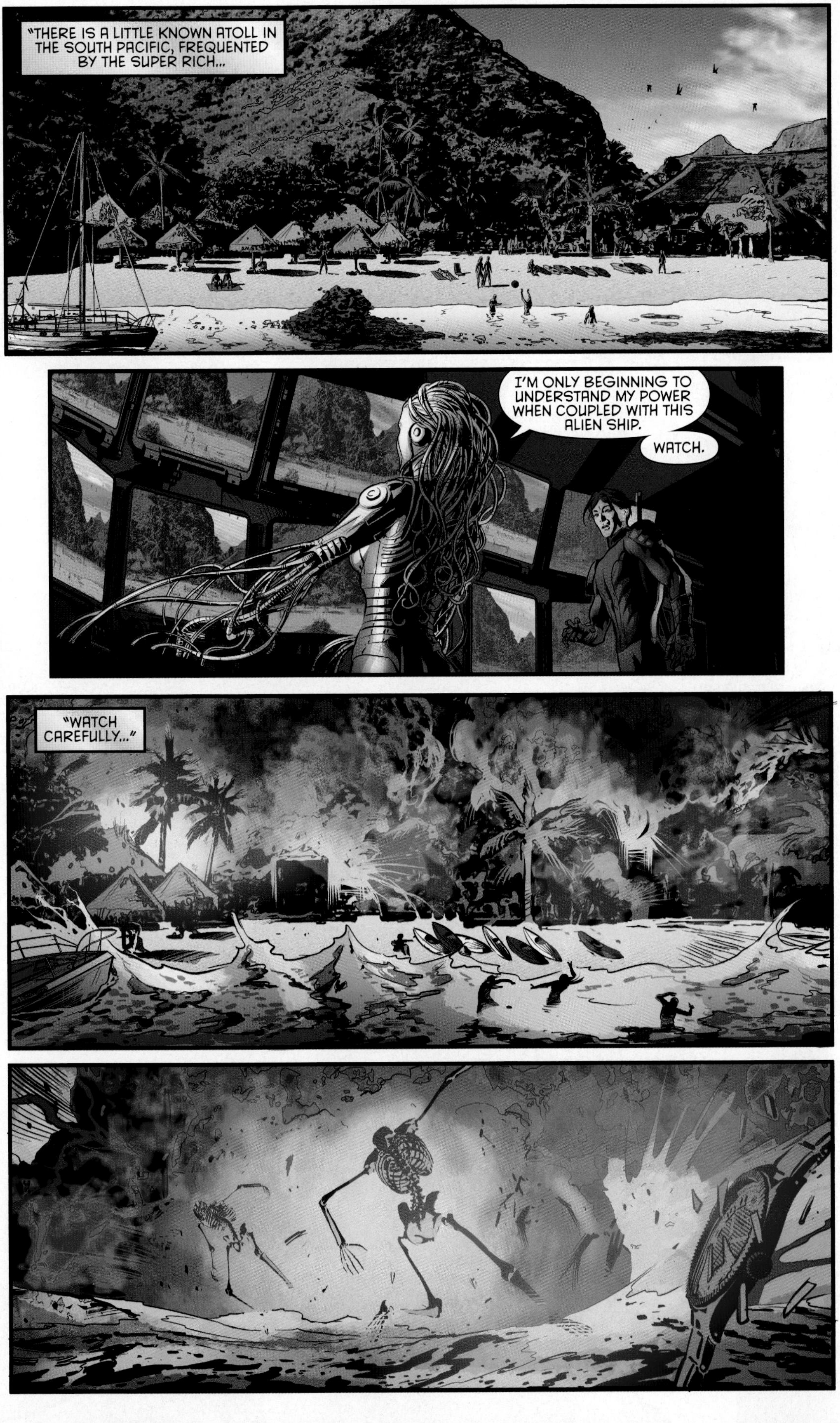
"THERE IS A LITTLE KNOWN ATOLL IN THE SOUTH PACIFIC, FREQUENTED BY THE SUPER RICH...
I'M ONLY BEGINNING TO UNDERSTAND MY POWER WHEN COUPLED WITH THIS ALIEN SHIP.
WATCH.
"WATCH CAREFULLY..."

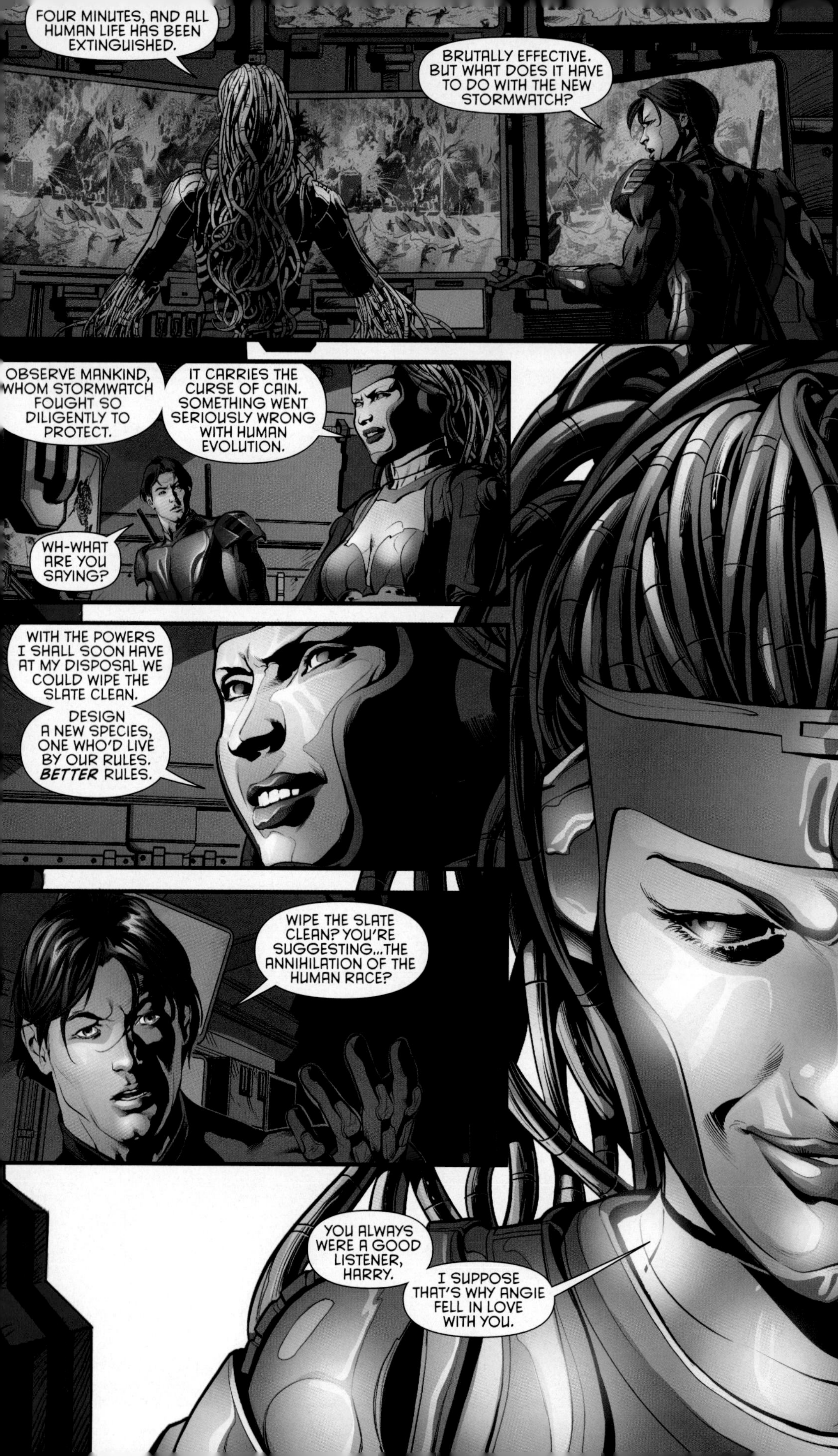
FOUR MINUTES, AND ALL HUMAN LIFE HAS BEEN EXTINGUISHED.
BRUTALLY EFFECTIVE. BUT WHAT DOES IT HAVE TO DO WITH THE NEW STORMWATCH?
OBSERVE MANKIND, WHOM STORMWATCH FOUGHT SO DILIGENTLY TO PROTECT.
IT CARRIES THE CURSE OF CAIN. SOMETHING WENT SERIOUSLY WRONG WITH HUMAN EVOLUTION.
WH-WHAT ARE YOU SAYING?
WITH THE POWERS I SHALL SOON HAVE AT MY DISPOSAL WE COULD WIPE THE SLATE CLEAN.
DESIGN A NEW SPECIES, ONE WHO'D LIVE BY OUR RULES. *BETTER* RULES.
WIPE THE SLATE CLEAN? YOU'RE SUGGESTING...THE ANNIHILATION OF THE HUMAN RACE?
YOU ALWAYS WERE A GOOD LISTENER, HARRY.
I SUPPOSE THAT'S WHY ANGIE FELL IN LOVE WITH YOU.

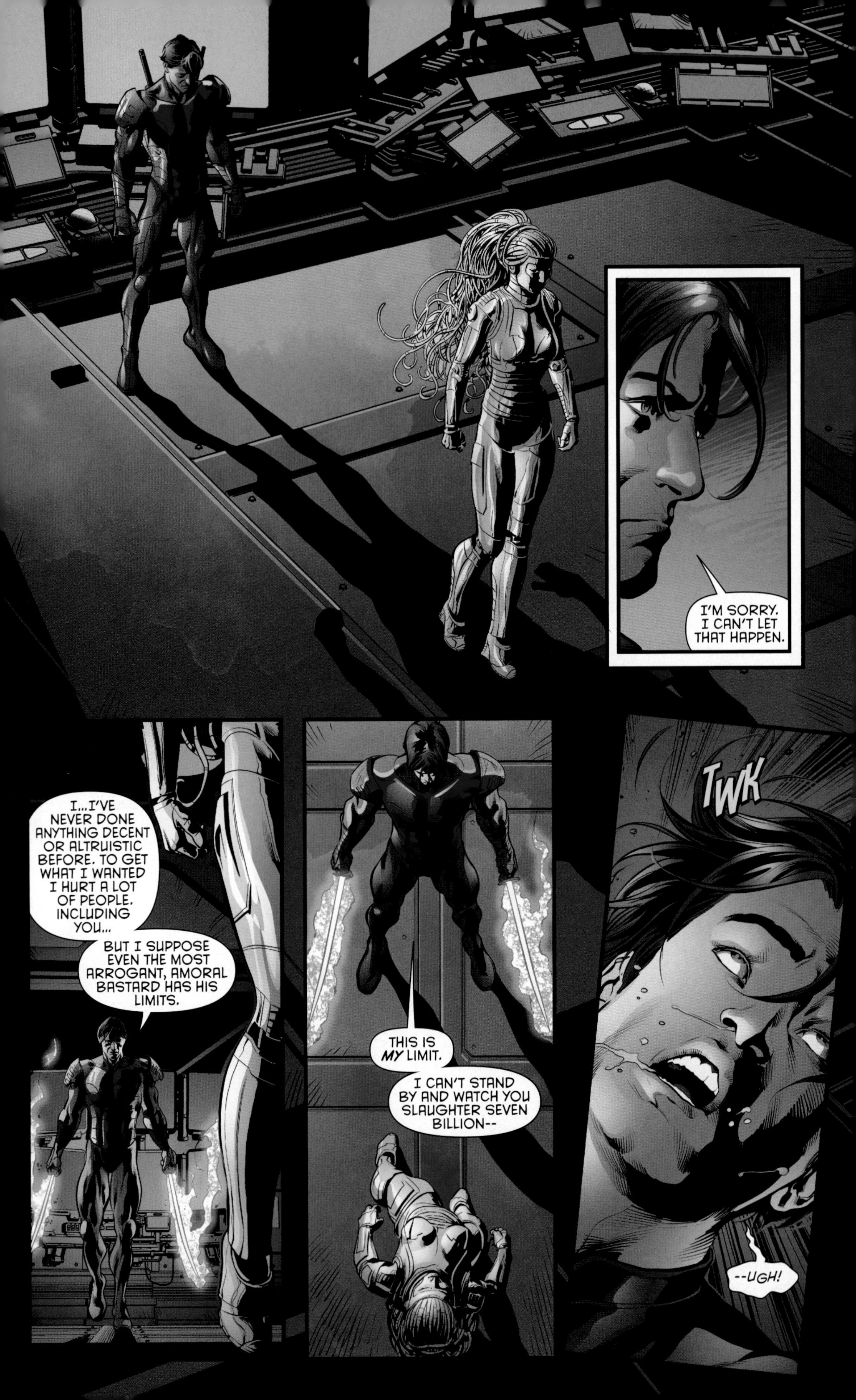
I'M SORRY. I CAN'T LET THAT HAPPEN.
I...I'VE NEVER DONE ANYTHING DECENT OR ALTRUISTIC BEFORE. TO GET WHAT I WANTED I HURT A LOT OF PEOPLE. INCLUDING YOU...
BUT I SUPPOSE EVEN THE MOST ARROGANT, AMORAL BASTARD HAS HIS LIMITS.
THIS IS MY LIMIT.
I CAN'T STAND BY AND WATCH YOU SLAUGHTER SEVEN BILLION--
TWK
--UGH!

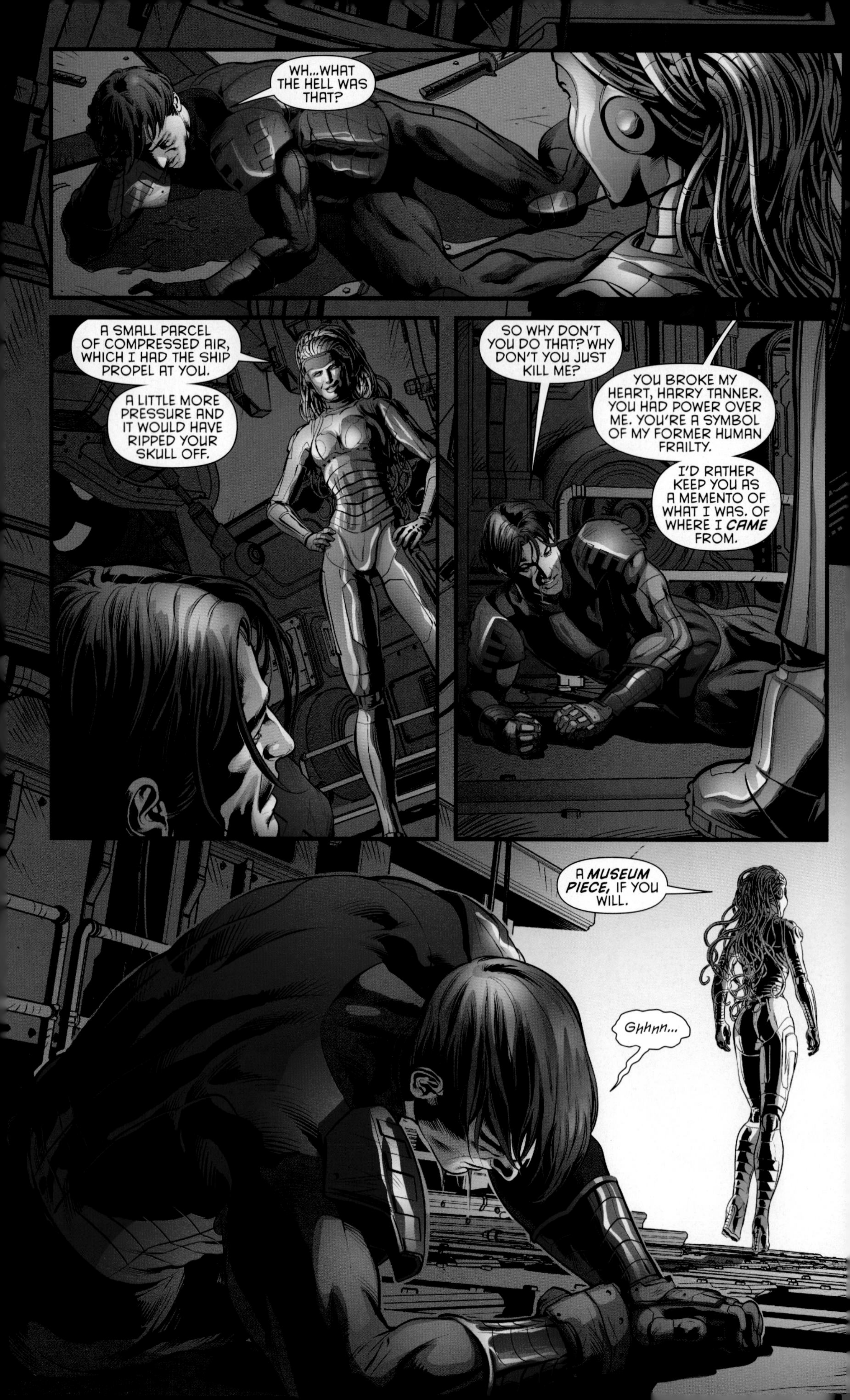
WH...WHAT THE HELL WAS THAT?
A SMALL PARCEL OF COMPRESSED AIR, WHICH I HAD THE SHIP PROPEL AT YOU.
A LITTLE MORE PRESSURE AND IT WOULD HAVE RIPPED YOUR SKULL OFF.
SO WHY DON'T YOU DO THAT? WHY DON'T YOU JUST KILL ME?
YOU BROKE MY HEART, HARRY TANNER. YOU HAD POWER OVER ME. YOU'RE A SYMBOL OF MY FORMER HUMAN FRAILTY.
I'D RATHER KEEP YOU AS A MEMENTO OF WHAT I WAS. OF WHERE I *CAME* FROM.
A ***MUSEUM PIECE,*** IF YOU WILL.
Ghhnn...

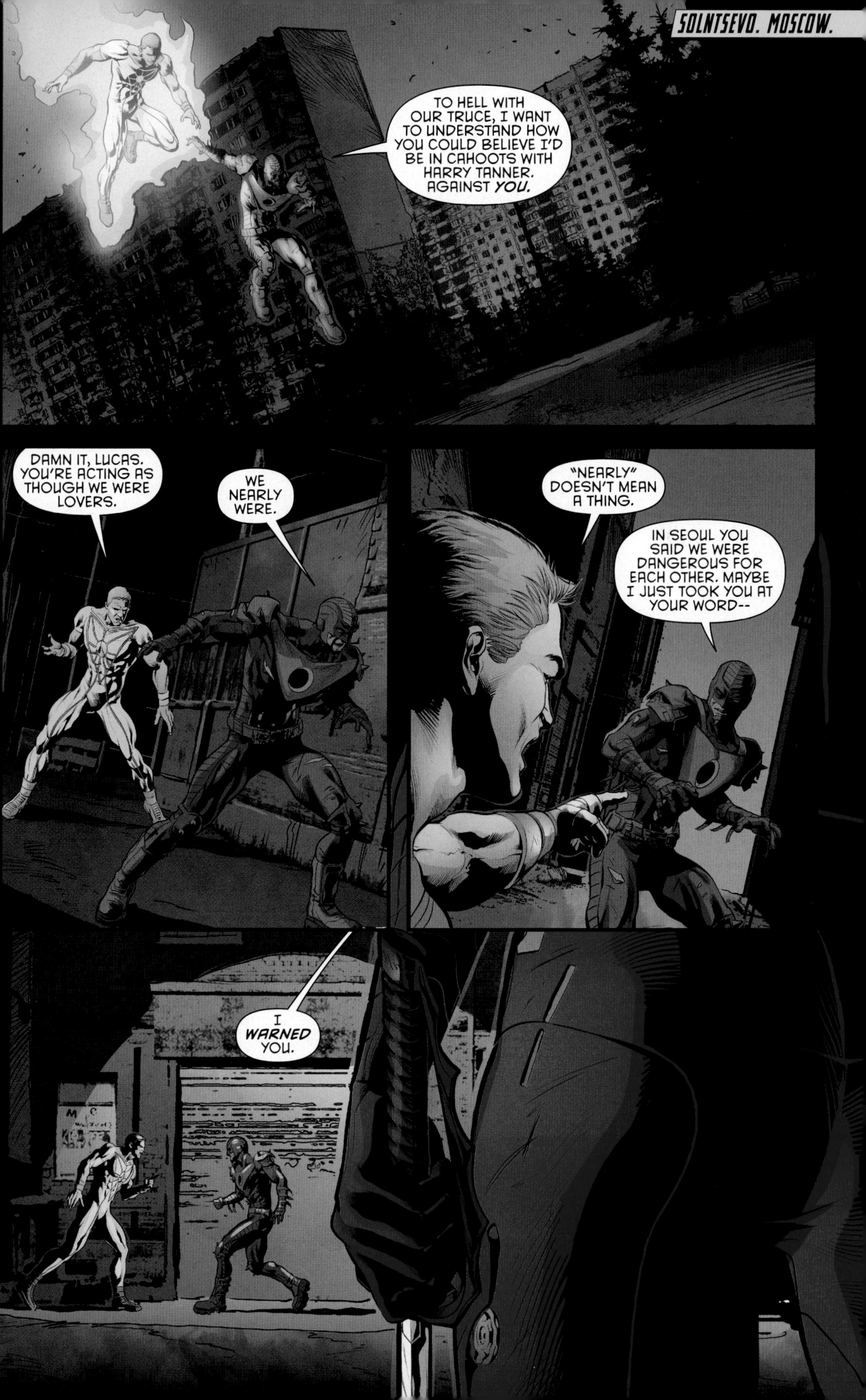
SOLNTSEVO. MOSCOW.
TO HELL WITH OUR TRUCE, I WANT TO UNDERSTAND HOW YOU COULD BELIEVE I'D BE IN CAHOOTS WITH HARRY TANNER. AGAINST *YOU.*
DAMN IT, LUCAS. YOU'RE ACTING AS THOUGH WE WERE LOVERS.
WE NEARLY WERE.
"NEARLY" DOESN'T MEAN A THING.
IN SEOUL YOU SAID WE WERE DANGEROUS FOR EACH OTHER. MAYBE I JUST TOOK YOU AT YOUR WORD--
I *WARNED* YOU.

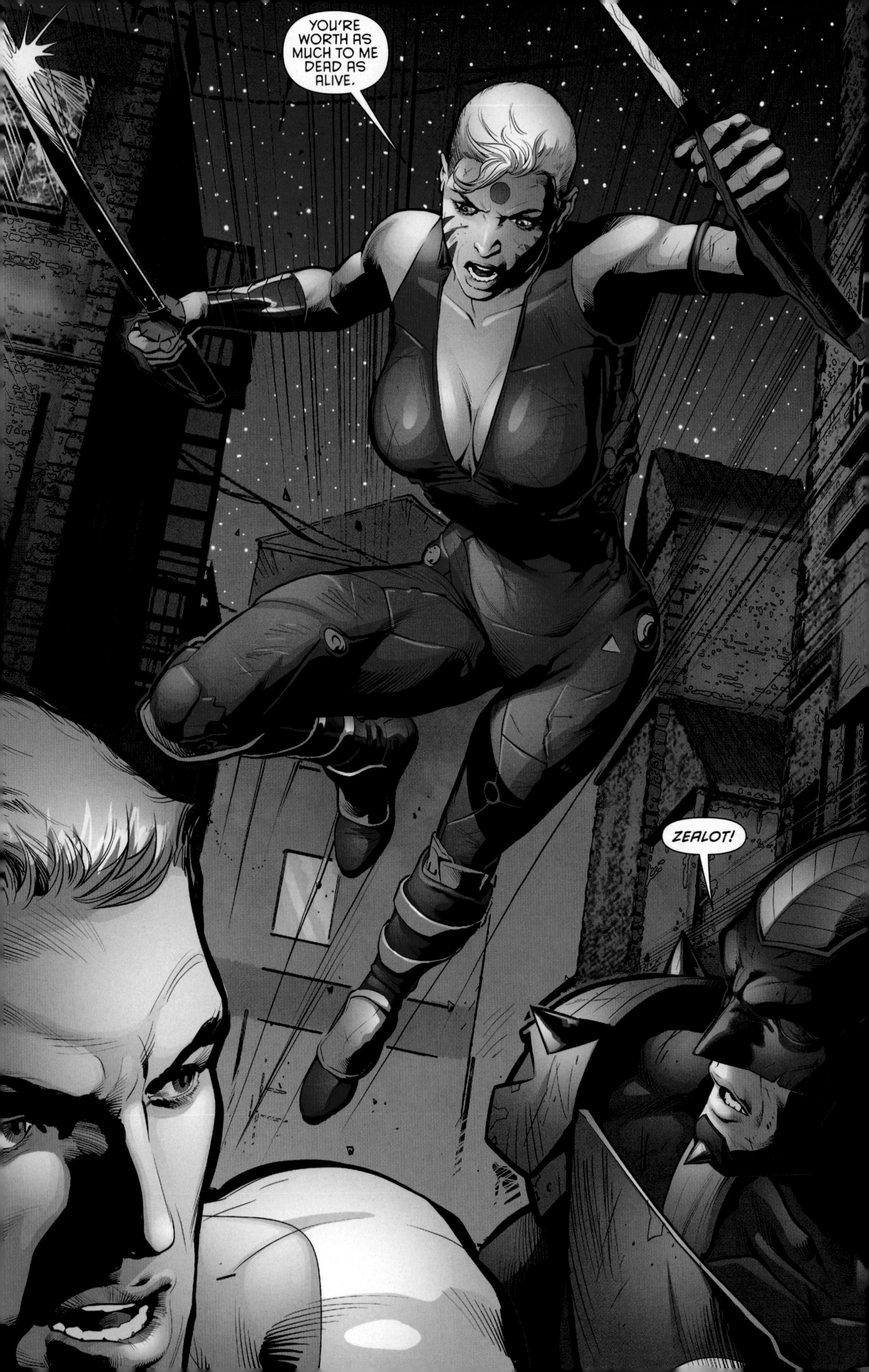
YOU'RE WORTH AS MUCH TO ME DEAD AS ALIVE.
ZEALOT!

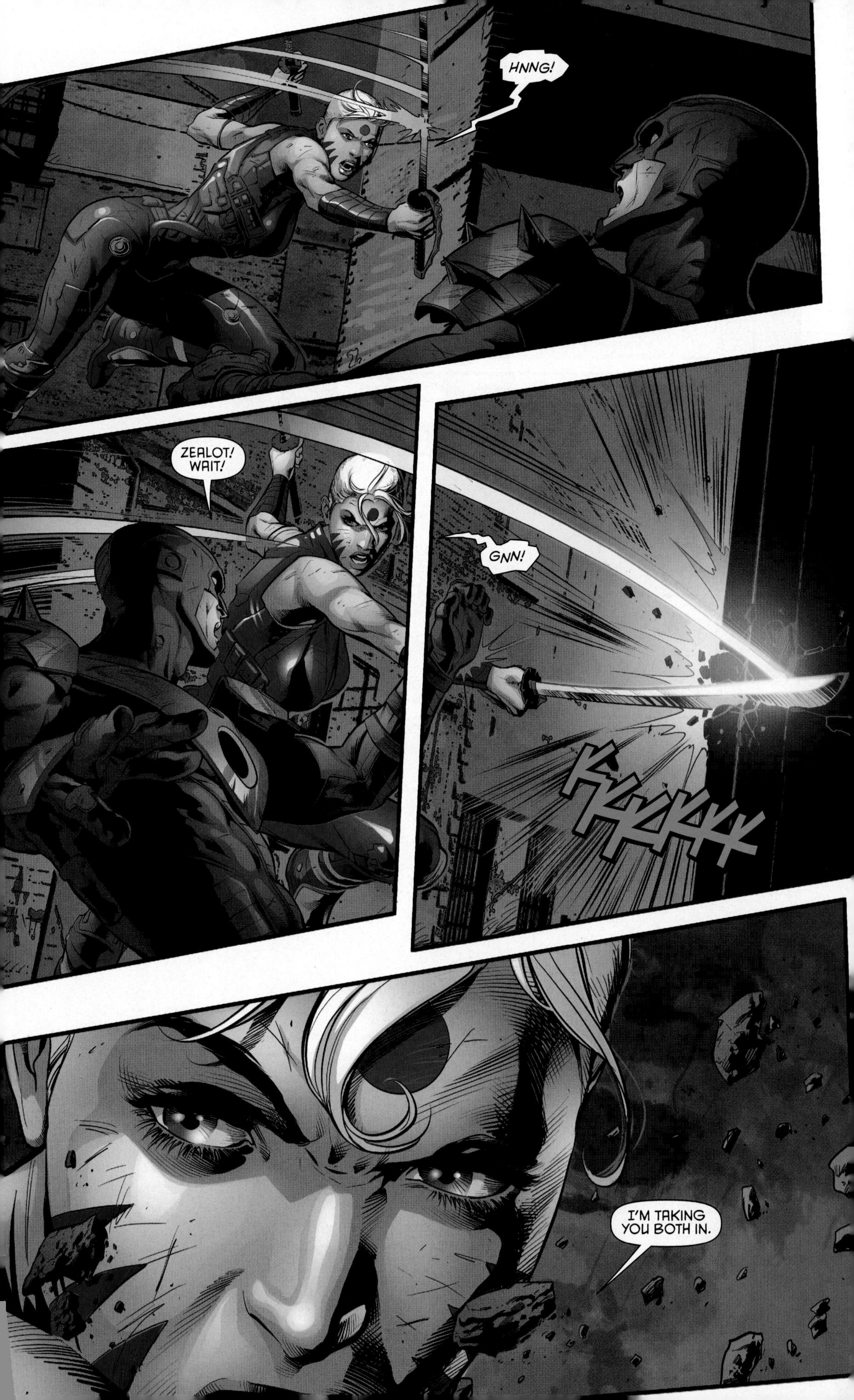
HNNG!
ZEALOT! WAIT!
GNN!
KKKKKKK
I'M TAKING YOU BOTH IN.

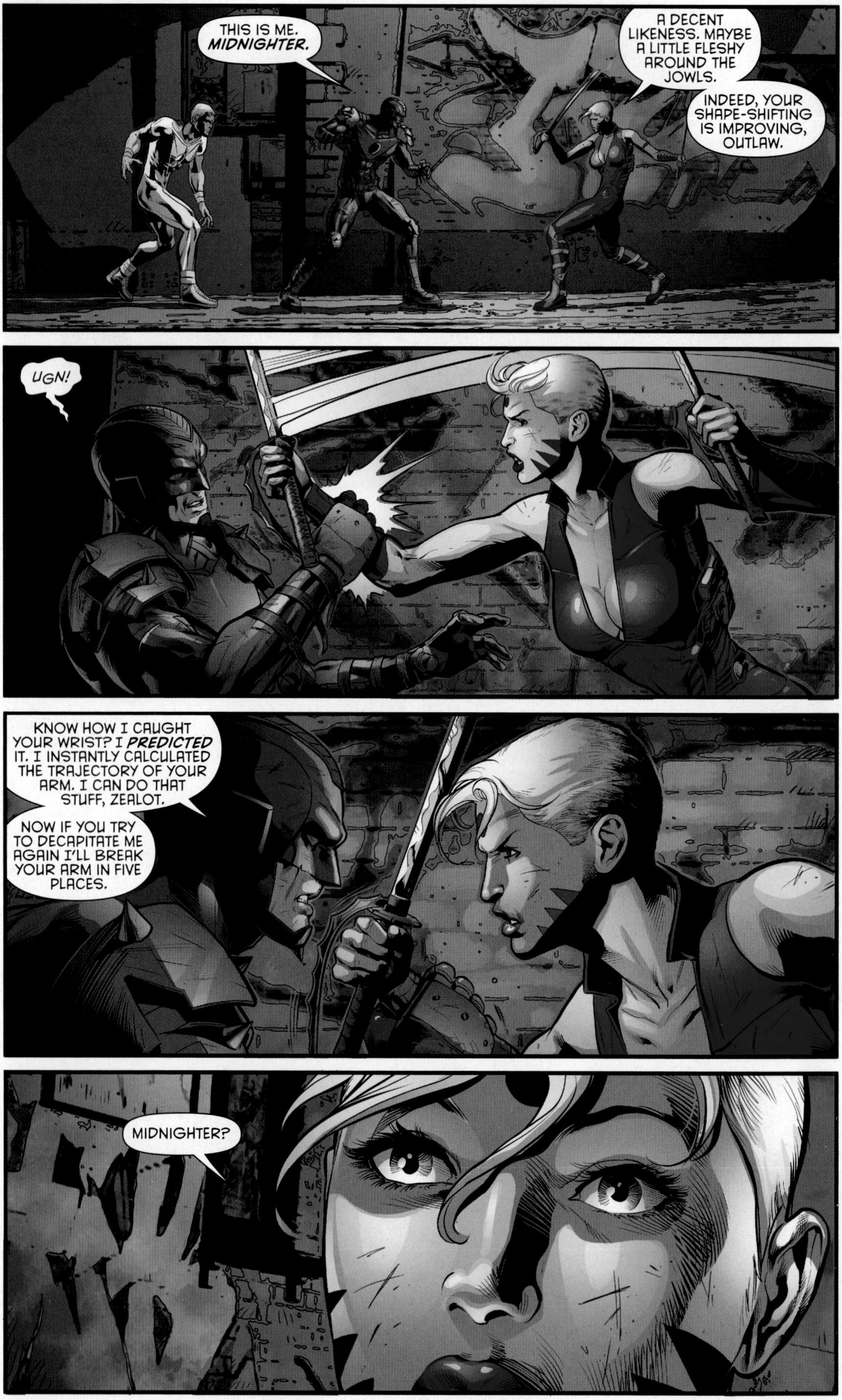
THIS IS ME. *MIDNIGHTER.*
A DECENT LIKENESS. MAYBE A LITTLE FLESHY AROUND THE JOWLS.
INDEED, YOUR SHAPE-SHIFTING IS IMPROVING, OUTLAW.
UGN!
KNOW HOW I CAUGHT YOUR WRIST? I *PREDICTED* IT. I INSTANTLY CALCULATED THE TRAJECTORY OF YOUR ARM. I CAN DO THAT STUFF, ZEALOT.
NOW IF YOU TRY TO DECAPITATE ME AGAIN I'LL BREAK YOUR ARM IN FIVE PLACES.
MIDNIGHTER?

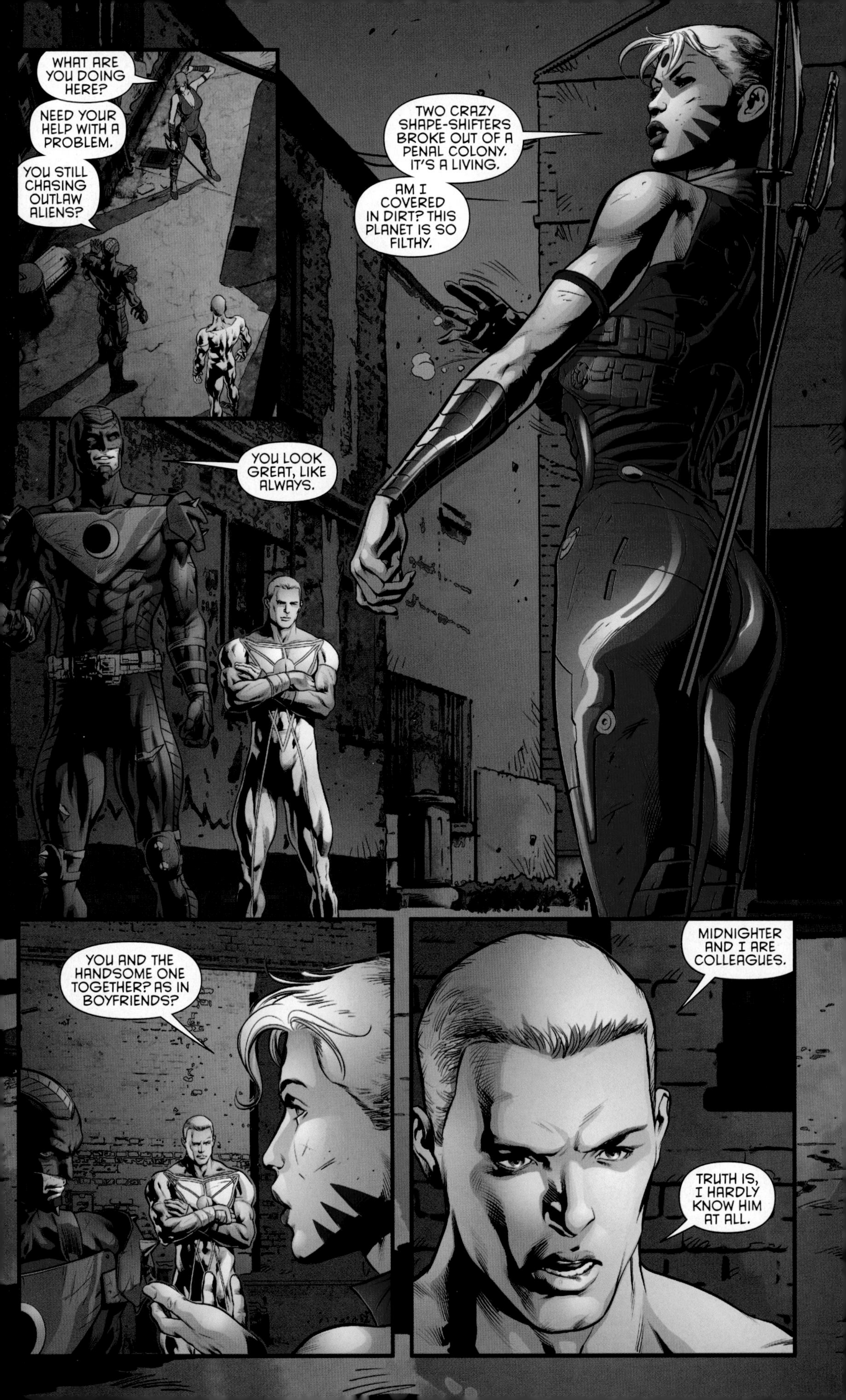
WHAT ARE YOU DOING HERE?
NEED YOUR HELP WITH A PROBLEM.
YOU STILL CHASING OUTLAW ALIENS?
TWO CRAZY SHAPE-SHIFTERS BROKE OUT OF A PENAL COLONY. IT'S A LIVING.
AM I COVERED IN DIRT? THIS PLANET IS SO FILTHY.
YOU LOOK GREAT, LIKE ALWAYS.
YOU AND THE HANDSOME ONE TOGETHER? AS IN BOYFRIENDS?
MIDNIGHTER AND I ARE COLLEAGUES.
TRUTH IS, I HARDLY KNOW HIM AT ALL.

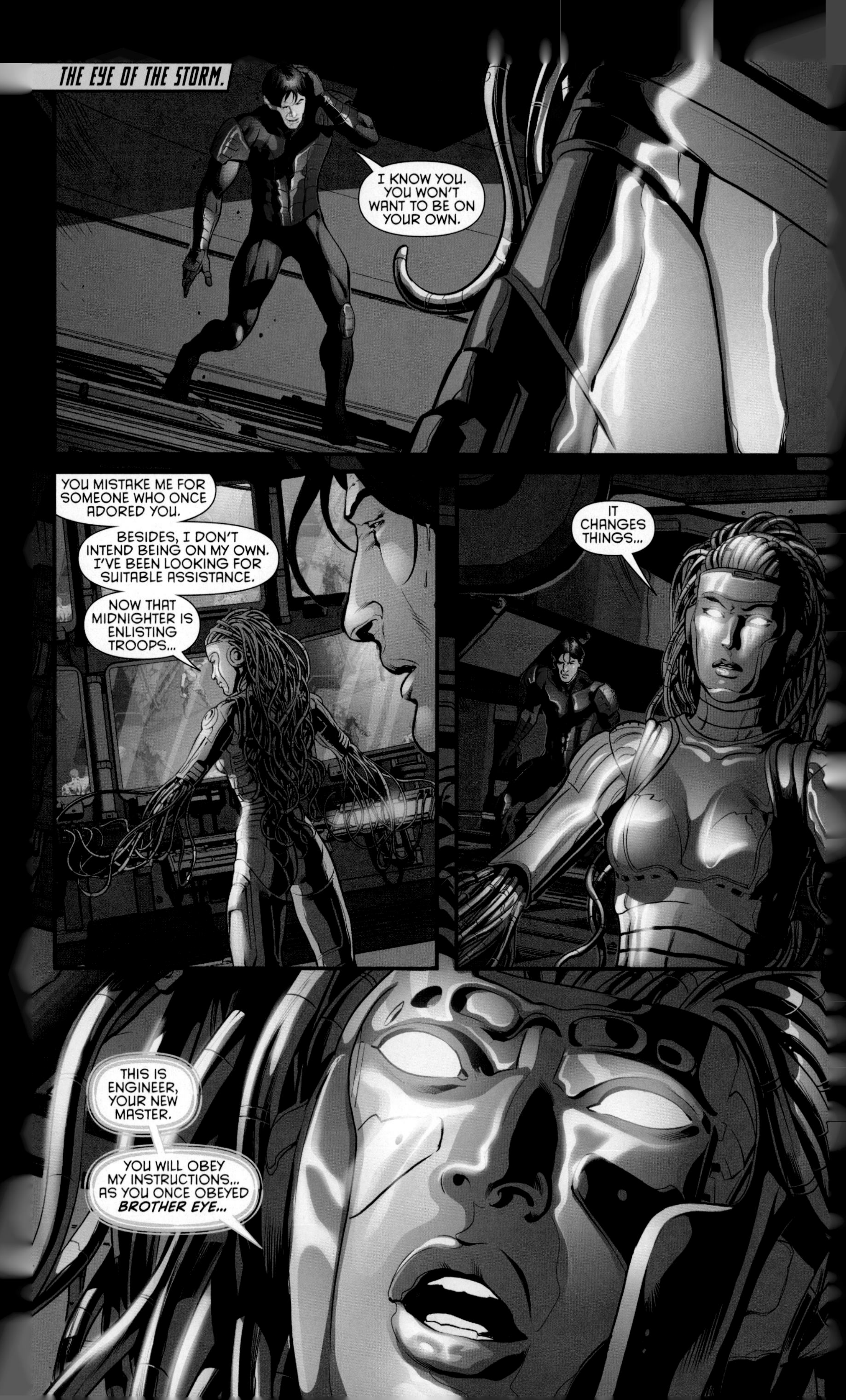
THE EYE OF THE STORM.
I KNOW YOU. YOU WON'T WANT TO BE ON YOUR OWN.
YOU MISTAKE ME FOR SOMEONE WHO ONCE ADORED YOU.
BESIDES, I DON'T INTEND BEING ON MY OWN. I'VE BEEN LOOKING FOR SUITABLE ASSISTANCE.
NOW THAT MIDNIGHTER IS ENLISTING TROOPS...
IT CHANGES THINGS...
THIS IS ENGINEER, YOUR NEW MASTER.
YOU WILL OBEY MY INSTRUCTIONS... AS YOU ONCE OBEYED *BROTHER EYE*...

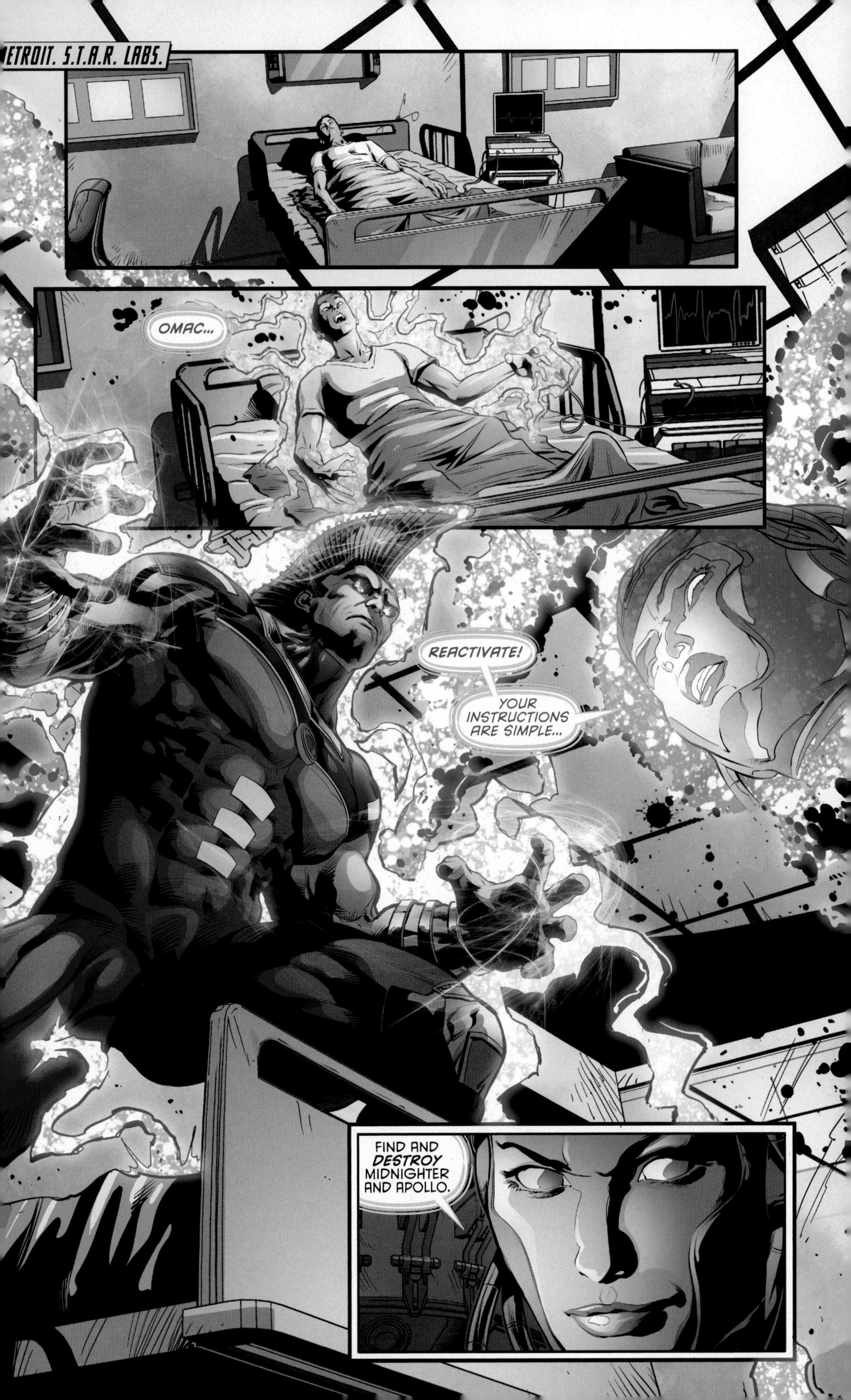
ETROIT. S.T.A.R. LABS.
OMAC...
REACTIVATE!
YOUR INSTRUCTIONS ARE SIMPLE...
FIND AND DESTROY MIDNIGHTER AND APOLLO.

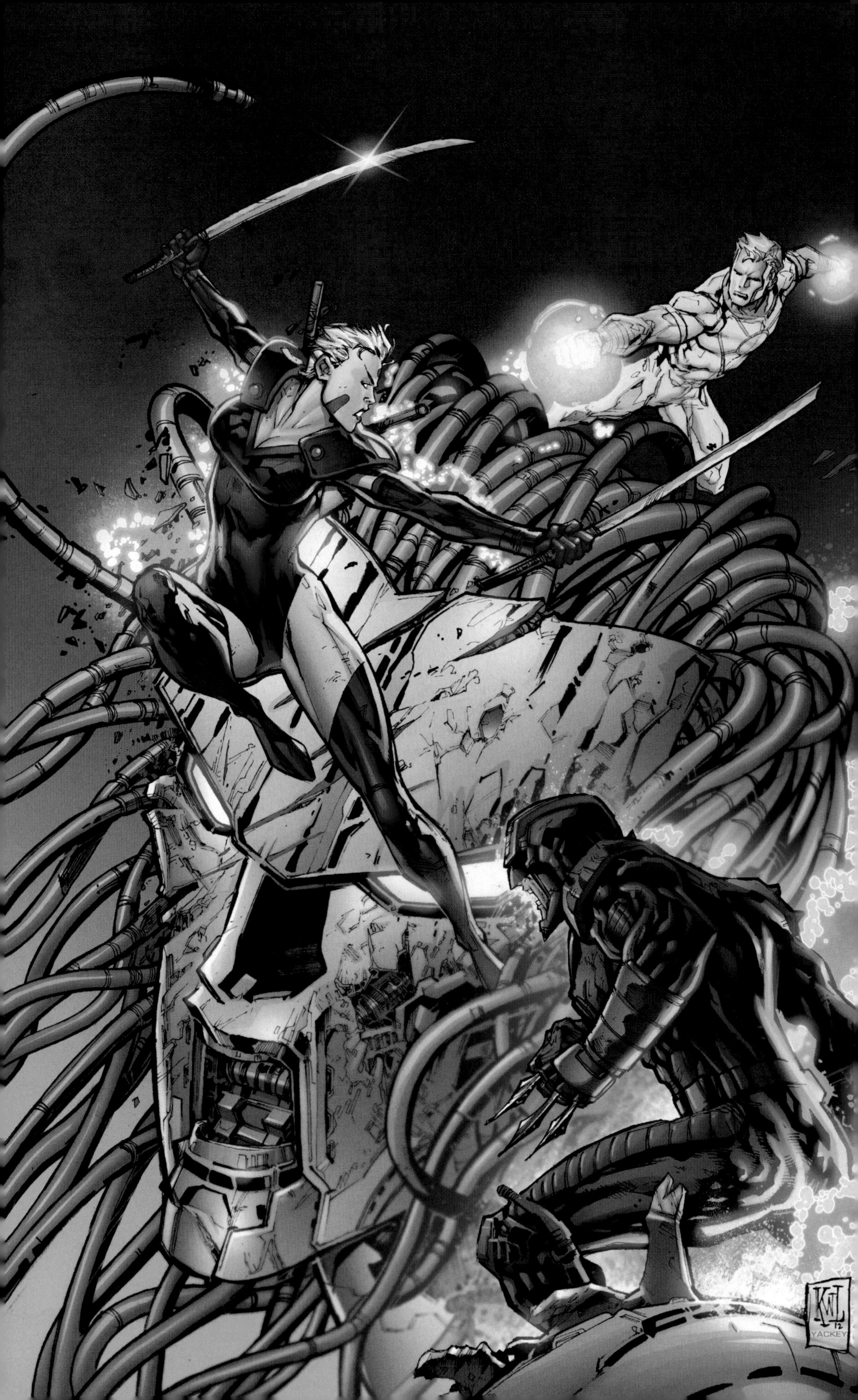
YACKEY

THE SCREAM

PETER MILLIGAN writer **WILL CONRAD** artist cover art by **KEN LASHLEY & MATT YACKEY**

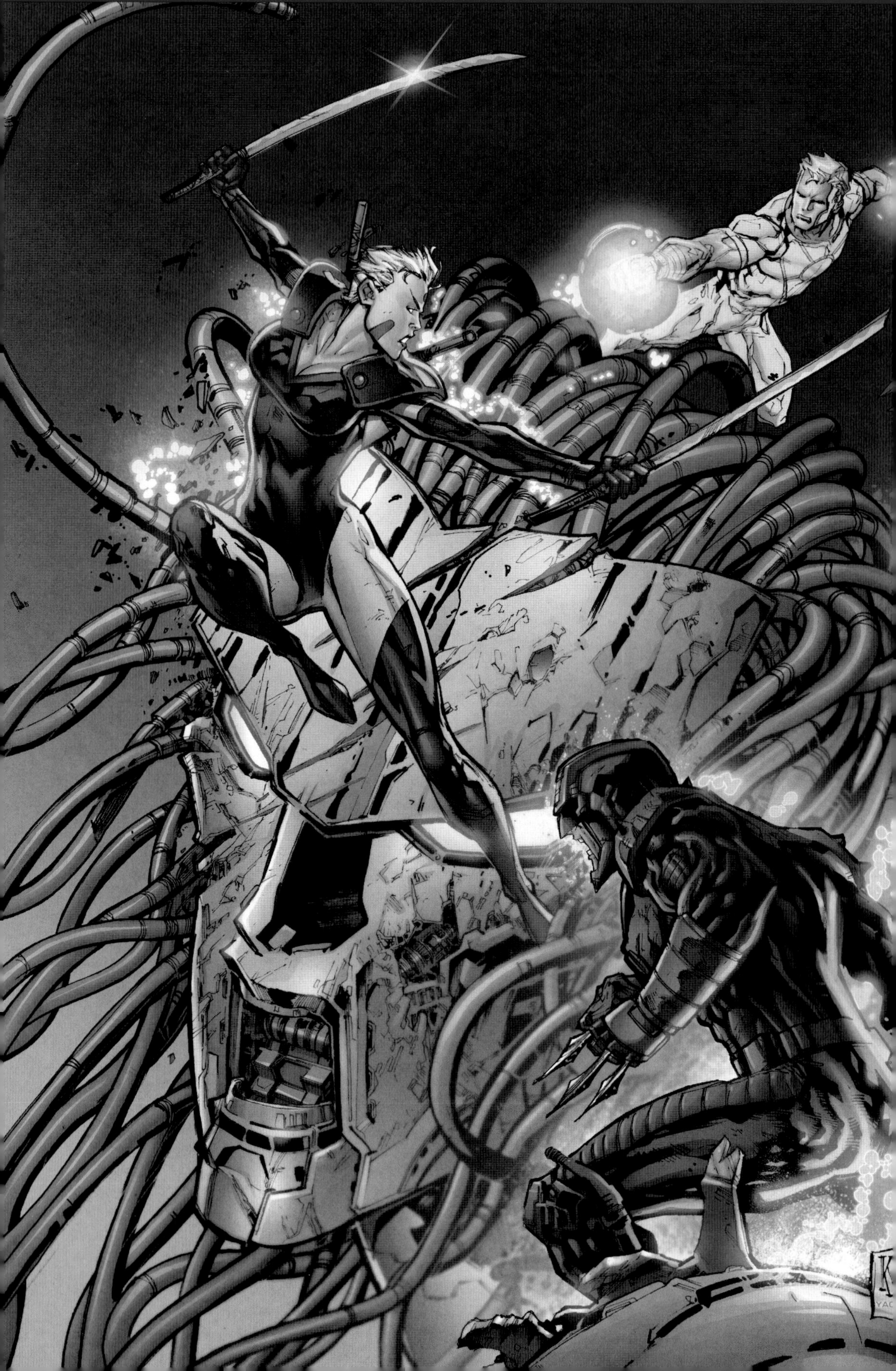

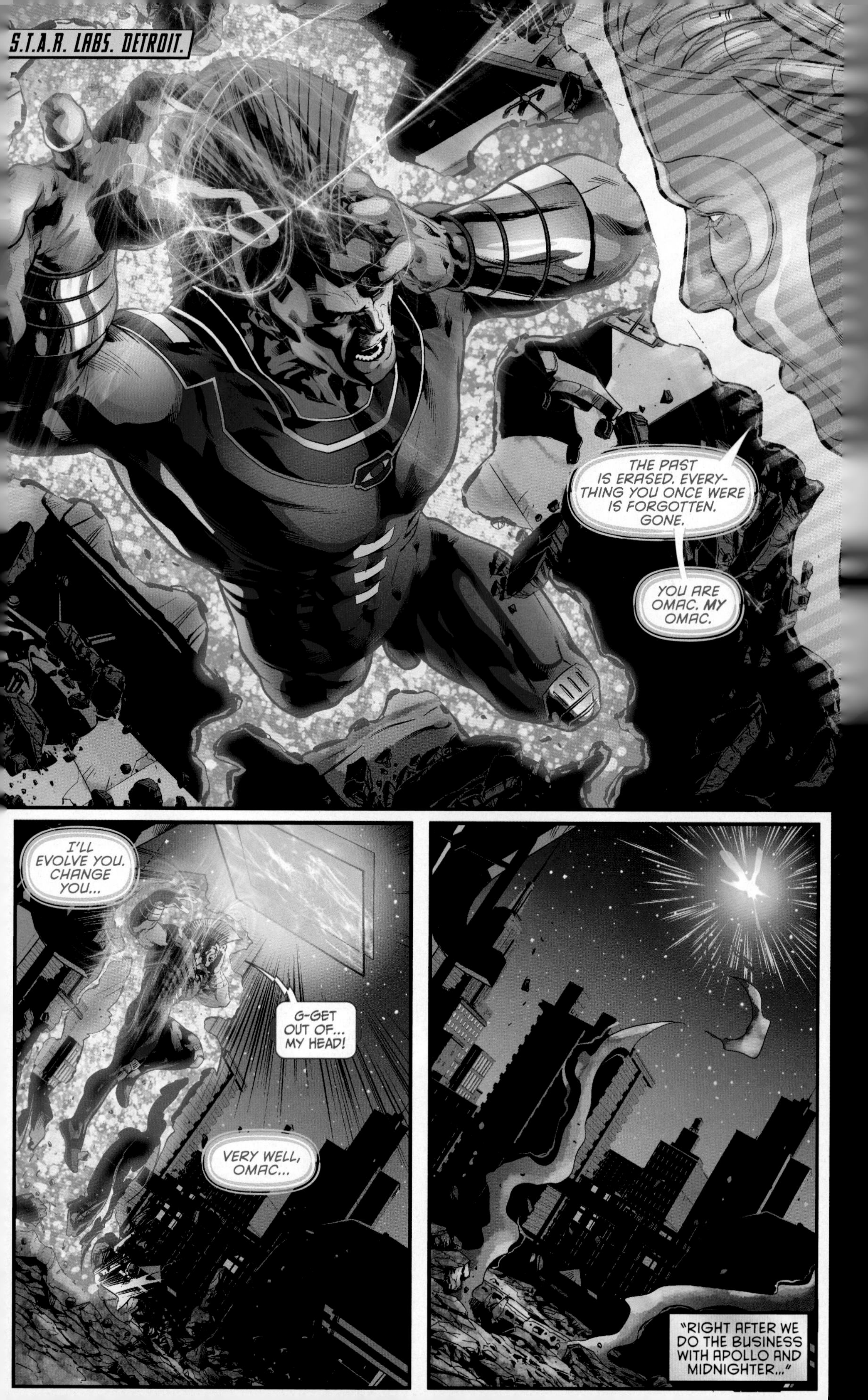
S.T.A.R. LABS. DETROIT.
THE PAST IS ERASED. EVERYTHING YOU ONCE WERE IS FORGOTTEN. GONE.
YOU ARE OMAC. MY OMAC.
I'LL EVOLVE YOU. CHANGE YOU...
G-GET OUT OF... MY HEAD!
VERY WELL, OMAC...
"RIGHT AFTER WE DO THE BUSINESS WITH APOLLO AND MIDNIGHTER..."

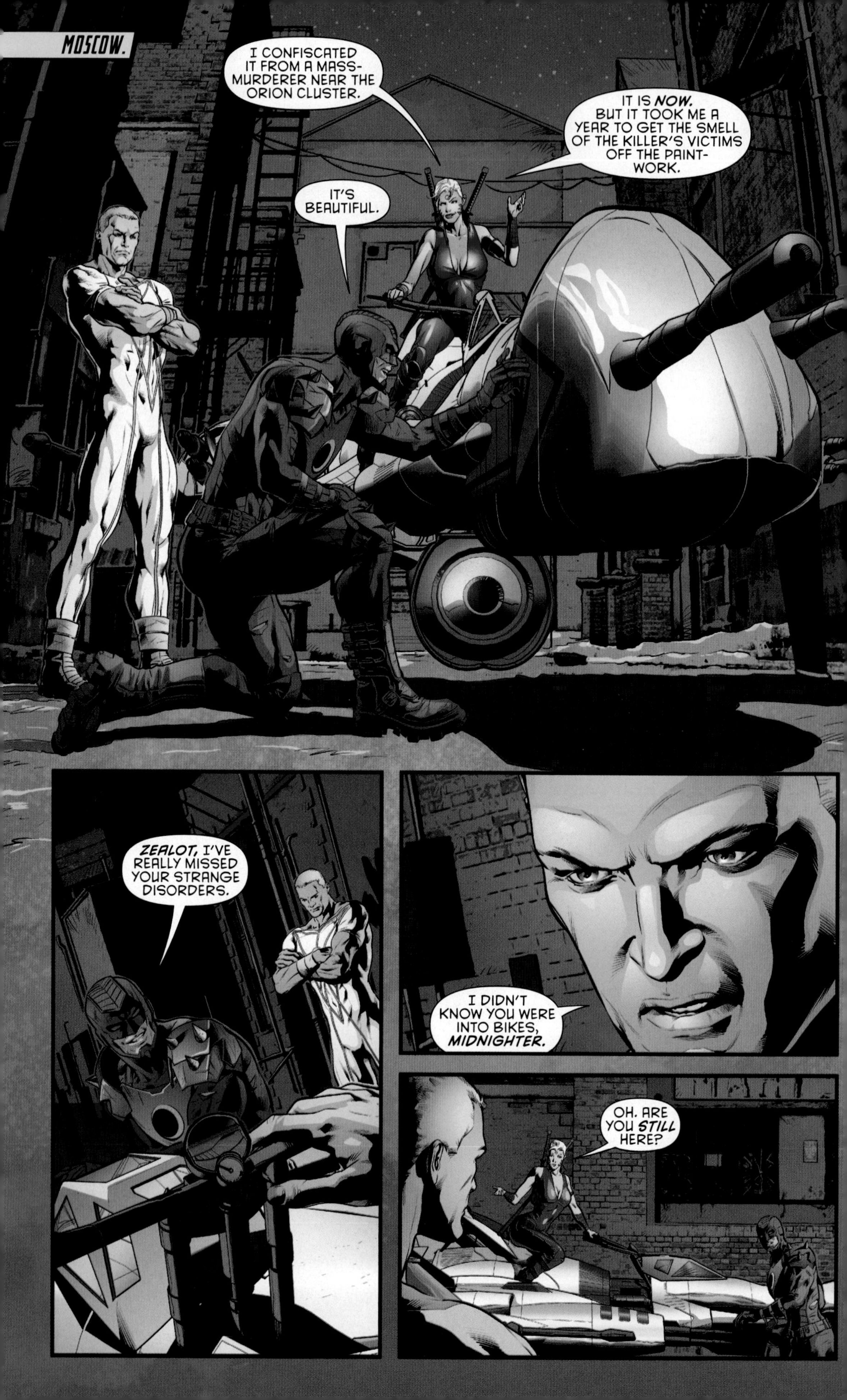
MOSCOW.
I CONFISCATED IT FROM A MASS-MURDERER NEAR THE ORION CLUSTER.
IT'S BEAUTIFUL.
IT IS NOW. BUT IT TOOK ME A YEAR TO GET THE SMELL OF THE KILLER'S VICTIMS OFF THE PAINT-WORK.
ZEALOT, I'VE REALLY MISSED YOUR STRANGE DISORDERS.
I DIDN'T KNOW YOU WERE INTO BIKES, MIDNIGHTER.
OH. ARE YOU STILL HERE?

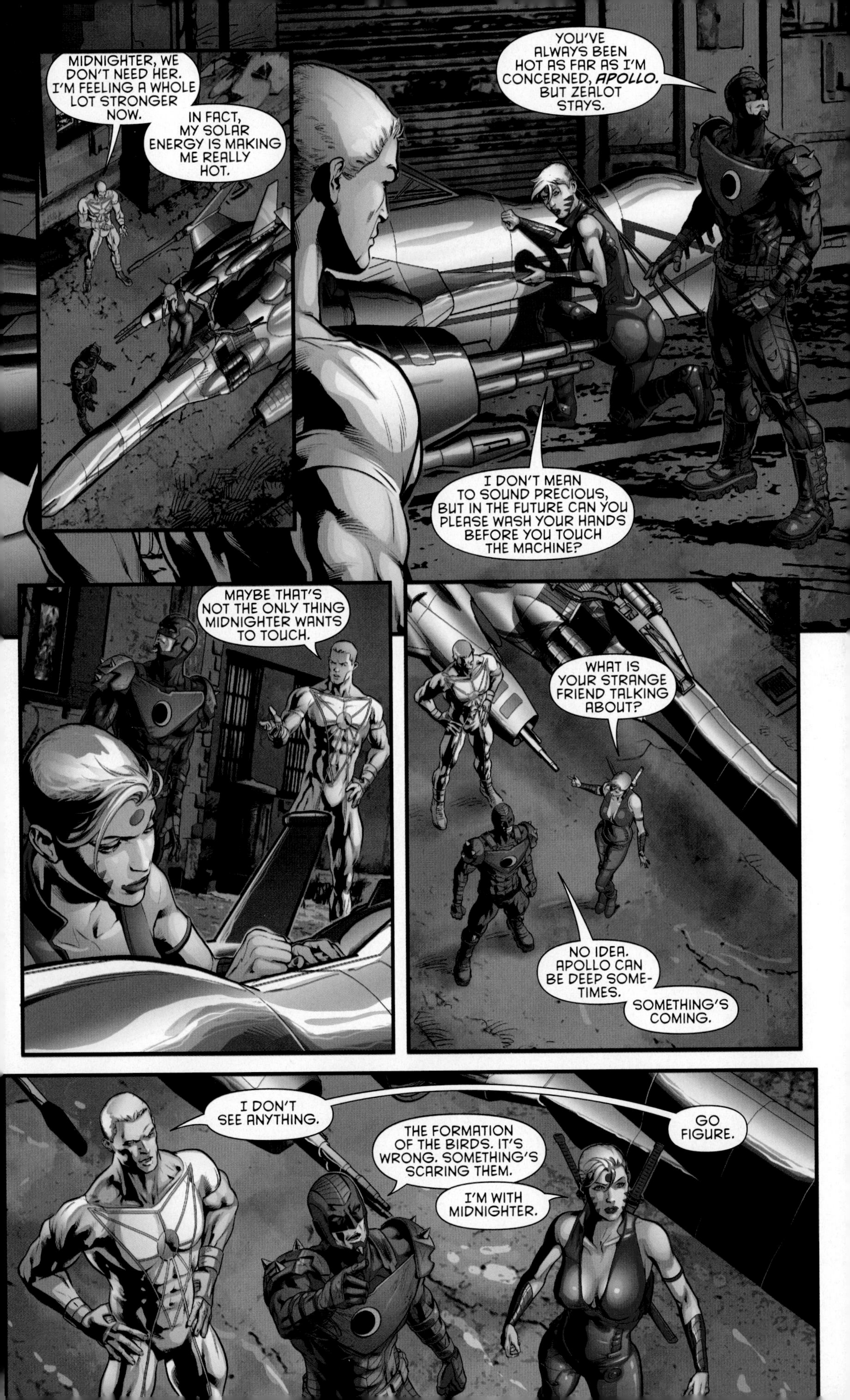
MIDNIGHTER, WE DON'T NEED HER. I'M FEELING A WHOLE LOT STRONGER NOW.
IN FACT, MY SOLAR ENERGY IS MAKING ME REALLY HOT.
YOU'VE ALWAYS BEEN HOT AS FAR AS I'M CONCERNED, APOLLO. BUT ZEALOT STAYS.
I DON'T MEAN TO SOUND PRECIOUS, BUT IN THE FUTURE CAN YOU PLEASE WASH YOUR HANDS BEFORE YOU TOUCH THE MACHINE?
MAYBE THAT'S NOT THE ONLY THING MIDNIGHTER WANTS TO TOUCH.
WHAT IS YOUR STRANGE FRIEND TALKING ABOUT?
NO IDEA. APOLLO CAN BE DEEP SOME-TIMES.
SOMETHING'S COMING.
I DON'T SEE ANYTHING.
GO FIGURE.
THE FORMATION OF THE BIRDS. IT'S WRONG. SOMETHING'S SCARING THEM.
I'M WITH MIDNIGHTER.

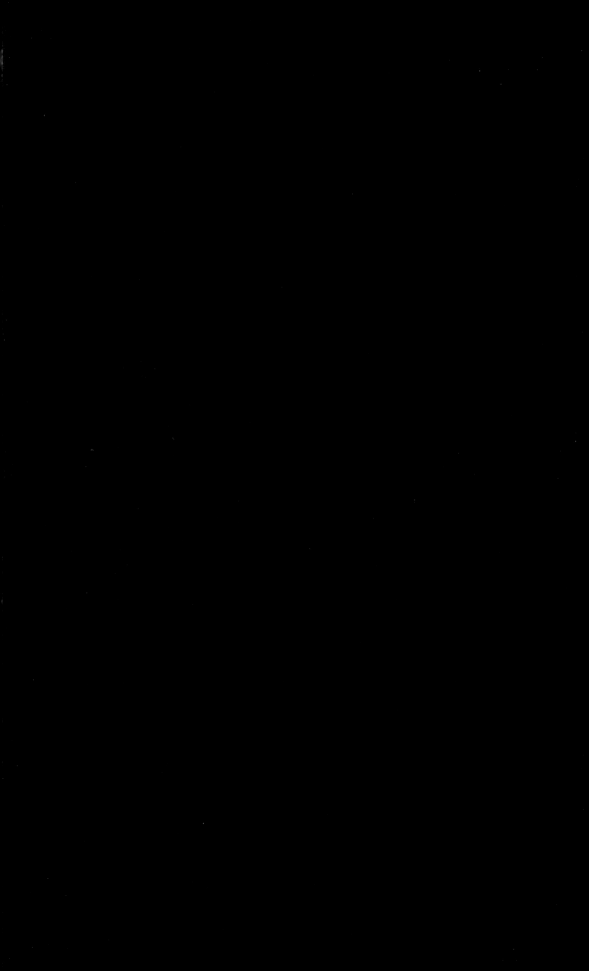

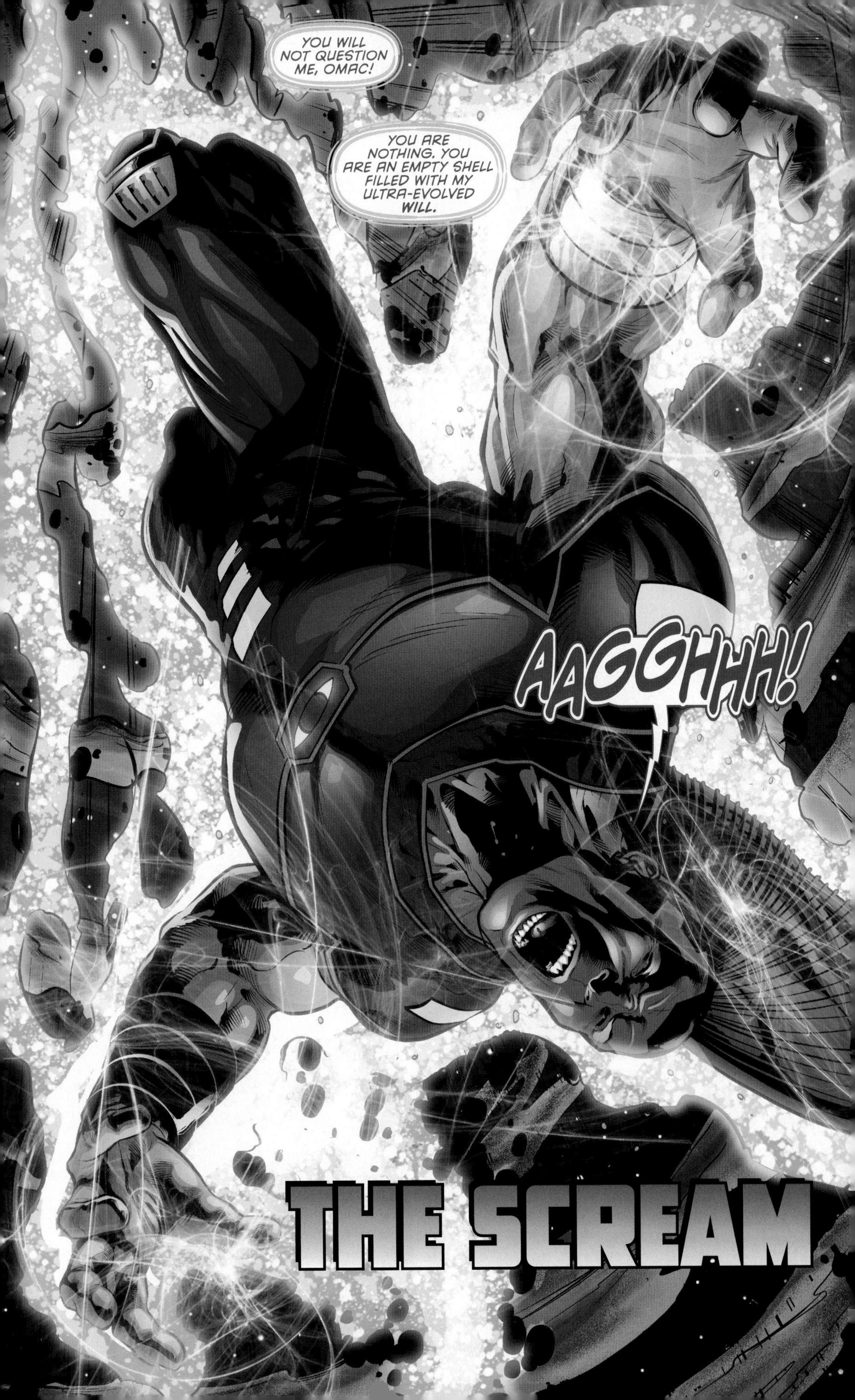
YOU WILL NOT QUESTION ME, OMAC!
YOU ARE NOTHING. YOU ARE AN EMPTY SHELL FILLED WITH MY ULTRA-EVOLVED WILL.
AAGGHHH!
THE SCREAM

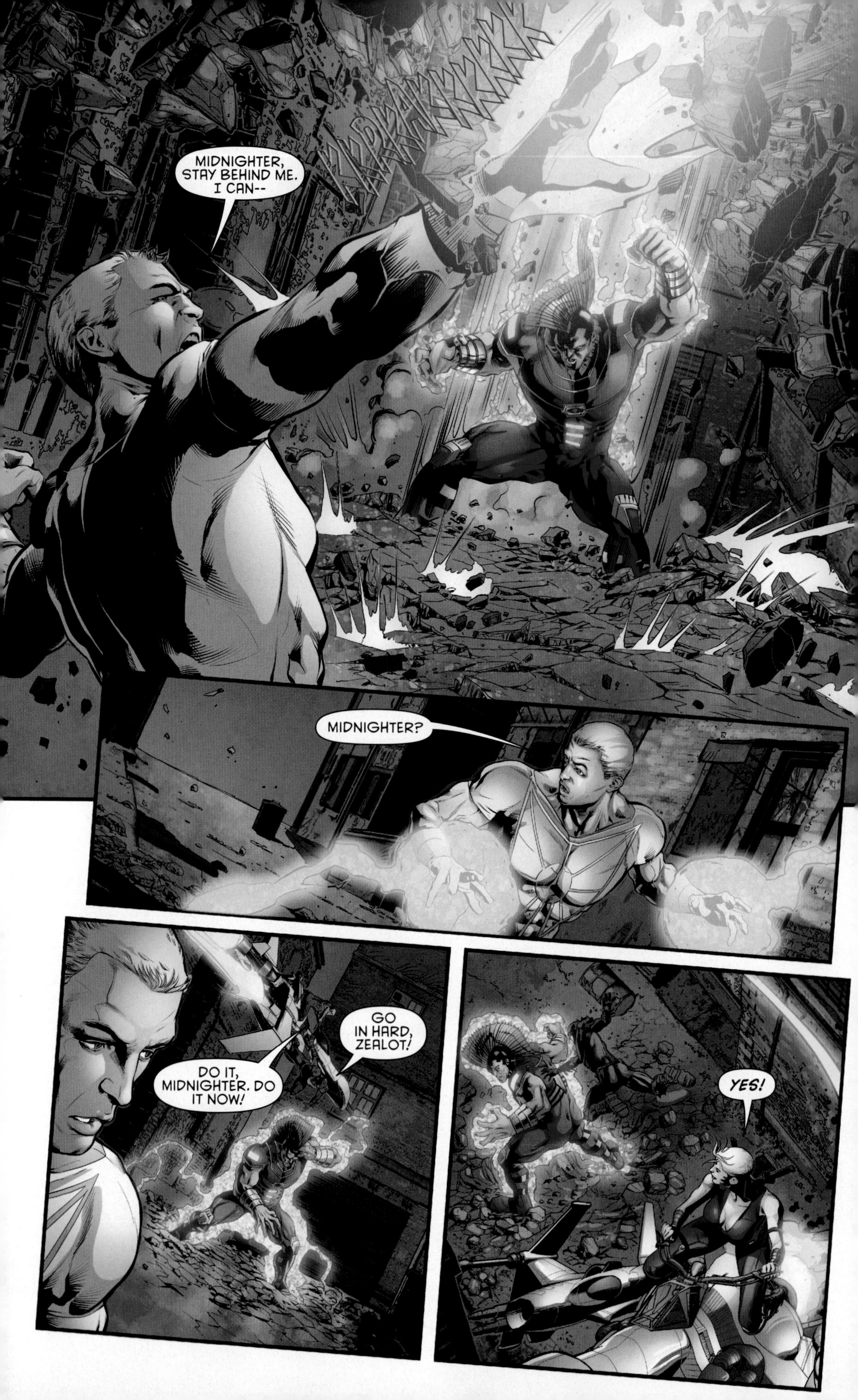
MIDNIGHTER, STAY BEHIND ME. I CAN--
MIDNIGHTER?
DO IT, MIDNIGHTER. DO IT NOW!
GO IN HARD, ZEALOT!
YES!

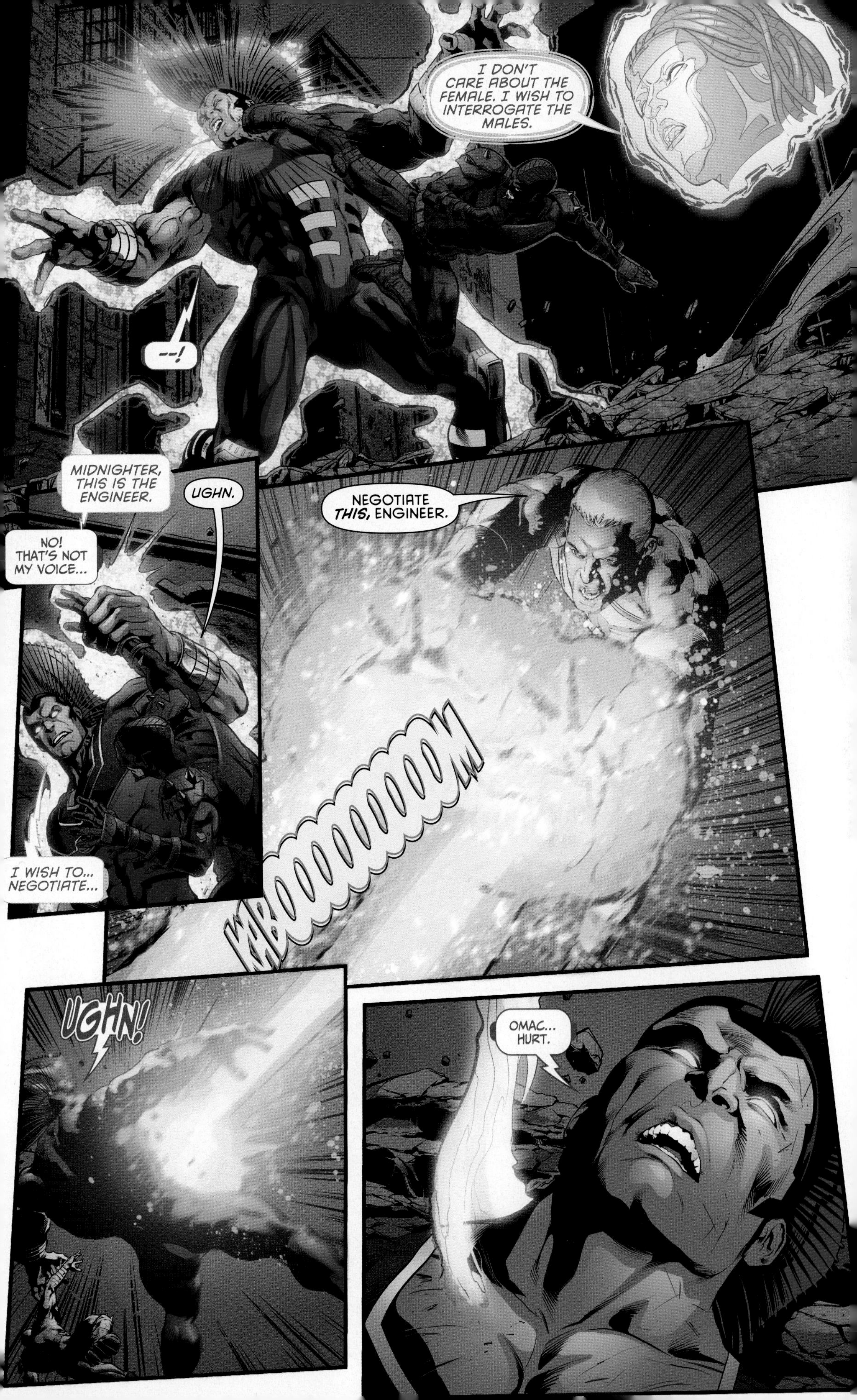
I DON'T CARE ABOUT THE FEMALE. I WISH TO INTERROGATE THE MALES.
--!
MIDNIGHTER, THIS IS THE ENGINEER.
NO! THAT'S NOT MY VOICE...
UGHN.
I WISH TO... NEGOTIATE...
NEGOTIATE *THIS,* ENGINEER.
KABOOOOOOOOOM
UGHN!
OMAC... HURT.

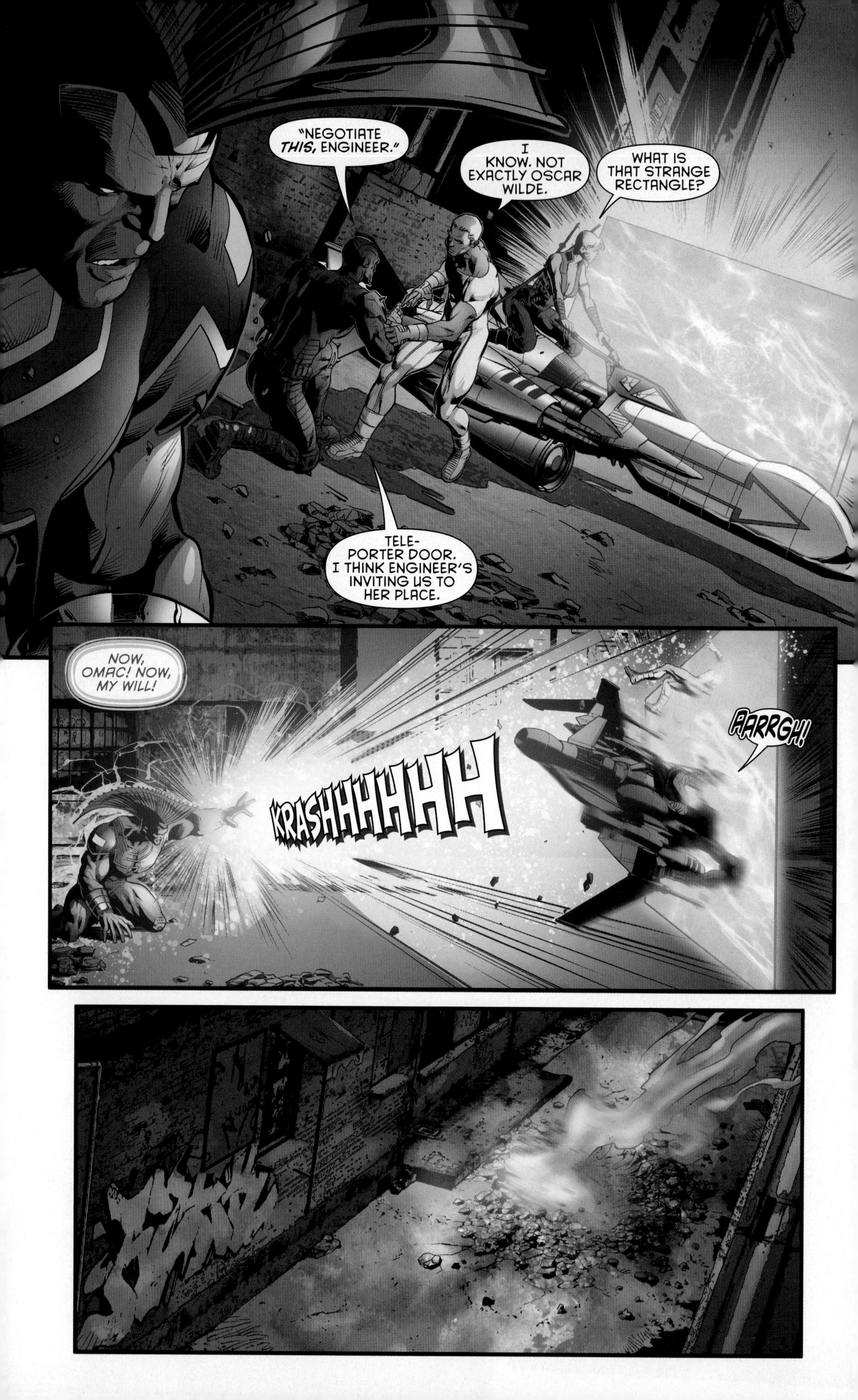
"NEGOTIATE THIS, ENGINEER."
I KNOW. NOT EXACTLY OSCAR WILDE.
WHAT IS THAT STRANGE RECTANGLE?
TELE-PORTER DOOR. I THINK ENGINEER'S INVITING US TO HER PLACE.
NOW, OMAC! NOW, MY WILL!
KRASHHHHHHH
AARRGH!

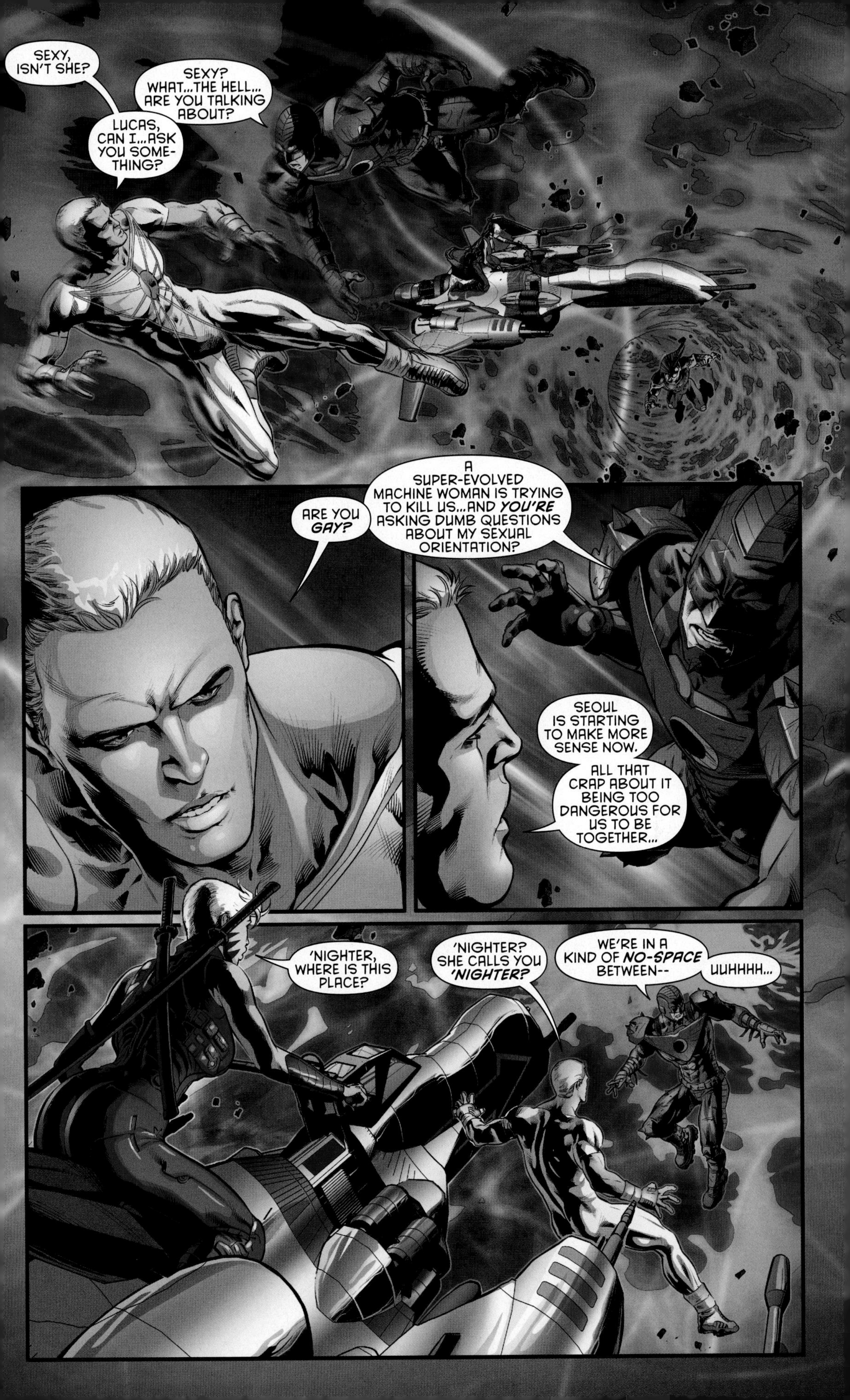
SEXY, ISN'T SHE?
SEXY? WHAT...THE HELL... ARE YOU TALKING ABOUT?
LUCAS, CAN I...ASK YOU SOME-THING?
ARE YOU GAY?
A SUPER-EVOLVED MACHINE WOMAN IS TRYING TO KILL US...AND YOU'RE ASKING DUMB QUESTIONS ABOUT MY SEXUAL ORIENTATION?
SEOUL IS STARTING TO MAKE MORE SENSE NOW.
ALL THAT CRAP ABOUT IT BEING TOO DANGEROUS FOR US TO BE TOGETHER...
'NIGHTER, WHERE IS THIS PLACE?
'NIGHTER? SHE CALLS YOU 'NIGHTER?
WE'RE IN A KIND OF NO-SPACE BETWEEN--
UUHHHH...

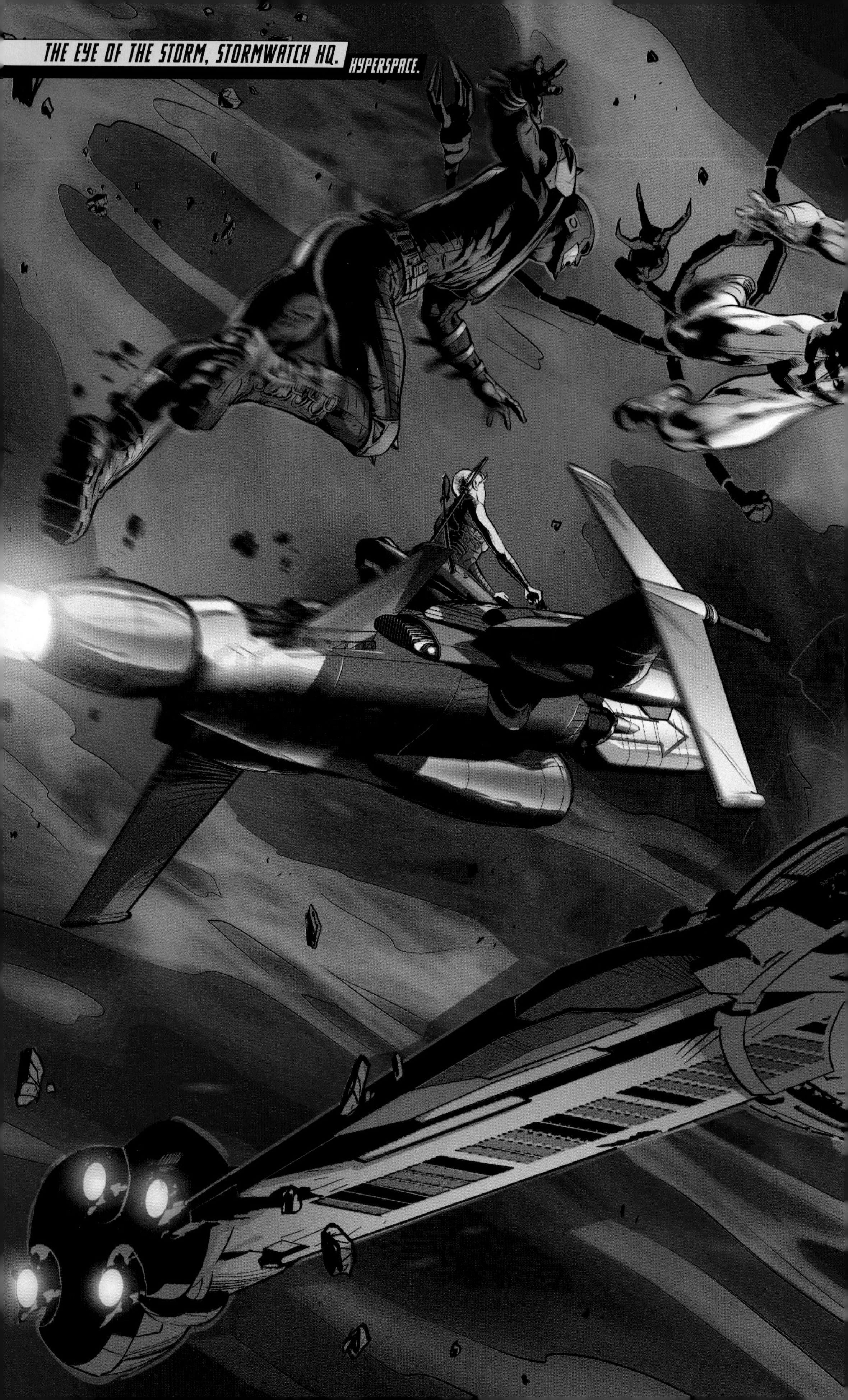
THE EYE OF THE STORM, STORMWATCH HQ.
HYPERSPACE.

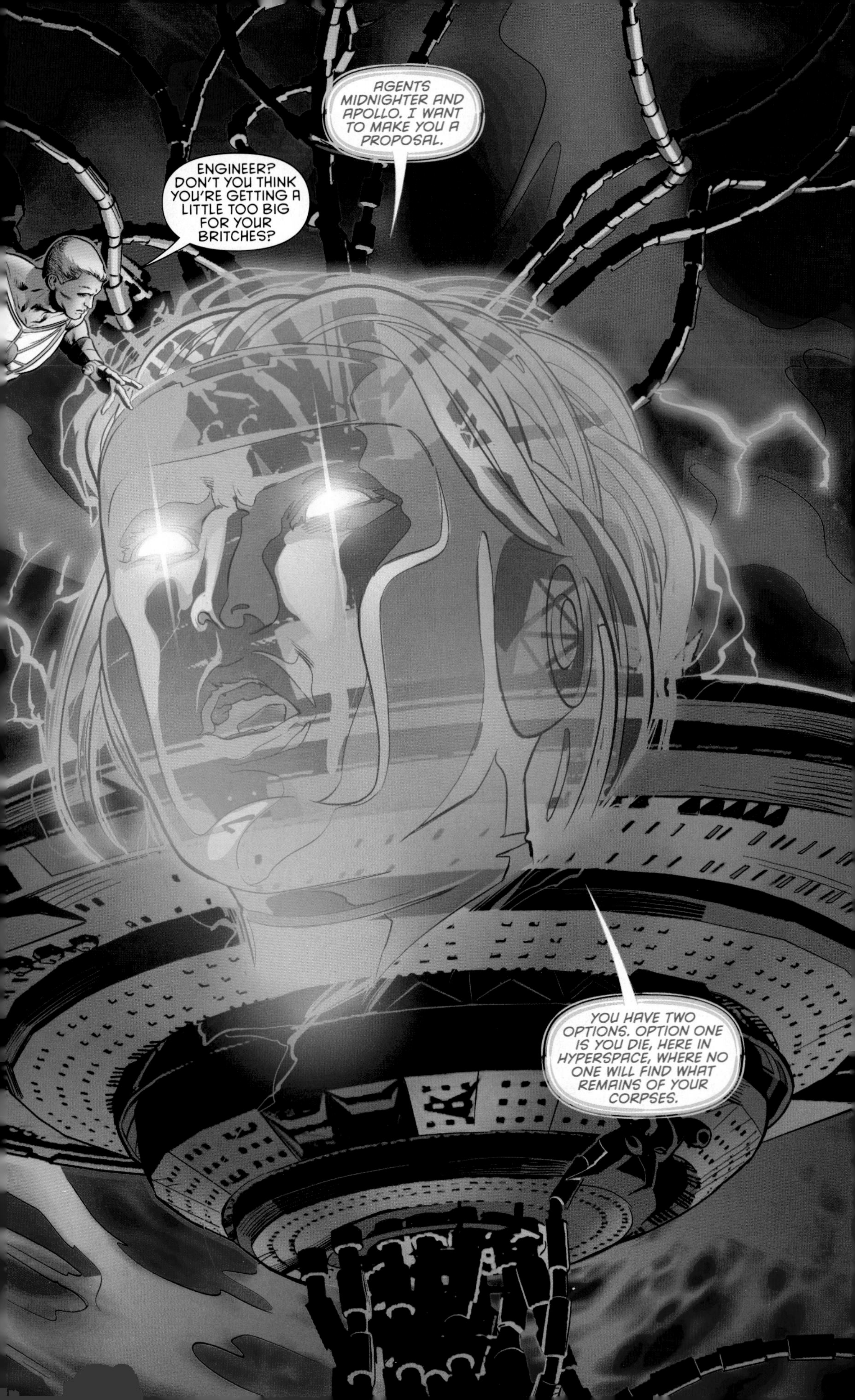
ENGINEER? DON'T YOU THINK YOU'RE GETTING A LITTLE TOO BIG FOR YOUR BRITCHES?
AGENTS MIDNIGHTER AND APOLLO. I WANT TO MAKE YOU A PROPOSAL.
YOU HAVE TWO OPTIONS. OPTION ONE IS YOU DIE, HERE IN HYPERSPACE, WHERE NO ONE WILL FIND WHAT REMAINS OF YOUR CORPSES.

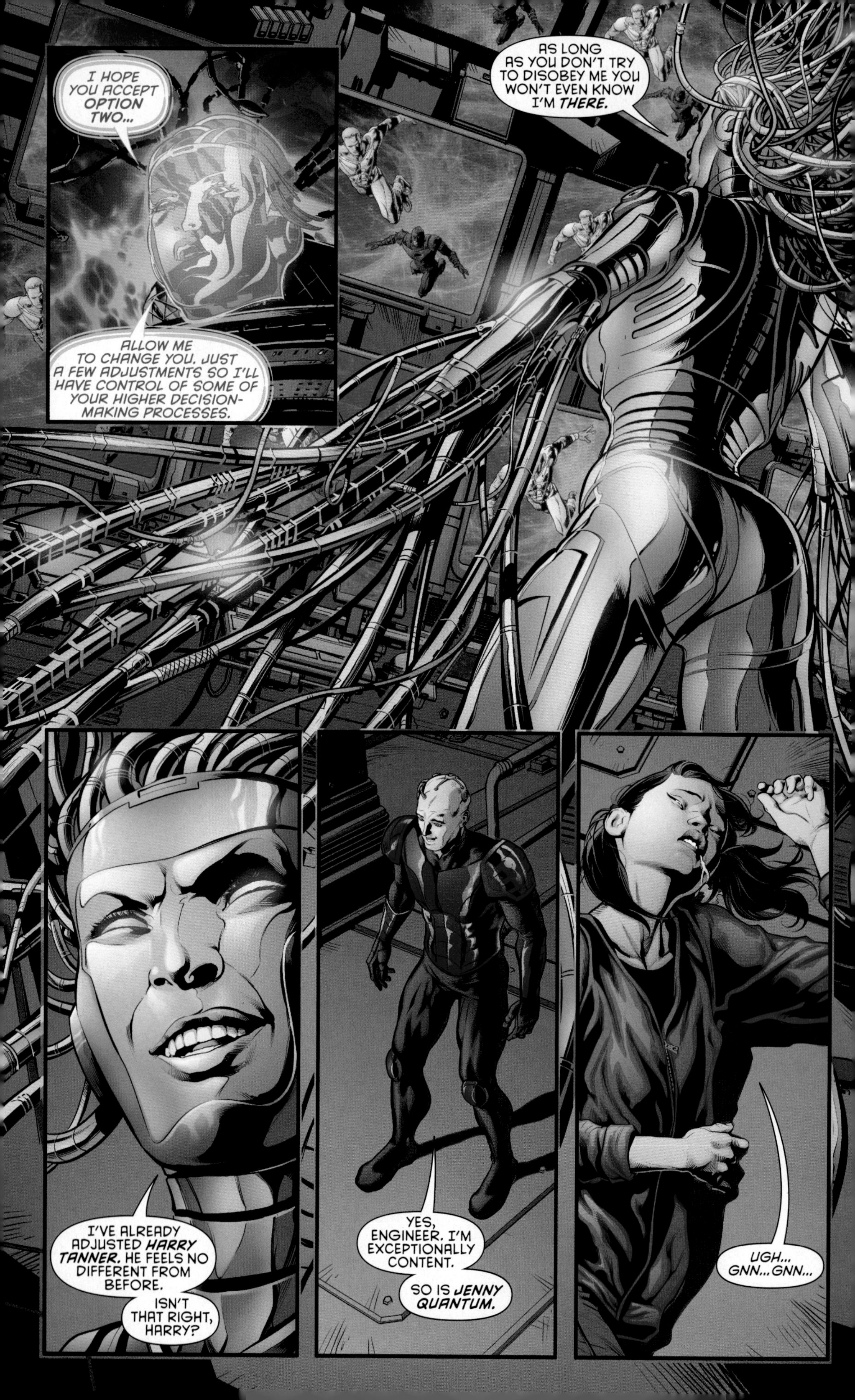

I HOPE YOU ACCEPT OPTION TWO...
ALLOW ME TO CHANGE YOU. JUST A FEW ADJUSTMENTS SO I'LL HAVE CONTROL OF SOME OF YOUR HIGHER DECISION-MAKING PROCESSES.
AS LONG AS YOU DON'T TRY TO DISOBEY ME YOU WON'T EVEN KNOW I'M THERE.
I'VE ALREADY ADJUSTED HARRY TANNER. HE FEELS NO DIFFERENT FROM BEFORE.
ISN'T THAT RIGHT, HARRY?
YES, ENGINEER. I'M EXCEPTIONALLY CONTENT.
SO IS JENNY QUANTUM.
UGH... GNN...GNN...

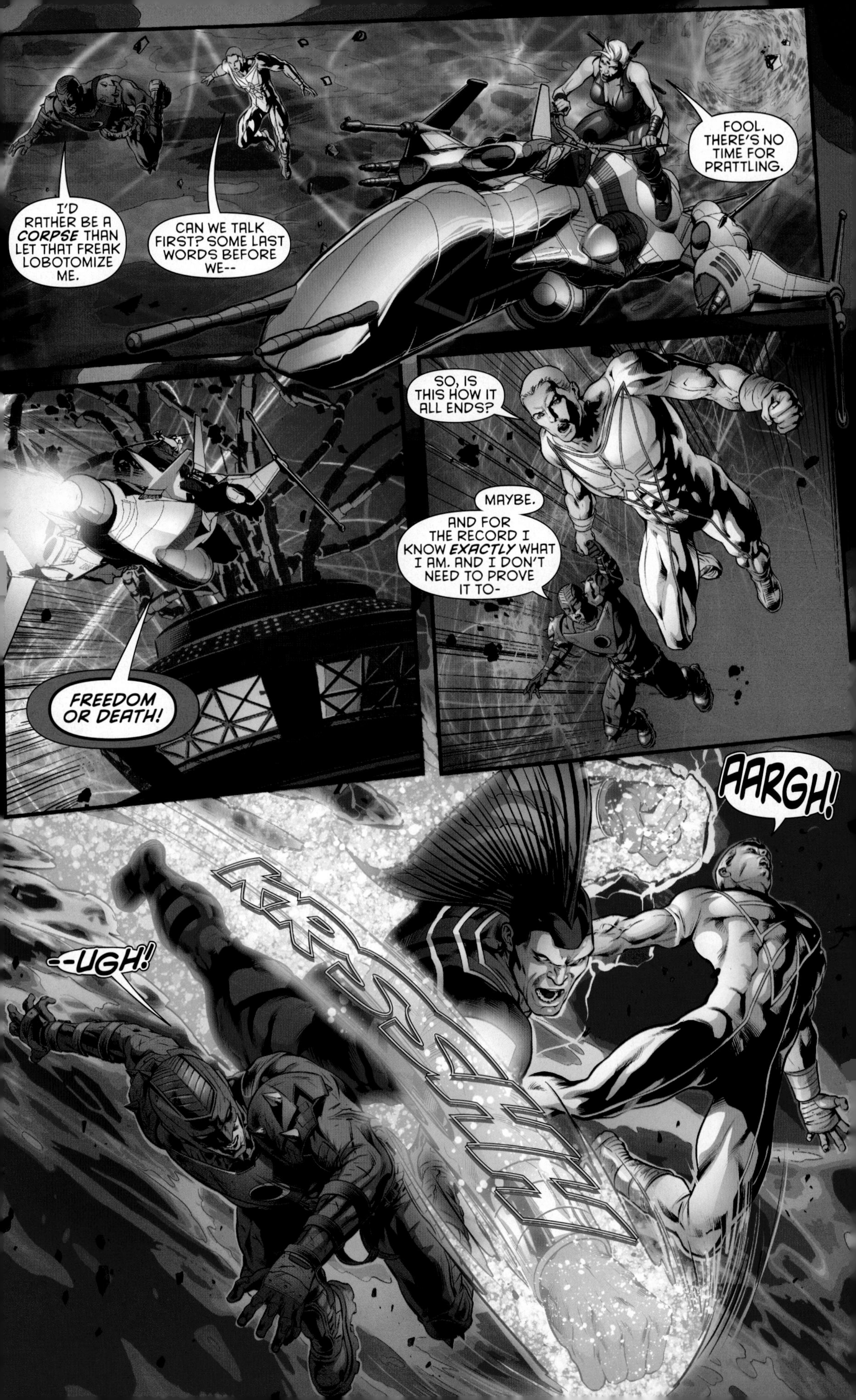
I'D RATHER BE A CORPSE THAN LET THAT FREAK LOBOTOMIZE ME.
CAN WE TALK FIRST? SOME LAST WORDS BEFORE WE--
FOOL. THERE'S NO TIME FOR PRATTLING.
FREEDOM OR DEATH!
SO, IS THIS HOW IT ALL ENDS?
MAYBE.
AND FOR THE RECORD I KNOW EXACTLY WHAT I AM. AND I DON'T NEED TO PROVE IT TO-
AARGH!
--UGH!

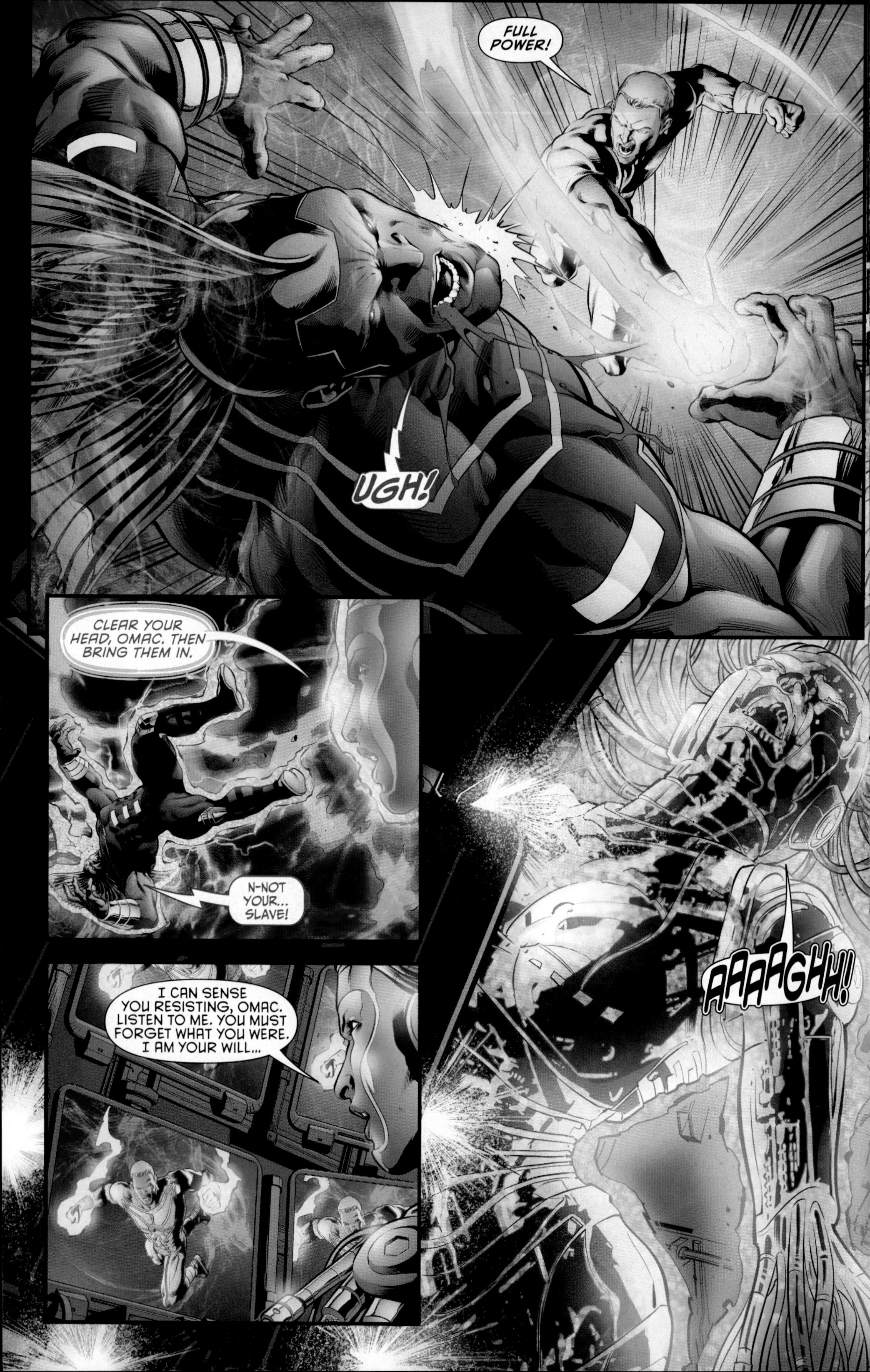
FULL POWER!
UGH!
CLEAR YOUR HEAD, OMAC. THEN BRING THEM IN.
N-NOT YOUR... SLAVE!
AAAAGHH!
I CAN SENSE YOU RESISTING, OMAC. LISTEN TO ME. YOU MUST FORGET WHAT YOU WERE. I AM YOUR WILL...

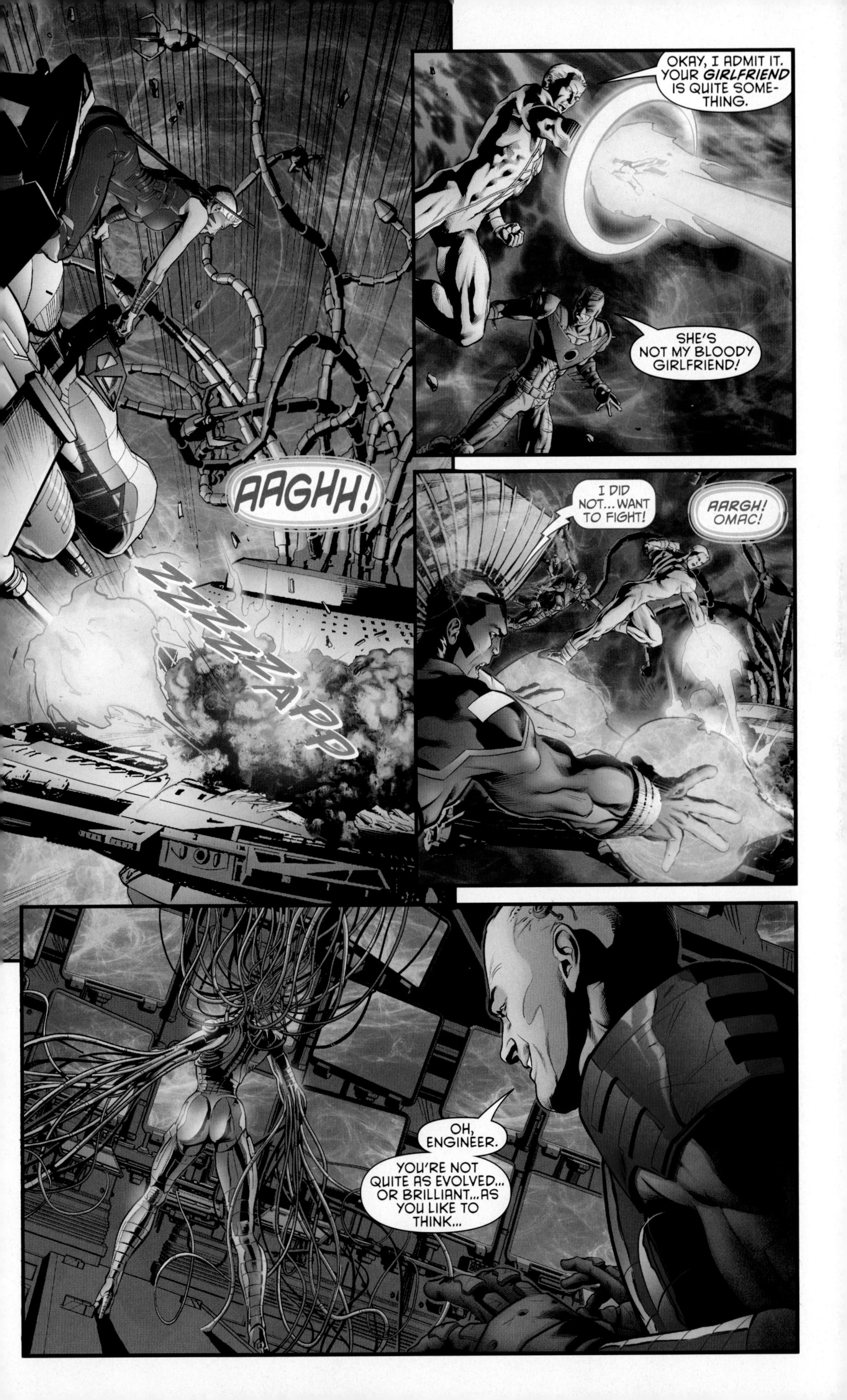
OKAY, I ADMIT IT. YOUR GIRLFRIEND IS QUITE SOME-THING.
SHE'S NOT MY BLOODY GIRLFRIEND!
AAGHH!
ZZZZZZAPP
I DID NOT... WANT TO FIGHT!
AARGH! OMAC!
OH, ENGINEER.
YOU'RE NOT QUITE AS EVOLVED... OR BRILLIANT...AS YOU LIKE TO THINK...

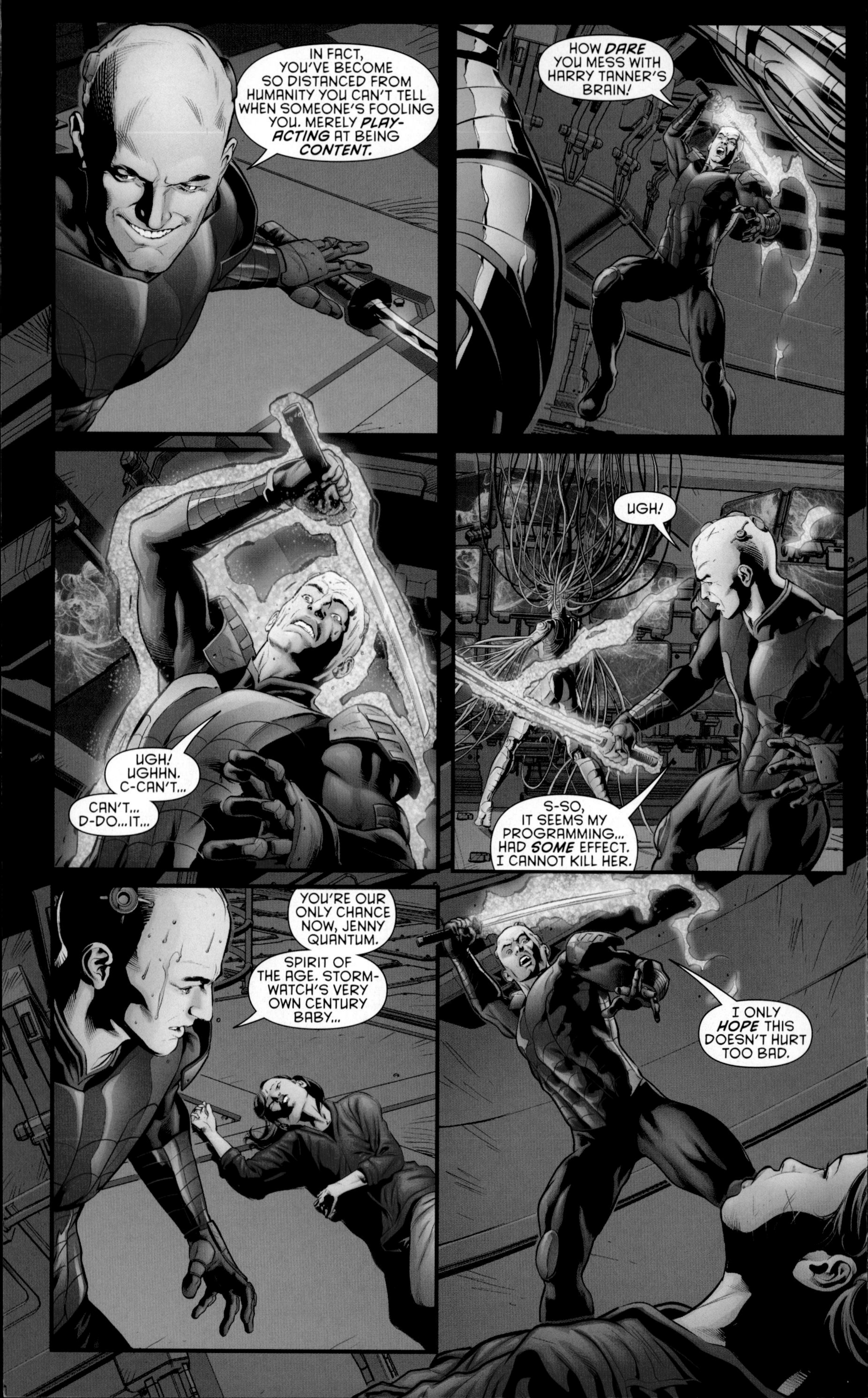
IN FACT, YOU'VE BECOME SO DISTANCED FROM HUMANITY YOU CAN'T TELL WHEN SOMEONE'S FOOLING YOU. MERELY PLAY-ACTING AT BEING CONTENT.
HOW DARE YOU MESS WITH HARRY TANNER'S BRAIN!
UGH! UGHHN. C-CAN'T...
CAN'T... D-DO...IT...
UGH!
S-SO, IT SEEMS MY PROGRAMMING... HAD SOME EFFECT. I CANNOT KILL HER.
YOU'RE OUR ONLY CHANCE NOW, JENNY QUANTUM.
SPIRIT OF THE AGE. STORM-WATCH'S VERY OWN CENTURY BABY...
I ONLY HOPE THIS DOESN'T HURT TOO BAD.

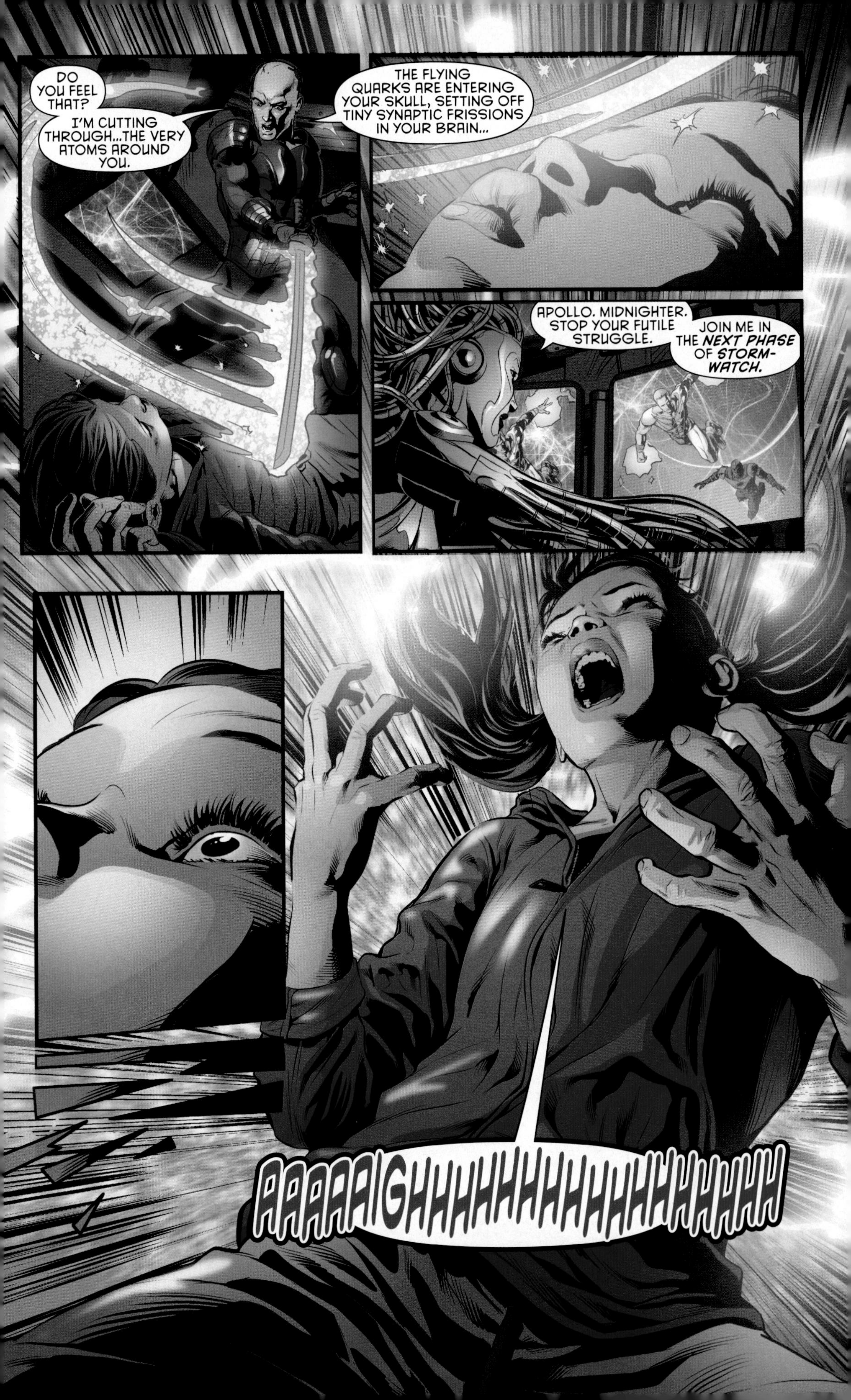
DO YOU FEEL THAT?
I'M CUTTING THROUGH...THE VERY ATOMS AROUND YOU.
THE FLYING QUARKS ARE ENTERING YOUR SKULL, SETTING OFF TINY SYNAPTIC FRISSIONS IN YOUR BRAIN...
APOLLO. MIDNIGHTER. STOP YOUR FUTILE STRUGGLE.
JOIN ME IN THE *NEXT PHASE* OF *STORM-WATCH.*
AAAAAIGHHHHHHHHHHHHHHHHHHH

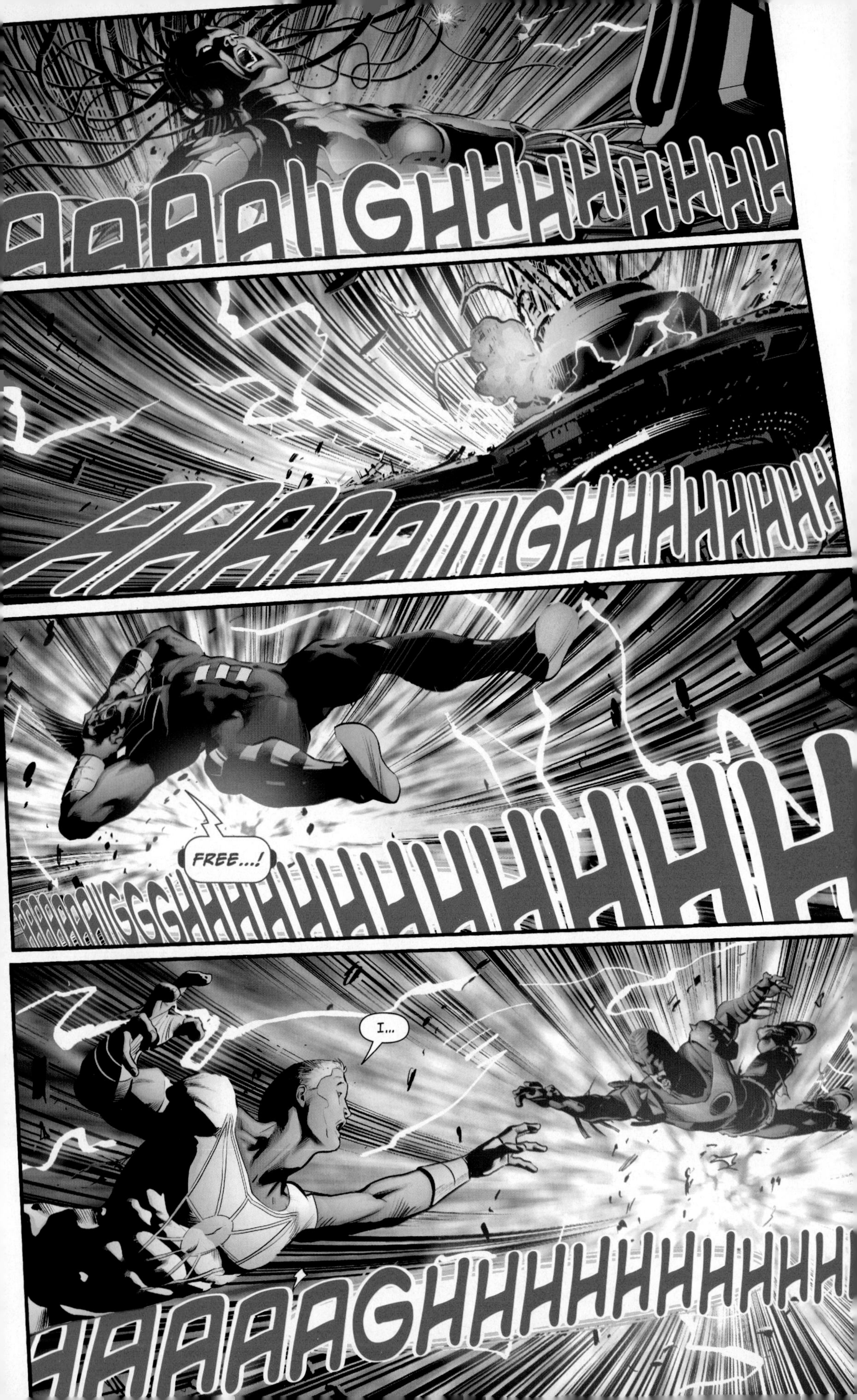
AAAAIIGHHHHHHHH
AAAAAIIIIGHHHHHHHHH
FREE...!
AAAAAAIGGHHHHHHHHHHHHHHHHH
I...
AAAAAGHHHHHHHHHHHH

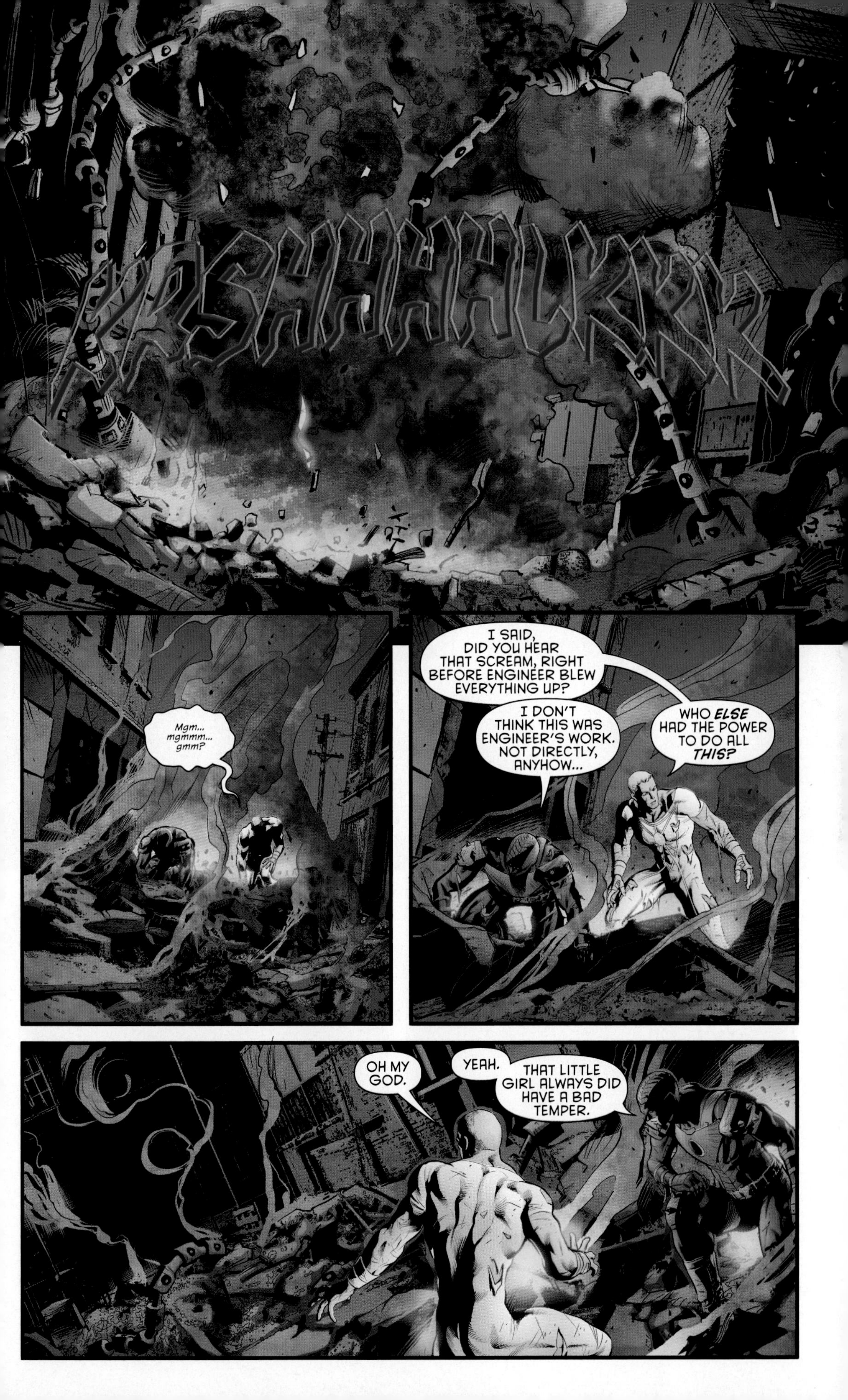
KRSHHHHHHHUKKKK
Mgm... mgmmm... gmm?
I SAID, DID YOU HEAR THAT SCREAM, RIGHT BEFORE ENGINEER BLEW EVERYTHING UP?
I DON'T THINK THIS WAS ENGINEER'S WORK. NOT DIRECTLY, ANYHOW...
WHO *ELSE* HAD THE POWER TO DO ALL *THIS?*
OH MY GOD.
YEAH.
THAT LITTLE GIRL ALWAYS DID HAVE A BAD TEMPER.

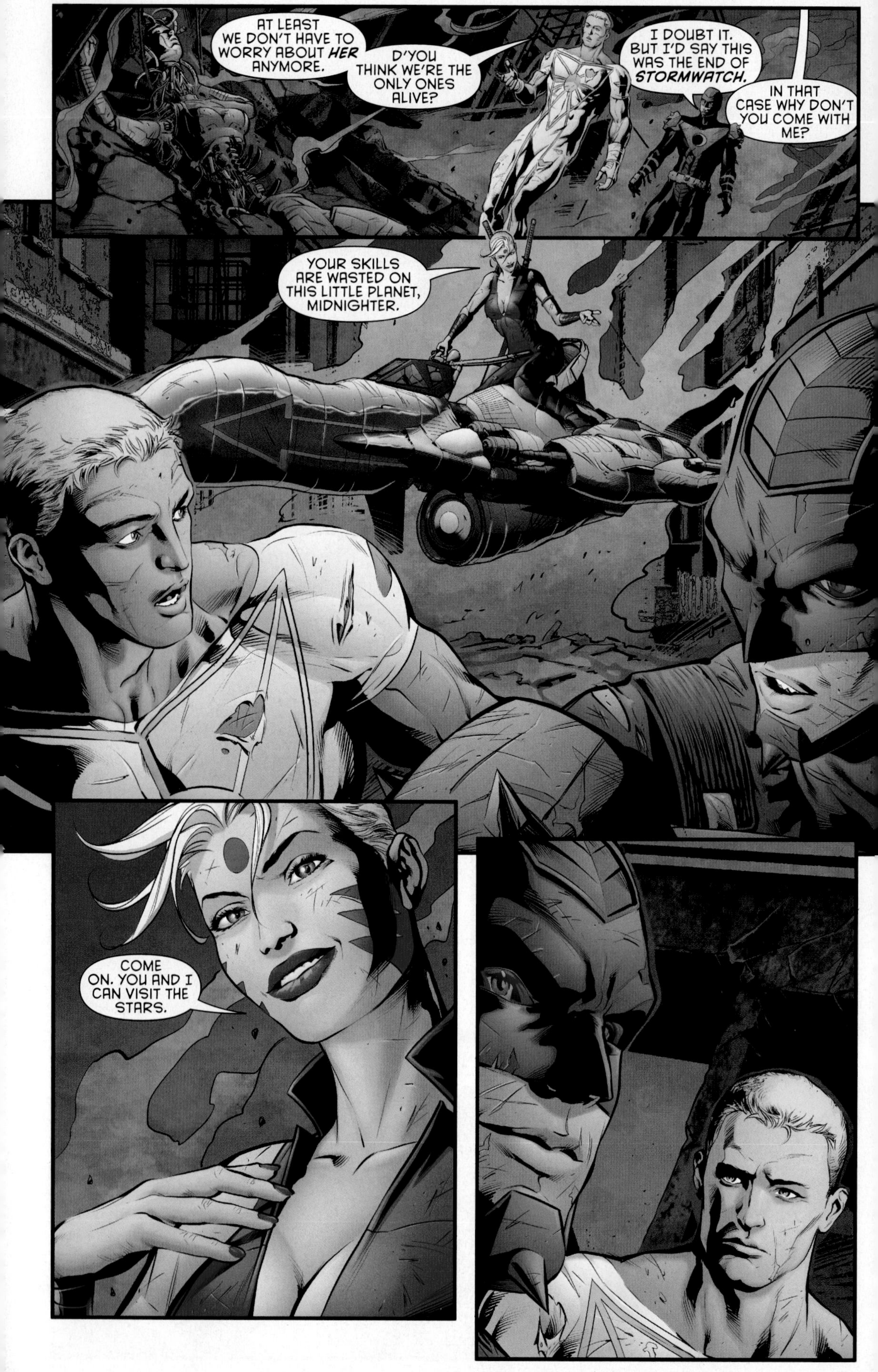
AT LEAST WE DON'T HAVE TO WORRY ABOUT HER ANYMORE.
D'YOU THINK WE'RE THE ONLY ONES ALIVE?
I DOUBT IT. BUT I'D SAY THIS WAS THE END OF STORMWATCH.
IN THAT CASE WHY DON'T YOU COME WITH ME?
YOUR SKILLS ARE WASTED ON THIS LITTLE PLANET, MIDNIGHTER.
COME ON. YOU AND I CAN VISIT THE STARS.

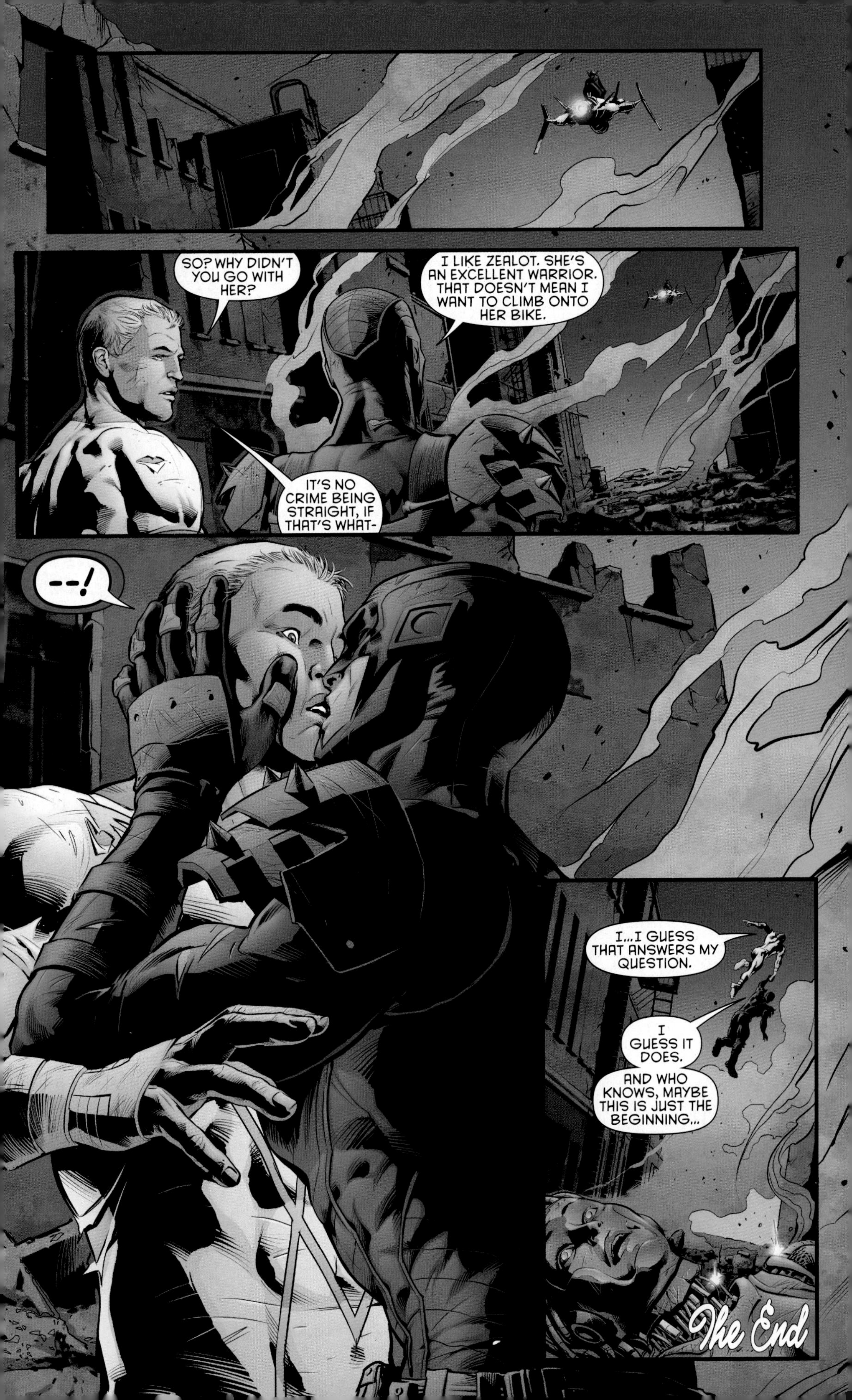
SO? WHY DIDN'T YOU GO WITH HER?
I LIKE ZEALOT. SHE'S AN EXCELLENT WARRIOR. THAT DOESN'T MEAN I WANT TO CLIMB ONTO HER BIKE.
IT'S NO CRIME BEING STRAIGHT, IF THAT'S WHAT-
--!
I...I GUESS THAT ANSWERS MY QUESTION.
I GUESS IT DOES.
AND WHO KNOWS, MAYBE THIS IS JUST THE BEGINNING...
The End

STORMWATCH

ISSUE #18 COVER SKETCHES BY KEN LASHLEY

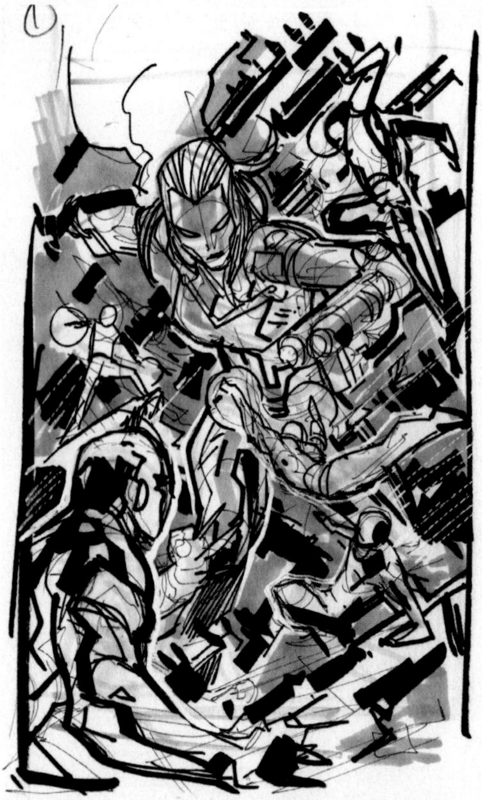
1

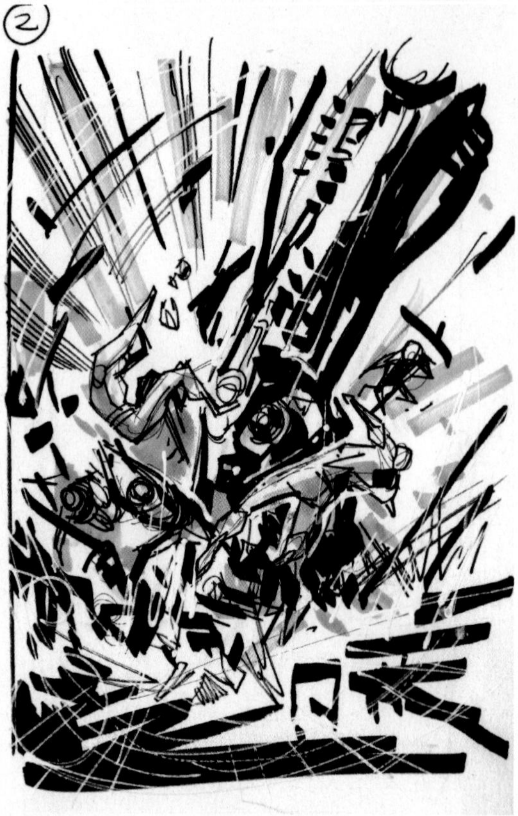
2

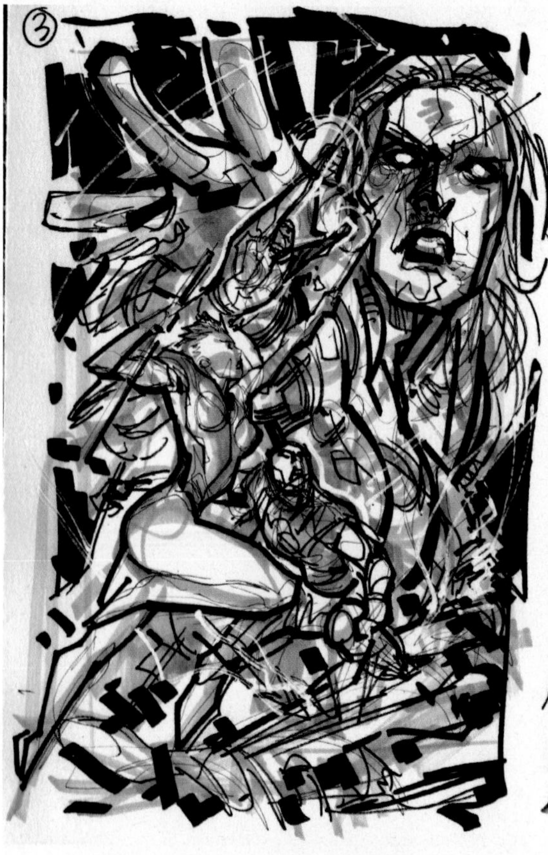
3

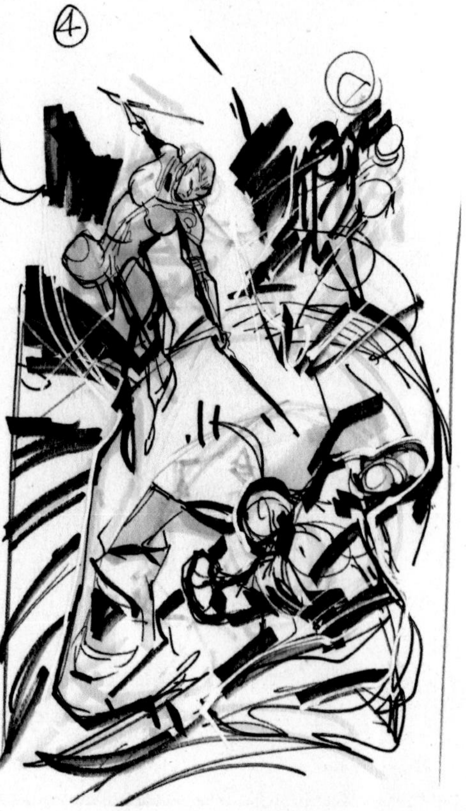
4

STORMWATCH
ISSUE #18 INTERIOR LAYOUTS BY WILL CONRAD

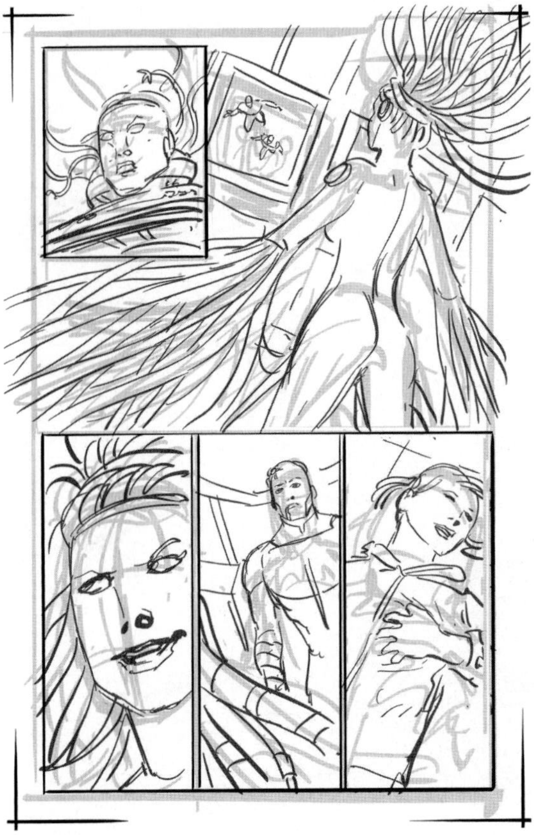

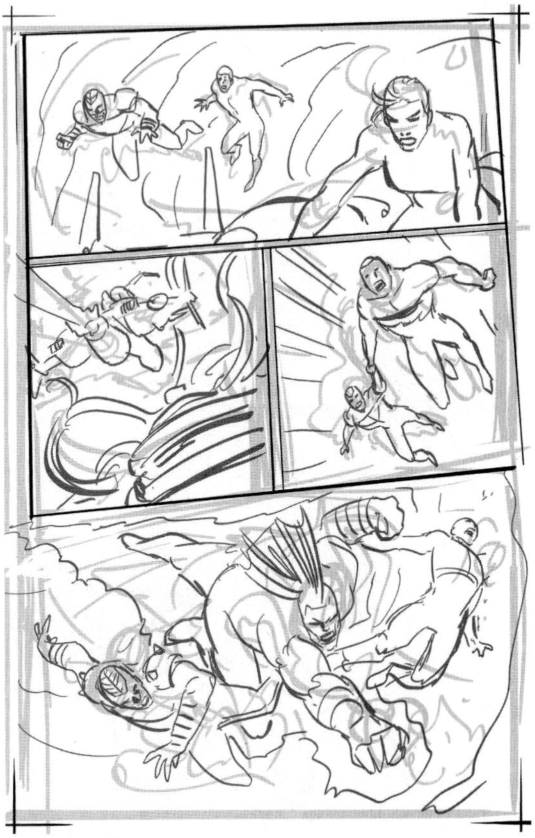

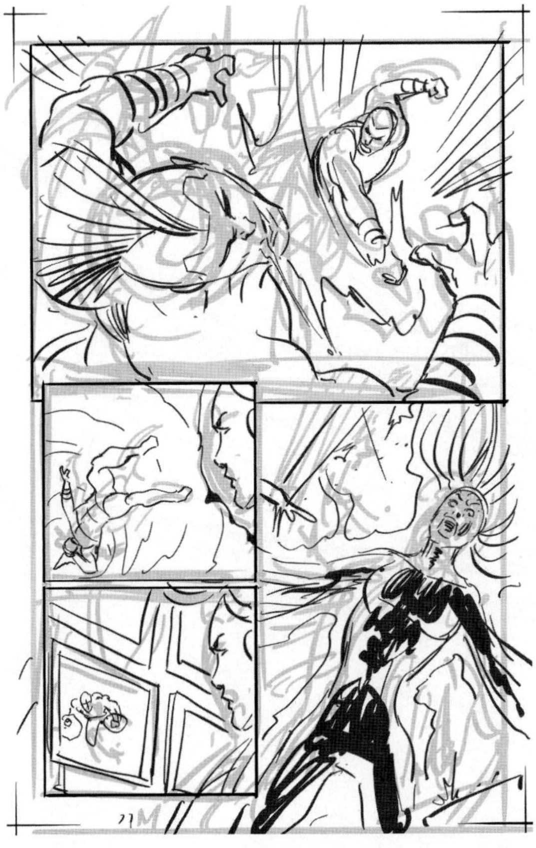

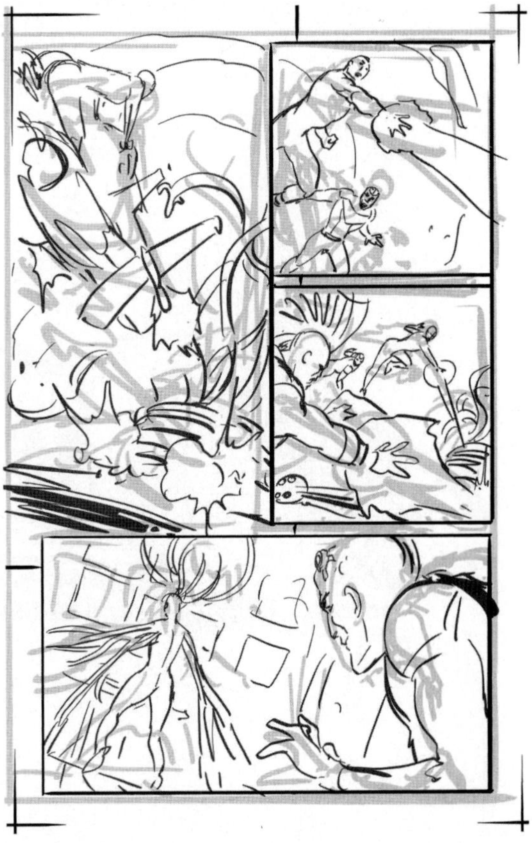

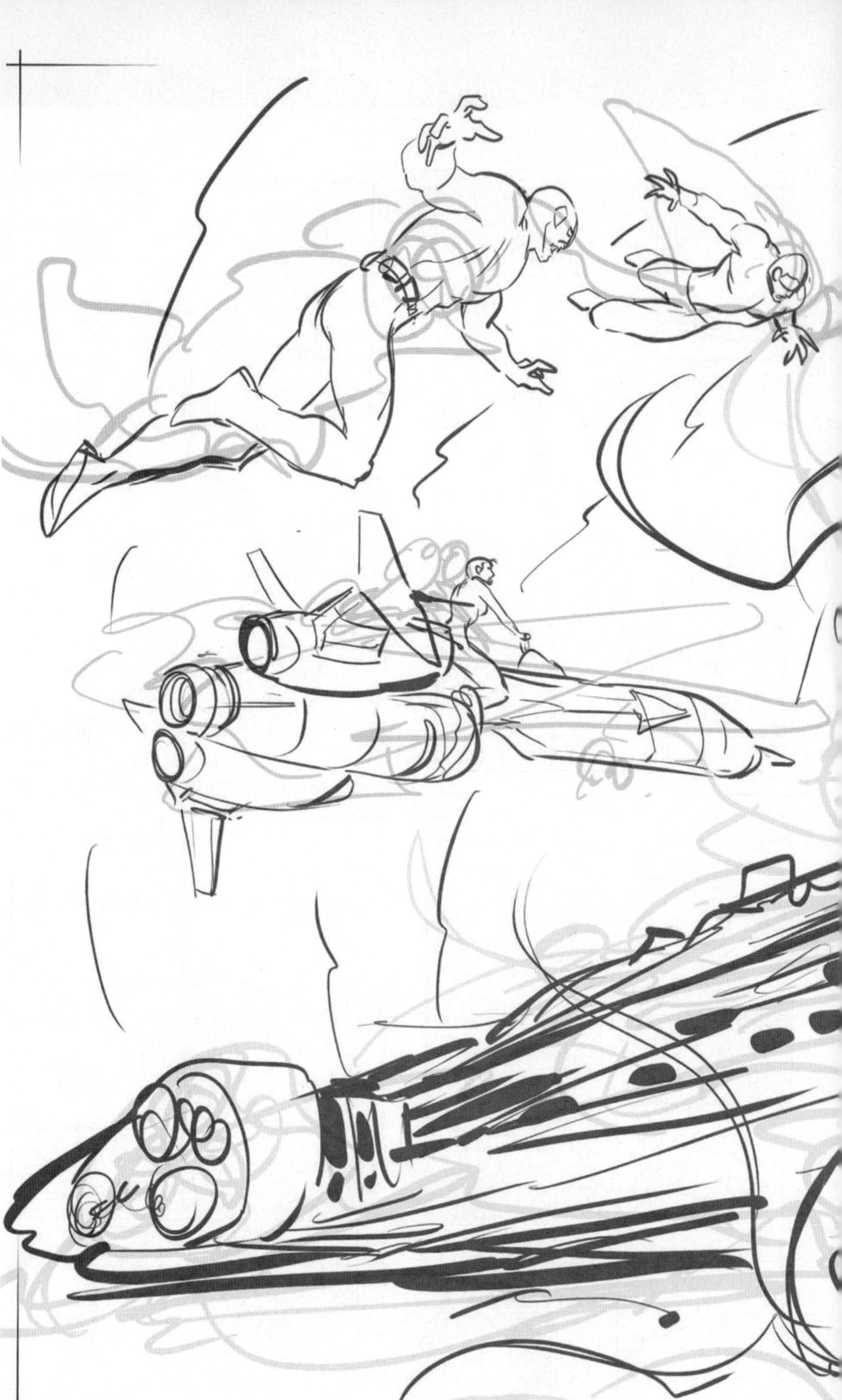